Frederick William Robertson

Sermons preached at Trinity Chapel Brighton

Frederick William Robertson

Sermons preached at Trinity Chapel Brighton

ISBN/EAN: 9783742802194

Manufactured in Europe, USA, Canada, Australia, Japa

Cover: Foto ©Thomas Meinert / pixelio.de

Manufactured and distributed by brebook publishing software (www.brebook.com)

Frederick William Robertson

Sermons preached at Trinity Chapel Brighton

COLLECTION

OF

BRITISH AUTHORS.

VOL. 556.

SERMONS

BY THE LATE

REV. FREDERICK W. ROBERTSON, M.A.

IN THREE VOLUMES.

VOL. I.

SERMONS,

PREACHED AT

TRINITY CHAPEL, BRIGHTON,

BY THE LATE

REV. FREDERICK W. ROBERTSON, M.A.,

THE INCUMBENT.

COPYRIGHT EDITION.

IN THREE VOLUMES.

VOL. I.

LEIPZIG

BERNHARD TAUCHNITZ

1861.

CONTENTS

OF VOLUME I.

SERMON I.

Preached April, 29, 1819.

GOD'S REVELATION OF HEAVEN.

SERMON II.

Preached June 6, 1819.

PARABLE OF THE SOWER.

CONFIRMATION LECTURE.

SERMON III.

Preached June 10, 1849.

SERMON IV.

Preached August 12, 1849.

SERMON V.

Preached October 20, 1850.

SERMON VI.

Preached October 28, 1849.

SERMON XI.

Preached December 6, 1849.

FIRST ADVENT LECTURE.

THE GREEK.

SERMON XII.

Preached December 13, 1849.

SECOND ADVENT LECTURE.

THE ROMAN.

SERMON XIII.

Preached December 20, 1849.

THIRD ADVENT LECTURE.

THE BARBARIAN.

SERMON XVIII.

Preached July 13, 1851.

FREEDOM BY THE TRUTH.

SERMON XIX.

Preached at the Autumn Assizes, held at Lewes, 1852.

THE KINGDOM OF THE TRUTH.

SERMON XX.

Preached November 7, 1852.

THE SCEPTICISM OF PILATE.

SERMON XXI.

Preached on the first day of Public Mourning for the Queen Dowager, Dec. 1849.

THE ISRAELITE'S GRAVE IN A FOREIGN LAND.

SERMONS.

I.

Preached April, 29, 1849.

GOD'S REVELATION OF HEAVEN.

1 Cor. ii. 9, 10. — "Eye hath not seen, nor ear heard, neither have entered into the heart of man, the things which God hath prepared for them that love him. But God hath revealed them unto us by his Spirit."

The preaching of the Apostle Paul was rejected by numbers in the cultivated town of Corinth. It was not wise enough, nor eloquent enough, nor was it sustained by miracles. The man of taste found it barbarous: the Jew missed the signs and wonders which he looked for in a new dispensation: and the rhetorician missed the convincing arguments of the schools. To all which the Apostle was content to reply, that his judges were incompetent to try the question. The princes of this world might judge in a matter of politics: the leaders in the world of literature were qualified to pronounce on a point of taste: the counsellors of this world to weigh an amount of evidence. But in matters spiritual, they were as unfit to judge as a man without ear is to decide respecting harmony; or a man judging alone by sensation, to supersede the higher truth of science by an appeal to his own estimate of appearances. The world, to sense, seems stationary. To the eye of Reason it moves with lightning speed;

and the cultivation of reason alone can qualify for an opinion on the matter. The judgment of the senses is worth nothing in such matters. For every kind of truth a special capacity or preparation is indispensable.

For a revelation of spiritual facts two things are needed: — First, a Divine Truth; next, a spirit which can receive it.

Therefore the Apostle's whole defence resolved itself into this: The natural man receiveth not the things which are of the Spirit of God. The world by wisdom knew not God. And his vindication of his teaching was — These Revealed Truths cannot be seen by the eye, heard by the ear, nor guessed by the heart: they are visible, audible, imaginable only to the spirit. By the spiritually prepared, they are recognised as beautiful, though they be folly to all the world beside, — as his Master had said before him, "Wisdom is justified by her children." In whatever type of life she might be exhibited, whether in the austere Man of the Desert, or in the higher type of the social life of Christ, the Children of Wisdom recognised her lineaments, justified and loved her — She was felt by *them*.

Two things are contained in this verse: —

I. The inability of the lower parts of human nature — the natural man — to apprehend the higher truths.

II. The Nature and laws of revelation.

I. By the natural man is meant the lower faculties of man; and it is said of these that they cannot discover truth spiritual.

1. Eternal truth is not perceived through sensation.

"Eye hath not seen the things which God hath prepared for them that love Him."

There is a life of mere sensation. The degree of its enjoyment depends upon fineness of organization. The pleasures of sense arise from the vibration of a nerve, or the thrilling of a muscle — nothing higher.

The highest pleasure of sensation comes through the eye. She ranks above all the rest of the senses in dignity. He whose eye is so refined by discipline that he can repose with pleasure upon the serene outline of beautiful form, has reached the purest of the sensational raptures.

Now the Corinthians could appreciate this. Theirs was the land of Beauty. They read the Apostle's letter, surrounded by the purest conceptions of Art. In the orders of architecture, the most richly graceful of all columnar forms receives its name from Corinth. And yet it was to these men, living in the very midst of the chastely beautiful, upon whom the Apostle emphatically urged, — "*Eye* hath not seen the things which God hath prepared for them that love Him."

Let us not depreciate what God has given. There is a rapture in gazing on this wondrous world. There is a joy in contemplating the manifold Forms in which the All Beautiful has concealed His essence, — the Living Garment in which the Invisible has robed His mysterious loveliness. In every aspect of Nature there is joy; whether it be the purity of virgin morning, or the sombre gray of a day of clouds, or the solemn pomp and majesty of night; whether it be the chaste lines of the crystal, or the waving outline of distant hills, tremulously visible through dim vapours; the minute petals of the fringed daisy, or the overhanging form of mysterious forests. It is a pure delight *to see.*

But all this is bounded. The eye can only reach the finite Beautiful. It does not scan "the King in his beauty, nor the land that is very far off." The Kingdom, but not the King — something measured by inches, yards, and miles — not the land which is very far off in the Infinite.

Again, it is perishable beauty, — a sight to sadden rather than delight. Even while you gaze, and feel how fair it is, joy mingles with melancholy, from a consciousness that it all is fading: it is the transient — not the Eternal Loveliness for which our spirits pant.

Therefore, when He came into this world, who was the Truth and the Life, in the body which God had prepared for Him, He came not in the glory of form: He was "a root out of a dry ground: He had no form nor comeliness; when they saw Him, there was no beauty that they should desire Him." The eye did not behold, even in Christ, the things which God had prepared.

Now observe, this is an Eternal Truth; true at all times — true now and for ever. In the quotation of this verse, a false impression is often evident. It is quoted as if the Apostle by "the things prepared" meant heaven, and the glories of a world which is to be visible hereafter, but is at present unseen. This is manifestly alien from his purpose. The world of which he speaks is not a future, but a present revelation. God *hath* revealed it. He speaks not of something to be manifested hereafter, but of something already shown, only not to eye nor ear. The distinction lies between a kingdom which is appreciable by the senses, and another whose facts and truths are seen and heard only by the spirit. Never yet hath the eye seen the Truths of God — but then never shall it see them. In Heaven this shall be as true as now. Shape and colour give them not. God will never be visible — nor will His blessedness. He has no form. The pure in heart will see Him, but never with the eye; only in the same way, but in a different degree, that they see him now. In the anticipated Vision of the Eternal, what do you expect to see? A shape? Hues? You will never behold God. Eye hath not seen, and never shall see in finite form, the Infinite One, nor the Infinite of feeling or of Truth.

Again — no scientific analysis can discover the Truths of God. Science cannot give a Revelation. Science proceeds upon observation. It submits everything to the experience of the senses. Its law, expounded by its great lawgiver, is, that if you would ascertain its truth you must see, feel, taste. Experiment is the test of truth. Now, you cannot, by searching, find out the Almighty to perfection, nor a single one of the blessed Truths He has to communicate.

Men have tried to demonstrate Eternal Life, from an examination of the structure of the body. One fancies he has discovered the seat of life in the pineal gland — another in the convolution of a nerve — and thence each infers the continuance of the mystic principle supposed to be discovered there. But a third comes, and sees in it all nothing really immaterial: organization, cerebration, but not Thought or Mind separable from these; nothing that must necessarily subsist after the organism has been destroyed.

Men have supposed they discovered the law of Deity written on the anatomical phenomena of disease. They have exhibited the brain inflamed by intoxication, and the structure obliterated by excess. They have shown in the disordered frame the inevitable penalty of transgression. But if a man, startled by all this, gives up his sin, has he from this selfish prudence learned the law of Duty? The penalties of wrong-doing, doubtless: but not the sanction of Right and Wrong written on the conscience, of which penalties are only the enforcements. He has indisputable evidence that it is expedient not to commit excesses; but you cannot manufacture a conscience out of expediency: the voice of conscience says not, It is better not to do so; but "Thou shalt not."

No: it is vain that we ransack the world for probable evidences of God, and hypotheses of his existence. It is idle to look into the materialism of man for the Revelation of his immortality; or to examine the morbid anatomy of the body to find the rule of Right. If a man go to the eternal world with convictions of Eternity, the Resurrection, God, already in his spirit, he will find abundant corroborations of that which he already believes. But if God's existence be not thrilling every fibre of his heart, if the Immortal be not already in him as the proof of the Resurrection, if the law of Duty be not stamped upon his soul as an Eternal Truth, unquestionable, a thing that must be obeyed, quite separately from all considerations of punishment or impunity, science will never reveal these — observation pries in vain — the physician comes away from the laboratory an infidel. Eye hath not seen the truths which are clear enough to Love and to the Spirit.

2. Eternal truth is not reached by hearsay — "Ear hath not heard the things which God hath prepared for them that love Him."

No revelation can be adequately given by the address of man to man, whether by writing or orally, even if he be put in possession of the Truth itself. For all such revelation must be made through words: and words are but counters — the coins of intellectual exchange. There is as little resemblance between the silver coin and the bread it purchases, as between the word and the thing it stands for. Looking at the coin, the form of the loaf does not suggest itself. Listening to the word, you do not perceive the idea for which it stands, unless you are already in possession of it. Speak of ice to an inhabitant of the torrid zone, the word does not give him an idea, or if it does, it must be a false one. Talk of blueness to one who cannot distinguish colours, what can your most eloquent description present to him resembling the truth of your sensation? Similarly in matters spiritual, no verbal revelation can give a single simple idea. For instance, what means justice to the unjust — or purity to the man whose heart is steeped in licentiousness? What does infinitude mean to a being who has never stirred from infancy beyond a cell, never seen the sky, or the sea, or any of those *occasions* of thought which, leaving vagueness on the mind, suggest the idea of the illimitable? It means, explain it as you will, nothing to him but a room: vastly larger than his own, but still a room, terminated by a wall. Talk of God to a thousand ears, each has his own different conception. Each man in this congregation has a God before him at this moment, who is, according to his own attainment in goodness, more or less limited and imperfect. The sensual man hears of God, and understands one thing. The pure man hears, and conceives another thing. Whether you speak in metaphysical or metaphorical language, in the purest words of inspiration, or the grossest images of materialism, the conceptions conveyed by the same word are essentially different, according to the soul which receives.

So that apostles themselves, and prophets speaking to the ear, cannot reveal truth to the soul — no, not if God Himself were to touch their lips with fire. A verbal revelation is only a revelation to the ear.

Now see what a hearsay religion is. There are men who believe on authority. Their minister believes all this Christianity true: therefore so do they. He calls this doctrine essential: they echo it. Some thousands of years ago, men communed with God; they have heard this, and are content it should be so. They have heard with the hearing of the ear, that God is Love — that the ways of holiness are ways of pleasantness, and all her paths peace. But a hearsay belief saves not. The Corinthian philosophers heard Paul — Pharisees heard Christ. How much did the ear convey? To thousands exactly nothing. He alone believes truth who feels it. He has a religion whose soul knows by experience that to serve God and know Him is the richest treasure. And unless Truth come to you, not in word only, but in power besides — authoritative because true, not true because authoritative — there has been no real revelation made to you from God.

3. Truth is not discoverable by the heart — "neither have entered into the heart of man the things which God hath prepared for them that love Him."

The heart — two things we refer to this source: the power of imagining, and the power of loving.

Imagination is distinct from the mere dry faculty of reasoning. Imagination is creative — it is an immediate intuition; not a logical analysis — we call it popularly a kind of inspiration. Now imagination is a power of the heart: — Great thoughts originate from a large heart: a man must have a heart, or he never could create.

It is a grand thing, when in the stillness of the soul, thought bursts into flame, and the intuitive vision comes like an inspiration; when breathing thoughts clothe themselves in burning words, winged as it were with lightning — or when a great law of the universe reveals itself to the mind of Genius, and where all was darkness, his single word bids Light be, and all is Order where chaos and confusion were. Or when the truths of human nature shape themselves forth in the creative fancies of one like the million-minded Poet, and you recognise the rare power of *heart* which sympathizes with, and can reproduce all that is found in man.

But all this is nothing more than what the material man can achieve. The most etheral creations of fantastic fancy were shaped by a mind that could read the life of Christ, and then blaspheme the Adorable. The truest utterances, and some of the deepest ever spoken, revealing the unrest and the agony that lie hid in the heart of man, came from one whose life was from first to last selfish. The highest astronomer of this age, before whose clear eye Creation lay revealed in all its perfect order, was one whose spirit refused to recognise the Cause of Causes. The mighty heart of genius had failed to reach the things which God imparts to a humble spirit.

There is more in the heart of man — it has the power of affection. The highest moment known on earth by the merely natural, is that in which the mysterious union of heart with heart is felt. Call it friendship — love — what you will, that mystic blending of two souls in one, when self is lost and found again in the being of another; when, as it were, moving about in the darkness and loneliness of existence, we suddenly come in contact with something, and we find that spirit has touched spirit. This is the purest, serenest ecstasy of the merely human — more blessed than any sight that can be presented to the eye, or any sound that can be given to the ear: more sublime than the sublimest dream ever conceived by genius in its most gifted hour, when the freest way was given to the shaping spirit of imagination.

This has entered into the heart of man, yet this is of the lower still. It attains not to the things prepared by God — it dimly shadows them. Human love is but the faint type of that surpassing blessedness which belongs to those who love God.

II. We pass therefore to the Nature and Laws of Revelation.

First, Revelation is made by a Spirit to a spirit — "God hath revealed them to us by His Spirit." Christ is the voice of God *without* the man — the Spirit is the voice of God *within* the man. The highest Revelation is not made by Christ, but comes directly from the universal Mind to our minds. Therefore, Christ said Himself, "He, the Spirit, shall take of mine and shall show it unto you." And therefore it is written here "The *Spirit* searches all things, yea the deep things God."

Now the Spirit of God lies touching, as it we the soul of man — ever around and near. On the o side of earth, man stands with the boundless heav above him: nothing between him and space — sp around him and above him — the confines of the s touching him. So is the spirit of man to the Spirit the Ever Near. They mingle. In every man this true. The spiritual in him, by which he might beco a recipient of God, may be dulled, deadened, by a l of sense, but in this world never lost. All men not spiritual men; but all have spiritual sensibilit which might awake. All that is wanted is to beco conscious of the nearness of God. God has placed m here to feel after Him if haply they might find Hi albeit *He be not far* from any one of them. Our so float in the immeasurable ocean of Spirit. God l around us: at any moment we might be conscious the contact.

The *condition* upon which this Self-Revelation the Spirit is made to man, is Love. These things "prepared for them that love Him," or, which is t same thing, revealed to those who have the mind Christ.

Let us look into this word Love. Love to m may mean several things. It may mean love to l person, which is very different from himself — or may mean simply pity. Love to God can only me one thing: God is a Character. To love God is to lo His character. For instance — God is Purity. A to be pure in thought and look; to turn away from u hallowed books and conversation, to abhor the moments in which we have not been pure, is to love God.

God is Love — and to love men till private attachments have expanded into a philanthropy which embraces all — at last even the evil and enemies, with compassion — that is to love God. God is Truth. To be true — to hate every form of falsehood — to live a brave — true — real life — that is to love God. God is Infinite — and to love the boundless, reaching on from grace to grace, adding charity to faith, and rising upwards ever to see the Ideal still above us, and to die with it unattained, aiming insatiably to be perfect even as the Father is perfect — that is to love God.

This Love is manifested in obedience — Love is the life of which obedience is the form. "He that hath my commandments and keepeth them, he it is that loveth me. . . . He that loveth me not keepeth not my sayings." Now here can be no mistake. Nothing can be Love to God which does not shape itself into obedience. We remember the anecdote of the Roman commander who forbade an engagement with the enemy, and the first transgressor against whose prohibition was his own son. He accepted the challenge of the leader of the other host, met, slew, spoiled him, and then in triumphant feeling carried the spoils to his father's tent. But the Roman father refused to recognise the instinct which prompted this as deserving of the name of Love — Disobedience contradicted it, and deserved death: — weak sentiment, what was it worth?

So with God: — strong feelings, warm expressions, varied internal experience co-existing with disobedience, God counts not as Love. Mere weak feeling may not usurp that sacred name.

To this Love, adoring and obedient, God reveals His Truth — For such as love it is prepared: or rather, by the well-known Hebrew inversion, such are prepared for it. — Love is the condition without which revelation does not take place. As in the natural, so in the spiritual world: — By compliance with the laws of the universe, we put ourselves in possession of its blessings. — Obey the laws of health and you obtain health: — Temperance, sufficiency of light and air, and exercise, these are the conditions of health. Arm yourselves with the laws of nature, and you may call down the lightning from the sky: — surround yourself with glass, and the lightning may play innocuously a few inches from you — It cannot touch you — you may defy it — you have obeyed the conditions of nature, and nature is on your side against it.

In the same way, there are conditions in the world of Spirit, by compliance with which God's Spirit comes into the soul with all its Revelations, as surely as lightning from the sky, and as invariably: — such conditions as these. "The secret of the Lord is with them that *fear* Him." "No man hath seen God at any time." "If we *love* one another, God dwelleth in us." "With this man will I dwell, even with him that is of a *meek* and *contrite* spirit." "If any man will *do* His will, he shall know of the doctrine" — Reverence, love, meekness, contrition, obedience — these conditions having taken place, God enters into the soul, whispers His secret, becomes visible, imparts knowledge and conviction.

Now these laws are universal and invariable: — they are subject to no caprice. — There is no favourite child of nature who may hold the fire-ball in the hollow of his hand and trifle with it without being burnt: —

there is no selected Child of Grace who can live an irregular life without unrest; or be proud, and at the same time have peace: or indolent, and receive fresh inspiration: or remain unloving and cold, and yet see and hear and feel the things which God had prepared for them that love Him.

Therefore the apostle preached the Cross to men who felt, and to men who felt not, the Revelation contained in it. The Cross is humbleness: love: self-surrender — These the apostle preached. To conquer the world by loving it — To be blest by ceasing the pursuit of happiness, and sacrificing life instead of finding it — to make a hard lot easy by submitting to it — this was his divine philosophy of life. And the princes of this world, amidst scoffs and laughter, replied, Is that all? Nothing to dazzle — nothing to captivate. But the disciples of the inward life recognised the Divine Truth which this doctrine of the Cross contained. The humble of heart, and the loving, felt that in this lay the mystery of life, of themselves, and of God, all revealed and plain. It was God's own wisdom, felt by those who had the mind of Christ.

The application of all this is very easy: Love God and He will dwell with you. — Obey God, and He will reveal the truths of His deepest teaching to your soul. Not *perhaps:* — As surely as the laws of the spiritual world are irreversible, are these things prepared for obedient love: — An inspiration as true, as real, and as certain as that which ever prophet or apostle reached, is yours, if you will.

And if obedience were entire and love were perfect, then would the Revelation of the Spirit to the soul of man be perfect too. There would be trust expelling care, and enabling a man to repose: — there would be a love which would cast out fear: — there would be a sympathy with the mighty All of God: — selfishness would pass, Isolation would be felt no longer; — the tide of the universal and eternal Life would come with mighty pulsations throbbing through the soul. To such a man it would not matter where he was, nor what: — to live or die would be alike. If he lived, he would live unto the Lord; if he died, he would die to the Lord. The bed of down surrounded by friends, or the martyr's stake, girt round with curses — what matter which? Stephen, dragged, hurried, driven, felt the glory of God streaming on his face: when the shades of faintness were gathering round his eyes, and the world was fading away into indistinctness, "the things prepared" were given him. His spirit saw what "eye had never seen." The later martyr bathes his fingers in the flames, and while the flesh shrivels and the bones are cindered, says, in unfeigned sincerity, that he is lying on a bed of roses. It would matter little what he was, — the ruler of a kingdom, or a tailor grimed with the smoke and dust of a workshop. To a soul filled with God, the difference between these two is inappreciable: — as if, from a distant star, you were to look down upon a palace and a hovel, both dwindled into distance, and were to smile at the thought of calling one large and the other small.

No matter to such a man what he saw or what he heard; for every sight would be resplendent with beauty, and every sound would echo harmony: things common would become transfigured, as when the ecstatic state of the inward soul reflected a radiant cloud from the frame of Christ. The Human would become Divine,

Life — even the meanest — noble. In the hue of every violet there would be a glimpse of Divine affection, and a dream of Heaven. The forest would blaze with Deity, as it did to the eye of Moses. The creations of genius would breathe less of earth and more of Heaven. Human love itself would burn with a clearer and intenser flame, rising from the altar of self-sacrifice.

These are "the things which God had prepared for them that love Him." Compared with these, what are loveliness, — the eloquent utterances of man, — the conceptions of the heart of Genius? What are they all to the serene stillness of a spirit lost in Love: the full deep rapture of a soul into which the spirit of God is pouring itself in a mighty tide of Revelation?

II.

Preached June 6, 1849.

PARABLE OF THE SOWER.

MATT. xiii. 1-10. — "The same day went Jesus out of the house, and sat by the seaside. And great multitudes were gathered together unto him, so that he went into a ship, and sat; and the whole multitude stood on the shore. And he spake many things unto them in parables, saying, behold, a sower went forth to sow: And when he sowed, some seeds fell by the wayside, and the fowls came and devoured them up: Some fell upon stony places, where they had not much earth; and forthwith they sprang up, because they had no deepness of earth: And when the sun was up, they were scorched; and because they had no root, they withered away. And some fell among thorns; and the thorns sprung up and choked them: But other fell into good ground, and brought forth fruit, some an hundred-fold, some sixty-fold, some thirty-fold. Who hath ears to hear, let him hear."

BEFORE the reception of the Lord's Supper on Sunday next, I have been anxious to address you, my young friends, once more, in order to carry on the thoughts, and, if possible, deepen the impressions of Tuesday last. During the last few weeks, you have been subjected to much that is exciting; and in proportion to the advantage is the danger of that excitement. A great part of the value of the rite of Confirmation consists in its being a season of excitement or impression. The value of excitement is, that it breaks up the old mechanical life which has become routine. It stirs the stagnancy of our existence, and causes the stream of life to flow more fresh and clear. The danger of excitement is the probability of reaction. The heart, like the body and the mind, cannot be long exposed to extreme tension, without giving way afterwards. Strong impressions are succeeded by corresponding listlessness. Your work, to which you have so long looked forward, is done. The profession has been made; and now, left suddenly, as it were, with nothing before you, and apparently no answer to the question — What are we to do now? — insensibly you will feel that all is over, and the void within your hearts will be inevitably filled, unless there be great vigilance, by a very different class of excitements. This danger will be incurred most by those precisely who felt most deeply the services of the past week.

The parable I have selected dwells upon such a class of dangers.

No one who felt, or even thought, could view the scene of Tuesday last without emotion. Six or seven hundred young persons solemnly pledged themselves to renounce evil in themselves and in the world, and to become disciples of the Cross. The very colour of their garments, typical of purity, seemed to suggest the hope and the expectation that the day might come when they shall be found clothed with that inward righteousness, of which their dress was but a symbol, when "they shall walk with Him in white, for they are worthy." As yet fresh in feeling, as yet untainted by open sin, who could see them without hoping that?

My young friends, experience forces us to correct that sanguine anticipation. Of the seven hundred who were earnest then, it were an appalling question to ask how many will have retained their earnestness six months hence, and how much of all that which seemed so real, will be recognised as pure, true gold, at the last Great Day. Soon some will have lost their innocence — and some will have become frivolous and artificial — and the world will have got its cold deadening hand on some. Who shall dare to guess in how many the best raised hopes will be utterly disappointed?

Now, the question which presents itself is, — How comes so much promise to end in failure? And to this the parable of the sower returns a reply.

Three causes are conceivable: It might be the will — or, if you venture so to call it — the fault of him who gave the Truth: Or it might be some inherent impotency in the Truth itself: Or, lastly, the fault might lie solely in the soil of the heart.

This parable assures us that the fault does not lie in God, the sower. God does not predestinate men to fail. That is strikingly told in the history of Judas — "From a ministry and apostleship Judas fell, that he might go to his own place." The ministry and apostleship were that to which God had destined him. To work out that, was the destiny appointed to him, as truly as to any of the other apostles. He was called, elected to that. But when he refused to execute that mission, the very circumstances which, by God's decree, were leading him to blessedness, hurried him to ruin. Circumstances prepared by Eternal Love, became the destiny which conducted him to everlasting doom. He was a predestined man — crushed by his Fate. But he went to his "*own* place." He had shaped his own destiny. So the ship is wrecked by the winds and waves — hurried to its fate. But the winds and waves were in truth its best friends. Rightly guided, it would have made use of them to reach the port; wrongly steered, they became the destiny which drove it on the rocks. Failure — the wreck of life, is not to be impiously traced to the Will of God. God will have all men to be saved, and come to a knowledge of the Truth. God willeth not the death of a sinner.

Nor, again, can we find the cause in any impotency of Truth: — an impotency, doubtless, there is somewhere. The old Thinkers accounted for it by the depravity of matter. God can do anything, they said. Being good, God would do all good. If He do not, it is because of the materials He has to deal with. Matter thwarts Him: Spirit is pure, but matter is essentially evil and unspiritual: the body is corrupt. Against this doctrine, St Paul argues, 2 Cor. v. 4.

The true account is this, — God has created in man a will which has become a cause. "God can do any thing." — I know not that. God cannot deny Himself — God cannot do wrong — God cannot create a number less than one — God cannot make a contradiction true. It is a contradiction to let man be free, and force him to do right. God has performed this marvel, of creating a Being with free will, independent, so to speak, of Himself — a real cause in His universe. To say that He has created such a one, is to say that He has given him the power to fail. Without free-will there could be no human goodness. It is wise, therefore, and good in God, to give birth to free-will. But once acknowledge free-will in man, and the origin of evil does not lie in God.

And this leads us to the remaining cause of failure which is conceivable. In our own free-will — in the grand and fearful power we have to ruin ourselves — lies the real and only religious solution of the mystery. In the soil of the heart is found all the nutriment of spiritual life, and all the nutriment of the weeds and poisons which destroy spiritual life. And it is this which makes Christian character, when complete a thing, so inestimably precious. There are things precious, not from the materials of which they are made, but from the risk and difficulty of bringing them to perfection. The speculum of the largest telescope foils the optician's skill in casting. Too much or too little heat — the interposition of a grain of sand, a slight alteration in the temperature of the weather, and all goes to pieces — it must be recast. Therefore, when successfully finished, it is a matter for almost the congratulation of a country. Rarer, and more difficult still than the costliest part of the most delicate of instruments, is the completion of Christian character. Only let there come the heat of persecution — or the cold of human desertion — a little of the world's dust — and the rare and costly thing is cracked, and becomes a failure.

In this parable are given to us the causes of failure; and the requirements which are necessary in order to enable impressions to become permanent.

I. The causes of failure.

1. The first of these is want of spiritual perception Some of the seed fell by the wayside. There are persons whose religion is all outside — it never penetrates beyond the intellect. Duty is recognised in word — not felt. They are regular at church — understand the Catechism and Articles — consider the Church a most venerable institution — have a respect for religion — but it never stirs the deeps of their being. They feel nothing in it beyond a safeguard for the decencies and respectabilities of social life; valuable, as parliaments and magistrates are valuable, but by no means

the one awful question which fills the soul with fearful grandeur.

Truth of life is subject to failure in such hearts, in two ways, — By being trodden down: — wheat, dropped by a harvest cart upon a road lies outside. There comes a passenger's foot, and crushes some of it; then wheels come by — the wheel of traffic and the wheel of pleasure — crushing it grain by grain. It is "trodden down."

The fate of religion is easily understood from the parallel fate of a single sermon. Scarcely has its last tone vibrated on the ear, when a fresh impression is given by the music which dismisses the congregation. That is succeeded by another impression, as your friend puts his arm in yours, and talks of some other matter, irrelevant, obliterating any slight seriousness which the sermon produced. Another, and another, and another — and the word is *trodden down*. Observe, there is nothing wrong in these impressions. The farmer's cart which crushes the grain by the wayside is rolling by on rightful business — and the stage and the pedestrian are in their place — simply the seed is not. It is not the wrongness of the impressions which treads religion down; but only this, that outside religion yields in turn to other outside impressions which are stronger.

Again, conceptions of religious life, which are only conceptions outward, having no lodgment in the heart, *disappear*. Fowls of the air came and devoured the seed. Have you ever seen grain scattered on the road? The sparrow from the housetop, and the chickens from the barn, rush in and within a minute after it has been scattered, not the shadow of a grain is left. This is the picture: not of thought crushed by degrees —

but of thought dissipated, and no man can tell when or how it went. Swiftly do these winged thoughts come, when we pray, or read, or listen; in our inattentive, sauntering, wayside hours: and before we can be upon our guard, the very trace of holier purposes has disappeared. In our purest moods, when we kneel to pray, or gather round the altar, down into the very Holy of Holies sweep these foul birds of the air, villain fancies, demon thoughts. The germ of life, the small seed of impression, is gone — where, you know not. But it is gone. Inattentiveness of spirit, produced by want of spiritual interest, is the first cause of disappointment.

2. A second cause of failure is want of depth in character. Some fell on stony ground. Stony ground means often the soil with which many loose stones are intermixed; but that is not the stony ground meant here: this stony ground is the thin layer of earth upon a bed of rock. Shallow soil is like superficial character. You meet with such persons in life. There is nothing deep about them — all they do and all they have is on the surface. The superficial servant's work is done; but lazily, partially — not thoroughly. The superficial workman's labour will not bear looking into — but it bears a showy outside. The very dress of such persons betrays the slatternly, incomplete character of their minds. When religion comes in contact with persons of this stamp, it shares the fate of everything else. It is taken up in a superficial way.

There is deep knowledge of human nature and exquisite fidelity to truth in the single touch by which the impression of religion on them is described. The seed sprang up quickly; and then withered away as quickly, because it had no depth of root. There is a quick easily-moved susceptibility, that rapidly exhibits the slightest breath of those emotions which play upon the surface of the soul, and then as rapidly passes off. In such persons words are ever at command — voluble and impassioned words. Tears flow readily. The expressive features exhibit every passing shade of thought. Every thought and every feeling plays upon the surface — everything that is sown springs up at once with vehement vegetation. But slightness and inconstancy go together with violence. "Out of the abundance of the heart the mouth speaketh." True; but also out of the emptiness of the heart the mouth can speak even more volubly. He who can always find the word which is appropriate and adequate to his emotions, is not the man whose emotions are deepest: warmth of feeling is one thing — permanence is another. On Tuesday last, they who went to the table most moved and touched were not necessarily those who raised in a wise observer's breast the strongest hope of persistence in the life of Christ. Rather those who where calm and subdued; — that which springs up quickly often does so merely from this, that it has no depth of earth to give it room to strike its roots down and deep.

A young man of this stamp came to Christ — running, kneeling, full of warm expressions, engaging gestures, and professed admiration, worshipping and saying, "Good Master!" Lovable and interesting as such always are — Jesus loved him. But it lay all upon the surface, withered away when the depth of its meaning was explored. The test of self-sacrifice was applied to his apparent love. He was ready for anything. Well, "Go, sell that thou hast." It had sprung up quickly: but it withered because it had no root.

And that is another stroke of truth in the delineation of this character. Not wealth nor comfort is the bane of its religion: but "When tribulation or persecution ariseth because of the word, by and by they are offended." A pleasant, sunny religion would be the life to suit them. "They receive the Word with joy." So long as they have happiness they can love God — feel very grateful, and expand with generous emotions. But when God speaks as he spoke to Job out of the whirlwind, and the sun is swept from the face of their heaven, and the sharp Cross is the only object left in the dreary landscape, and the world blames, and friends wound the wounded with cold speech and hollow commonplaces: what is there in superficial religion to keep the heart in its place and vigorous still?

Another point. Not without significance is it represented that the superficial character is connected with the hard heart. Beneath the light thin surface of easily stirred dust lies the bed of rock. The shallow ground was stony ground. And it is among the children of light enjoyment and unsettled life that we must look for stony heartlessness: — not in the world of business — not among the poor, crushed to the earth by privation and suffering. These harden the character, but often leave the heart soft. If you wish to know what hollowness and heartlessness are, you must seek for them in the world of light, elegant, superficial Fashion — where frivolity has turned the heart into a rockbed of selfishness. Say what men will of the heartlessness of Trade, it is nothing compared with the heartlessness of Fashion. Say what they will of the atheism of science, it is nothing to the atheism of that round of pleasure in which many a heart lives: — dead while it lives.

3. Once more, impressions come to nothing when the mind is subjected to dissipating influences, and yields to them. "Some fell among thorns."

There is nutriment enough in the ground for thorns, and enough for wheat; but not enough, in any ground, for both wheat and thorns. The agriculturist thins his nursery-ground, and the farmer weeds his field, and the gardener removes the superfluous grapes, for that very reason: in order that the dissipated sap may be concentrated in a few plants vigorously.

So, in the same way, the heart has a certain power of loving. But love, dissipated on many objects, concentrates itself on none. God *or* the world — not both. "No man can serve two masters." "If any man love the world, the love of the Father is not in him." He that has learned many accomplishments or sciences, generally knows none thoroughly. Multifariousness of knowledge is commonly opposed to depth — variety of affections is generally not found with intensity.

Two classes of dissipating influences distract such minds. "The cares of this world, and the deceitfulness of riches, choke the Word." The *cares* of this world — its petty trifling distractions — not wrong in themselves — simply dissipating — filling the heart with paltry solicitudes and mean anxieties — *wearing*. Martha was "cumbered with much serving." Her household and her domestic duties, real duties, divided her heart with Christ. The time of danger, therefore, is when life expands into new situations and larger spheres, bringing with them new cares. It is not in the earlier stages of existence that these *distractions* are felt. Thorns sprang up and choked the wheat as they grew together. You see a religious man taking up a new pursuit with eagerness. At first no danger is suspected. But it is a *distraction* — something that distracts or divides — he has become dissipated, and by and by you remark that his zest is gone — he is no longer the man he was. He talks as before — but the life is gone from what he says: — his energies are frittered. The Word is "choked."

Again, the deceitfulness of riches dissipate. True as always to nature, never exaggerating, never one-sided: Christ does not say, that such religion brings forth no fruit, but only that it brings none to perfection. A fanatic bans all wealth and all worldly care as the department of the devil, — Christ says, "How hardly shall they that *trust* in riches enter into the Kingdom of Heaven." He does not say the divided heart has no religion, but it is a dwarfed, stunted, feeble religion. Many such a Christian do you find among the rich and the titled, who, as a less encumbered man, might have been a resolute soldier of the Cross; but he is only now a realization of the old Pagan fable — a spiritual giant buried under a mountain of gold. Oh! many, many such we meet in our higher classes, pining with a nameless want, pressed by a heavy sense of the weariness of existence, strengthless in the midst of affluence, and incapable even of tasting the profusion of comfort which is heaped around them.

There is a way God their Father has of dealing

with such which is no pleasant thing to bear. In agriculture it is called *weeding*. In gardening it is done by *pruning*. It is the cutting off the over-luxuriant shoots, in order to call back the wandering juices into the healthier and more living parts. In religion it is described thus, — "Every branch that beareth fruit He purgeth" . . . . Lot had such a danger, and was subjected to such a treatment. A quarrel had arisen between Abraham's herdsmen and his. It was necessary to part. Abraham, in that noble way of his, gave him the choice of the country when they separated. Either hand for Abraham: either the right hand or the left: — what cared the Pilgrim of the Invisible for fertile lands or rugged sands? Lot chose wisely, as they of the world speak. Well, if this world be all: — he got a rich soil — became a prince, had kings for his society and neighbours. It was nothing to Lot that "the men of the land were sinners before the Lord exceedingly" — enough that it was well watered everywhere. But his wife became enervated by voluptuousness, and his children tainted with ineradicable corruption — the moral miasma of the society wherein he had made his home. Two warnings God gave him — First, his home and property were spoiled by the enemy; then came the fire from heaven; and he fled from the cities of the plain a ruined man. His wife looked back with lingering regret upon the splendid home of her luxury and voluptuousness, and was overwhelmed in the encrusting salt: his children carried with them into a new world the plague-spot of that profligacy which had been the child of affluence and idleness; and the spirit of that rain of fire — of the buried Cities of the Plain — rose again in the darkest of the crimes which the Old Testament records, to poison the new society at its very fountain. And so the old man stood at last upon the brink of the grave, a blackened ruin scathed by lightning, over the grave of his wife, and the shame of his family — saved, but only "so as by fire."

It is a painful thing, that weeding work. "Every branch in me that beareth fruit, He purgeth it, that it may bring forth more fruit." The keen edge of God's pruning-knife cuts sheer through. No weak tenderness stops Him whose love seeks Goodness, not Comfort, for His servants. A man's distractions are in his wealth — and perhaps fire or failure make him bankrupt: what he feels is God's sharp knife. Pleasure has dissipated his heart, and a stricken frame forbids his enjoying pleasure — shattered nerves and broken health wear out the life of Life. Or perhaps it comes in a sharper, sadder form: the shaft of death goes home — there is heard the wail of danger in his household. And then, when sickness has passed on to hopelessness, and hopelessness has passed on to death, the crushed man goes into the chamber of the dead; and there, when he shuts down the lid upon the coffin of his wife, or the coffin of his child, his heart begins to tell him the meaning of all this. Thorns had been growing in his heart, and the sharp knife has been at work making room — but by an awful desolation — tearing up and cutting down, that the Life of God in the soul may not be choked.

II. For the permanence of religious impressions this parable suggests three requirements: "They on the good ground are they which, in an honest and good heart, having heard the word keep it, and bring forth fruit with patience."

1. "An honest and good heart." Earnestness: that is, sincerity of purpose. Now, sincerity is reckoned, by an exaggeration, sometimes the only virtue. So that a man be sincere, they say, it matters little what he thinks or what he is: but in Truth is the basis of all goodness; without which goodness of any kind is impossible. There are faults more heinous, but none more ruinous, than insincerity. Subtle minds, which have no broad firm footing in reality, lose everything by degrees, and may be transformed into any shape of evil — may become guilty of anything, and excuse it to themselves. To this sincerity is given, in the parable, success: A harvest thirty-fold, sixty-fold, an hundred-fold.

This earnestness is the first requisite for real success in everything. Do you wish to become rich? You may become rich: that is, if you desire it in no half-way, but thoroughly. A miser sacrifices all to this single passion; hoards farthings, and dies possessed of wealth. Do you wish to master any science or accomplishment? — Give yourself to it, and it lies beneath your feet. Time and pains will do anything. This world is given as the prize for the men in earnest; and that which is true of this world is truer still of the world to come. "The kingdom of heaven suffereth violence, and the violent take it by force." Only there is this difference. In the pursuit of wealth, knowledge, or reputation, circumstances have power to mar the wisest schemes. The hoard of years may be lost in a single night. The wisdom hived up by a whole life may perish when some fever impairs memory. But in the kingdom of Christ, where inward *character* is the prize, no chance can rob earnestness of its exactly proportioned due of success. "*Whatsoever* a man soweth, that shall he also reap." There is no blight, nor mildew, nor scorching sun, nor rain-deluge, which can turn that harvest into a failure. "Lay not up for yourselves treasures on earth." . . . Sow for time, and *probably* you will succeed in time. Sow the seeds of Life — Humbleness, Pure-heartedness, Love; and in the long Eternity which lies before the soul, every minutest grain will come up again with an increase of thirty, sixty, or an hundred-fold.

2. Meditation is a second requisite for permanence. They *keep* the word which they have heard

Now, meditation is often confounded with something which only partially resembles it. Sometimes we sit in a kind of day-dream, the mind expatiating far away into vacancy, whilst minutes and hours slip by, almost unmarked, in mere vacuity. This is not meditation, but reverie, — a state to which the soul resigns itself in pure passivity. When the soul is absent and dreaming, let no man think that *that* is spiritual meditation, or anything that is spiritual.

Meditation is partly a passive, partly an active state. Whoever has pondered long over a plan which he is anxious to accomplish, without distinctly seeing at first the way, knows what meditation is. The subject itself presents itself in leisure moments spontaneously: but then all this sets the mind at work — contriving, imagining, rejecting, modifying. It is in this way that one of the greatest of English engineers, a man uncouth and unaccustomed to regular discipline of mind, is said to have accomplished his most marvellous triumphs. He threw bridges over almost impracticable torrents, and pierced the eternal mountains for his viaducts. Sometimes a difficulty brought all the work to a pause: then he would shut himself up in his room, eat nothing, speak to no one, abandon himself intensely to the contemplation of that on which his heart was set; and at the end of two or three days, would come forth serene and calm, walk to the spot, and quietly give orders which seemed the result of superhuman intuition. This was meditation.

Again, he knows what it is, who has ever earnestly and sincerely loved one living human being. The image of his friend rises unbidden by day and night, stands before his soul in the street and in the field, comes athwart his every thought, and mixes its presence with his every plan. So far all is passive. But besides this he plans and contrives for that other's happiness — tries to devise what would give pleasure — examines his own conduct and conversation, to avoid that which can by any possibility give pain. This is meditation.

So, too, is meditation on religious truths carried on. If it first be loved, it will recur spontaneously to the heart.

But then it is dwelt on till it receives innumerable applications — is again and again brought up to the sun and tried in various lights, and so incorporates itself with the realities of practical existence.

Meditation is done in silence. By it we renounce our narrow individuality, and expatiate into that which is infinite. Only in the sacredness of inward silence does the soul truly meet the secret, hiding, God. The strength of resolve, which afterwards shapes life and mixes itself with action, is the fruit of those sacred, solitary moments. There is a divine depth in silence. We meet God alone.

For this reason, I urged it upon so many of you to spend the hours previous to your Confirmation separate from friends, from books, from everything human, and to force yourselves into the Awful Presence.

Have we never felt how human presence, if frivolous, in such moments frivolises the soul, and how impossible it is to come in contact with any thoughts which are sublime, or drink in one inspiration which is from Heaven, without degrading it, even though surrounded by all that would naturally suggest tender and awful feeling, when such are by?

It is not the number of books you read; nor the variety of sermons which you hear; nor the amount of religious conversation in which you mix: but it is the frequency and the earnestness with which you meditate on these things, till the truth which may be in them becomes your own, and part of your own being, that ensures your spiritual growth.

3. The third requisite is endurance. "They bring forth fruit with patience." Patience is of two kinds. There is an active and there is a passive endurance. The former is a masculine, the latter for the most part a feminine virtue. Female patience is exhibited chiefly in fortitude; in bearing pain and sorrow meekly without complaining. In the old Hebrew life, female endurance shines almost as brightly as in any life which Christianity itself can mould. Hannah, under the provocations and taunts of her rival, answering not again her husband's rebuke, humbly replying to Eli's unjust

blame, is true to the type of womanly endurance. For the type of man's endurance you may look to the patience of the early Christians under persecution. They came away from the Sanhedrim to endure and bear; but it was to bear as conquerors rushing on to victory, preaching the truth with all boldness, and defying the power of the united world to silence them. These two diverse qualities are joined in One, and only One of woman born, in perfection. One there was in whom human nature was exhibited in all its elements symmetrically complete. One in whom, as I lately said, there met all that was manliest and all that was most womanly. His endurance of pain and grief was that of the woman rather than the man. A tender spirit dissolving into tears, meeting the dark hour not with the stern defiance of the man and the stoic, but with gentleness, and trust, and love, and shrinking, like a woman. But when it came to the question in Pilate's judgment-hall, or the mockeries of Herod's men of war, or the discussion with the Pharisees, or the exposure of the hollow falsehoods by which social, domestic, and religious life were sapped, the Woman has disappeared, and the hardy resolution of the Man, with more than manly daring, is found in her stead. This is the "patience" for us to cultivate: To bear and to persevere. However dark and profitless, however painful and weary existence may have become, however any man like Elijah may be tempted to cast himself beneath the juniper-tree and say, "It is enough: now, O Lord!" — life is not done, and our Christian character is not won, so long as God has anything left for us to suffer, or anything left for us to do.

Patience, however, has another meaning. It is the opposite of that impatience which cannot *wait*. This is one of the difficulties of spiritual life. We are disappointed if the harvest do not come at once.

Last Tuesday, doubtless, you thought that all was done, and that there would be no more falling back.

Alas! a little experience will correct that. If the husbandman, disappointed at the delay which ensues before the blade breaks the soil, were to rake away the earth to examine if germination were going on, he would have a poor harvest. He must have "long patience, till he receive the early and the latter rain." The winter frost must mellow the seed lying in the genial bosom of the earth: the rains of spring must swell it, and the suns of summer mature it. So with you. It is the work of a long life to become a Christian. Many, oh! many a time, are we tempted to say, "I make no progress at all. It is only failure after failure. Nothing grows." Now look at the sea when the flood is coming in. Go and stand by the sea-beach, and you will think that the ceaseless flux and reflux is but retrogression equal to the advance. But look again in an hour's time, and the whole ocean has advanced. Every advance has been beyond the last, and every retrograde movement has been an imperceptible trifle less than the last. This is progress: to be estimated at the end of hours, not minutes. And this is *Christian* progress. Many a fluctuation — many a backward motion with a rush at times so vehement that all seems lost: — but if the Eternal work be real, every failure has been a real gain, and the next does not carry us so far back as we were before. Every advance is a real gain, and part of it is never lost. Both when we advance and when we fail, we gain. We are nearer to God than we were. The flood of spirit-life has carried us up higher on the everlasting shores, where the waves of life beat no more, and its fluctuations end, and all is safe at last. "This is the faith and patience of the saints."

It is because of the second of these requirements, Meditation, that I am anxious we should meet on Sunday next for an early Communion, at eight o'clock. I desire that the candidates may have a more solemn and definite Communion of their own, with few others present except their own relations and friends. In silence and quietness, we will meet together then. Before the world has put on its full robe of light, and before the busy gay crowd have begun to throng our streets, — before the distractions of the day begin, we will consecrate the early freshness of our souls — untrodden, unhardened, undissipated — to God. We will meet in the simplicity of brotherhood and sisterhood. We will have Communion in a sacred meal, which shall exhibit as nearly as may be the idea of family affection. Ye that are beginning life, and we who know something of it — ye that offer yourselves for the first time at that table, and we who, after sad experience and repeated failure, still *desire* again to renew our aspirations and our vows to Him — we will come and breathe together that prayer, which I commended to you at your confirmation, — "Our Father, which art in Heaven, lead us not into temptation, but deliver us from evil."

III.

Preached June 10, 1849.

JACOB'S WRESTLING.

GEN. xxxii. 28, 29. — "And he said, Thy name shall be called no more Jacob, but Israel: for as a prince hast thou power with God and with men, and hast prevailed. And Jacob asked him, and said, Tell me, I pray thee, thy name. And he said, Wherefore is it that thou dost ask after my name? And he blessed him there."

THE complexion of this story is peculiarly Jewish. It contains three points which are specially interesting to every Jew in a national point of view. It explained to him why he was called Israelite. It traces the origin of his own name, Israelite, to a distant ancestor, who had signally exhibited religious strength, and been, in the language of those times, a wrestler with God, from whence he had obtained the name Israel. It casts much deep and curious interest round an otherwise insignificant village, Peniel, where this transaction had taken place, and which derived its name from it: Peniel, the face of God. And, besides, it explained the origin of a singular custom, which might seem a superstitious one, of not suffering a particular muscle to be eaten, and regarding it with a kind of religious awe, as the part in which Jacob was said by tradition to have been injured, by the earnest tension of his frame during this struggle. So far all is Jewish, narrow, merely of local interest. Besides this, much of the story is evidently mythical.

It is clear at once, that it belongs to that earlier period of literature when traditions were preserved in a poetical shape, adapted to the rude conceptions of the day; but enshrining an inner and a deeper truth.

To disengage this truth from the form in which it is encased, is the duty of the expositor.

Now, putting aside the form of this narrative, and looking into the heart and meaning of it, it will become apparent that we have no longer anything infantine, or Jewish, or of limited interest, but a wide truth, wide as human nature; and that there is before us the record of an inward spiritual struggle, as real now in the nineteenth century as then: as real in every earnest man as it was in the history of Jacob.

We take these points:

I. The nameless secret of Existence.

II. The revelation of that secret to the Soul.

The circumstances which preceded this event were these: more than twenty years before, Jacob had been guilty of a deliberate sin. He had deceived his father; he had over-reached his free-spirited, impetuous, open-hearted brother Esau. Never, during all those twenty years, had he seen the man whom he had injured. But now, on the point of returning to his native country, news was brought to him of his brother's approach, which made a meeting inevitable. Jacob made all his dispositions and arrangements to prepare for the worst. He sent over the brook Jabbok first the part of his family whom he valued least, and who would be the first to meet Esau; then those whom he loved most, that, in the event of danger, they might have the greatest facility in escaping; then Jacob was left alone, in the still dark night. It was one of those moments in existence when a crisis is before us, to which great and pregnant issues are linked — when all has been done that foresight can devise, and the hour of action being past, the instant of reaction has come. Then the soul is left passive and helpless, gazing face to face upon the anticipated and dreadful moment which is slowly moving on. It is in those hours that, having gone through in imagination the whole circle of resources, and found them nothing, and ourselves powerless, as in the hands of a Destiny, there comes a strange and nameless dread, a horrible feeling of insecurity, which gives the consciousness of a want, and forces us to feel out into the abyss for something that is mightier than flesh and blood to lean upon.

Then, therefore, it was that there came the moment of a conflict within the soul of Jacob, so terrible and so violent that it seemed an actual struggle with a living man. In the darkness he had heard a Voice, and came in contact with a Form, and felt a Presence, the reality of which there was no mistaking. Now, to the unscientific mind, that which is real seems to be necessarily material too. What wonder if, to the unscientific mind of Jacob, this conflict, so real, and attended in his person with such tangible results, seemed all human and material — a conflict with a tangible antagonist? What wonder if tradition preserved it in such a form? Suppose we admit that the Being, whose awful presence Jacob felt, had no Form which could be grappled by a human hand, is it less real for that? Are there no realities but those which the hand can touch and the eye see?

Jacob in that hour felt the dark secret and mystery of existence.

Upon this I shall make three remarks.

1. The first has reference to the contrast observable between this and a former revelation made to Jacob's soul. This was not the first time it had found itself

face to face with God. Twenty years before, he had seen in vision a ladder reared against the sky, and angels ascending and descending on it. Exceedingly remarkable. Immediately after his transgression, when leaving his father's home, a banished man, to be a wanderer for many years, this first meeting took place. Fresh from his sin, God met him in tenderness and forgiveness. He saw the token which told him that all communication between heaven and earth was not severed. The way was clear and unimpeded still. Messages of reciprocated love might pass between the Father and His sinful child, as the angels in the dream ascended and descended on the visionary ladder. The possibility of saintliness was not forfeited. All *that* the Vision taught him. Then took place that touching Covenant, in which Jacob bound himself to serve gratefully his father's God, and vowed the vow of a consecrated heart to Him. All that was now past. After twenty years God met him again; but this second intercourse was of a very different character. It was no longer God the Forgiver, God the Protector, God the covenanting Love, that met Jacob; but God the Awful, the Unnameable, whose breath blasts, at whose touch the flesh of the mortal shrinks and shrivels up. This is exactly the reverse of what might have been anticipated. You would have expected the darker vision of experience to come first. First the storm-struggle of the soul; then the Vision of Peace. It was exactly the reverse.

Yet all this, tried by experience, is a most true and living account. The awful feelings about Life and God are *not* those which characterise our earlier years. It is quite natural that in the first espousals of the soul in its freshness to God, bright and hopeful feelings should be the predominant or the only ones. Joy marks, and ought to mark, early religion. Nay, by God's merciful arrangement, even sin is not that crushing thing in early life which it sometimes becomes in later years, when we mourn not so much a calculable number of sinful acts, as a deep pervading sinfulness. Remorse does not corrode with its evil power then. Forgiveness is not only granted, but consciously and joyfully felt. It is as life matures, that the weight of life, the burden of this unintelligible world, and the mystery of the hidden God, are felt.

A vast amount of insincerity is produced by mistaking this. We expect in the religion of the child the experience which can only be true in the religion of the man. We force into their lips the language which describes the wrestling of the soul with God. It is twenty years too soon. God, in His awfulness, the thought of mystery which scathes the soul — how can they know *that* yet, before they have got the thews and sinews of the man's heart to master such a thought? They know nothing yet — they *ought* to know nothing yet of God but as the Father who is around their beds — they *ought* to see nothing yet but Heaven, and angels ascending and descending.

This morning, my young brethren, you presented yourselves at the Communion Table for the first time. Some of you, we trust, were conscious of meeting God. Only let us not confound the dates of Christian experience. If you did, it was not as Jacob met God on this occasion, but rather as he met Him on the earlier one. It were only a miserable forcing of insincerity upon you to require that this solemn, fearful sensation of his should be yours. Rather, we trust, you felt God present as the Lord of Love. A ladder was raised for you to heaven. Oh! we trust that the feeling in some cases at least was this — as of angels ascending and descending upon a Child of God.

2. Again, I remark, that the end and aim of Jacob's struggle was to know the name of God. "Tell me, I pray thee, thy name." A very unimportant desire at first sight. For what signifies a name? In these days, when names are only epithets, it signifies nothing. "Jehovah, Jove, or Lord," as the "Universal Prayer" insinuates, are all the same. Now, to assert that it matters not whether God be called Jehovah, Jove, or Lord, is true, if it mean this that a devout and earnest heart is accepted by God, let the name be what it will by which He is addressed. But if it mean that Jove and Jehovah express the same Being — that the character of Him whom the Pagan worshipped was the same as the character of Him whom Israel adored under the name of Jehovah — that they refer to the same group of ideas — or that *always* names are but names, then we must look much deeper.

In the Hebrew history are descernible three periods distinctly marked, in which names and words bore very different characters. These three, it has been observed by acute philologists, correspond to the periods in which the nation bore the three different appellations of Hebrews, Israelites, Jews.

In the first of these periods, names meant truths, and words were the symbols of realities. The characteristics of the names given then were simplicity and sincerity. They were drawn from a few simple sources:

either from some characteristic of the individual, as Jacob, the supplanter, or Moses, drawn from the water; or from the idea of family, as Ben-jamin, the son of my right hand; or from the conception of the tribe or nation, then gradually consolidating itself; or, lastly, from the religious idea of God. But in this case not the highest notion of God — not Jah or Jehovah, but simply the earlier and simpler idea of Deity: El. — Israel, the prince of El; Peniel, the face of El.

In these days names were real, but the conceptions they contained were not the loftiest.

The second period begins about the time of the departure from Egypt, and it is characterised by unabated simplicity, with the addition of sublimer thought and feeling more intensely religious. The heart of the nation was big with mighty and new religious truth — and the feelings with which the national heart was swelling found vent in the names which were given abundantly. God, under His name Jah, the noblest assemblage of spiritual truths yet conceived, became the adjunct to names of places and persons. Oshea's name is changed into Je-hoshua.

Observe moreover, that in this period there was no fastidious, over-refined chariness in the use of that name. Men, conscious of deep and real reverence, are not fearful of the appearance of irreverence. The word became a common word, as it always may, so long as it is *felt*, and awe is *real*. A mighty cedar was called a cedar of Jehovah — a lofty mountain, a mountain of Jehovah. Human beauty even was praised by such an epithet. Moses was divinely fair, beautiful to God. The Eternal Name became an adjunct. No beauty —

no greatness — no goodness, was conceivable, except as emanating from Him: therefore His name was freely but most devoutly used.

Like the earlier period, in this too, words mean realities; but, unlike the earlier period, they are impregnated with deeper religious thought.

The third period was at its zenith in the time of Christ: — words had lost their meaning, and shared the hollow unreal state of all things. A man's name might be Judas, and still he might be a traitor. A man might be called Pharisee, exclusively religious, and yet the name might only cover the hollowness of hypocrisy; or he might be called most noble Festus, and be the meanest tyrant that ever sat upon a proconsular chair. This is the period in which every keen and wise observer knows that the decay of national religious feeling has begun. That decay in the meaning of words, that lowering of the standard of the ideas for which they stand, is a certain mark of this. The debasement of a language is a sure mark of the debasement of a nation. The insincerity of a language is a proof of the insincerity of a nation: for a time comes in the history of a nation when words no longer stand for things; when names are given for the sake of an euphonious sound; and when titles are but the epithets of unmeaning courtesy: — a time when Majesty — Defender of the Faith — Most Noble — Worshipful, and Honourable — not only mean nothing, but do not flush the cheek with the shame of convicted falsehood when they are worn as empty ornaments.

The Name of God shares this fate. A nation may reach the state in which the Eternal Name can be used to point a sentence, or adorn a familiar conversation, and no longer shock the ear with the sound of blasphemy, because in good truth the Name no longer stands for the Highest, but for a meaner conception, an idol of the debased mind. For example, in a foreign language, the language of a light and irreligious people, the Eternal Name can be used as a light expletive and conversational ejaculation, and not shock any religious sensibility. You could not do that in English. It would sound like a blasphemy to say, in light talk, My God! or Good God! Your flesh would creep at hearing it. But in that language the word has lost its sacredness, because it has lost its meaning. It means no more than Jove or Baal. It means a Being whose existence has become a nursery fable. No marvel that we are taught to pray, "Hallowed be Thy name." We cannot pray a deeper prayer for our country than to say — Never may that Name in English stand for a lower idea than it stands for now. There is a solemn power in words, because words are the expression of character. "By thy words thou shalt be justified, and by thy words thou shalt be condemned."

Yet in this period, exactly in proportion as the solemnity of the idea was gone, reverence was scrupulously paid to the corpse-like word which remained and had once enclosed it. In that hollow, artificial age, the Jew would wipe his pen before he ventured to write the Name — he would leave out the vowels of the sacred Jehovah, and substitute those of the less sacred Elohim. In that kind of age, too, men bow to the name of Jesus, often just in that proportion in which they have ceased to recognise His true grandeur and majesty of character.

In such an age, it would be indeed preposterous to

spend the strength upon an inquiry such as this: "Tell me Thy Name?" Jehovah, Jove, or Lord — what matter? But Jacob did not live in this third period, when names meant nothing: nor did he live in the second, when words contained the deepest truth the nation is ever destined to receive. But he lived in the first age, when men are sincere, and truthful and earnest, and names exhibit character. To tell Jacob the Name of God was to reveal to him What God is, and Who.

3. I observe a third thing. This desire of Jacob was not the one we should naturally have expected on such an occasion. He is alone — his past fault is coming retributively on a guilty conscience — he dreads the meeting with his brother. His soul is agonized with *that*, and *that* we naturally expect will be the subject and the burden of his prayer. No such thing! Not a word about Esau — not a word about personal danger at all. All that is banished completely for the time, and deeper thoughts are grappling with his soul. To get safe through to-morrow? No, no, no! To be blessed by God — to know Him, and what He is — that is the battle of Jacob's soul from sunset till the dawn of day.

And this is our struggle — *the* struggle. Let any true man go down into the deeps of his own being, and answer us, — what is the cry that comes from the most real part of his nature? Is it the cry for daily bread? Jacob asked for that in his *first* communing with God — preservation, safety. Is it even this, — to be forgiven our sins? Jacob had a sin to be forgiven, and in that most solemn moment of his existence he did not say a syllable about it. Or is it this —

"Hallowed be Thy Name?" No, my brethren. Out of our frail and yet sublime humanity, the demand that rises in the earthlier hours of our religion may be this — Save my soul; but in the most unearthly moments it is this — "Tell me thy Name." We move through a world of mystery; and the deepest question is, What is the being that is ever near, sometimes felt, never seen, — That which has haunted us from childhood with a dream of something surpassingly fair, which has never yet been realized — That which sweeps through the soul at times as a desolation, like the blast from the wings of the Angel of Death, leaving us stricken and silent in our loneliness — That which has touched us in our tenderest point, and the flesh has quivered with agony, and our mortal affections have shrivelled up with pain — That which comes to us in aspirations of nobleness, and conceptions of superhuman excellence. Shall we say It or He? What is It? Who is He? Those anticipations of Immortality and God — what are they? Are they the mere throbbings of my own heart, heard and mistaken for a living something beside me? Are they the sound of my own wishes, echoing through the vast void of Nothingness? or shall I call them God, Father, Spirit, Love? A living Being within me or outside me? Tell me Thy Name, thou awful mystery of Loveliness! This is the struggle of all earnest life.

We come now to,

II. The revelation of the Mystery.

1. It was revealed by awe. Very significantly are we told, that the Divine antagonist seemed as it were anxious to depart as the day was about to dawn; and that Jacob held Him more convulsively fast, as if

aware that the daylight was likely to rob him of his anticipated blessing: in which there seems concealed a very deep truth. God is approached more nearly in that which is indefinite than in that which is definite and distinct. He is felt in awe, and wonder and worship, rather than in clear conceptions. There is a sense in which darkness has more of God than light has. He dwells in the thick darkness. Moments of tender, vague mystery often bring distinctly the feeling of His presence. When day breaks and distinctness comes, the Divine has evaporated from the soul like morning dew. In sorrow, haunted by uncertain presentiments, we feel the infinite around us. The gloom disperses, the world's joy comes again, and it seems as if God were gone — the Being who had touched us with a withering hand, and wrestled with us, yet whose presence even when most terrible, was more blessed than His absence. It is true, even literally, that the darkness reveals God. Every morning God draws the curtain of the garish light across His eternity, and we lose the Infinite. We look down on earth instead of up to heaven, on a narrower and more contracted spectacle — that which is examined by the microscope when the telescope is laid aside — smallness, instead of vastness. "Man goeth forth unto his work and to his labour till the evening;" and in the dust and pettiness of life we seem to cease to behold Him: then at night He undraws the curtain again, and we see how much of God and Eternity the bright distinct day has hidden from us. Yes, in solitary, silent, vague darkness, the Awful One is near.

This morning, young brethren, we endeavoured to act on this belief — we met in stillness, before the full broad glare of day had rested on our world. Your first communion implored His blessing in the earlier hour which seems so peculiarly His. Before the dull, and deadening, and earthward influences of the world had dried up the dew of fresh morning feeling, you tried to fortify your souls with a sense of His presence. This night, before to-morrow's light shall dawn, pray that He will not depart until he has left upon your hearts the blessing of a strength which shall be yours through the garish day, and through dry, scorching life, even to the close of your days.

2. Again; this revelation was made in an unsyllabled blessing. Jacob requested two things. He asked for a blessing — and he prayed to know the Name of God. God gave him the blessing. "He blessed him there," but refused to tell His Name. "Wherefore dost thou ask after my Name?"

In this, too, seems to lie a most important truth. Names have a power, a strange power, of hiding God. Speech has been bitterly defined as the art of hiding thought. Well, that sarcastic definition has in it a truth. The Eternal Word is the Revealer of God's thought; and every *true* word of man is *originally* the expression of a thought; but by degrees the word hides the thought. Language is valuable for the things of this life; but for the things of the other world it is an encumbrance almost as much as an assistance. Words often hide from us our ignorance of even earthly truth. The child asks for information, and we satiate his curiosity with words. Who does not know how we satisfy ourselves with the name of some strange bird or plant, or the name of some new law in nature? It is a mystery perplexing us before. We get the name, and fancy we understand something more than we did before; but, in truth, we are more hopelessly ignorant: for before we felt there was a something we had not attained, and so we inquired and searched — now, we fancy we possess it, because we have got the name by which it is known: and the word covers over the abyss of our ignorance. If Jacob had got a *word*, that word might have satisfied him. He would have said, Now I understand God, and know all about Him.

Besides, names and words soon lose their meaning. In the process of years and centuries the meaning dies off them like the sunlight from the hills. The hills are there — the colour and life are gone. The words of that creed, for example, which we read last Sunday (the Athanasian), were living words a few centuries ago. They have changed their meaning, and are, to ninety-nine out of every hundred, only dead words. Yet men tenaciously hold to the expression of which they do not understand the meaning, and which have a very different meaning now from what they had once — Person, Procession, Substance; and they are almost worse with them than without them — for they conceal their ignorance, and place a barrier against the earnestness of inquiry. We repeat the creed by rote, but the profound truths of Being which the creed contains, how many of us understand?

All this affords an instructive lesson to parents and to teachers. In the education of a pupil or a child, the wise way is to deal with him as God dealt with His pupil, the child-man Jacob: for before the teaching of God, the wisest man — what is he but a child? God's plan was not to give names and words, but truths of feeling. That night, in that strange scene, He impressed on Jacob's soul a religious awe which was hereafter to develop, — not a set of formal expressions, which would have satisfied with husks the cravings of the intellect, and shut up the soul: — Jacob felt the Infinite, who is more truly felt when least named. Words would have reduced that to the Finite; for, oh! to know all about God is one thing — to know the living God is another. Our rule seems to be this: Let a child's religion be expansive — capable of expansion — as little systematic as possible: let it lie upon the heart like the light loose soil, which can be broken through as the heart bursts into fuller life. If it be trodden down hard and stiff in formularies, it is more than probable that the whole must be burst through, and broken violently and thrown off altogether, when the soul requires room to germinate.

And in this way, my young brethren, I have tried to deal with you. Not in creeds, nor even in the stiffness of the catechism, has truth been put before you. Rather has it been trusted to the impulses of the heart; on which, we believe, God works more efficaciously than we can do. A few simple truths: and then these have been left to work, and germinate, and swell. Baptism reveals to you this truth for the heart, that God is your Father, and that Christ has encouraged you to live as your Father's children. It has revealed that Name which Jacob knew not — Love. Confirmation has told you another truth, that of self-dedication to Him. Heaven is the service of God. The highest blessedness of life is, powers and self consecrated to His will. These are the germs of truth: but it would have been miserable self-delusion, and most pernicious teaching, to have aimed at exhausting truth, or systematizing it. We are jealous of over-systematic teaching. God's love to you — the sacrifice of your lives to God — but the *meaning* of that? Oh! a long, long life will not exhaust the meaning — the Name of God. Feel Him more and more — all else is but empty words.

Lastly, the effect of this Revelation was to change Jacob's character. His name was changed from Jacob to Israel, because himself was an altered man. Hitherto there had been something subtle in his character — a certain cunning and craft — a want of breadth, as if he had no firm footing upon reality. The forgiveness of God twenty years before had not altered this. He remained Jacob, the subtle supplanter still. For, indeed, a man whose religion is chiefly the sense of forgiveness, does not thereby rise into integrity or firmness of character — a certain tenderness of character may very easily go along with a great deal of subtlety. Jacob was tender and devout, and grateful for God's pardon, and only half honest still. But this half-insincere man is brought into contact with the awful God, and his subtlety falls from him. He becomes real at once. Every insincere habit of mind shrivels in the face of God. One clear true glance into the depths of Being, and the whole man is altered. The name changes because the character has changed. No longer Jacob the supplanter, but Israel the Prince of God — the champion of the Lord, who had fought *with* God and conquered; and who, henceforth, will fight *for* God and be His true loyal soldier: a larger, more unselfish name — a larger and more unselfish man — honest and true at last. No man becomes honest till he has got face to face with God. There is a certain insincerity about us all — a something dramatic. One of those dreadful moments which throw us upon ourselves, and strip off the hollowness of our outside show, must come before the insincere is true.

And again, young brethren, such a moment, at least of truthfulness, ought to have been this morning. Let the old pass. Let the name of the world pass into the Christian name. Baptism and Confirmation, the one gives, and the other reminds us of the giving of a better name and a truer. Henceforth be men. Lose the natural frailty, whatever it is. See God, and you *will* lose it.

To conclude, here is a question for each man separately — What is the name of your God? Not in the sense of this age, but in the sense of Jacob's age. What is the *Name* of the Deity you worship? In the present modern sense of Name, by which nothing more than epithet is meant, of course the reply is easy. The name of yours is the God of Christian worship — the threefold One — the Author of Existence, manifested in Divine humanity, commingling with us as pure spirit — the Father, Son and Holy Ghost. That, of course, you say is the Name of your God. Now, put away names — give words to the winds. What do you adore in your heart of hearts? What is the name oftenest on your lips in your unfettered, spontaneous moments? If we overheard your secret thoughts, who and what is it which is to you the greatest and the best that you would desire to realize? The character of the rich man, or the successful, or the admired? Would the worst misery which could happen to you be the wreck of property — the worst shame, not to have done wrong, but to have sunk in the estimation of society? Then in the classifications of earth, which separate men into Jews, Christians, Mahometans, you may rank as a worshipper of the Christian's God. But in the nomenclature of Heaven, where names cannot stand for things, God sees you as an idolator — your highest is not His highest. The Name that is above every name is not the description of your God.

For life and death we have made our choice. The life of Christ — the life of Truth and Love; and if it must be, as the result of that, the Cross of Christ, with the obloquy and shame that wait on truth — that is the Name before which we bow. In this world "there are Gods many, and Lords many: but to us there is one Lord, the Father of our Lord Jesus Christ."

IV.

Preached August 12, 1849.

CHRISTIAN PROGRESS BY OBLIVION OF THE PAST.

PHIL. iii. 13, 14. — "Brethren, I count not myself to have apprehended; but this one thing I do, forgetting those things which are behind, and reaching forth unto those things which are before, I press toward the mark, for the prize of the high calling of God in Christ Jesus."

THE first thing which strikes us on reading these verses is, that the Apostle Paul places himself on a level with the persons whom he addresses. He speaks to them as frail, weak men; and he gives them in himself a specimen of what frailty and weakness can achieve in the strength of Christ. And it is for this reason that the passage before us is one of the most encouraging in all the writings of St. Paul. For there is one aspect in which the apostle is presented to us which is perhaps a depressing one. When we look at his almost superhuman career, reverence and admiration we must feel; but so far does he seem removed from ordinary life, that imitation appears out of the question. Let us select but two instances of this discouraging aspect of the apostle's life. Most of us know the feeling of unaccountable depression which rests upon us when we find ourselves alone in a foreign town, with its tide of population ebbing and flowing past us, a mass of human life, in which we ourselves are nothing. But that was Paul's daily existence. He had consecrated himself to an almost perpetual exile. He had given up the endearments of domestic life for ever. Home, in this world, St. Paul had none. With a capacity for the tenderest feelings of our nature, he had chosen for his lot the task of living among strangers, and as soon as they ceased to be strangers, quitting them again. He went on month by month, attaching congregations to himself, and month by month dooming himself to severance. And yet I know not that we read of one single trace of depression or discouragement suffered to rest on the apostle's mind. He seems to have been ever fresh and sanguine, the salient energy of his soul rising above the need of all human sympathy. It is the magnificent spectacle of missionary life, with more than missionary loneliness. There is something almost awful in the thought of a man who was so thoroughly in the next world that he needed not the consolations of this world. And yet, observe, there is nothing encouraging for us in this. It is very grand to look upon, very commanding, very full of awe; but it is so much above us, so little like anything human that we know of, that we content ourselves with gazing on him as on the gliding swallow's flight, which we wonder at, but never think of imitating.

Now, let us look at one other feature in St Paul's character — his superiority to those temptations which are potent with ordinary men. We say nothing of his being above the love of money: of his indifference to a life of comfort and personal indulgence. Those temptations only assail the lower part of our nature; and it is not saintliness to be above these: common excellence is impossible otherwise. But when we come to look for those temptations which master the higher and the nobler man, ambition, jealousy, pride, it is not that we see them conquered by the apostle; they scarcely seem to have even lodged in his bosom at all. It was open to the apostle, if he had felt the ambition, to make for himself a name, to become the leader of a party in Corinth and in the world. And yet remember we not how sternly he put down the thought, and how he laboured to merge his individuality in the Cause, and make himself an equal of inferior men? "Who, then, is Paul, and who is Apollos, but ministers, servants, by whom ye believed?"

Again, in respect of jealousy. Jealousy seems almost inseparable from human love. It is but the other side of love, the shadow cast by the light when the darker body intervenes. There came to him in prison that most cutting of all news to a minister's heart, that others were trying to supplant him in the affection of his converts. But his was that lofty love which cares less for reciprocation than for the well-being of the objects loved. The rival teachers were teaching from emulation; still they could not but bless by preaching to his disciples. What then? Notwithstanding every way, whether in pretence or in truth, "Christ is preached; and I therein do rejoice, yea, and will rejoice." Not a trace of jealousy in these words.

Once more — Degrading things were laid to his charge. The most liberal-minded of mankind was charged with bigotry. The most generous of men was suspected of avarice. If ever pride were venial, it had been then. Yet read through the whole of the Second Epistle of the Corinthians, and say if one spark of pride be visible. He might have shut himself up in high and dignified silence. He might have refused to condescend to solicit a renewal of the love which had once grown cold; and yet we look in vain for the symptoms of offended pride. Take this one passage as a specimen. "Behold this third time I am willing to come unto you . . . . and I will very gladly spend and be spent for you, though the more abundantly I love you, the less I am beloved."

In this there in very little encouragement. A man so thoroughly above human resentment, human passions, human weakness, does not seem to us an example. The nearer humanity approaches a perfect standard, the less does it command our sympathy. A man must be weak before we can feel encouraged to attempt what he has done. It is not the Redeemer's sinlessness, nor His unconquerable fidelity to duty, nor His superhuman nobleness, that win our desire to imitate. Rather His tears at the grave of friendship, His shrinking from the sharpness of death; — and the feeling of human doubt which swept across his soul like a desolation. These make Him one of us, and therefore our example.

And it is on this account that this passage seems to us so full of encouragement. It is the precious picture of a frail and struggling apostle — precious both to the man and to the minister. To the man, because it tells him that what he feels Paul felt, imperfect, feeble, far from what he would wish to be; yet with sanguine hope, expecting progress in the saintly life. Precious to the minister because it tells him that his very weakness may be subservient to a people's strength. Not in his transcendent gifts — not in his saintly endowments — not even in his apostolic devotedness, is St. Paul so close to our hearts, as when he makes himself one with us, and says, "Brethren, I count not myself to have apprehended." And we know not how otherwise any minister could hope to do good, when he addresses men who are infinitely his superiors in almost everything. We know not how else he could urge on to a sanctity which he has not himself attained: we know not how he could dare to speak severely of weaknesses by which he himself is overpowered, and passions of which he feels himself all the terrible tyranny, if it were not that he expects to have tacitly understood *that* in his own case which the apostle urged in every form of expression: Brethren, be as I am, for I am as ye are — struggling, baffled, but panting for emancipation.

We confine ourselves to two subjects:

I. The apostle's object in this life.

II. The means which he used for attaining it.

I. The apostle's object or aim in this life was "perfection." In the verse before — "Not as though I had already attained, either were already perfect." — Perfection was his unreached mark.

And less than this no Christian can aim at. There are given to us "exceeding great and precious promises," that by means of these we might be partakers of the Divine nature. Not to be equal to the standard of our day, nor even to surpass it. Not to be superior to the men amongst whom we live. Not to forgive those who have little to be forgiven. Not to love our friends — But to be the children of our Father — to be pure even as Christ is pure — to be "perfect even as our Father which is in Heaven is perfect."

It is easily perceivable why this perfection is unattainable in this life. Faultlessness is conceivable, being merely the negation of evil. But perfection is positive, the attainment of all conceivable excellence. It is long as Eternity — expansive as God. Perfection is our mark: yet never will the aim be so true and steady as to strike the golden centre. Perfection of character, yet even to the dying hour, it will be but this, "I count not myself to have apprehended." Christian life is like those questions in mathematics which never can be exactly answered. All you can attain is an approximation to the truth. You may labour on for years and never reach it; yet your labour is not in vain. Every figure you add makes the fraction nearer than the last to the million millionth; and so it is with holiness. Christ is our mark — the perfect standard of God in Christ. But be as holy as you will, there is a step nearer, and another, and another, and so infinitely on.

To this object the apostle gave himself with singleness of aim. "*This one thing I do.*" The life of man is a vagrant changeful desultoriness; like that of children sporting on an enamelled meadow, chasing now a painted butterfly, which loses its charm by being caught — now a wreath of mist, which falls damp upon the hand with disappointment — now a feather of thistledown, which is crushed in the grasp. In the midst of all this fickleness, St. Paul had found a purpose to which he gave the undivided energy of his soul. "This one thing I do — I press toward the mark."

This is intelligible enough in the case of a minister; for whether he be in the pulpit or beside a sick man's bed — or furnishing his mind in the study, evidently and unmistakably it is his profession to be doing only one thing. But in the manifold life of the man of the world, and business, it is not so easy to understand how this can be carried out. To answer this, we observe, there is a difference between doing and being. Perfection is being, not doing — it is not to effect an act but to achieve a character. If the aim of life were to do something, then, as in an earthly business, except in doing this one thing the business would be at a standstill. The student is not doing the one thing of student-life when he has ceased to think or read. The labourer leaves his work undone when the spade is not in his hand, and he sits beneath the hedge to rest. But in Christian life, every moment and every act is an opportunity for doing the one thing of *becoming* Christ-like. Every day is full of a most impressive experience. Every temptation to evil temper which can assail us to-day will be an opportunity to decide the question whether we shall gain the calmness and the rest of Christ, or whether we shall be tossed by the restlessness and agitation of the world. Nay, the very vicissitudes of the seasons, day and night, heat and cold, affecting us variably, and producing exhilaration or depression, are so contrived as to conduce towards the being which we become, and decide whether we shall be masters of ourselves, or whether we shall be swept at the mercy of accident and circumstance, miserably susceptible of merely outward influences. Infinite as are the varieties of life, so manifold are the paths to saintly character; and he who has not found out how directly or indirectly to make everything converge towards his soul's sanctification, has as yet missed the meaning of this life.

In pressing towards this "mark," the apostle attained a prize; and here I offer an observation, which is not one of mere subtlety of refinement, but deeply practical. The mark was perfection of character — the prize was blessedness. But the apostle did not aim at the prize of blessedness: he aimed at the mark of perfectness. In becoming perfect he attained happiness, but his primary aim was not happiness.

We may understand this by an illustration. In student-life there are those who seek knowledge for its own sake, and there are those who seek it for the sake of the prize, and the honour, and the subsequent success in life that knowledge brings. To those who seek knowledge for its own sake the labour is itself reward. Attainment is the highest reward. Doubtless the prize stimulates exertion; encourages and forms a part of the motive; but only a subordinate one: and knowledge would still have "a price above rubies," if there were no prize at all. They who seek knowledge for the sake of the prize are not genuine lovers of knowledge —they only love the rewards of knowledge; had it no honour or substantial advantage connected with it, they would be indolent.

Applying this to our subject, I say this it a spurious goodness which is good for the sake of reward. The child that speaks truth for the sake of the praise of truth, is not truthful. The man who is honest because honesty is the best policy, has not integrity in his heart. He who endeavours to be humble, and holy, and perfect, in order to win heaven, has only a counterfeit religion. God for His own sake — Goodness because it is good — Truth because it is lovely — this is the Christian's aim. The prize is only an incentive; inseparable from success, but not the aim itself.

With this limitation, however, we remark that it is a Christian duty to dwell much more on the thought of future blessedness than most men do. If ever the apostle's step began to flag, the radiant diadem before him gave new vigour to his heart; and we know how at the close of his career the vision became more vivid and more entrancing. "Henceforth there is laid up for me a crown of glory!" It is our privilege, if we are on our way to God, to keep steadily before us the thought of Home. Make it a matter of habit. Force yourself at night, alone, in the midst of the world's bright sights, to pause to think of the heaven which is yours. Let it calm you and ennoble you, and give you cheerfulness to endure. It was so that Moses was enabled to live amongst all the fascinations of his courtly life, with a heart unseduced from his laborious destiny. By faith ... "esteeming the reproach of Christ greater riches than the treasures of Egypt." Why? "for he had respect unto the recompense of the reward." It was so that our Master strengthened his Human Soul for its sharp earthly endurance. "For the joy that was set before him, He endured the cross, despising the shame." If we would become heavenly-minded, we must let the imagination realize the blessedness to which we are moving on. Let us think much of rest, — the rest which is not of indolence, but of powers in perfect equilibrium. The rest which is deep as summer midnight, yet full of life and force as summer sunshine, the sabbath of Eternity. Let us think of the love of God, which we shall feel in its full tide upon our souls. Let us think of that marvellous career of sublime occupation which shall belong to the spirits of just men made perfect; when we shall fill a higher place in God's universe, and more consciously, and with more distinct insight, co-operate with God in the rule over His Creation. "I press toward the mark — for the prize."

II. We pass to our second topic. The means which Paul found available for the attainment of Divine and perfect character. His great principle was to forget the things which were behind, and to reach forward to the things which were before. The wisdom of a divine life lies hid in this principle. I shall endeavour to expand the sentiment to make it intelligible.

What are the things behind, which are to be forgotten?

1. If we would progress in Christian life, we must forget the days of innocence that lie behind us. Let not this be misunderstood. Innocent, literally, no man ever is. We come into the world with tendencies to evil; but there was a time in our lives when those were only tendencies. A proneness to sin we had; but we had not yet sinned. The moment had not yet arrived when that cloud settles down upon the heart, which in all of after life is never entirely removed: the sense of guilt, the anguish of lost innocence, the restless feeling of a heart no longer pure. Popularly, we call that innocence; and when men become bitterly aware that early innocence of heart is gone, they feel as if all were lost, and so look back to what they reckon holier days with a peculiar fondness of regret. I believe there is much that is merely feeble and sentimental in this regret. Our early innocence is nothing more than ignorance of evil. Christian life is not a retaining of that ignorance of evil: nor even a returning of it again. We lose our mere negative sinlessness. We put on a firm manly holiness. Human innocence is not to know evil: — Christian saintliness is to know evil and good, and prefer good. It is possible for a parent, with over-fastidious refinement, to prolong the duration of this innocence unnaturally. He may lock up his library, and prevent the entrance to forbidden

books: — he may exercise a jealous censorship over every book and every companion that comes into the house; — he may remove the public journal from the table, lest an eye may chance to rest upon the contaminating portion of its pages; but he has only put off the evil hour. He has sent into the world a young man of eighteen or twenty, ignorant of evil as a child, but not innocent as an angel who abhors the evil. No, we cannot get back our past ignorance, neither is it desirable we should. No sane mind wishes for that which is impossible. And it is no more to be regretted than the blossom is to be regretted when fruit is hardening in its place; — no more to be regretted than the slender gracefulness of the sapling, when you have got instead the woody fibre of the heart of oak of which the ship is made; — no more to be regretted than the green blade when the ear has come instead, bending down in yellow ripeness. Our innocence is gone, withered with the business-like contact with the great world. It is one of the things behind. Forget it. It was worth very little. And now for something of a texture more firm, more enduring. We will not mourn over the loss of simplicity, if we have got instead souls indurated by experience, disciplined, even by fall, to refuse the evil and to choose the good.

2. In the next place, it is wise to forget our days of youth. Up to a certain period of life it is the tendency of man to look forwards. There is a marvellous prodigality with which we throw away our present happiness when we are young, which belongs to those who feel that they are rich in happiness, and never expect to be bankrupts. It almost seems one of the signatures of our immortality that we squander time as

if there were a dim consciousness that we are in possession of an eternity of it; but as we arrive at middle age, it is the tendency of man to look back. To a man of middle life, existence is no longer a dream, but a reality. He has not much more new to look forward to, for the character of his life is generally fixed by that time. His profession, his home, his occupations, will be for the most part what they are now. He will make few new acquaintances — no new friends. It is the solemn thought connected with middle age that life's last business is begun in earnest; and it is then, midway between the cradle and the grave, that a man begins to look back and marvel with a kind of remorseful feeling that he let the days of youth go by so half-enjoyed. It is the pensive autumn feeling, — it is the sensation of half sadness that we experience when the longest day of the year is past, and every day that follows is shorter, and the lights fainter, and the feebler shadows tell that nature is hastening with gigantic footsteps to her winter grave. So does man look back upon his youth. When the first grey hairs become visible — when the unwelcome truth fastens itself upon the mind, that a man is no longer going up the hill, but down, and that the sun is already westering, he looks back on things behind. Now this is a natural feeling, but is it the high Christian tone of feeling? In the spirit of this verse, we may assuredly answer, No. We who have an inheritance incorruptible and undefiled, and that fadeth not away, what have we to do with things past? When we were children we thought as children. But now there lies before us manhood, with its earnest work: and then old age, and then the grave, and then home. And so manhood in the Christian life is a better thing than boyhood, because it is a riper thing; and old age ought to be a brighter, and a calmer, and a more serene thing than manhood. There is a second youth for man, better and holier than his first, if he will look on and not back. There is a peculiar simplicity of heart and a touching singleness of purpose in Christian old age, which has ripened gradually and not fitfully. It is then that to the wisdom of the serpent is added the harmlessness of the dove; it is then that to the firmness of manhood is joined almost the gentleness of womanhood; it is then that the somewhat austere and sour character of growing strength, moral and intellectual, mellows into the rich ripeness of an old age, made sweet and tolerant by experience; it is then that man returns to first principles. There comes a love more pure and deep than the boy could ever feel; there comes a conviction, with a strength beyond that which the boy could ever know, that the earliest lesson of life is infinite, Christ is all in all.

3. Again; it is wise to forget past errors. There is a kind of temperament which, when indulged, greatly hinders growth in real godliness. It is that rueful, repentant, self-accusing temper, which is always looking back, and microscopically observing how that which is done might have been better done. Something of this we ought to have. A Christian ought to feel always that he has partially failed, but that ought not to be the only feeling. Faith ought ever to be a sanguine, cheerful thing; and perhaps in practical life we could not give a better account of faith than by saying, that it is, amidst much failure, having the heart to *try again*. Our best deeds are marked by imperfec-

tion; but if they really were our best, "forget the things that are behind" — we shall do better next time.

Under this head we include all those mistakes which belong to our circumstances. We can all look back to past life and see mistakes that have been made, to a certain extent, perhaps, irreparable ones. We can see where our education was fatally misdirected. The profession chosen for you perhaps was not the fittest, or you are out of place, and many things might have been better ordered. Now, on this apostolic principle, it is wise to forget all that. It is not by regretting what is irreparable that true work is to be done, but by making the best of what we are. It is not by complaining that we have not the right tools, but by using well the tools we have. What we are, and where we are, is God's providential arrangement — God's doing, though it may be man's misdoing; and the manly and the wise way is to look your disadvantages in the face, and see what can be made out of them. Life, like war, is a series of mistakes, and he is not the best Christian nor the best general who makes the fewest false steps. Poor mediocrity may secure that; but he is the best who wins the most spendid victories by the retrieval of mistakes. Forget mistakes: organize victory out of mistakes.

Finally; Past guilt lies behind us, and is well forgotten. There is a way in which even sin may be banished from the memory. If a man looks forward to the evil he is going to commit, and satisfies himself that it is inevitable, and so treats it lightly, he is acting as a fatalist. But if a man partially does this, looking backward, feeling that sin when it is past has become part of the history of God's universe, and is not to be wept over for ever, he only does that which the Giver of the Gospel permits him to do. Bad as the results have been in the world of making light of sin, those of brooding over it too much have been worse. Remorse has done more harm than even hardihood. It was remorse which fixed Judas in an unalterable destiny; it was remorse which filled the monasteries for ages with men and women whose lives became useless to their fellow-creatures; it is remorse which so remembers bygone faults as to paralyse the energies for doing Christ's work; for when you break a Christian's spirit, it is all over with progress. Oh! we want everything that is hopeful and encouraging for our work, for, God knows, it is not an easy one. And therefore it is that the Gospel comes to the guiltiest of us all at the very outset with the inspiring news of pardon. You remember how Christ treated sin. Sin of oppression and hypocrisy indignantly, but sin of frailty — "'Hath no man condemned thee?' 'No man, Lord.' 'Neither do I condemn thee; go, and sin no more.'" As if he would bid us think more of what we may be than of what we have been. There was the wisdom of life in the proverb with which the widow of Tekoah pleaded for the restoration of Absolom from banishment before David. Absolom had slain his brother Amnon. Well, Amnon was dead before his time; but the severity of revenge could never bring him back again. "We must all die," said the wise woman, "and are as water spilt upon the ground, which cannot be gathered up again." Christian brethren, *do not stop too long to weep over spilt water.* Forget your guilt, and wait to see what eternity has to say to it. You have other work to do now.

So let us work out the spirit of the apostle's plan. Innocence, youth, success, error, guilt — let us forget them all.

> Not backward are our glances bent,
> But onwards to our Father's home.

In conclusion, remember Christian progress is only possible in Christ. It is a very lofty thing to be a Christian; for a Christian is a man who is restoring God's likeness to his character; and therefore the apostle calls it here a high calling. High as heaven is the calling wherewith we are called. But this very height makes it seem impracticable. It is natural to say — All that was well enough for one so transcendently gifted as Paul to hope for: but I am no gifted man — I have no iron strength of mind — I have no sanguine hopefulness of character — I am disposed to look on the dark side of things — I am undetermined, weak, vacillating; and then I have a whole army of passions and follies to contend with. We have to remind such men of one thing they have forgotten. It is the high calling of God if you will; but it is the high calling of God in Christ Jesus. What the world calls virtue is a name and a dream without Christ. The foundation of all human excellence must be laid deep in the blood of the Redeemer's cross, and in the power of His Resurrection. First let a man know that all his past is wrong and sinful; then let him fix his eye on the love of God in Christ loving him, even him, the guilty one. Is there no strength in that? no power in the knowledge that all that is gone by *is gone*, and that a fresh, clear future is open? It is not the progress of virtue that God asks for, but progress in saintliness, empowered by hope and love.

Lastly, let each man put this question to himself, "Dare I look on?" With an earnest Christian, it is "reaching forth to those things which are before." Progress ever. And then just as we go to rest in this world tired, and wake up fresh and vigorous in the morning, so does the Christian go to sleep in the world's night, weary with the work of life, and then on the resurrection-day he wakes in his second and his brighter morning. It is well for a believer to look on. — Dare you? Remember, out of Christ it is not wisdom, but madness, to look on. You must look back, for the longest and the best day is either past or passing. It will be winter soon — desolate, uncheered, hopeless, winter — cold age, with its dreariness and its disappointments, and its querulous broken-heartedness; and there is no second spring for you — no resurrection morning of blessedness to dawn on the darkness of your grave. God has only one method of salvation, the Cross of Christ. God can have only one; for the Cross of Christ means death to evil, life to good. There is no other way to salvation but that, for that in itself is, and alone is, salvation. Out of Christ, therefore, it is woe to the man who reaches forth to the things which are before. To such I say — My unhappy brethren, Omnipotence itself cannot change the darkness of your destiny.

V.

Preached October 20, 1850.

TRIUMPH OVER HINDRANCES — ZACCHEUS.

LUKE xix. 8. — "And Zaccheus stood, and said unto the Lord, Behold, Lord, the half of my goods I give to the poor; and if I have taken anything from any man by false accusation, I restore him fourfold."

THERE are persons to whom a religious life seems smooth and easy. Gifted by God constitutionally with a freedom from those inclinations which in other men are tyrannous and irresistible — endued with those aspirations which other men seem to lack — it appears as if they were born saints.

There are others to whom it is all a trial — a whole world of passions keep up strife within. The name of the Spirit which possesses them is Legion. It is a hard fight from the cradle to the grave — up-hill work — toil all the way; and at the last it seems as if they had only just kept their ground.

There are circumstances which seem as if intended as a very hotbed for the culture of religious principle, in which the difficulty appears to be to escape being religious.

There are others in which religious life seems impossible. For the soul, tested by temptation, is like iron tried by weights. No iron bar is absolutely infrangible. Its strength is tested by the weight which it will bear without breaking. No soul is absolutely impeccable. It seems as if all we can dare to ask even of the holiest is how much temptation he can bear without giving way. There are societies amidst which some are forced to dwell daily, in which the very idea of Christian rest is negatived. There are occupations in which purity of heart can scarcely be conceived. There are temptations to which some are subjected in a long series, in which to have stood upright would have demanded not a man's but an angel's strength.

Here are two cases: one in which temperament and circumstances are favourable to religion; another in which both are adverse. If life were always the brighter side of these pictures, the need of Christian instruction and Christian casuistry — *i. e.*, the direction for conduct under various supposable cases, would be superseded. The end of the institution of a Church would be gone; for the Church exists for the purposes of mutual sympathy and mutual support. But the fact is, life is for the most part a path of varied trial. How to lead the life divine, surrounded by temptations from within and from without — how to breathe freely the atmosphere of heaven, while the feet yet touch earth — how to lead the life of Christ, who shrunk from no scene of trying duty, and took the temptations of man's life as they came; or how even to lead the ordinary saintly life, winning experience from fall, and permanent strength out of momentary weakness, and victory out of defeat — this is the problem.

The possibility of such a life is guaranteed by the history of Zaccheus. Zaccheus was tempted much, and Zaccheus contrived to be a servant of Christ. If we wanted a motto to prefix to this story, we should append this — The successful pursuit of religion under dificulties.

These, then, are the two branches of our thoughts to-day.

I. The hindrances to a religious life.

II. The Christian triumph over difficulties.

I. The hindrances of Zaccheus were two-fold: Partly circumstantial — partly personal. Partly circumstantial, arising from his riches and his profession of a publican.

Now the publican's profession exposed him to temptation in these three ways. First of all in the way of *opportunity*. A publican was a gatherer of the Roman public imposts. Not however as now, when all is fixed, and the Government pays the gatherer of the taxes. The Roman publican paid so much to the government for the privilege of collecting them; and then indemnified himself, and appropriated what overplus he could from the taxes which he gathered. There was therefore, evidently, a temptation to overcharge, and a temptation to oppress. To overcharge, because the only redress the payer of the taxes had was an appeal to law, in which his chance was small before a tribunal where the judge was a Roman, and the accused an official of the Roman Government. A temptation to oppress, because the threat of law was nearly certain to extort a bribe. Besides this, most of us must have remarked that a certain harshness of manner is contracted by those who have the rule over the poor. They come in contact with human souls only in the way of business. They have to do with their ignorance, their stupidity, their attempts to deceive; and hence the tenderest-hearted men become impatient and apparently unfeeling. Hard men, knowing that redress is difficult, become harder still, and exercise their authority with the insolence of office; so that, when to the insolence of office and the likelihood of impunity there was superadded the pecuniary advantage annexed to a tyrannical extortion, any one may understand how great the publican's temptation was.

Another temptation was presented: to live satisfied with a low morality. The standard of right and wrong is eternal in the heavens — unchangeably one and the same. But here on earth it is perpetually variable — it is one in one age or nation, another in another. Every profession has its conventional morality, current nowhere else. That which is permitted by the peculiar standard of truth acknowledged at the bar, is falsehood among plain men — that which would be reckoned in the army purity and tenderness, would be elsewhere licentiousness and cruelty. There is a parliamentary honour quite distinct from honour between man and man. Trade has its honesty; which rightly named is fraud. And in all these cases the temptation is to live content with the standard of a man's own profession or society; and this is the real difference between the worldly man and the religious man. He is the worldling who lives below that standard, or no higher — he is the servant of God who lives *above* his age. But you will perceive, that amongst publicans a very little would count much — that which would be laxity to a Jew, and shame to a Pharisee, might be reckoned very strict morality among the Publicans.

Again, Zaccheus was tempted to that hardness in evil which comes from having no character to support. But the extent to which sin hardens depends partly on the estimate taken of it by society. The falsehood of Abraham, the guilt and violence of David, were very different in their effect on character in an age when truth and purity and gentleness were scarcely recognised, from what they would be now. Then, Abraham and David had not so sinned against their conscience as a man would sin now in doing the same acts; because their consciences were less enlightened. A man might be a slave-trader in the Western hemisphere, and in other respects a humane, upright, honourable man. In the last century, the holy Newton of Olney trafficked in slaves, after becoming religious. A man who had dealings in this way in this country could not remain upright and honourable, even if it were conceivable that he began as such; because he would either conceal from the world his share in the traffic, and so doing it secretly, would become a hypocrite; or else he must cover his wickedness by effrontery, doing it in defiance of public shame, and so getting seared in conscience. Because in the one case, the sin, remaining sin, yet countenanced by society, does not degrade the man, nor injure his conscience, even to the same extent to which it would ruin the other, whose conscience must become seared by defiance of public shame. It is scarcely possible to unite together the idea of an executioner of public justice and a humble holy man. And yet assuredly, not from anything that there is unlawful in the office: an executioner's trade is as lawful as a soldier's. A soldier is placed there by his country to slay his country's enemies; and a doomster is placed there to slay the transgressors of his country's laws. Wherein lies the difference which leaves the one a man of honour, and almost necessitates the other to be taken from the rank of reprobates, or else gradually to become such? Simply the difference of public opinion — public scorn. Once there was no shame in the office of the executioner, and the Judge of Israel, with his own hands, hewed Agag to pieces before the Lord in Gilgal. Phinehas executed summary and sanguinary vengeance, and his name has been preserved in a hymn by his country's gratitude. The whole congregation became executioners in the case of blasphemy, and no abandonment was the result. But the voice of public opinion pronouncing an office or a man scandalous, either finds or else makes them what it has pronounced them. The executioner is or becomes an outcast, because reckoned such.

More vile and more degraded than even the executioner's office with us, was the office of publican among the Jews. A penitent publican could not go to the house of God without the risk of hearing muttered near him the sanctimonious thanksgiving of Pharisaism: "God, I thank Thee that I am not as this publican." A publican, even though high in office, and rich besides, could not receive into his house a teacher of religion without being saluted by the murmurs of the crowd, as in this case: "He is gone to eat with a man that is a sinner." A sinner! The proof of that? The only proof was that he was *a publican*. There are men and women in this congregation who have committed sins that never have been published to the world; and therefore, though they be still untouched by the love of God, they have never sunk down to degradation; whereas the very same sins, branded with public shame, have sunk others not worse than them down to the lowest infamy. There is no principle in education and in life more sure than this — to stigmatize is to ruin: to take away character is to take away all. There is no power committed to man, capable of use and abuse, more certain and more awful than this: "Whose-soever sins ye remit, they are remitted unto them."

This, then, was a temptation arising out of Zaccheus' circumstances — to become quite hardened by having no character to support.

The *personal* hindrance to a religious life lay in the recollection of past guilt. Zaccheus had done wrong, and no fourfold restitution will undo that, where remorse only exists.

There is a difference between remorse and penitence. Remorse is the consciousness of wrong-doing with no sense of love. Penitence is that same consciousness, with the feeling of tenderness and gratefulness added.

And pernicious as have been the consequences of self-righteousness, more destructive still have been the consequences of remorse. If self-righteousness has slain its thousands, remorse has slain its tens of thousands; for, indisputably, self-righteousness secures a man from degradation. Have you never wondered at the sure walk of these persons who, to trust their own estimate of themselves, are always right? They never sin — their children are better brought up than any other children — their conduct is irreproachable. Pride saves them from a fall. That element of self-respect, healthful always, is their safeguard. Yes, the Pharisee was right. He is not an extortioner, nor unjust, and he is regular in his payments and his duties. That was self-righteousness: it kept him from saintliness; but it saved him from degradation too. Remorse, on the contrary, crushes. If a man lose the world's respect, he can retreat back upon the consciousness of the God within. But if a man lose his own respect, he sinks down and down, and deeper yet, until he can get it back again by feeling that he is sublimely loved, and he dares at last to respect that which God vouchsafes to care for. Remorse is like the clog of an insoluble debt. The debtor is proverbially extravagant — one more, and one more expense. What can it matter when the great bankruptcy is near? And so, in the same way, one sin, and one more. Why not? why should he pause when all is hopeless? what is one added to that which is already infinite?

Past guilt becomes a hindrance too in another way — It makes fresh sin easier. Let any one, out of a series of transgressions, compare the character of the first and the last. The first time there was the shudder and the horror, and the violent struggle, and the feeling of impossibility. I cannot — *cannot* do that. The second time there was faint reluctance, made more faint by recollection of the facility and the pleasantness of the first transgression; and the last time there is neither shudder nor reluctance, but the eager plunge down the precipice on the brink of which he trembled once. All this was against Zaccheus. A publican had lost self-respect, and sin was easy.

II. Pass we on to the triumph over difficulties. In this there is man's part, and God's part.

Man's part in Zaccheus' case was exhibited in the discovery of expedients. The Redeemer came to Jericho, and Zaccheus desired to see that blessed Countenance, whose very looks, he was told, shed peace upon restless spirits and fevered hearts. But Zaccheus was small of stature, and a crowd surrounded him. Therefore he ran before, and climbed up into a sycamore-tree. You must not look on this as a mere act of curiosity. They who thronged the steps of Jesus were a crowd formed of different materials from the crowd which would have been found in the amphitheatre. He was there as a religious Teacher or Prophet; and they who took pains to see Him, at least were the men who looked for salvation in Israel. This, therefore, was a *religious* act.

We have heard of the "pursuit of knowledge under difficulties." The shepherd, with no apparatus besides his thread and beads, has lain on his back on the starry night, mapped the heavens, and unconsciously become a distinguished astronomer. The peasant boy, with no tools but his rude knife, and a visit now and then to the neighbouring town, has begun his scientific education by producing a watch that would mark the time. The blind man, trampling upon impossibilities, has explored the economy of the beehive, and, more wondrous still, lectured on the laws of light. The timid stammerer, with pebbles in his mouth, and the roar of the sea-surge in his ear, has attained correctest elocution, and swayed as one man the changeful tides of the mighty masses of the Athenian democracy. All these were *expedients*. It is thus in the life religious. No man ever trod exactly the path that others trod before him. There is no exact chart laid down for the voyage. The rocks and quicksands are shifting; he who enters upon the ocean of existence arches his sails to an untried breeze. He is "the first that ever burst into that lonely sea." Every life is a *new* life. Every day is a *new* day — like nothing that ever went before, or can ever follow after. No books — no systems — no forecast — set of rules, can provide for all cases; every case is a new case. And just as in any earthly enterprise, the conduct of a campaign, or the building of a bridge, unforeseen difficulties and unexpected disasters must be met by that inexhaustible fertility of invention which belongs to those who do not live to God *second-hand.* We must live to God first-hand. If we are in earnest, as Zaccheus was, we must invent peculiar means of getting over peculiar difficulties.

There are times when the truest courage is shown in retreating from a temptation. There are times when, not being on a level with other men in qualifications of temper, mind, character, we must compensate by inventions and Christian expedients. You must climb over the crowd of difficulties which stand between your soul and Christ — you must "run before" and forecast trials, and get into the sycamore solitude. Without a living life like this you will never get a glimpse of the King in his beauty: you will never see it. You will be just on the point of seeing Him, and shut out by some unexpected hindrance.

Observe, again, an illustration of this, Zaccheus' habit of restoration. "Behold, Lord, the half of my goods I give to the poor; and if I have taken anything from any man by false accusation, I restore him fourfold." There are two ways of interpreting this; it may have reference to the future. It commonly is so interpreted. It is supposed that, touched by the love of Christ, Zaccheus proclaimed this as his resolve — I hereby promise to give the half of my goods to the poor. But it is likely that this interpretation has been put upon it in order to make it square with the evangelical order of emotions — Grace first, liberality after. The interpretation seems rather put on the passage than found there. The word is not future, but singular: Behold, Lord, I give. And it seems more natural to take it as a statement of the habit of Zaccheus' previous life. If so, then all is plain. This man, so maligned, had been leading a righteous life after all, according to the Mosaic standard. On the day of defence he stands forward and vindicates himself from the aspersion. "These are my habits." And the Son of Man vindicates him before all. Yes, publican as he is, he too is a "son of Abraham."

Here then were *expedients* by which he overcame the hindrances of his position. The tendency to the hardness and selfishness of riches he checked by a rule of giving half away. The tendency to extortion he met by fastening on himself the recollection, that when the hot moment of temptation had passed away, he would be severely dealt with before the tribunal of his own conscience, and unrelentingly sentenced to restore fourfold.

God's part in this triumph over difficulties is exhibited in the address of Jesus: "Zaccheus, make haste and come down; for to-day I must abide at thy house."

Two things: Invitation and sympathy. Invitation — "come down." Say what we will of Zaccheus seeking Jesus, the truth is Jesus was seeking Zaccheus. For what other reason but the will of God had Jesus come to Jericho, but to seek Zaccheus and such as he? Long years Zaccheus had been living in only a dim consciousness of being a servant of God and goodness. At last the Saviour is born into the world — appears in Judea — comes to Jericho, Zaccheus' town — passes down Zaccheus' street, and by Zaccheus' house, and up to Zaccheus' person. What is all this but seeking? what the Bible calls election? Now there is a specimen in this of the ways of God with men in this world. We do not seek God — God seeks us. There is a Spirit pervading Time and Space Who seeks the souls of men. At last the seeking becomes reciprocal — the Divine Presence is felt afar, and the soul begins to turn towards it. Then when we begin to seek God, we become conscious that God is seeking us. It is at that period that we distinguish the voice of personal invitation — "Zaccheus!" It is then that the Eternal Presence makes its abode with us, and the hour of unutterable joy begins, when the banquet of Divine Love is spread within the soul, and the Son of God abides there as at a feast. "Behold I stand at the door and knock: If any man hear my voice, I will come in and sup with him, and he with Me."

This is Divine Grace. We are saved by grace, not will. "It is not of him that willeth, nor of him that runneth, but of God that showeth mercy." In the matter of man's salvation God is first. He comes to us self-invited — He names us by name — He isolates us from the crowd, and sheds upon us the sense of personal recognition — He pronounces the benediction, till we feel that there is a mysterious blessing on our house, and on our meal, and on our heart. This day is salvation come to this house, forasmuch as he also is a son of Abraham.

Lastly, the Divine part was done in sympathy. By sympathy we commonly mean little more than condolence. If the tear start readily at the voice of grief, and the purse-strings open at the accents of distress, we talk of a man's having great sympathy.

To weep with those who weep: — Common sympathy does not mean much more.

The sympathy of Christ was something different from this. Sympathy to this extent, no doubt, Zaccheus could already command. If Zaccheus were sick, even a Pharisee would have given him medicine. If Zaccheus had been in need, a Jew would not have scrupled to bestow an alms. If Zaccheus had been bereaved, many even of that crowd that murmured when they saw him treated by Christ like a son of Abraham, would have given to his sorrow the tribute of a sigh.

The sympathy of Jesus was fellow-feeling for all that is human. He did not condole with Zaccheus upon his trials, — He did not talk to him "about his soul," — He did not preach to him about his sins, — He did not force His way into his house to lecture him, — He simply said, "I will abide at thy house:" thereby identifying himself with a publican: thereby acknowledging a publican for a brother. Zaccheus a publican? Zaccheus a sinner? Yes; but Zaccheus is a man. His heart throbs at cutting words. He has a sense of human honour. He feels the burning shame of the world's disgrace. Lost? Yes: — but the Son of Man, with the blood of the human race in His veins, is a Brother to the lost.

It is in this entire and perfect sympathy with all Humanity that the heart of Jesus differs from every other heart that is found among the sons of men. And it is this — oh! it is this, which is the chief blessedness of having such a Saviour. If you are poor, you can only get a miserable sympathy from the rich; with the best intentions they cannot understand you. Their sympathy is awkward. If you are in pain, it is only a factitious and constrained sympathy you get from those in health — feelings forced, adopted kindly, but imperfect still. They sit, when the regular condolence is done, beside you, conversing on topics with each other that jar upon the ear. *They* sympathise? Miserable comforters are they all. If you are miserable, and tell out your grief, you have the shame of feeling that you were not understood; and that you have bared your inner self to a rude gaze. If you are in doubt, you cannot tell your doubts to religious people; not, not even to the ministers of Christ — for they have no place for doubts in their largest system. They ask, What right have you to doubt? They suspect your character. They shake the head; and whisper it about gravely, that you read strange books — that you are verging on infidelity. If you are depressed with guilt, to whom shall you tell out your tale of shame? The confessional, with its innumerable evils, and yet indisputably soothing power, is passed away; and there is nothing to supply its place. You cannot speak to your brother man, for you injure him by doing so, or else weaken yourself. You cannot tell it to society, for society judges in the gross, by general rules, and cannot take into account the delicate differences of transgression. It banishes the frail penitent, and does homage to the daring hard transgressor.

Then it is that, repulsed on all sides and lonely, we turn to Him whose mighty Heart understands and feels all. "Lord, to whom shall we go? Thou hast the words of eternal life." And then it is that, exactly like Zaccheus, misunderstood, suspected by the world, suspected by our own hearts — the very voice of God apparently against us — isolated and apart, we speak to Him from the loneliness of the sycamore-tree, heart to heart, and pulse to pulse. "Lord, Thou knowest all things:" Thou knowest my secret charities, and my untold self-denials. "*Thou* knowest that I love thee."

Remark, in conclusion, the power of this sympathy on Zaccheus' character. Salvation that day came to Zaccheus' house. What brought it? What touched him? Of course, "the gospel." Yes; but what is the gospel? What was his gospel? Speculations or revelations concerning the Divine Nature? The scheme of the atonement? or of the incarnation? or baptismal regeneration? Nay, but the Divine sympathy of the Divinest Man. The personal love of God, manifested in the face of Jesus Christ. The floodgates of his soul were opened, and the whole force that was in the man flowed forth. Whichever way you take that expression, "Behold, Lord, the half of my goods I give to the poor:" If it referred to the future, then, touched by unexpected sympathy, finding himself no longer an outcast, he made that resolve in gratefulness. If to the past, then, still touched by sympathy, he who had never tried to vindicate himself before the world, was softened to tell out the tale of his secret munificence. This is what I have been doing all the time they slandered me, and none but God knew it.

It required something to make a man like that talk of things which he had not suffered his own left hand to know, before a scorning world. But any how, it was the manifested Fellowship of the Son of Man, which brought salvation to that house.

Learn this: When we live the gospel so, and preach the gospel so, sinners will be brought to God. We know not yet the gospel power; for who trusts, as Jesus did, all to that? Who ventures, as he did, upon the power of Love, in sanguine hopefulness of the most irreclaimable? who makes *that*, the divine humility of Christ, "the gospel?" More than by eloquence, more than by accurate doctrine, more than by ecclesiastical order, more than by any doctrine trusted to by the most earnest and holy men, shall we and others, sinful rebels, outcasts, be won to Christ, by that central truth of all the gospel — the entireness of the Redeemer's sympathy. In other words, the Love of Jesus.

VI.

Preached October 28, 1849.

THE SHADOW AND THE SUBSTANCE OF THE SABBATH.

COL. ii. 16, 17. — "Let no man, therefore, judge you in meat, or in drink, or in respect of an holyday, or of the new moon, or of the sabbath-days: which are a shadow of things to come; but the body is of Christ."

No sophistry of criticism can explain away the obvious meaning of these words. The apostle speaks of certain institutions as Jewish: shadowy: typical: and among these we are surprised to find the sabbath-days. It has been contended that there is here no allusion to the seventh day of rest, but only to certain Jewish holydays, not of Divine institution. But, in the first place, the "holydays" have been already named in the same verse; in the next we are convinced that no plain man, reading this verse for the first time, without a doctrine to support, would have put such an interpretation upon the word: and we may be sure that St. Paul would never have risked so certain a misconstruction of his words by the use of an ambiguous phrase. This, then, is the first thing we lay down — a very simple postulate, one would think — when the apostle *says* the sabbath-days, he *means* the sabbath-days.

Peculiar difficulties attend the discussion of the subject of the sabbath. If we take the strict and ultra ground of sabbath observance, basing it on the rigorous requirements of the fourth commandment, we take ground which is not true; and all untruth, whether it be an over-statement or a half-truth, recoils upon itself. If we impose on men a burden which cannot be borne, and demand a strictness which, possible in theory, is impossible in practice, men recoil; we have asked too much, and they give us nothing — the result is an open, wanton, and sarcastic desecration of the Day of Rest.

If, on the other hand, we state the truth, that the sabbath is obsolete — a shadow which has passed — without modification or explanations, evidently there is a danger no less perilous. It is true to spiritual, false to unspiritual men; and a wide door is opened for abuse. And to recklessly loosen the hold of a nation on the sanctity of the Lord's day would be most michievous — to do so wilfully would be an act almost diabolical. For if we must choose between Puritan over-precision on the one hand, and on the other that laxity which, in many parts of the Continent, has marked the day from other days only by more riotous worldliness, and a more entire abandonment of the whole community to amusement, no Christian would hesitate: no English Christian at least; to whom that day is hallowed by all that is endearing in early associations, and who feels how much it is the very bulwark of his country's moral purity.

Here, however, as in other cases, it is the half-truth which is dangerous — the other half is the corrective; the whole truth alone is safe. If we say the sabbath is shadow, this is only half the truth. The apostle adds, "the body is of Christ."

There is, then, in the sabbath that which is shadowy and that which is substantial; that which is transient and that which is permanent; that which is temporal and typical, and that which is eternal. The shadow and the body.

Hence, a very natural and simple division of our subject suggests itself.

I. The transient shadow of the sabbath which has passed away.

II. The permanent substance which cannot pass.

I. The transient shadow which has passed away.

The history of the sabbath-day is this. It was given by Moses to the Israelites, partly as a sign between God and them, marking them off from all other nations by its observance; partly as commemorative of their deliverance from Egypt. And the reason why the seventh day was fixed on, rather than the sixth or eighth, was, that on that day God rested from His labour. The soul of man was to form itself on the model of the Spirit of God. It is not said, that God at the creation gave the sabbath to man, but that God rested at the close of the six days of creation: whereupon He had blessed and sanctified the seventh day to the Israelites. This is stated in the fourth commandment, and also in Gen. i., which was written for the Israelites; and the history of creation naturally and appropriately introduces the reason and the sanction of their day of rest.

Nor is there in the Old Testament a single trace of the observance of the sabbath before the time of Moses. After the Deluge, it is not mentioned in the covenant made with Noah. The first account of it occurs after the Israelites had left Egypt; and the fourth commandment consolidates it into a law, and explains the principle and sanctions of the institution.

The observance of one day in seven, therefore, is

purely Jewish. The Jewish obligation to observe it rested on the enactment given by Moses.

The spirit of its observance, too, is Jewish, and not Christian. There is a difference between the spirit of Judaism and that of Christianity. The spirit of Judaism is separation — that of Christianity is permeation. To separate the evil from the good was the aim and work of Judaism: — to sever one nation from all other nations; certain meats from other meat; certain days from other days. Sanctify means to set apart. The very essence of the idea of Hebrew holiness lay in sanctification in the sense of separation.

On the contrary, Christianity is permeation — it permeates all evil with good — it aims at overcoming evil by good — it desires to transfuse the spirit of the day of rest into all other days, and to spread the holiness of one nation over all the world. To saturate life with God, and the world with Heaven, that is the genius of Christianity.

Accordingly, the observance of the sabbath was entirely in the Jewish spirit. No fire was permitted to be made on pain of death: Exod. xxxv. 3. No food was to be prepared: xvi. 5, 23. No buying nor selling: Nehem. x. 31. So rigorously was all this carried out, that a man gathering sticks was arraigned before the congregation, and sentenced to death by Moses.

This is Jewish, typical, shadowy; — it is all to pass away. Much already has passed: even those who believe our Lord's day to be the descendant of the sabbath admit this. The day is changed. The first day of the week has taken the place of the seventh. The computation of hours is altered. The Jews reckoned from sunset to sunset — modern Christians reckon from midnight to midnight. The spirit of its observance, too, is altered. No one contends now for Jewish strictness in its details.

Now, observe, all this implies the abrogation of a great deal more — nay, of the whole Jewish sabbath itself. We have altered the day — the computation of the hours — the mode of observance: What remains to keep? Absolutely nothing of the literal portion except one day in seven: and that is abrogated, if the rest be abrogated. For by what right do we say that the order of the day, whether it be the first or the seventh, is a matter of indifference, because only formal, but that the proportion of days, one in seven, instead of one in eight or nine, is moral, and unalterable? On what intelligible principle do we produce the fourth commandment as binding upon Christians, and abrogate so important a clause of it as, "In it thou shalt do *no manner of work?*" On what self-evident ground is it shown that the Jew might not light a fire, but the Christian may; yet that if the postal arrangements of a country permit the delivery of a letter, it is an infraction of the sabbath?

Unquestionably on no scriptural authority. Let those who demand a strict observance of the letter of scripture remember that the Jewish sabbath is distinctly enforced in the Bible, and nowhere in the Bible repealed. You have changed the seventh day to the first on no clear scriptural permission. Two or three passages tell us that, after the resurrection, the apostles were found together on the first day of the week (which, by the way, may have been Saturday evening after sunset). But it is concluded that therefore *probably* the change was apostolic. You have only a probability to go on — and that probability, except with the aid of tradition, infinitesimally small — for the abrogation of a single iota of the Jewish fourth commandment.

It will be said, however, that works of necessity and works of mercy are excepted by Christ's example.

Tell us, then, ye who are servants of the letter, and yet do not scruple to use a carriage to convey you to some church where a favourite minister is heard, is that a spiritual necessity or a spiritual luxury? Part of the Sunday meal of all of you is the result of a servant's work. Tell us, then, ye accurate logicians, who say that nothing escapes the rigour of the prohibition — which is not necessary or merciful? Is a hot repast a work of necessity or a work of mercy? Oh! it rouses in every true soul a deep and earnest indignation to hear men who drive their cattle to church on Sundays, because they are too emasculated to trudge through cold and rain on foot, invoke the severity of an insulted Law of the Decalogue on those who provide facilities of movement for such as cannot afford the luxury of a carriage. What, think you, would He who blighted the Pharisees with such burning words, have said, had He been present by, while men, whose servants clean their houses, and prepare their meals, and harness their horses, stand up to denounce the service on some railway by which the poor are helped to health and enjoyment? Hired service for the rich is a necessity — hired service for the poor is a desecration of the sabbath! It is right that a thousand should toil for the few in private! It is past bearing in a Christian country that a few should toil for thousands on the sabbath day!

There is only this alternative: if the fourth commandment be binding still, that clause is unrepealed — "no manner of work;" and so, too, is that other important part, the sanctification of the seventh day and not the first. If the fourth commandment be not binding in these points, then there is nothing left but the broad, comprehensive ground taken by the apostle. The whole sabbath is a shadow of things to come. In consistency, either hold that none of the formal part is abrogated, or else all. The whole of the letter of the commandment is moral, or else none.

II. There is, however, in the sabbath a substance, a permanent something — "a body" — which cannot pass away.

"The body is of Christ;" the spirit of Christ is the fulfilment of the law. To have the spirit of Christ is to have fulfilled the law. Let us hear the mind of Christ in this matter.

"The sabbath was made for man, not man for the sabbath." In that principle, rightly understood, lies the clue for the unravelling of the whole matter. The religionists of that day maintained that the necessities of man's nature must give way to the rigour of the enactment; He taught that the enactment must yield to man's necessities. They said that the sabbath was written in the book of the Law; He said that it was written on man's nature, and that the law was merely meant to be in accordance with that nature. They based the obligation to observe the sabbath on the sacredness of an enactment; He on the sacredness of the nature of man.

An illustration will help us to perceive the difference between these two views. A wise physician prescribes a regimen of diet to a palate which has become diseased: he fixes what shall be eaten, the quantity, the hours, and number of times. On what does the obligation to obey rest? On the arbitrary authority of the physician? or on the nature with which that prescription is in accordance? When soundness and health are restored, the prescription falls into disuse: but the nature remains unalterable, which has made some things nutritious, others unwholesome, and excess for over pernicious. Thus the spirit of the prescription may be still in force when the prescriptive authority is repealed.

So Moses prescribed the sabbath to a nation spiritually diseased. He gave the regimen of rest to men who did not feel the need of spiritual rest. He fenced round his rule with precise regulations of detail — one day in seven, no work, no fire, no traffic. On what does the obligation to obey it rest? On the authority of the rule? or on the necessities of that nature for which the rule was divinely adapted? Was man made for the sabbath, to obey it as a slave? or, Was the sabbath made for man? And when spiritual health has been restored, the Law regulating the details of rest may become obsolete; but the nature which demands rest never can be reversed.

Observe, now, that this a far grander, safer, and more permanent basis on which to rest the sabbath than the mere enactment. For if you allege the fourth commandment as your authority, straightway you are met by the objection "no *manner* of work." Who gave you leave to alter that? And if you reply, works of necessity and works of mercy I may do, for Christ excepted these from the stringency of the rule, again the rejoinder comes, is there one in ten of the things that all Christians permit as lawful, really a matter of necessity?

Whereas, if the sabbath rest on the needs of human nature, and we accept His decision that the sabbath was made for *man*, then you have an eternal ground to rest on from which you cannot be shaken, A son of man may be lord of the sabbath-day, but he is not lord of his own nature. He cannot make one hair white or black. You may abrogate the formal Rule, but you cannot abrogate the needs of your own soul. Eternal as the constitution of the soul of man is the necessity for the existence of a day of rest. Further, still, on this ground alone can you find an impregnable defence of the *proportion*, one day in seven. On the other ground it is unsafe. Having altered the seventh to the first, I know not why one in seven might not be altered to one in ten. The thing, however, has been tried; and by the necessities of human nature the change has been found pernicious. One day in ten, prescribed by revolutionary France, was actually pronounced by physiologists insufficient. So that we begin to find that, in a deeper sense than we at first suspected, "the sabbath was made for man." Even in the contrivance of one day in seven, it was arranged by unerring wisdom. Just because the sabbath was made for man, and not because man was ordained to keep the sabbath-day, you cannot tamper even with the iota, one day in seven.

That necessity on which the observance leans is the need of Rest. It is the deepest want in the soul of man. If you take off covering after covering of the nature which wraps him round, till you come to the central heart of hearts, deep lodged there you find the requirement of Repose. All men do not hanker after pleasure — all men do not crave intellectual food. But all men long for rest; the most restless that ever pursued a turbulent career on earth did by that career only testify to the need of the soul within. They craved for something which was not given: there was a thirst which was not slaked: their very restlessness betokened that — restless because not at rest It is this need which sometimes makes the quiet of the grave an object of such deep desire. "There the wicked cease from troubling, and there the weary are at rest." It is this which creates the chief desirableness of Heaven: "There remaineth a rest for the people of God." And it is this which, consciously or unconsciously, is the real wish that lies at the bottom of all others. — Oh! for tranquillity of heart — Heaven's profound silence in the soul, "a meek and quiet spirit, which in the sight of God is of great price!"

The rest needed by man is twofold. Physical repose of the body — a need which he shares with the animals through the lower nature which he has in common with them. "Thou shalt do no work, nor thy cattle," — so far man's sabbath-need places him only on a level with the ox and with the ass.

But, besides this, the rest demanded is a repose of spirit. Between these two kinds of rest there is a very important difference. Bodily repose is simply inaction: the rest of the soul is exercise, not torpor. To do nothing is physical rest — to be engaged in full activity is the rest of the soul.

In that hour, which of all the twenty-four is most emblematical of heaven, and suggestive of repose, the eventide, in which instinctively Jacob went into the fields to meditate — when the work of the day is done, when the mind has ceased its tension, when the passions are lulled to rest in spite of themselves, by the spell of the quiet star-lit sky — it is then, amidst the silence of the lull of all the lower parts of our nature, that the soul comes forth to do its work. Then the peculiar, strange work of the soul, which the intellect cannot do — meditation, begins. Awe, and worship, and wonder are in full exercise; and Love begins then in its purest form of mystic adoration and pervasive and undefined tenderness — separate from all that is coarse and earthly — swelling as if it would embrace the All in its desire to bless, and lose itself in the sea of the love of God. This is the Rest of the soul — the *exercise* and play of all the nobler powers.

Two things are suggested by this thought.

First, the mode of the observance of the day of Rest. It has become lately a subject of very considerable attention. Physiologists have demonstrated the necessity of cessation from toil: they have urged the impossibility of perpetual occupation without end. Pictures, with much pathos in them, have been placed before us, describing the hard fate of those on whom no sabbath dawns. It has been demanded as a right, entreated as a mercy, on behalf of the labouring man, that he should have one day in seven for recreation of his bodily energies. All well and true. But there is a great deal more than this. He who confines his conception of the need of rest to that, has left man on a level with the brutes. Let a man take merely lax and liberal notions of the fourth commandment — let him give his household and dependants immunity from toil, and wish for himself and them no more — he will find that there is a something wanting still. Experience tell us, after a trial, that those Sundays are the happiest, the purest, the most rich in blessing, in which the spiritual part has been most attended to; — those in which the business letter was put aside till evening, and the profane literature not opened, and the ordinary occupations entirely suspended; — those in which, as in the temple of Solomon, the sound of the earthly hammer has not been heard in the temple of the soul: for this is, in fact, the very distinction between the spirit of the Jewish sabbath and the spirit of the Christian Lord's day. The one is chiefly for the body — "Thou shalt do no manner of work." The other is principally for the soul — "I was in the spirit on the Lord's day."

The other truth suggested by that fact, that the repose of the soul is exercise, not rest, is, that it conveys an intimation of man's immortality. It is only when all the rest of our human nature is calmed that the spirit comes forth in full energy: all the rest tires, the spirit never tires. Humbleness, awe, adoration, love, these have in them no weariness: so that when this frame shall be dissolved into the dust of the earth, and the mind, which is merely fitted for this time world, learning by experience, shall have been superseded, then, in the opening out of an endless career of love, the spirit will enter upon that sabbath of which all earthly sabbaths are but the shadow, the sabbath of Eternity, the immortal Rest of the Father's Home.

Two observations in concluding.

1. When is a son of man lord of the sabbath-day? To whom may the sabbath safely become a shadow? I reply, he that has the mind of Christ may exercise discretionary lordship over the sabbath-day. He who

is in possession of the substance may let the shadow go. A man in health has done with the prescriptions of the physician. But for an unspiritual man to regulate his hours and amount of rest by his desires, is just as preposterous as for an unhealthy man to rule his appetites by his sensations. Win the mind of Christ — be like Him — and then, in the reality of Rest in God, the sabbath form of rest will be superseded. Remain apart from Christ, and then you are under the law again — the fourth commandment is as necessary for you as it was for the Israelite: the prescriptive regimen which may discipline your soul to a sounder state. It is at his peril that the worldly man departs from the *rule* of the day of rest. Nothing can make us free from the law but the Spirit.

2. The rule pronounced by the apostle is a rule of liberty, and at the same time a rule of charity: "Let no man judge you in respect of the sabbath-days." It is very difficult to discuss this question of the sabbath. Heat, vehemence, acrimony, are substituted for argument. When you calmly ask to investigate the subject, men apply epithets, and call them reasons: — they stigmatise you as a breaker of the sabbath, pronounce you "dangerous;" with sundry warnings against you in private, and pregnant hints in public.

The apostle urges charity: "One man esteemeth one day above another: another man esteemeth every day alike." . . . . "He that regardeth the day, regardeth it to the Lord; and he that regardeth not the day, to the Lord he regardeth it not." Carry out that spirit. In the detail of this question there is abundant difficulty. It is a question of degree. Some work must be done on the sabbath-day: — some must sacrifice their rest to the rest of others; for all human life is sacrifice, voluntary or involuntary.

Again, that which is rest to one man is not rest to another. To require the illiterate man to read his Bible for some hours would impose a toil upon him, though it might be a relaxation to you. To the labouring man a larger proportion of the day must be given to the recreation of his physical nature than is necessary for the man of leisure, to whom the spiritual observance of the day is easy, and seems all. Let us learn large, charitable considerateness. Let not the poor man sneer at his richer neighbour, if, in the exercise of his Christian liberty, he uses his horses to convey him to church and not to the mere drive of pleasure; but then, in fairness, let not the rich man be shocked and scandalized if the over-wearied shopkeeper and artisan breathe the fresh air of heaven with their families in the country. "The sabbath was made for man." Be generous, consistent, large minded. A man may hold stiff, precise Jewish notions on this subject; but do not stigmatise that man as a formalist. Another may hold large, Paul-like views of the abrogation of the fourth commandment, and yet he may be sincerely and zealously anxious for the hallowing of the day in his household and through his country. Do not call that man a sabbath-breaker. Remember, the Pharisees called the Son of God a sabbath-breaker. They kept the law of the sabbath — they broke the law of love. Which was the worst to break? which was the higher law to keep? Take care lest, in the zeal which seems to you to be for Christ, ye be found indulging their spirit, and not His.

VII.

Preached November 4, 1849.

THE SYMPATHY OF CHRIST.

HEB. iv. 15, 16. — "For we have not an high priest which cannot be touched with the feeling of our infirmities; but was in all points tempted like as we are, yet without sin. Let us therefore come boldly unto the throne of grace, that we may obtain mercy, and find grace to help in time of need."

ACCORDING to these verses, the Priesthood of Jesus Christ is based upon the perfection of His Humanity. Because tempted in all points like as we are, therefore He can show mercy, and grant help. Whatever destroys the conception of His Humanity does in that same degree overthrow the notion of His Priesthood.

Our subject is the Priestly Sympathies of Christ. But we make three preliminary observations.

The perfection of Christ's Humanity implies that He was possessed of a human soul as well as a human body. There was a view, held in early times, and condemned by the church as a heresy, according to which the body of Christ was an external framework animated by Deity, as our bodies are animated by our souls. What the soul is to us Deity was to Christ. His body was flesh, blood, bones, — moved, guided, ruled by indwelling Divinity.

But you perceive at once that this destroys the notion of complete humanity. It is not this tabernacle of material elements which constitutes our humanity: you cannot take the pale corpse from which life has fled, and call *that* Man. And if Deity were to take up that form and make it its abode, that would not be an union of the Divine and Human. It would only be the union of Deity with certain materials, that might have passed into man, or into an animal, or a herb. Humanity implies a body and a soul.

Accordingly, in the life of Christ we find two distinct classes of feeling. When He hungered in the wilderness — when He thirsted on the cross — when He was weary by the well at Sychar, — He experienced sensations which belong to the bodily department of human nature. But when out of twelve He selected one to be His bosom friend, when He looked round upon the crowd in anger, when the tears streamed down His cheeks at Bethany, and when He recoiled from the thought of approaching dissolution, these — grief, friendship, fear, — were not the sensations of the body, much less were they the attributes of Godhead. They were the affections of an acutely sensitive human soul, alive to all the tenderness, and hopes, and anguish with which human life is filled, qualifying Him to be tempted *in all* points like as we are.

The second thought which presents itself is, that the Redeemer not only was but *is* man. He *was* tempted in all points like us. He *is* a high priest which can be touched. Our conceptions on this subject, from being vague, are often very erroneous. It is fancied that in the history of Jesus' existence, once, for a limited period and for definite purposes, He took part in frail humanity; but that when that purpose was accomplished, the man for ever perished, and the Spirit reascended, to unite again with pure unmixed Deity. But Scripture has taken peculiar pains to give assurance of the continuance of His Humanity. It has carefully recorded His resurrection. After that He passed through space from spot to spot: when He was in one place, He was not in another. His body was sustained by the ordinary aliments: broiled fish and honeycomb. The prints of suffering were on Him. His recognitions were human still. Thomas and Peter were especially reminded of incidents before His death, and connected with His living interests. To Thomas — "Reach hither thy hand." To Peter — "Lovest thou me?"

And this typifies to us a very grand and important truth. It is this, if I may venture to so express myself — the truth of the Human Heart of God. We think of God as a Spirit, infinitely removed from and unlike the creatures He has made. But the truth is, man resembles God: all spirits, all minds are of the same family. The Father bears a likeness to the Son whom He has created. The mind of God is similar to the mind of man. Love does not mean one thing in man, and another thing in God. Holiness, Justice, Pity, Tenderness — these are in the Eternal the same in kind which they are in the Finite Being. The present Manhood of Christ conveys this deeply important truth, that the Divine Heart is human in its sympathies.

The third observation upon these verses is, that there is a connection between what Jesus was and what Jesus is. He can be touched now, *because* He was tempted then. The incidents and the feelings of that part of the existence which is gone have not passed away without results which are deeply entwined with His present being. His past experience has left certain effects durable in His nature as it is now. It has endued Him with certain qualifications and certain susceptibilities, which He would not have had but for that experience. Just as the results remained upon His body, the prints of the nails in His palms, and the spear-gash in His side, so do the results remain upon His soul, enduing Him with a certain susceptibility, for He can be touched with the feeling of our infirmities: with certain qualifications, for He is able to show mercy, and to impart grace to help in time of need.

To turn now to the subject itself. It has two branches.

I. The Redeemer's preparation for his priesthood.
II. The Redeemer's priestly qualifications.

I. His preparation.

The preparation consisted in being tempted. But here a difficulty arises. Temptation, as applied to a Being perfectly free from tendencies to evil, is not easy to understand. See what the difficulty is. Temptation has two senses: It means test or probation: it means also trial, involving the idea of pain or danger. A common acid applied to gold, tests it: but there is no risk or danger to the most delicate golden ornament. There is one acid, and only one, which tries it, as well as tests it. The same acid applied to a shell endangers the delicacy of its surface. A weight hung from a bar of iron only tests its strength; the same, depending from a human arm, is a trial, involving it may be the risk of pain or fracture. Now, trial placed before a sinless being is intelligible enough in the sense of probation: it is a test of excellence: but it is not easy to see how it can be temptation in the sense of pain, if there be no inclination to do wrong.

However, Scripture plainly asserts this as the character of Christ's temptation. Not merely test, but trial.

First, you have passages declaring the immaculate nature of His mind; as here, "without sin." Again, He was "holy, harmless, undefiled, separate from sinners." And again, "The prince of this world cometh, and hath nothing in Me." The spirit of evil found nothing which it could claim as its own in Christ. It was the meeting of two elements which will not amalgamate. Oil and water could as easily blend, as the mind of Christ with evil. Temptation glanced from His heart as the steel point does from the surface of the diamond. It was not that evil propensities were kept under by the power of the Spirit in Him: — He had no evil propensities at all. Obedience was natural to Him.

But then we find another class of passages, such as this: "He *suffered*, being tempted." There was not merely test in the temptation, but there was also painfulness in the victory. How could this be without any tendency to evil?

To answer this, let us analyse sin. In every act of sin there are two distinct steps: There is the rising of a desire which is natural, and, being natural, is not wrong: — there is the indulgence of that desire in forbidden circumstances; and that is sin. Let injury, for example, be inflicted, and resentment will arise. It must arise spontaneously. It is as impossible for injustice to be done, and resentment not to follow, as it is for the flesh not to quiver on the application of intense torture. Resentment is but the sense of injustice, made more vivid by its being brought home to ourselves: — resentment is beyond our control, so far.

There is no sin in this: but let resentment rest there; let it pass into, not justice, but revenge — let it smoulder in vindictive feeling till it becomes retaliation, and then a natural feeling has grown into a transgression. You have the distinction between these two things clearly marked in Scripture. "Be ye angry" — here is the allowance for the human, "and sin not" — here is the point where resentment passes into retaliation.

Take, again, the natural sensation of hunger. Let a man have been without food: let the gratification present itself, and the natural desire will arise involuntarily. It will arise just as certainly in a forbidden as in a permitted circumstance. It will arise whether what he looks on be the bread of another or his own. And it is not here, in the sensation of hunger, that the guilt lies. But it lies in the wilful gratification of it after it is known to be forbidden.

This was literally one of the cases in which Christ was tried. The wish for food was in His nature in the wilderness. The very mode of gratifying it was presented to His imagination: by using Divine power in an unlawful way. And had He so been constituted that the lower wish was superior to the higher will, there would have been an act of sin; had the two been nearly balanced, so that the conflict hung in doubt, there would have been a tendency to sin: what we call a sinful nature. But it was in the entire and perfect subjugation of desire to the will of Right that a sinless nature was exhibited.

Here, then, is the nature of sin. Sin is not the possession of desires; but the having them in uncontrolled ascendancy over the higher nature. Sinfulness does not consist in having *strong* desires or passions:

in the strongest and highest natures, all, including the desires, is strong. Sin is not a real *thing*. It is rather the absence of a something, the will to do right. It is not a disease or taint, an actual substance projected into the constitution. It is the absence of the spirit which orders and harmonizes the whole; so that what we mean when we say the natural man must sin inevitably is this, that he has strong natural appetites, and that he has no bias from above to counteract those appetites: exactly as if a ship were deserted by her crew, and left on the bosom of the Atlantic with every sail set and the wind blowing. No one forces her to destruction — yet on the rocks she will surely go, just because there is no pilot at the helm. Such is the state of ordinary men. Temptation leads to fall. The gusts of instincts, which, rightly guided, would have carried safely into port, dash them on the rocks. No one forces them to sin; but the spirit-pilot has left the helm. — Fallen Nature.

Sin, therefore, is not in the appetites, but in the absence of a controlling Will.

Now, contrast this state with the state of Christ. There were in Him all the natural appetites of mind and body. Relaxation and friendship were dear to Him — so were sunlight and life. Hunger — pain — death — He could feel all, and shrunk from them. Conceive then a case in which the gratification of any one of those inclinations was inconsistent with His Father's will. At one moment is was unlawful to eat, though hungry: and without one tendency to disobey, did fasting cease to be severe? It was demanded that He should endure anguish; and willingly as He subdued Himself, did pain cease to be pain? Could the spirit of obedience reverse every feeling in human nature? When the brave man gives his shattered arm to the surgeon's knife, will may prevent even the quiver of an eyelid; but no will and no courage can reverse his sensations, or prevent the operation from inflicting pain. When the heart is raw, and smarting from recent bereavement, let there be the deepest and most reverential submission to the Highest Will, is it possible not to wince? Can any cant demand for submission extort the profession that pain is pleasure?

It seems to have been in this way that the temptation of Christ caused suffering. He suffered from the force of desire. Though there was no hesitation whether to obey or not, no strife in the will, in the act of mastery there was pain. There was self-denial: — there was obedience at the expense of tortured natural feeling. He shrunk from St. Peter's suggestion of escape from ignominy as from a thing which did not shake His determination, but made Him feel, in the idea of bright life, vividly the cost of His resolve. "Get thee behind me, Tempter, for thou art an offence." In the garden, unswervingly: "Not as I will, but as thou wilt." No reluctance in the *will*. But was there no struggling? No shudder in the inward sensations? No remembrance that the Cross was sharp? No recollection of the family at Bethany, and the pleasant walk, and the dear companionship which he was about to leave? "My soul is exceeding sorrowful to die."....

So that in every one of these cases — not by the reluctancy of a sinful sensation, but by the quivering and the anguish of natural feeling when it is trampled upon by lofty will — Jesus *suffered*, being tempted. He was "tempted like as we are." Remember this.

For the way in which some speak of the sinlessness of Jesus, reduces all His suffering to physical pain, destroys the reality of temptation, reduces that glorious heart to a pretence, and converts the whole of His history into a mere fictitious drama, in which scenes of trial were represented, not felt.

Remember that, "in all points," the Redeemer's *soul* was tempted.

II. The second point we take is the Redeemer's Priesthood.

Priesthood is that office by which He is the medium of union between man and God. The capacity for this has been indelibly engraven on His nature by His experience here. All this capacity is based on His sympathy: — He can be "touched with the feeling of our infirmities."

Till we have reflected on it, we are scarcely aware how much the sum of human happiness in the world is indebted to this one feeling — sympathy. We get cheerfulness and vigour, we scarcely know how or when, from mere association with our fellow-men; and from the looks reflected on us of gladness and employment, we catch inspiration and power to go on, from human presence and from cheerful looks. The workman works with added energy from having others by. The full family circle has a strength and a life peculiarly its own. The substantial good and the effectual relief which men extend to one another is trifling. It is not by these, but by something far less costly, that the work is done. God has ensured it by a much more simple machinery. He has given to the weakest and the poorest, power to contribute largely to the common stock of gladness. The child's smile and laugh are mighty powers in this world. When bereavement has left you desolate, what substantial benefit is there which makes condolence acceptable? It cannot replace the loved ones you have lost. It can bestow upon you nothing permanent. But a warm hand has touched yours, and its thrill told you that there was a living response there to your emotion. One look — one human sigh, has done more for you than the costliest present could convey.

And it is for want of remarking this, that the effect of public charity falls often so far short of the expectations of those who give. The springs of men's generosity are dried up by hearing of the repining, and the envy and the discontent which have been sown by the general collection and the provision establishment among cottages where all was harmony before. The famine and the pestilence are met by abundant liberality; and the apparent return for this is riot and sedition. But the secret lies all in this. It is not in channels such as these that the heart's gratitude can flow. Love is not bought by money, but by love. There has been all the machinery of a public distribution: but there has been no exhibition of individual, personal interest. The rich man who goes to his poor brother's cottage, and without affectation of humility, naturally, and with the respect which man owes to man, enters into his circumstances, inquiring about his distresses, and hears his homely tale, has done more to establish an interchange of kindly feeling than he could have secured by the costliest present, by itself. Public donations have their value and their uses. Poor-laws keep human beings from starvation: but in the point of eliciting gratitude, all these fail. Man has not been brought into contact close enough with man for this. They do not work by sympathy.

Again, when the electric touch of sympathetic feeling has gone among a mass of men, it communicates itself, and is reflected back from every individual in the crowd, with a force exactly proportioned to their numbers. The speech or sermon read before the limited circle of a family, and the same discourse uttered before closely crowded hundreds, are two different things. There is strange power even in the mere presence of a common crowd, exciting almost uncontrollable emotion.

It is on record that the hard heart of an oriental conqueror was unmanned by the sight of a dense mass of living millions engaged in one enterprise. He accounted for it by saying, that it suggested to him that within a single century not one of those millions would be alive. But the hard-hearted bosom of the tyrant mistook its own emotions: his tears came from no such far-fetched inference of reflection: they rose spontaneously, as they will rise in a dense crowd, you cannot tell why. It is the thrilling thought of numbers engaged in the same object. It is the idea of our own feelings reciprocated back to us, and reflected from many hearts. It is the mighty presence of Life.

And, again, it seems partly to avail itself of this tendency within us, that such stress is laid on the injunction of united prayer. Private devotion is essential to the spiritual life — without it there is no life. But it cannot replace united prayer: for the two things have different aims. Solitary prayer is feeble in comparison with that which rises before the throne echoed by the hearts of hundreds, and strengthened by the feeling that other aspirations are mingling with our own. And whether it be the chanted litany, or the more simply read service, or the anthem producing one emotion at the same moment in many bosoms, the value and the power of public prayer seem chiefly to depend on this mysterious affection of our nature — sympathy.

And now, having endeavoured to illustrate this power of sympathy, it is for us to remember that of this in its fulness He is susceptible. There is a vague way of speaking of the Atonement which does not realize the tender, affectionate, personal love by which that daily, hourly reconciliation is effected. The sympathy of Christ was not merely love of men in masses: He loved the masses, but he loved them because made up of individuals. He "had compassion on the multitude;" but He had also discriminating, special tenderness for erring Peter and erring Thomas. He felt for the despised lonely Zaccheus in his sycamore-tree. He compassionated the discomfort of His disciples. He mixed His tears with the stifled sobs by the grave of Lazarus. He called the abashed children to His side. Amongst the numbers, as He walked, He detected the individual touch of faith. "Master, the multitude throng thee, and sayest thou, *Who* touched me?" — "Somebody hath touched me."

Observe, how He is touched by our infirmities — with a separate, special, discriminating love. There is not a single throb, in a single human bosom, that does not thrill at once with more than electric speed up to the mighty heart of God. *You* have not shed a tear or sighed a sigh, that did not come back to you exalted and purified by having passed through the Eternal bosom.

The priestly powers conveyed by this faculty of sympathising, according to the text, are two — The power of mercy: and the power of having grace to help. "Therefore" — because He can be touched — "let us come boldly," expecting mercy — and grace.

1. We may boldly expect mercy from Him who has learned to sympathise. He learned sympathy by being tempted: but it is by being tempted, *yet without sin*, that He is specially able to show mercy.

There are two who are unfit for showing mercy:— He who has never been tried; and he who, having been tempted, has fallen under temptation. The young, untempted, and upright, are often severe judges. They are for sanguinary punishment: they are for expelling offenders from the bosom of society. The old, on the contrary, who have fallen much, are lenient: but it is a leniency which often talks thus: Men must be men — a young man must sow his wild oats and reform.

So young ardent Saul, untried by doubt, persecuted the Christians with severity; and Saul the King, on the contrary, having fallen himself, weakly permitted Agag to escape punishment. David, again, when his own sin was narrated to him under another name, was unrelenting in his indignation: "The man that hath done this thing shall surely die."

None of these were qualified for showing mercy aright. Now this qualification "without sin," is very remarkable: for it is the one we often least should think of. Unthinkingly we should say that to have erred would make a man lenient: — it is not so.

That truth is taught with deep significance in one

of the incidents of the Redeemer's life. There stood in His presence a tempted woman, covered with the confusion of recent conviction. And there stood beside her the sanctimonious religionists of that day, waiting like hell-hounds to be let loose upon their prey. Calm words came from the lips of Him "who spake as man never spake," and whose heart felt as man never felt. "He that is without sin among you let him first cast a stone." A memorable lesson of eternal truth. Sinners are not fit to judge of sin: — their justice is revenge — their mercy is feebleness. He alone can judge of sin — he alone can attemper the sense of what is due to the offended Law with the remembrance of that which is due to human frailty — he alone is fit for showing manly mercy, who has, like his Master, felt the power of temptation in its might, and come scathless through the trial.

"In all points tempted — *yet without sin*;" therefore, to Him you may "boldly go to find mercy."

2. The other priestly power is the grace of showing "help in time of need."

We must not make too much of sympathy, as mere feeling. We do in things spiritual as we do with hothouse plants. The feeble exotic, beautiful to look at, but useless, has costly sums spent on it. The hardy oak, a nation's strength, is permitted to grow, scarcely observed, in the fence and copses. We prize feeling and praise its possessor. But feeling is only a sickly exotic in itself — a passive quality, having in it nothing moral, no temptation and no victory. A man is no more a good man for having feeling, than he is for having a delicate ear for music, or a far-seeing optic nerve. The Son of man had feeling — He could be "touched." — The tear would start from His eyes at the sight of human sorrow. But that sympathy was no exotic in His soul, beautiful to look at, too delicate for use. Feeling with Him led to this, "He went about doing good." Sympathy with Him was this, "Grace to help in time of need."

And this is the blessing of the thought of Divine sympathy. By the sympathy of man, after all, the wound is not healed: it is only stanched for a time. It can make the tear flow less bitterly; it cannot dry it up. So far as permanent good goes, who has not felt the deep truth which Job taught his friends — "Miserable comforters are ye all?"

The sympathy of the Divine Human! He knows what strength is needed. He gives grace to help; and when the world, with its thousand forms of temptation, seems to whisper to us as to Esau, Sell me thy birthright, the other voice speaks, Shall I barter blessedness for happiness? the inward peace for the outward thrill? the benediction of my Father for a mess of pottage? There are moments when we seem to tread above this earth, superior to its allurements, able to do without its kindness, firmly bracing ourselves to do our work as He did His. Those moments are not the sunshine of life. They did not come when the world would have said that all round you was glad: but it was when outward trials had shaken the soul to its very centre, then there came from Him. . . "Grace to help in time of need."

From this subject, I draw, in concluding, two inferences.

1. He who would sympathise must be content to be tried and tempted. There is a hard and boisterous rudeness in our hearts by nature, which requires to be

softened down. We pass by suffering gaily, carelessly, not in cruelty, but unfeelingly, just because we do not know what suffering is. We wound men by our looks and our abrupt expressions without intending it, because we have not been taught the delicacy, and the tact, and the gentleness which can only be learnt by the wounding of our own sensibilities. There is a haughty feeling in uprightness which has never been on the verge of fall, that requires humbling. There is an inability to enter into difficulties of thought which marks the mind to which all things have been presented superficially, and which has never experienced the horror of feeling the ice of doubt crashing beneath the feet

Therefore, if you aspire to be a son of consolation — if you would partake of the priestly gift of sympathy — if you would pour something beyond common-place consolation into a tempted heart — if you would pass through the intercourse of daily life, with the delicate tact which never inflicts pain — if to that most acute of human ailments, mental doubt, you are ever to give effectual succour, you must be content to pay the price of the costly education. Like Him, you must suffer — being tempted.

But remember, it is being tempted in all points, *yet without* sin, that makes sympathy real, manly, perfect, instead of a mere sentimental tenderness. Sin will teach you to *feel* for trials. It will not enable you to judge them; to be merciful to them — nor to help them in time of need with any certainty.

Lastly, it is this same human sympathy which qualifies Christ for judgment. It is written that the Father hath committed all judgment to Him, *because* He is the Son of Man. The sympathy of Christ extends to the frailties of human nature; not to its hardened guilt: He is "touched with the feeling of our *infirmities*." There is nothing in His bosom which can harmonize with malice — He cannot feel for envy — He has no fellow-feeling for cruelty: oppression: hypocrisy; bitter censorious judgments. Remember, He could look round about Him with anger. The sympathy of Christ is a comforting subject. It is, besides, a tremendous subject; for on sympathy the awards of heaven and hell are built. "Except a man be born again" — not he *shall* not, but — "he *cannot* enter into heaven." There is nothing in him which has affinity to anything in the Judge's bosom. A sympathy for that which is pure implies a repulsion of that which is impure. Hatred of evil is in proportion to the strength of love for good. To love good intensely, is to hate evil intensely. It was in strict accordance with the laws of sympathy that He blighted Pharisaism in such ungentle words as these: "Ye serpents, ye generation of vipers! how can ye escape the damnation of hell?" Win the mind of Christ now — or else His sympathy for human nature will not save you from, but only ensure, the recoil of abhorrence at the last — "Depart from me! I never knew you."

VIII.

Preached November 11, 1849.

THE PHARISEES AND SADDUCEES AT JOHN'S BAPTISM.

MATT. iii. 7. — "But when he saw many of the Pharisees and Sadducees come to his baptism, he said unto them, O generation of vipers, who hath warned you to flee from the wrath to come?"

IT seems that the Baptist's ministry had been attended with almost incredible success, as if the population of the country had been roused in mass by the tidings of his doctrine. "Then went out to him Jerusalem, and all Judea, and all the region round about Jordan, and were baptized by him in Jordan, confessing their sins."

The success of his ministry was tested by the numbers that he baptized. Not so a modern ministry. Ministerial success is not shown now by the numbers who listen. Not impression, but altered character, marks success. Not by startling, nor by electrifying, congregations, but by turning men from darkness unto light, from the power of Satan unto God, is the work done. With John, however, it was different. He was on earth to do a special work — the work of the axe, not the trowel; to throw down, not to build; to startle, not to instruct; and therefore his baptism was simply symbolized by water, the washing away of the past: whereas that of Christ was symbolized by fire, the touching of the life and heart with the living flame of a heavenlier life. Whoever, therefore, came to John for baptism, possessed conviction of the truth of that which John taught, and thereby so far tested the fidelity and success of his ministry.

Bearing, then, in mind, that coming to John's baptism was the seal of his success, and that his baptism contained, in symbolical form, the whole substance of his teaching, these are the two topics of the text: —

I. The meaning wrapped up in John's message.
II. The Baptist's astonishment at his own success.

I. The meaning of John's message. His baptism implied to those who came to put themselves under its protection that they were in danger, for it was connected with the warning, "Flee from the wrath to come!"

Future retribution has become to us a kind of figment. Hell is in the world of shadows. The tone in which educated men speak of it still, is often only that good-humoured condescension which makes allowance for childish superstition.

Part of this incredulity arises from the confessedly symbolical intimations of Scripture on the subject. We read of the fire and the worm: of spirits being salted with fire: of a lake of fire and brimstone. All this tells solely of physical suffering. And accordingly, for centuries, this was the predominant conception of Christendom on the subject. Scarcely any other element was admitted. Whoever has seen those paintings on which the master-spirits have thrown down the conceptions of their age, will remember that hideous demons, distorted countenances, and waves of flame represent the whole idea. And in that immortal work in which he who sang of hell, purgatory, and heaven, has embodied the belief of his day, still the same fact prevails. You read of the victims of unchaste life hurried on the dark whirlwind for ever; of the heretics in their coffins of intense fire; and of the guilty spirits who are plunged deep down in "thick-ribbed ice." But in those harrowing pictures which his genius has painted with such vividness, there is not one idea of mental suffering embodied. It is all bodily, awful, intolerable torture. Now all this we believe no longer. The circles of hell and the mountain of purgatory are as fabulous to us as the Tartarus of the heathens. Singular, that in an age in which the chief aim of science appears to be to get rid of physical pain and discomfort, as if these were the worst evils conceivable, the idea of a bodily hell should be just the one at which we have learnt to smile. But with the form, we have also dispossessed ourselves of belief in the reality of retribution at all.

Now Scripture language is symbolical. There is no salt, no worm, no fire to torture. I say not that a diseased soul may not form for itself a tenement hereafter, as here, peculiarly fitted to be the avenue of suffering; but unquestionably we cannot build upon these expressions a material hell.

Hell is the infinite terror of the soul, whatever that may be. To one man it is pain. Rid him of that, he can bear all degradation. To another it is public shame. Save him from that, and he will creep and crawl before you to submit to any reptile meanness. "Honour me now, I pray thee, before the people," till Samuel turns from the abject thing in scorn. To others, the infinite terror is *that*, compared with which, all these would be a bed of roses. It is the hell of having done wrong — the hell of having had a spirit from God, pure, with high aspirations, and to be conscious of having dulled its delicacy, and degraded its desires — the hell of having quenched a light brighter than the sun's — of having done to another an injury that through time and through eternity never can be undone — infinite, maddening remorse — the hell of knowing that every chance of excellence, and every opportunity of good, has been lost for ever. This is the infinite terror: — this is wrath to come.

You doubt that? Have you ever marked that striking fact, the connection of the successive stages of the soul? How sin can change the countenance, undermine the health, produce restlessness? Think you the grave will end all that? That by some magic change, the moral being shall be buried there, and the soul rise again so changed in every feeling that the very identity of being would be lost, and it would amount to the creation of a new soul? Say you that God is love? Oh! but look round this world. The aspect of things is stern; very stern. If they be ruled by love, it is a love which does not shrink from human agony. There is a law of infinite mercy here, but there is a law of boundless rigour too. Sin, and you will suffer — that law is not reversed. The young, and the gentle, and the tender, are inexorably subjected to it. We would shield them if we could: but there is that which says they shall not be shielded. They shall weep, and fade, and taste of mortal anguish, even as others. Carry that out into the next world, and you have "wrath to come."

John's baptism, besides, implied the importance of confession. "They were baptized . . . confessing their sins." On the eve of a promised new life, they were required to acknowledge the iniquity of past life. In the cure of our spiritual maladies there is a wondrous efficacy, to use a homely phrase, in making a "clean breast." There is something strengthening, something soothing, and at the same time something humbling, in acknowledging that we have done wrong. There is a pride in us which cannot bear pity. There is a diseased sensitiveness which shrinks from the smart of acknowledgment; and yet that smart must be borne before we can be truly soothed. When was it that the younger son in the parable received the ring, and the robe, and the banquet, which represent the rapture of the sense of being forgiven? When he had fortitude enough to go back, mile by mile, step by step, every inch of the way he had gone wrong, borne unflinchingly the sneer of his father's domestics, and, worse than all, the sarcasms of his immaculate brother, and manfully said out, "Father, I have sinned against heaven and before thee." When was it that the publican went down *justified* to his house? When he said, even before a supercilious Pharisee, "God be merciful to me a sinner!" When did the royal delinquent hear the words, "The Lord hath also put away thy sin?" When he gave the sacrifice of his lips — "I have sinned before the Lord." And when did the church of Ephesus rise into the brightest model of a perfect church that has yet been exhibited on earth? After her converts had publicly come forward, burnt those manuscripts which were called "Ephesian letters" to the value of 50,000 pieces of silver, "confessed and showed their deeds." There is a profound truth in the popular anxiety, that a murderer should confess before he dies. It is an instinctive feeling that a true death is better than a false life — that to die with unacknowledged guilt is a kind of lie. To acknowledge his sin is to put it from him, to abjure it — to refuse to acknowledge it as part of himself — to separate it from him — to say, I will keep it as mine no more: then it is gone. Who has a secret of guilt lying like lead upon his heart? As he values serenity of soul, let that secret be made known. And if there be one to-day who is impressed or touched by all this, let him beware how he procrastinates that which was done when John baptized. The iron that once was cooled may never be warmed again — the heart that once had its flood-gates open, and has delayed to pour out the stagnation of its wretchedness, may be closed for ever.

Once more, John's baptism implied the necessity of a renewal of heart. We lose part of the significance of that ceremony from its transplantation away from a climate in which it was natural and appropriate.

Ablution in the East is almost a religious duty: the dust and heat weigh upon the spirits and heart like a load: the removal is refreshment and happiness. And it was impossible to see that significant act — in which the convert went down into the water, travel-worn and soiled with dust, disappeared for one moment, and then emerged pure and fresh — without feeling that the symbol answered to, and interpreted a strong craving of the human heart. It is the desire to wash away that which is past and evil. We would fain go to another country and begin life afresh. We look upon the grave almost with complacency, from the fancy that there we shall lie down to sleep and wake fresh and new. It was this same longing that expressed itself in heathenism by the fabled river of forgetfulness, of which the dead must drink before they can enter into rest.

Now to that craving John gave reality and meaning when he said, "Behold the Lamb of God!" For else that craving is but a sick fond wish. Had John merely said, "Flee from the wrath to come!" he would have filled man's life with the terrors of anticipated hell. Had he only said, My baptism implies that ye must be pure, he would have crushed men's hearts with the feeling of impossibility: for excellence without Christ is but a dream. He gave meaning and promise to all when he said, "Behold the Lamb of God, which taketh away the sins of the world."

Sin-laden and guilty men — the end of all the Christian ministry is to say that out with power, "Behold the Lamb of God!" Divine life and death! to have had one glimpse of which, with its ennobling impulses, it were worth while to have endured a life of suffering. When we believe that the sacrifice of that Lamb meant love to us, our hearts are lightened of their load: the past becomes as nothing, and life begins afresh. Christ is the River of Forgetfulness in which bygone guilt is overwhelmed.

II. The Baptist's astonishment at his own success. It was a singular scene which was exhibited in those days on the banks of Jordan. There was a crowd of human beings, each having a history of his own, men who have long mouldered in Earth's dust, but who were living then in fresh and vigorous existence. Think of it. Busy life was moving there, beings who had their hopes and fears about time and eternity: to whom life was dear as it is to us at this day. They had come to be cured of that worst of human maladies, the aching of a hollow heart; and a single mortified man was bending over them, whose countenance bore all that peculiar aspect of saintliness which comes from spare diet and austere habits, and all that unruffled composure which comes from lonely communings with God: — a solitary man, who had led a hermit's life, but was possessed of rare sagacity in worldly matters; — for hermit as he was, John took no half-views of men and things: there was nothing morbid in his view of life: there was sound common sense in the advice he gave the different classes which came to him. "Repent," with him, did not mean — Come with me into the wilderness to live away from the world, but it meant this: Go back to the world, and live above it, each doing his work in an unworldly spirit. It was a strange spectacle, men of the world coming with implicit reverence to learn the duties of active life from a man whose world was the desert, and who knew nothing of active life except by hearsay.

Now what was the secret of this power by which he chained the hearts of men as by a spell?

One point in the secret of this success was a thing which we see every day. Men of thought and quiet contemplation exercise a wonderful influence over men of action. We admire that which we are not ourselves. The man of business owns the control of the man of religious thoughtfulness. Like coalesces in this world with unlike. The strong and the weak, the contemplative and the active, bind themselves together. They are necessary for each other. The active soldiers and the scheming publicans came to the lonely ascetic John, to hear something of that still, inner life, of which their own career could tell them nothing.

A second cause of this success appears to have been that it was a ministry of terror. Fear has a peculiar fascination. As children love the tale of the supernatural which yet makes them shudder, so do men, as it would seem, find a delight in the pictures of eternal woe which terrify them. Partly from the pleasure which there is in vivid emotions, and partly perhaps from a kind of feeling of expiation in the horror which is experienced. You could not go among the dullest set of rustics and preach graphically and terribly of hell-fire without ensuring a large audience. The preaching of John in this respect differed from the tone of Christ's. Christ taught much that God is Love. He spoke a great deal of the Father which is in Heaven. He instructed in those parables which required thoughtful attention, exercise of mind, and a gently sensitive conscience. He spoke didactic, calm discourses, very engaging, but with little excitement in them: such discourses as the Sermon on the Mount, respecting goodness, purity, duties; which assuredly, if any one were to venture so to speak before a modern congregation, would be stigmatized as a moral essay. Accordingly, His success was much less marked than that of John's. No crowds were baptized as His followers: one hundred and twenty, in an upper chamber, appear to have been the fruits of His life-work. To teach so, is assuredly not the way to make strong impressions; but it is the way to work deeply, gloriously — for eternity. How many of John's terrified Pharisees and Sadducees, suppose we, retained the impression six months?

What is your religion? Excitability, romance, impression, fear? Remember, excitement has its uses; impression has its value. John, in all circumstances of his appearance and style of teaching, impressed by excitement. Excitement, warmed feelings, make the first actings of religious life and the breaking of inveterate habits easier. But excitement and impression are not religion. Neither can you trust to the alarm produced by the thought of eternal retribution. Ye that have been impressed, beware how you let those impressions die away. Die they will, and must: we cannot live in excitement for ever; but beware of their leaving behind them nothing except a languid, jaded heart. If God ever gave you the excitements of religion, breaking in upon your monotony, as John's teaching broke in upon that of Jerusalem, take care. There is no restoring of elasticity to the spring that has been overbent. Let impression pass on at once to acting.

We have another cause to assign for John's success. Men felt that he was real. Reality is the secret of all success. Religion in Jerusalem had long become a thing of forms. Men had settled into a routine of externals, as if all religion centred in these. Decencies and proprieties formed the substance of human life. And here was a man in God's world once more who felt that religion is an everlasting reality. Here was a man once more, to tell the world that life is sliding into the abyss; that all we see is but a shadow; that the invisible Life within is the only real life. Here was a man who could feel the splendours of God shining into his soul in the desert without the aid of forms. His locust-food, his hair-garment, his indifference to earthly comforts, spoke out once more that one at least could make it a conviction to live and die upon, that man does not live on bread alone, but on the living Word which proceedeth out of the mouth of God. And when that crowd dispersed at sunset, and John was left alone in the twilight, with the infinite of darkness deepening round him, and the roll of Jordan by his side, reflecting the chaste clear stars, there was something there higher than Pharisaic forms to speak to him: — There was heaven and eternity to force him to be real. This life was swiftly passing. What is it to a man living like John, but a show and a dream? He was homeless upon earth. Well — but beyond — beyond — in the blue eternities above, there was the prophet's home. He had cut himself off from the solaces of life. He was to make an enemy of the man of honour, Herod. He had made an enemy of the man of religion, the Pharisee. But he was passing into that country, where it matters little whether a man has been clothed in finest linen or in coarsest camel's hair, that still country, where the struggle-storm of life is over, and such as John find their rest at last in the home of God, which is reserved for the True and Brave. If perpetual familiarity with such thoughts as these cannot make a man real, there is nothing in this world that can.

And now, look at this man, so disciplined. Life to John was a reality. The citizens of Jerusalem could not go to him, as they might have gone to the schools of their rabbis, for learned subtleties, or to the groves of Athenian literature for melting imagery. Speech falls from him, sharp — rugged — cutting: — a word and no more. "Repent!" — "wrath to come." "The axe is laid at the root of the trees." "Fruitless trees will be cast into the fire." He spoke as men speak when they are in earnest, simply and abruptly, as if the graces of oratory were out of place. And then, that life of his! The world could understand it. There was written on it, in letters that needed no magnifying glass to read, "Not of this world."

It is, after all, this which tells — the reality of

unworldliness. The world is looking on to see what religious people mean. It has a most profound contempt for unreality. Such a man as John comes before them. Well, we understand that: — we do not like him: get him out of the way, and kill him if he interferes with us — but it is genuine. They then turn and see other men drawing ingenious distinctions between one kind of amusement and another — indulging themselves on the sabbath-day and condemning others who do similar things, and calling that unworldliness. They see that a religious man has a shrewd eye to his interests — is quick at making a bargain — captivated by show and ostentation — affects titled society. The world is very keen-sighted: it looks through the excitement of your religious meetings, quietly watches the zest of your scandal, scans your consciousness, and the question which the world keeps putting pertinaciously is, Are these men in earnest? Is it any marvel if Christian unreality is the subject of scoffs and bitter irony?

Let men see that you are real — inconsistent, it may be, sinful: oh! full of sin — impetuous — hasty — perhaps stern — John was. But compel them to feel that you are in earnest. This it the secret of influence.

So much, then, for the causes of success. Now let us analyse that success a little more closely, by considering the classes of men on whom that influence told.

First of all, we read of soldiers, publicans, and the poor people, coming to John for advice, and with the acknowledgment of guilt; and we do not read that their arrival excited the smallest emotion of astonishment in John's bosom. The wonder was not *there*. No wonder that the poor, whose lot in this world is hard, should look wistfully for another. No wonder that soldiers, with their prompt habits of obedience and their perpetual opportunities of self-devotion, should recognise with reverence the type of heroic life which John presented. No wonder that the guilty publicans should come for purification of heart. For is it not true that the world's outcasts may be led by their very sin to Christ? It is no wonder to see a saddened sinner seeking in the disappointment and weariness of solitary age that which he rejected in the heat of youth. Why, even the world is not astonished when it sees the sinner become the saint. Of course, the world has its own sarcastic account to give. Dissipation leads to weariness, and weariness to satiety, and satiety to devotion, and so your great sinner becomes a great saint, and serves God when all his emotions are exhausted. Be it so. He who knew our nature well, knew that marvellous revolutions go on in the soul of a man whom the world counts lost. In our wildest wanderings there is sometimes a Love, strong as a father's, tender as a mother's, watching over us, and bringing back the erring child again. Know you not the law of nature? Have you never seen how out of chaos and ferment nature brings order again? Life out of death, beauty out of corruption? Such, gainsay it who will, often is the history of the rise of saintliness and purity out of a disappointed, bruised, and penitent spirit. When the life-hopes have become a wreck — when the cravings of the heart for keen excitement have been ministered to so abundantly as to leave nothing but loathing and self-reproach behind — when innocence of heart is gone

9*

— yes — even then — scoff who will — the voice of Him is heard, who so dearly purchased the right to say it: "Come unto me, all ye that labour and are heavy laden, and I will give you rest."

John was not surprised that such came to him, owning the power of life-giving truth.

But among those who came, there were two classes who did move him to marvel. The first was the moral, self-satisfied formalist. The second was the calm, metaphysical, reasoning infidel. When he saw the Pharisees and Sadducees coming, he said: "Who hath warned *you?*"

Now who were these men?

The Pharisees were men who rested satisfied with the outward. The form of religion, which varies in all ages, *that* they wanted to stereotype. The inner heart of religion — the unchangeable — justice — mercy — truth — that they could not feel. They had got their two schools of orthodoxy — the school of Shammai and the school of Hillel; and, under the orthodoxy of these popular idols of the day, they were content to lose their own power of independent thought: souls that had shrunk away from all goodness and nobleness, and withered into the mummy of a soul. They could jangle about the breadth of a phylactery. They could discuss, as if it were a matter of life and death, ecclesiastical questions about tithe. They could decide to a furlong the length of journey allowable on the sabbath-day. But they could not look with mercy upon a broken heart pouring itself out to God in His temple — nor suffer a hungry man to rub an ear of corn on the Sabbath — nor cover the shame of a tempted sister or an erring brother. Men without souls, from whose narrow hearts the grandeur of everlasting truth was shut out.

There was another class in Israel as different from the Pharisees as man can be from man. The Sadducees could not be satisfied with the creed of Pharisaism, and had begun to cross-examine its pretensions. They felt that the thing which stood before them there, challenging the exclusive name of religion, with its washing of cups, its fastings, its parchment texts, this had nothing in it of the Eternal and the Infinite. This comes not from the Almighty God, and so from doubt they passed on to denial. The usual order had taken place. The reaction from superstition is infidelity. The reaction from ultra-strictness is laxity. The reaction from Pharisaism was the Sadducee. And the Sadducee, with a dreadful daring, had had the firmness to say: "Well, then, there is no life to come. That is settled. I have looked into the abyss without trembling. There is no phantom there. There is neither angel, spirit, nor life to come. And this glorious thing, man, with his deep thoughts, and his great, unsatisfied heart, his sorrows and his loves, godlike and immortal as he seems, is but dust animated for a time, passing into the nothingness out of which he came." That cold and hopeless creed was the creed of Sadduceeism. Human souls were trying to live on that and find it enough.

And the strange thing was, that these men, so positive in their creed, so distinct in their denial, so intolerant of the very name of future existence, crowded to John to make those confessions, and promise that new life, which were meet for men who desired to flee from the wrath to come. Wrath to come! What had the infidel to do with that? Repentance unto life! Why should the denier of life listen to that? Fruits meet for repentance! What had the formalist to do with that rebuke, whose life was already all that could be needed? "O generation of vipers," said the prophet, in astonishment, "who hath warned *you* to flee from the wrath to come?"

I deduce, from those facts which astonished John, two truths. Formalism, even morality, will not satisfy the conscience of man. Infidelity will not give rest to his troubled spirit. It is a pregnant lesson, if we will only read it thoughtfully, to consider those two classes going up for baptism. That heart of man which the moralist tells us is so pure and excellent, the light of day has shone into it, and behold, in the moralist's self, it is not pure, but polluted and miserable: else, what has that Pharisee to do with the symbol of new life which he is gone to John to use? That clear, unbiassed intellect with which the sceptic reached his conclusions, behold it is not clear nor unbiassed! It has been warped by an evil life. His heart is restless, and dark, and desolate: else, why is that Sadducee trembling on Jordan's brink? There is a something which they want, both Pharisee and Sadducee, and they come to see if baptism will give it them. Strangely moved indeed must those men have been — ay, shaken to the inmost soul — before they could so contradict their own profession as to acknowledge that there was a hollowness in their hearts. We almost fancy we can stand at the water's edge and hear the confession which was wrung from their lips, hot-burning and choked with sobs, during the single hour in which reality had forced itself upon their souls: — "It is a lie! — we are *not* happy — we are miserable — Prophet of the Invisible! what hast thou got to tell us of that awful other world?"

For when man comes to front the everlasting God, and look the splendour of His judgments in the face, personal integrity, the dream of spotlessness and innocence, vanish into thin air: your decencies, and your church-goings, and your regularities, and your attachment to a correct school and party, your gospel formulas of sound doctrine — what is all that in front of the blaze of the wrath to come?

And scepticism, too, how philosophical soever, and how manly it may appear, will it rock the conscience with an everlasting lullaby? Will it make, with all its reasonings, the tooth of the worm less sharp, and the fire less fierce that smoulders inwardly? Let but the plain, true man speak. We ask from him no rhetoric. We require no eloquence. Let him but say, in his earnestness, Repent — or — Wrath to come — and then what has infidelity to fall back upon?

There is rest in this world nowhere except in Christ, the Manifested Love of God. Trust in excellence, and the better you become, the keener is the feeling of deficiency. Wrap up all in doubt, and there is a stern voice that will thunder at last out of the wilderness upon your dream.

A heart renewed — a loving heart — a penitent and humble heart — a heart broken and contrite, purified by love — that and only that is the rest of man. Spotlessness may do for angels — Repentance unto Life is the highest that belongs to man.

IX.

Preached November 25, 1849.

CAIAPHAS' VIEW OF VICARIOUS SACRIFICE.

JOHN xi. 49-53. — "And one of them, named Caiaphas, being the high priest that same year, said unto them, Ye know nothing at all, nor consider that it is expedient for us, that one man should die for the people, and that the whole nation perish not. And this spake he not of himself: but being high priest that year, he prophesied that Jesus should die for that nation; and not for that nation only, but also that he should gather together in one the children of God, that were scattered abroad. Then, from that day forth they took counsel together for to put him to death."

ON this occasion, the first resolution passed the Jewish Sanhedrim to compass the death of Jesus. The immeditate occasion of their meeting was the fame of the resurrection of Lazarus. There were many causes which made the Saviour obnoxious to the Priests and Pharisees. If that teaching were once received, their reign was over: a teaching which abolished the pretensions of a priesthood, by making every man his own priest, to offer spiritual sacrifices *to* God — which identified Religion with Goodness — making spiritual excellence, not ritual regularity, the righteousness which God accepts — which brought God within the reach of the sinner and the fallen — which simplified the whole matter by making Religion a thing of the heart, and not of rabbinical learning or theology: — such teaching swept away all the exclusive pretensions of Pharisaism, made the life which they had been building up with so much toil for years, time wasted, and reduced their whole existence to a lie.

This was the ground of their hatred to the Son of Man. But this was not the ground which they put forward. He was tried chiefly on the charge of treason against the Emperor; and the argument by which the mind of the judge was principally swayed, was, "If thou let this man go, thou art not Cæsar's friend." The present passage contains the first trace of the adoption of that ground. "If we let him alone, the Romans will come and take away both our place and nation."

Be it observed, then, the real ground of opposition was hatred of the light. The ostensible ground was patriotism, public zeal, loyalty, far-sighted policy: and such is life. The motive on which a deed of sin is done is not the motive which a man allows to others, or whispers to himself. Listen to the criminal receiving sentence, and the cause of condemnation is not the enormity of the crime, but the injustice of the country's law. Hear the man of disorderly life, whom society has expelled from her bosom, and the cause of the expulsion is not his profligacy, but the false slander which has misrepresented him. Take his own account of the matter, and he is innocent — injured — pure. For there are names so tender, and so full of fond endearment, with which this world sugars over its dark guilt towards God, with a crust of superficial whiteness, that the Sin on which eighteen centuries have looked back appalled, was, to the doers of that Sin, nothing atrocious, but respectable, defensible, nay, even, under the circumstances, necessary.

The judgment of one of these righteous murderers was given in remarkable terms. Apparently there were some in the council, such men as Nicodemus, who could not acquiesce in the view given of the matter. Doubtless they alleged the unfairness of the proceeding, and the innocence of the Accused; upon which Caiaphas replied, "Ye know nothing at all, nor consider that it is expedient that one man die for the people, and that the whole nation perish not." The remarkable point in this judgment is, that it contained the very central doctrine of Christianity: unconsciously, Caiaphas had uttered the profoundest of all truths, the necessity of the suffering of the innocent for the guilty. He had stated it in the very words which St. John could have himself adopted. But they meant one thing in the lips of holy Love, and quite another thing in the lips of tyrannical Policy. Yet St. John, contemplating that sentence years after, could not but feel that there was something in those words deeper than met the ear, a truth almost inspired, which he did not hesitate to call prophetic. "Being high priest that year, he *prophesied.*"

We must not, therefore, call this merely a singular coincidence. It was the same truth viewed from different sides: the side of Caiaphas, and the side of John; the side of the world, and the side of God. — That truth was the vicarious Sacrifice of Christ.

And there are two ways in which you may contemplate that Sacrifice. Seen from the world's point of view, it is unjust, gross, cruel. Seen as John saw it, and as God looks at it, it was the sublimest of all truths; one which so entwines itself with our religious consciousness, that you might as soon tear from us our very being, as our convictions of the reality of Christ's Atonement. Our subject, then, is the vicarious sacrifice of Christ. The words of Caiaphas contain a formal falsehood and a material truth: the outward statement, and an inspired or prophetic inward verity — so that the subject branches into two topics: —

I. The human form, in which the words are false.
II. The divine principle or spirit, in which they are true.

I. The human form, in which the words are false.

Vicarious means in the stead of. When the Pope calls himself the vicar of Christ, he means that he is empowered in the stead of Christ to absolve, decree, &c. When we speak of vicarious suffering, we mean that suffering which is endured in another's stead, and not as the sufferer's own desert.

1. The first falsity in the human statement of that truth of vicarious sacrifice is its injustice. Some one said the Accused is innocent. The reply was — Better that one should die than many. "It is expedient for us, that one man should die for the people, and that the whole nation perish not." It was simply with Caiaphas a question of numbers: the unjust expediency of wresting the law a little to do much apparent good. The reply to that was plain. Expediency cannot obliterate Right and Wrong. Expediency may choose the best possible when the conceivable best is not attainable; but in right and wrong there is no better and best. Thou *shalt* not do wrong. Thou *must* not: you may not tell a lie to save life. Better that the whole Jewish nation should perish than that a Jewish legislature should steep its hand in the blood of one innocent. It is *not* expedient to do injustice.

There are cases in which it is expedient to choose the sacrifice of one instead of that of many — when a whole army or regiment has mutinied, the commander, instead of general butchery, many select a few to perish as examples to the rest. There is nothing here unjust. The many escape, but the few who die deserved to die. But no principle could justify a commander in selecting an innocent man, condemning him by unjust sentence, and affecting to believe that he was guilty, while the transgressors escaped, and learned the enormity of their transgressions by seeing execution done upon the guiltless. No principle can justify — nothing can do more than palliate the conduct of the ship's crew upon the raft who slay one of their number to support their existence on his flesh. No man would justify the parent, pursued in his chariot by wolves over Siberian snows, who throws out one of his children to the pack, that the rest may escape while their fangs are buried in their victim. You feel at once, expediency has no place here. Life is a trifle compared with Law. Better that all should perish by a visitation of God than that they should be saved by one murder.

I do not deny that this aspect has been given to the sacrifice of Christ. It has been represented as if the majesty of Law demanded a victim: and so as it glutted its insatiate thirst, one victim would do as well as another — the purer and the more innocent the better. It has been exhibited as if Eternal Love resolved in fury to strike, and so as He had His blow, it mattered not whether it fell on the whole world, or on the precious head of His own chosen Son.

Unitarianism has represented the Scriptural view in this way; or, rather, perhaps, we should say, it has been so represented to Unitarians — and, from a view so horrible, no wonder if Unitarianism has recoiled.

But it is not our fault if some blind defenders of the truth have converted the self-devotion of Love into a Brahminical sacrifice. If the work of redemption be defended by parallels drawn from the most atrocious records and principles of Heathenism, let not the fault be laid upon the Bible. We disclaim that as well as they. It makes God a Caiaphas. — It makes Him adopt the words of Caiaphas in the sense of Caiaphas. It represents Him in terms which better describe the ungoverned rage of Saul, missing his stroke at David, who has offended, and in disappointed fury dashing his javelin at his own son Jonathan.

You must not represent the Atonement as depending on the justice of unrighteous expediency.

2. This side of viewing the truth was the side of selfishness. It was not even the calm resolve of men balancing whether it be better for one to die or many; but whether it is better that He or *we* should perish. It is conceivable in the case supposed above, that a parent in the horrible dilemma should be enough bewildered to resolve to sacrifice one rather than lose all; but it is not conceivable that the doubt in his mind should be this — Shall *I* and the rest perish or this one? — yet this was the spirit in which the party of Caiaphas spoke. The Romans will come and take away *our* place and *our* nation.

And this spirit, too, is in human nature. The records of antiquity are full of it. If a fleet could not sail, it was assumed that the deities were offended. The purest and tenderest maiden of the royal household was selected to bleed upon the altar: and when the sharp knife passed to her innocent heart, this was the feeling in the bosoms of those stern and unrelenting warriors — of the blood and of the stock of Caiaphas — Better she than we.

This *may* be the way in which the sacrifice of Christ is regarded by us. There is a kind of acquiescence in the Atonement which is purely selfish. The more bloody the representation of the character of God, the greater, of course, the satisfaction in feeling sheltered from it. The more Wrath instead of Love is believed to be the Divine name, the more may a man find joy in believing that he is safe. It is the feeling of the Siberian story: the innocent has glutted the wolves; and we may pursue our journey in safety. Christ has suffered, and I am safe. He bore the agony — I take the reward: I may now live with impunity: and, of course, it is very easy to call acquiescence in that arrangement humility, and to take credit for the abnegation of self-righteousness: but who ever can acquiesce in that thought chiefly in reference to *personal safety*, and, without desiring to share the Redeemer's Cross, aspire to enjoy the comforts and the benefits of the Redeemer's sacrifice, has but something of the spirit of Caiaphas after all, the spirit which contentedly sacrifices Another for self — selfishness assuming the form of wisdom.

II. We pass to the prophetic or hidden spirit in which these words are true.

I observe, first, that vicarious sacrifice is the Law of Being. It is a mysterious and fearful thing to observe how all God's universe is built upon this law, how it penetrates and pervades all Nature, so that if it were to cease, Nature would cease to exist. Hearken to the Saviour himself expounding this principle: — "Except a corn of wheat fall into the ground and die, it abideth alone: but if it die, it bringeth forth much fruit." We are justified, therefore, in assuming the Law of Nature to be the Law of His own Sacrifice, for He himself represents it as the parallel.

Now observe this world of God's. The mountain-rock must have its surface rusted into putrescence and become dead soil, before the herb can grow. The destruction of the mineral is the life of the vegetable. Again the same process begins. The "corn of wheat dies," and out of death more abundant life is born. Out of the soil in which deciduous leaves are buried, the young tree shoots vigorously, and strikes its roots deep down into the realm of decay and death. Upon the life of the vegetable world, the myriad forms of higher life sustain themselves — still the same law: the sacrifice of life to give life. Further still. Have we never pondered over that mystery of nature — the dove struck down by the hawk — the deer trembling beneath the stroke of the lion — the winged fish falling into the jaws of the dolphin? It is the solemn law of vicarious sacrifice again. And as often as man sees his table covered with the flesh of animals slain, does he behold, whether he think of it or not, the deep mystery and law of being. They have surrendered their innocent lives that he may live. Nay, further still — it it as impossible for man to live as it is for man to be redeemed, except through vicarious suffering. The anguish of the mother is the condition of the child's life. His very being has its roots in the law of sacrifice; and from his birth onwards, instinctively this becomes the law which rules his existence. There is no blessing which was ever enjoyed by man which did not come through this. There was never a country cleared for civilization, and purified of its swamps and forests, but the first settlers paid the penalty of that which their successors enjoy. There never was a victory won, but the conquerors who took possession of the conquest passed over the bodies of the noblest slain, who died that they might win.

Now observe, all this is the Law obeyed, either unconsciously or else instinctively. But in the redemption of our humanity, a moment comes when that law is recognised as the will of God adopted *consciously*, and voluntarily obeyed as the law of man's existence. Then it is that man's true nobleness, his only possible blessedness, and his redemption from blind instincts and mere selfishness, begin. You may evade that law — you may succeed in living as Caiaphas did, sacrificing others, instead of yourself — and men will call you wise, and prudent, and respectable. But you are only a Caiaphas: — Redeemed you are not. Your proper humanity has not begun.

The Highest Man recognised that Law, and joyfully embraced it as the law of His existence. It was the consciousness of His surrender to that as God's will, and the voluntariness of the act, which made it Sacrifice. Hear Him: "No man taketh my life from me. I have power to lay it down, and I have power to take it up again." "*This commandment have I received from my Father.*" Had he been by the wiles of Caiaphas simply surprised and dragged struggling and reluctant to doom, He would have been a victim, but not a sacrifice — He would have been an object of our compassion, but by no means of our admiring wonder. It was the foresight of all the result of His opposition to the world's sin, and His steady uncompromising battle against it notwithstanding, in every one of its forms, knowing that He must be its victim at the last, which prevented His death from being merely the death of a lamb slain unconsciously on Jewish altars, and elevated it to the dignity of a true and proper Sacrifice.

We go beyond this, however. It was not merely a sacrifice, it was a sacrifice for sin. "His soul was made on offering for sin." Neither was it only a sacrifice for sin — it was a sacrifice for the *world's* sin. In the text, "that Jesus should die for that nation; and not for that nation only, but that also He should gather together in one the children of God that were scattered abroad."

Two ideas are necessary to be distinctly apprehended by us in order to understand that — the first is the notion of punishment, the second is the idea of the world's sin.

By punishment is simply meant the penalty annexed to transgression of a law. Punishment is of two kinds: the penalty which follows ignorant transgression, and the chastisement which ensues upon wilful disobedience. The first of these is called imputed guilt, the second is actual guilt. By imputed guilt is meant, in theological language, that a person is treated as if he were guilty: — if, for example, you approach too near the whirling wheel of steam machinery, the mutilation which follows is the punishment of temerity. If the traveller ignorantly lays his hand on the cockatrice's den, the throb of the evenomed fang is the punishment of his ignorance. He has broken a law of nature — and the guilt of the infraction is imputed to him — there is penalty: but there is none of the chastisement which follows sin. His conscience is not made miserable. He only suffers. Further, — according to the constitution of this world, it is not only our own transgressions of ignorance, but besides, the faults of others, which bring pain and sorrow on us. The man of irritable and miserably nervous temperament owes that often to a father's intemperance. Many a man has to struggle all his life with the penury which he reaps as the harvest of a distant ancestor's extravagance. In the strictest sense of the word, these are punishments; the consequences annexed to transgression: and, in the language of theology, they are called imputed guilt. But there is an all-important distinction between them and the chastisements of personal iniquity. If a man suffer ill health or poverty as the results of his own misconduct, his conscience forces him to refer this to the wrath of God. He is reaping as he had sown, and the miseries of conscious fault are added to his penalty. But if such things come as the penalty of the wrong of others, then, philosophically though you may call them punishment, in the popular sense of the word they are no punishments at all, but rather corrective discipline, nay, even richest blessings, if they are received from a Father's hand, and transmuted by humbleness into the means of spiritual growth.

Apply all this to the sacrifice of Christ. Let no man say that Christ bore the wrath of God. Let no man say that God was angry with His Son. We are sometimes told of a mysterious anguish which Christ endured, the consequence of Divine wrath, the sufferings of a heart laden with the conscience of the world's transgressions, which He was bearing as if they were

His own sins. Do not add to the Bible what is not in the Bible. The Redeemer's conscience was not bewildered to feel *that* His own, which was *not* His own. He suffered no wrath of God. Twice came the voice from heaven, "This is my beloved Son in whom I am *well pleased.*" There was seen an angel strengthening Him. Nay, even to the last, never did the consciousness of purity and the Father's Love forsake Him. "Father, into Thy hands I commend my spirit."

Christ came into collision with the world's evil, and He bore the penalty of that daring. He approached the whirling wheel, and was torn in pieces. He laid His hand upon the cockatrice's den, and its fangs pierced Him. It is the law which governs the conflict with evil. It can be only crushed by suffering from it. .... The Son of man who puts His naked foot on the serpent's head, crushes it: but the fang goes into His heel.

The Redeemer bore imputed sin. He bore the penalty of others' sin. He was punished. Did He bear the anger of the Most High? Was His the hell of an accusing conscience? In the Name of Him who is God, not Caiaphas, *never*. Something more, however, is necessary to complete our notion of punishment. It is a right estimate of Law. We are apt to think of punishment as something quite arbitrary, which can be remitted or changed at will. Hence, we almost always connect it with the idea of wrath. Hence, the heathen tried to bribe and coax their deities to spare. And hence the sacrifice of Christ comes to be looked upon in the light of a sagacious or ingenious contrivance, a mere "scheme." Now remember what Law is. The moral Laws of this universe are as immutable as God Himself. Law is the Being of God. God cannot alter those laws: He cannot make wrong right. He cannot make Truth falsehood, nor falsehood truth. He cannot make sin blessed, nor annex hell to innocence. Law moves on its majestic course irresistible. If His chosen Son violates Law, and throws himself from the pinnacle, He dies. If you resist a law in its eternal march, the universe crushes you, that is all. Consider what Law is, and then the idea of bloody vengeance passes away altogether from the Sacrifice. It is not "an eye for an eye," and "a tooth for a tooth," in the sanguinary spirit of the old retaliatory legislation. It is the eternal impossibility of violating that law of the universe whereby penalty is annexed to transgression, and must fall, either laden with curse, or rich in blessing.

The second idea which it behoves us to master is that of the world's sin. The apostle John always viewed sin as a great connected principle: *One;* a single world-spirit — exactly as the electricity with which the universe is charged, is indivisible, imponderable, one, so that you cannot separate it from the great ocean of fluid. The electric spark that slumbers in the dew-drop is part of the flood which struck the oak. Had that spark not been there, it could be demonstrated that the whole previous constitution of the universe might have been different, and the oak not struck.

Let us possess ourselves of this view of sin, for it is the true one. Separate acts of sin are but manifestations of one great principle. It was thus that the Saviour looked on the sins of His day. The Jews of that age had had no hand in the murder of Abel or

Zacharias; but they were of kindred spirit with the men who slew them. Condemning their murderers, they imitated their act. In that imitation they "allowed the deeds of their fathers;" they shared in the guilt of the act which had been consummated, because they had the spirit which led to it. "The blood of them all shall come on this generation." It was so, too, that Stephen looked on the act of his assassins. When God's glory streamed upon his face, he felt that the transaction going on then was not simply the violence of a mob in an obscure corner of the world: it was an outbreak of the Great Principle of evil — He saw in their act the resurrection of the spirit of those who had "resisted the Holy Ghost," in their day, slain the prophets, opposed Moses, crucified "the just one," and felt that their genuine descendants were now opposing themselves to the form in which Truth and Goodness were appearing in his day.

It is in this way only that you will be able with any reality of feeling to enter into the truth that your sins nailed Him to the cross: that the Lord hath laid on Him the iniquity of us all: that He died "not for that nation only, but that also He should gather together in one the children of God that were scattered abroad." If, for instance, indisputable evidence be given of the saintliness of a man whose creed and views are not yours, and rather than admit that Good in him *is* Good, you invent all manner of possible motives to discredit his excellence, then let the thought arise — This is the resurrection of the spirit which was rampant in the days of Jesus; the spirit of those who saw the purest Goodness, and rather than acknowledge it to be good, preferred to account for it as a diabolical power. Say to yourself — I am verging on the spirit of the sin that was unpardonable — I am crucifying the Son of God afresh. If in society you hear the homage unrebuked, — Honour to the rich man's splendid offering, instead of glory to the widow's humble mite — if you see the weak and defenceless punished severely for the sins which the great and strong do unblushingly, and even with the connivance and admiration of society — if you find sins of frailty placed on the same level with sins of pride and presumption — or if you find guilt of any kind palliated instead of mourned, then let the dreadful thought arise in the fulness of its meaning — I allow the deeds of those days — His blood shall come upon this generation. My sin and your sin, the sin of all, bears the guilt of the Redeemer's sacrifice. It *was* vicarious — He suffered for what He never did. "Not for that nation only, but that also He should gather together in one the children of God that were scattered abroad."

To conclude — Estimate rightly the death of Christ. It was not simply the world's example — it was the world's Sacrifice. He died not merely as a Martyr to the Truth. His death is the world's life. Ask ye what life is? Life is not exemption from penalty. Salvation is not escape from suffering and punishment. The Redeemer suffered punishment: but the Redeemer's soul had blessedness in the very midst of punishment. Life is elevation of soul — nobleness — Divine character. The spirit of Caiaphas was death: to receive all, and give nothing: to sacrifice others to himself. The spirit of Christ was life: to give and not receive: to be sacrificed, and not to sacrifice. Hear Him again — "He that loseth his life, the same shall find it." That is life: the spirit of losing all for Love's sake. That is the soul's life which alone is blessedness and heaven. By realizing that ideal of humanity, Christ furnished the life which we appropriate only when we enter into His spirit.

Listen: — Only by renouncing sin is His death to sin yours — only by quitting it are you free from the guilt of His blood, only by voluntary acceptance of the law of the Cross, self-surrender to the will of God, and self-devotion to the good of others as the law of your being, do you enter into that present and future heaven which is the purchase of His vicarious sacrifice.

X.

Preached December 2, 1849.

REALIZING THE SECOND ADVENT.

JOB xix. 25-27. — "For I know that my Redeemer liveth, and that he shall stand at the latter day upon the earth: And though after my skin worms destroy this body, yet in my flesh shall I see God: Whom I shall see for myself, and mine eyes shall behold, and not another; though my reins be consumed within me."

THE hardest, the severest, the last lesson which man has to learn upon this earth, is submission to the will of God. It is the hardest lesson, because to our blinded eyesight it often seems a cruel will. It is a severe lesson, because it can be only taught by the blighting of much that has been most dear. It is the last lesson, because when a man has learned that, he is fit to be transplanted from a world of wilfulness, to a world in which one Will alone is loved, and only one is done. All that saintly experience ever had to teach, resolves itself into this, the lesson how to say affectionately, "Not as I will, but as Thou wilt." Slowly and stubbornly our hearts acquiesce in that. The holiest in this congregation, so far as he has mastered the lesson, will acknowledge that many a sore and angry feeling against his God had to be subdued, many a dream of earthly brightness broken, and many a burning throb stilled in a proud resentful heart, before he was willing to suffer God to be sovereign in His own world, and do with him and his as seemed to Him best. The earliest record that we have of this struggle in the human bosom is found in this book of Job. It is the most ancient statement we have of the perplexities and miseries of life, so graphic, so true to nature, that it proclaims at once that what we are reading is drawn not from romance but life. It has been said, that religious experience is but the fictitious creation of a polished age, when fanciful feelings are called into existence by hearts bent back, in reflex action and morbid, on themselves. We have an answer to that in this book. Religion is no morbid fancy. In the rough rude ages when Job lived, when men did not dwell on their feelings as in later centuries, the heart-work of religion was, manifestly, the same earnest, passionate thing that it is now. The heart's misgivings were the same beneath the tent of an Arabian Emir which they are beneath the roof of a modern Christian. Blow after blow fell on the Oriental Chieftain: — one day he was a father — a prince — the lord of many vassals and many flocks, and buoyant in one of the best of blessings, health; the next, he was a childless, blighted, ruined man. And then it was that there came from Job's lips those yearnings for the quiet of the grave, which are so touching, so real; and, considering that some of the strongest of the Elect of God have yielded to them for a moment, we might almost say so pardonable: "I should have been at rest — where the wicked cease from troubling and the weary are at rest. There the prisoners rest together: they hear not the voice of the oppressor. Wherefore is light given unto him that is in misery, and life unto the bitter of soul — which long for death, but it cometh not, and dig for it more than for hid treasures — which rejoice exceedingly, and are glad when they can find the grave?" What is the book of Job but the record of an earnest soul's perplexities? The double difficulty of life solved there, the existence of moral evil — the question whether suffering is a mark of wrath or not.

What falls from Job's lips is the musing of a man half-stunned, half-surprised, looking out upon the darkness of life, and asking sorrowfully — why are these things so? And all that falls from his friends' lips is the commonplace remarks of men upon what is inscrutable, maxims learned second-hand by rote and not by heart, fragments of deep truths, but truths misapplied, distorted, torn out of all connection of time and place, so as to become actual falsehoods, only blistering a raw wound. It was from these awkward admonitions that Job appealed in the text. He appealed from the tribunal of man's opinion to a tribunal where sincerity shall be cleared and vindicated. He appealed from a world of confusion, where all the foundations of the earth are out of course, to a world where all shall be set right. He appealed from the dark dealings of a God whose way it is to hide Himself, to a God who shall stand upon this earth in the clear radiance of a love on which suspicion's self cannot rest a doubt. It was faith straining through the mist, and discerning the firm land that is beyond. "I know that my Redeemer liveth, and that he shall stand at the latter day upon the earth."

We take two points: —

I. The certainty of God's interference in the affairs of this world.

II. The means of realizing that interference.

God's interference, again, is contemplated in this passage in a twofold aspect: A present superintendence — "I know that my Redeemer liveth." A future, personal, visible interference — "He shall stand at the latter day upon the earth."

I. His present superintendence.

1. The first truth contained in that is God's personal existence. It is not chance, nor fate, which sits at the wheel of this world's revolutions. It was no fortuitous concourse of atoms which massed themselves into a world of beauty. It was no accidental train of circumstances which has brought the human race to their present state. It was a living God. And it is just so far as *this* is the conviction of every day, and every hour, and every minute — "My Redeemer *liveth*," — that one man deserves to be called more religious than another. To be religious is to feel that God is the Ever Near. It is to go through life with this thought coming instinctively and unbidden, "Thou, God, seest me." A life of religion is a life of faith: and faith is that strange faculty by which man feels the presence of the invisible; exactly as some animals have the power of seeing in the dark. That is the difference between the Christian and the world. Most men know nothing beyond what they see. Their lovely world is all in all to them: its outer beauty: not its hidden Loveliness. — Prosperity — struggle — sadness — it is all the same:— They struggle through it all alone, and when old age comes, and the companions of early days are gone, they feel that they are solitary. In all this strange deep world, they never meet, or but for a moment, the Spirit of it all, who stands at their very side. And it is exactly the opposite of this that makes a Christian. Move where he will, there is a Thought and a Presence which he cannot put aside. He is haunted for ever by

the Eternal Mind. God looks out upon him from the clear sky, and through the thick darkness — is present in the rain-drop that trickles down the branches, and in the tempest that crashes down the forest. A Living Redeemer stands beside him — goes with him — talks with him, as a man with his friend. The emphatic description of a life of spirituality is: "Enoch walked with God:" and it seems to be one reason why a manifestation of God was given us in the flesh, that this Livingness of God might be more distinctly felt by us. We must not throw into these words of Job a meaning which Job had not. Reading these verses, some have discovered in them all the Christian doctrine of the Second Advent — of a resurrection — of the humanity of Christ. This is simply an anachronism. Job was an Arabian Emir, not a Christian. All that Job meant by these words was, that he knew he had a vindicator in God above: that though his friends had the best of it then, and though worms were preying on his flesh, yet at last God Himself would interfere to prove his innocence. But God has given to us, for our faith to rest on, something more distinct and tangible than He gave to Job. There has been one on earth through whose lips God's voice spoke; and from whose character was reflected the character of God. A living Person manifesting Deity. It is all this added meaning gained from Christ with which we use these words: "I know that my Redeemer liveth." But we must remember that all that was not revealed to Job.

2. The second truth implied in the personal existence of a Redeemer is sympathy. It was the keenest part of Job's trial that no heart beat pulse to pulse with his. His friends misunderstood him; and his wife, in a

moment of atheistic bitterness, in the spirit of our own infidel poet, "Let no man say that God in mercy gave that stroke," — addressed him thus: "Curse God and die." In the midst of this, it seems to have risen upon his heart with a strange power to soothe, that he was not alone: gall and bitterness were distilling from the lips of man; and molten lead was dropping from the hand of God. But there was a great difference between the two inflictions. Men were doing their work, unknowing of the pain they gave: God was meting out His in the scales of a most exquisite compassion, not one drop too much, and every drop that fell had a meaning of love in it. "Affliction," said the tried man, "cometh not out of the dust, neither doth trouble spring out of the ground" — superintending all this, "I know that my Redeemer liveth."

And here there is one word full of meaning, from which we collect the truth of sympathy. It is that little word of appropriation, "My" Redeemer. Power is shown by God's attention to the vast: Sympathy by His condescension to the small. It is not the thought of heaven's sympathy by which we are impressed, when we gaze through the telescope on the mighty world of space, and gain an idea of what is meant by infinite. Majesty and power are there — but the very vastness excludes the thought of sympathy. It is when we look into the world of insignificance, which the microscope reveals, and find that God has gorgeously painted the atoms of creation, and exquisitely furnished forth all that belongs to minutest life, that we feel that God sympathises and individualizes. When we are told that God is the Redeemer of the *world*, we know that love dwells in the bosom of the Most High; but if we want to know that God feels for us individually and separately, we must learn by heart this syllable of endearment, "*My* Redeemer." Child of God! if you would have your thought of God something beyond a cold feeling of His presence, let faith *appropriate* Christ. You are as much the object of God's solicitude as if none lived but yourself. He has counted the hairs of your head. In Old Testament language, "He has put your tears into His bottle." He has numbered your sighs and your smiles. He has interpreted the desires for which you have not found a name nor an utterance yourself. If you have not learned to say *My* Redeemer, then just so far as there is anything tender or affectionate in your disposition, you will tread the path of your pilgrimage with a darkened and a lonely heart; and when the day of trouble comes, there will be none of that triumphant elasticity which enabled Job to look down, as from a rock, upon the surges which were curling their crests of fury at his feet, but could only reach his bosom with their spent spray.

3. The third thing implied in the present superintendence is God's vindication of wrongs. The word translated here Redeemer, is one of quite peculiar signification. In all the early stages of society, the redress of wrongs is not a public, but a private act. It was then as now — blood for blood. But the executioner of the law was invested with something of a sacred character. Now he is the mere creature of a country's law: then he was the delegated Hand of God; for the next of kin to the murdered man stood forward solemnly in God's name as the champion of the defenceless, the *goel*, or Avenger of Blood. Goel is the word here! so that, translated into the language of those far-

back days, Job was professing his conviction that there was a champion, or an Avenger, who would one day do battle for his wrongs.

It is a fearful amount of this kind of work which is in arrear for the Avenger to execute, accumulating century by century and year by year. From the days of Cain and Abel there have been ever two classes, the oppressor and the oppressed, the gentle humble ones who refuse to right themselves, and the unscrupulous who force them aside. The Church has ever had the world against it. The world struck its first deadly blow by the hand of Cain, and it has been striking ever since: from the battle-field — and the martyr's stake — and the dungeons of the inquisition — and the prisons of the lordly tyrant — the blood of the innocent has cried for vengeance. By taunt and sneer, the world has had her triumph. And the servants of the Meekest have only had *this* to cheer them, "I know that my Redeemer liveth."

There is a persecution sharper than that of the axe. There is an iron that goes into the heart deeper than the knife. Cruel sneers, and sarcasms, and pitiless judgments, and cold-hearted calumnies — these are persecution. There is the tyrant of the nursery, and the playground, and the domestic circle, as well as of the judgment-hall. "Better were it," said the Redeemer, "for that man if a millstone had been hanged about his neck." Did you ever do that? — Did you ever pour bitterness into a heart that God was bruising, by a cold laugh, or a sneer, or a galling suspicion? — Into a sister's heart, or a friend's, or even a stranger's? — Remember — when you sent them, as Job's friends sent him, to pour out their griefs alone before their Father, your name went up to the Avenger's ears, mingled with the cries of His own elect.

There is a second mode in which God interferes in this world's affairs. There is a present superintendence perceived by faith. But there is a future redress which will be made manifest to sight. "He shall stand at the latter day upon the earth." I shall see Him.

First of all, there will be a visible, personal interference. All that Job meant was in the case of his own wrongs. But if *we* use those words, we must apply them in a higher sense. The Second Advent of Christ is supposed by some to mean an appearance of Jesus in the flesh to reign and triumph visibly. Others who feel that the visual perception of His Form would be a small blessing, and that the highest and truest Presence is always spiritual and realized by the spirit, believe that His advent will be a coming in Power. We will not dispute: — controversy whets the intellect, and only starves, or worse, poisons the heart. We will take what is certain. Every signal manifestation of the right, and vindication of the truth in judgment, is called in Scripture a coming of the Son of Man. A personal Advent of the Redeemer is one which can be perceived by foes as well as recognised by friends. The destruction of Jerusalem, recognised by the heathen themselves as judgment, is called in the Bible a coming of Christ. In the Deluge — in the destruction of the cities of the plain — in the confusion of tongues — God is said to have come down to visit the earth. There are two classes, then, who shall see that sight. Men like Job, who feel that their

Redeemer liveth; and men like Balaam, from whose lips words of truth, terrible to him, came: "I shall see Him, but not now; I shall behold Him, but not nigh."—"Every eye shall see Him." — *You* will see the triumph of the Right — the destruction of the Wrong. The awful question is: As Balaam — or as Job? Besides this, it will be unexpected: every judgment coming of Christ is as the springing of a mine. There is a moment of deep suspense after the match has been applied to the fuse which is to fire the train. Men stand at a distance, and hold their breath. There is nothing seen but a thin, small column of white smoke, rising fainter, and fainter, till it seems to die away. Then men breathe again: and the inexperienced soldier would approach the place thinking that the thing has been a failure. It is only faith in the experience of the commander, or the veterans, which keeps men from hurrying to the spot again — till just when expectation has begun to die away, the low, deep thunder sends up the column of earth majestically to heaven, and all that was on it comes crashing down again in its far circle, shattered and blackened with the blast.

It is so with this world. By God's Word the world is doomed. The moment of suspense is past: the first centuries in which men expected the convulsion to take place at once; and even Apostles were looking for it in their lifetime. We have fallen upon days of scepticism. There are no signs of ruin yet. We tread upon it like a solid thing fortified by its adamantine hills for ever. There is nothing against that, but a few words in a printed book. But the world is mined: and the spark has fallen; and just at the moment when serenity is at its height, "the heavens shall pass away with a great noise, and the elements shall melt with fervent heat," and the feet of the Avenger shall stand on Earth.

II. The means of realizing this interference.

There is a difference between knowing a thing and realizing it. When a poor man becomes suddenly the possessor of a fortune or of dignity, it is some time before the thing becomes so natural to him that he can act in his new sphere like his proper self — it is all strangeness at first. When the criminal hears the death-sentence in the dock, his cheeks are tearless. He hears the words, but scarcely understands that they have anything to do with him. He has not realized that it is he himself that has to die. When bereavement comes, it is not at the moment when the breath leaves the body that we feel what has been lost: — we know, but we must have it in detail: see the empty chair — and the clothes that will never be worn again — and perceive day after day pass — and he comes not. Then we realize.

Job *knew* that God was the vindicator of wrongs — that he said. But why did he go on repeating in every possible form the same thing: — "I shall see God — see Him for myself — mine eyes shall behold Him — yes, mine and not another's?" It would seem as if he were doing what a man does when he repeats over and over to himself a thing which he cannot picture out in its reality. It was true: but it was strange, and shadowy, and unfamiliar.

It is no matter of uncertainty to any one of us whether he himself shall die. He knows it. Every time the funeral bell tolls, the thought in some shape suggests himself — I am a mortal, dying man. That is knowing it. Which of us has realized it? Who can shut his eyes, and bring it before him as a reality, that the day will come when the hearse will stand at the door for him, and that all this bright world will be going on without him, and that the very flesh which now walks about so complacently, will have the coffin-lid shut down upon it, and be left to darkness, and loneliness, and silence, and the worm? Or, take a case still more closely suggested by the text — out of the grave we must rise again — long after all that is young, and strong, and beautiful before me, shall have mouldered into forgetfulness. Earth shall hear her Master's voice breaking the long silence of the centuries, and our dust shall hear it, and stand up among the myriads that are moving on to judgment. Each man in his own proper identity, his very self, must see God, and be seen by Him — looking out on the strange new scene, and doomed to be an actor in it for all eternity. We all *know* that — on which of our hearts is it stamped, not as a doctrine to be proved by texts, but as one of those things which must be hereafter, and in sight of which we are to live now?

There are two ways suggested to us by this passage for realizing these things. The first of these is meditation. No man forgets what the mind has dwelt long on. It is not by a passing glance that things become riveted in the memory. It is by forcing the memory to call them up again and again in leisure hours. It is in the power of meditation to bring danger in its reality so vividly before the imagination, that the whole frame can start instinctively as if the blow were falling, or as if the precipice were near. It is in the power of meditation so to engrave scenes of loveliness on a painter's eye, that he transfers to the canvas a vivid picture that was real to him before it was real to others. It is in the power of meditation so to abstract the soul from all that is passing before the bodily eye, that the tongue shall absently speak out the words with which the heart was full, not knowing that others are standing by. It seems to have been this that Job was doing — he was realizing by meditation. You can scarcely read over these words without fancying them the syllables of a man who was thinking aloud.

It is like a soliloquy rather than a conversation. "I shall see him." Myself. Not another. My own eyes.

This is what we want. It is good for a man to get alone, and then in silence think upon his own death, and feel how time is hurrying him along: that a little while ago and he was not — a little while still and he will be no more. It is good to take the Bible in his hands, and read those passages at this season of the year which speak of the Coming and the end of all, till from the printed syllables there seems to come out something that has life, and form, and substance in it, and all things that are passing in the world group themselves in preparation for that, and melt into its outline. Let us try to live with these things in view. God our Friend — Christ our living Redeemer; our sympathising Brother; our conquering Champion: — The Triumph of Truth: the End of Wrong. We shall live upon realities then: and this world will fade away into that which we know it is, but cannot realize — an Appearance, and a Shadow.

Lastly, God ensures that His children shall realize all this by affliction. Job had admitted these things before, but this time he spoke from the ashes on which he was writhing. And if ever a man is sincere, it is when he is in pain. If ever that superficial covering of conventionalities falls from the soul, which gathers round it as the cuticle does upon the body, and the rust upon the metal, it is when men are suffering. There are many things which nothing but sorrow can teach us. Sorrow is the great Teacher. Sorrow is the Realizer. It is a strange and touching thing to hear the young speak truths which are not yet within the limits of their experience: to listen while they say that life is sorrowful, that friends are treacherous, that there is quiet in the grave. When we are boys we adopt the phrases that we hear. In a kind of prodigal excess of happiness, we say that the world is a dream, and life a nothing — that eternity lasts for ever, and that all here is disappointment. But there comes a day of sharpness, when we find to our surprise that what we said had a meaning in it; and we are startled. That is the sentimentalism of youth passing into reality. In the lips of the young such phrases are only sentimentalities. What we mean by sentimentalism is that state in which a man speaks things deep and true, not because he feels them strongly, but because he perceives that they are beautiful, and that it is touching and fine to say them — things which he fain *would* feel, and fancies that he *does* feel. Therefore, when all is well, when friends abound, and health is strong, and the comforts of life are around us, religion becomes faint, and shadowy. Religious phraseology passes into cant — the gay, and light, and trifling, use the same words as the holiest; till the earnest man, who *feels* what the world is sentimentalising about, shuts up his heart, and either coins other phrases or else keeps silence. And then it is that if God would rescue a man from that unreal world of names and mere knowledge, He does what he did with Job — He strips him of his flocks, and his herds, and his wealth; or else, what is the equivalent, of the power of enjoying them — the desire of his eyes falls from him at a stroke. Things become real then. Trial brings man face to face with God — God and he touch; and the flimsy veil of bright cloud that hung between him and the sky is blown away: he feels that he is standing outside the earth with nothing between him and the Eternal Infinite. Oh! there is something in the sick-bed, and the aching heart, and the restlessness and the languor of shattered health, and the sorrow of affections withered, and the stream of life poisoned at its fountain, and the cold, lonely feeling of utter rawness of heart which is felt when God strikes home in earnest, that forces a man to feel what is real and what is not.

This is the blessing of affliction to those who will lie still, and not struggle in a cowardly or a resentful way. It is God speaking to Job out of the whirlwind, and saying — In the sunshine and the warmth you cannot meet Me: but in the hurricane and the darkness, when wave after wave has swept down and across the soul, you shall see My Form, and hear My Voice, and know that your Redeemer liveth.

XI.

Preached December 6, 1849.

FIRST ADVENT LECTURE.

THE GRECIAN.

ROM. i. 14-17. — "I am debtor both to the Greeks and to the Barbarians, both to the wise and to the unwise. So, as much as in me is, I am ready to preach to Gospel the you that are at Rome also. For I am not ashamed of the Gospel of Christ: for it is the power of God unto salvation to every one that believeth; to the Jew first, and also to the Greek. For therein is the righteousness of God revealed from faith to faith: as it is written, The just shall live by faith."

The season of Advent commemorates three facts. 1. That the Lord has come. 2. That He is perpetually coming. 3. That He will yet come in greater glory than has yet appeared. And these are the three Advents — The first in the flesh, which is past: the second in the spirit: the third, His judgment Advent.

The first occupies our attention in these lectures.

We live surrounded by Christian institutions; breathe an atmosphere saturated by Christianity. It is exceedingly difficult even to imagine another state of things. In the enjoyment of domestic purity, it is difficult to conceive the debasing effects of polygamy: in the midst of political liberty to conceive of the blighting power of slavery: in scientific progress to imagine mental stagnation: in religious liberty and free goodness to fancy the reign of superstition.

Yet to realize the blessings of health, we must sit by the sick-bed: to feel what light is, we must descend into the mine and see the emaciated forms which dwindle away in darkness: to know what the blessing of sunshine is, go down into the valleys where stunted vegetation and dim vapours tell of a scene on which the sun scarcely shines two hours in the day. And to know what we have from Christianity, it is well to cast the eyes sometimes over the darkness from which the Advent of Christ redeemed us.

There are four departments of human nature spoken of in these verses, on which the Light shined. The apostle felt that the Gospel was the power of God unto salvation to the Greeks, the Romans, the Barbarians, and the Jews. In the present lecture we consider Christianity presented to the Grecian character, and superseding the Grecian religion.

Four characteristics marked Grecian life and Grecian religion. Restlessness — Worldliness — The worship of the Beautiful — The worship of the Human.

1. Restlessness.

Polytheism divided the contemplation over many objects: and as the outward objects were manifold, so was there a want of unity in the inward life. The Grecian mind was distracted by variety. He was to obtain wisdom from one Deity: eloquence from that Mercurius for whom Paul was taken: purity from Diana for whom Ephesus was zealous: protection for his family or country from the respective tutelary deities: success by a prayer to Fortune.

Hence dissipation of mind: that fickleness for which the Greeks were famous: and the restless love of novelty which made Athens a place of literary and social gossip — "some new thing."

All stability of character rests on the contemplation of changeless unity.

So, in modern science, which is eminently Christian,

having exchanged the bold theorizing of ancient times for the patient humble willingness to be taught by the facts of nature, and performing its wonders by exact imitation of them — on the Christian principle — the Son of man can do nothing of Himself, but what He seeth the Father do.

And all the results of science have been to simplify and trace back the manifold to unity. Ancient science was only a number of insulated facts and discordant laws; modern science has gradually ranged these under fewer and ever fewer laws. It is ever tending towards unity of law.

For example — Gravitation. The planet's motion, and the motion of the atom of water that dashes tumultuously, and as it seems lawlessly, down the foam of the cataract: the floating of the cork, the sinking of the stone, the rise of the balloon, and the curved flight of the arrow, are all brought under one single law — diverse and opposite as they seem.

Hence science is calm and dignified, reposing upon uniform fact. The philosopher's very look tells of repose, resting, as he does, on a few changeless principles.

So also in religion. Christianity proclaimed "One God and one Mediator between God and men, the man Christ Jesus." Observe the effect in the case of two apostles. St. Paul's view of the Gospel contemplated it as an eternal divine purpose. *His* Gospel, the salvation of the Gentiles, was the eternal purpose which had been hidden from ages and generations. His own personal election was part of an eternal counsel. All the children of God had been predestinated before the creation "unto the adoption of children by Jesus Christ to

Himself." Now see the effect on character. First, on veracity — 2 Cor. i. 18, &c. He contemplated the changeless "yea" of God — His own yea became fixed as God's — changeless, and calmly unalterable.

Again, in orthodoxy — "Jesus Christ, the same yesterday, to-day, and for ever." Be not carried about by divers and strange doctrines. Truth is one — Error manifold — many opinions, yet there can be but one faith. See how calm and full of rest all this spirit is.

Now consider St. John. His view of the Gospel recognised it rather as the manifestation of love than the carrying out of unity of an everlasting purpose. If you view the world as the Greek did, all is so various that you must either refer it to various deities, or to different modes of the same Deity. To-day you are happy — God is pleased: to-morrow miserable — God is angry. But St. John referred these all to unity of character — "God is Love." Pain and pleasure, the sigh and smile, the sunshine and the storm, nay hell itself, to him were but the result of Eternal love.

Hence came deep calm — the repose which we are toiling all our lives to find, and which the Greek never found.

II. Wordliness.

There are men and nations to whom this world seems given as their province, as if they had no aspiration above it. If ever there was a nation who understood the science of living, it was the Grecian. They had organized social and domestic life — filled existence with comforts: knew how to extract from everything its greatest measure of enjoyment. This world was their home — this visible world was the object of their worship. Not like the Orientals, who called all materialism bad, and whose highest object was to escape from it, "to be unclothed, not clothed upon," as St. Paul phrases it. The Greek looked upon this world in its fallen state, and pronounced it all "very good."

The results were threefold.

1. Disappointment. Lying on the infinite bosom of Nature, the Greek was yet unsatisfied. And there is an insatiable desire above all external forms and objects in man — all men — which they can never satisfy. Hence his craving too, like others, was from time to time, "Who will show us any good?" This dissatisfaction is exhibited in the parable of the prodigal, who is but the symbol of erring humanity. Away from his father's home, the famine came, and he fed on husks. Famine and husks are the world's unsatisfactoriness. A husk is a thing that seems full: is hollow: which stays the appetite for a time, but will not support the life. And such is this world: leaving a hollowness at heart, staying our craving but for a time. "He that drinketh of this water shall thirst again." And the worldly man is trying to satiate his immortal hunger upon husks.

Second result — Degradation. Religion aims at an ideal life above this actual one — to found a divine polity — a kingdom of God — a church of the best. And the life of worldliness pronounces this world to be all. This is to be adorned and beautified. Life as it is. Had you asked the Greek his highest wish, he would have replied, "This world, if it could only last — I ask no more." Immortal youth — and this bright existence. This is to feed on husks: but husks which the swine did eat. No degradation to the swine, for it is their nature; but degradation to man to rest in the outward, visible, and present, for the bosom of God is his home. The Greek, therefore, might be, in his own language, "a reasoning animal," but not one of the children of Heaven.

Third result — Disbelief in Immortality. The more the Greek attached himself to this world, the more the world unseen became a dim world of shades. The earlier traditions of the deep-thinking Orientals, which his forefathers brought from Asia, died slowly away; and any one who reminded him of them, was received as one would now be who were to speak of purgatory. The cultivated Athenians were for the most part sceptics in the time of Christ. Accordingly, when Paul preached at Athens the resurrection of the dead, they "mocked."

This bright world was all. Its revels — its dances — its theatrical exhibitions — its races — its baths — and academic groves, where literary leisure luxuriated, — these were blessedness; and the Greek's hell was death. Their poets speak pathetically of the misery of the wrench from all that is dear and bright. The dreadfulness of death is one of the most remarkable things that meet us in those ancient writings.

And these men were startled by seeing a new sect rise up to whom death was nothing — who almost courted it. They heard an apostle say at Miletus: "None of these things move me, neither count I my life dear unto myself, so that I might finish my course with joy." For the cross of Christ had crucified in their hearts the Grecian's world. To them life was honour, integrity, truth; that is, the soul: to this all other was to be sacrificed. This was the proper self, which could only die by sin, by denying its own existence. The rise of the higher life had made this life nothing, and delivered those who, though fear of death, were all their lifetime subject unto bondage.

Appeal to the worldy-minded. Melancholy spectacle! Men and women shutting out the idea of death, — the courtesies of society concealing from them the mention of their age, by all false appliances of dress, &c., &c., and staying the appearance of the hand of time. You must die. The day will come, and the coffin. Life in God alone robs that thought of dreadfulness: when the resurrection being begun within, you can look upon the decay of the outward man, and feel *I* am not dying.

III. The worship of the Beautiful.

The Greek saw this world almost only on its side of beauty. His name for it was Kosmos, divine order or regularity. He looked at actions in the same way. One and the same adjective expressed the noble and the beautiful. If he wanted to express a perfect man, he called him a musical or harmonious man.

What was the consequence? Religion degenerated into the arts. All the immortal powers of man were thrown upon the production of a work of the imagination. The artist who had achieved a beautiful statue was almost worshipped. The poet who had produced a noble poem was the prophet of the nation. The man who gave the richest strains of melody was half divine. This was their inspiration. The arts became religion, and religion ended in the arts.

Hence, necessarily, sensuality became religious; because all feelings produced by these arts, chiefly the voluptuous ones, were authorized by religion. There is a peculiar danger in refinement of sensuous enjoyments. Coarse pleasures disgust, and pass for what they are; but who does not know that the real danger and triumph of voluptuousness are when it approaches the soul voiled under the drapery of elegance? — They fancied themselves above the gross multitude: but their sensuality, disguised even from themselves, was sensuality still — ay, and even at times, in certain festivals, broke out into gross and unmistakeable licentiousness.

And hence, the greatest of the Greeks in his imaginary Republic banished from that perfect state all the strains which were soft and enfeebling — all the poems that represented any deeds of Deities unworthy of the Divine — all the statues which could suggest one single feeling of impurity. Himself a worshipper of the purest beautiful, it was yet given to his all but inspired heart, to detect the lurking danger before which Greece was destined to fall — the approach of sensuality through the worship of the graceful and the refined.

There is this danger now. Men are awakened from coarse rude life to the desire of something deeper. And the God or Spirit of this world can subtly turn that aside into channels which shall effectually enfeeble and ruin the soul. Refinement — melting imagery — dim religious light: all the witchery of form and colour — music — architecture: all these, even coloured with the hues of religion, producing feelings either religious or quasi-religious, may yet do the world's work. For all attempt to impress the heart through the senses, "to make perfect through the flesh," is fraught with that danger beneath which Greece sunk. There is a self-deception in these feelings: the thrill — and the sense of mystery — and the luxury of contemplation — and the impressions on the senses: all these lie very close to voluptuousness — enfeeblement of heart — yea, even impurity.

This, too, is the ruinous effect of an education of accomplishments. The education of the taste, and the cultivation of the feelings in undue proportion, destroys the masculine tone of mind. An education chiefly romantic or poetical, not balanced by hard practical life, is simply the ruin of the soul.

If any one ever felt the beauty of this world it was He. The beauty of the lily nestling in the grass — He felt it all: but the beauty which he exhibited in life was the stern loveliness of moral action. The King in His Beauty "had no form or comeliness:" it was the beauty of obedience — of noble deeds — of unconquerable fidelity — of unswerving truth, — of Divine self-devotion. The Cross! the Cross! We must have something of iron and hardness in our characters. The Cross tells us that is the true Beautiful which is Divine: an inward, not an outward beauty, which rejects and turns sternly away from the meretricious forms of the outward world, which have a corrupting or debilitating tendency.

IV. The worship of Humanity.

The Greek had strong human feelings and sympathies. He projected his own self on nature: humanized it: gave a human feeling to clouds, forests, rivers, seas.

In this he was a step above other idolatries. The Hindoo, for instance, worshipped monstrous emblems of physical power. Might: gigantic masses: hundred-handed deities, scarcely human, you find in Hindostan. In Egypt, again, Life was the thing sacred. Hence all that had life was in a way divine: the sacred ibis, crocodile, bull, cat, snake. All that produced and all that ended life. Hence death too was sacred. The Egyptian lived in the contemplation of death. His coffin was made in his lifetime; his ancestors embalmed: the sacred animals preserved in myriad heaps through generations in mummy pits. The sovereign's tomb was built to last for, not centuries, but thousands of years.

The Greek was above this. It was not merely power, but human power: not merely beauty, but human beauty; not merely life, but human life, which was the object of his profoundest veneration. His effort therefore was, in his conception of his god, to realize a beautiful human being. And not the animal beauty of the human only; but the intelligence which informs and shines through beauty. All his life he was moulding into shape visions of earth — a glorious human being. Light under the conditions of humanity: the "sun in human limbs arrayed" was the central object of Grecian worship.

Much in this had a germ of truth — more was false. This principle, which is true, was evidently stated: The Divine, under the limitations of humanity, is the only worship of which man is capable. Demonstrably: for man cannot conceive that which is not in his own mind. He may worship what is below himself, or that which is in himself resembling God; but attributes of which from his own nature he has no conception, he clearly cannot adore.

The only question therefore is, *What* he shall reckon divine and in alliance with God? If power, then he worships as the Hindoo — If life, then as the

Egyptian — If physical and intellectual beauty, then as the Greek.

Observe — they wanted some living image of God containing something more truly divine to supplant their own. For still, in spite of their versatile and multifarious conceptions, the illimitable Unknown remained: to which an altar stood in Athens. They wanted Humanity in its glory — they asked for a Son of Man.

Christ is Deity under the limitations of Humanity. But there is presented in Christ for worship, not power: nor beauty: nor physical life: but the moral image of God's perfections. Through the heart, and mind, and character of Jesus it was that the Divinest streamed. Divine *character*, that was given in Christ to worship.

Another error. The Greek worshipped *all* that was in man. Every feeling had its beauty, and its divine origin. Hence Thieving had its patron deity: and Treachery, and Cunning: and Lust had its temple erected for abominable worship. All that was human had its sanction in the example of some god.

Christ corrects. Not all that is human is divine. There is a part of our nature kindred with God: the strengthening of that, by mixture with God's spirit, is our true and proper humanity — regeneration of soul. There is another part whereby we are related to the brutes; our animal propensities; our lower inclinations; our corrupted will. And whoever lives in that, and strengthens that, sinks not to the level of the brutes, but below them, to the level of the demons: for he uses an immortal spirit to degrade himself: and the immortal joined with evil, as the life to the body, is demoniacal.

In conclusion, remark: In all this system one thing was wanting — the sense of sin. The Greek worshipped the beautiful — adored the human — deified the world: of course this worship found no place for sin. The Greek would not have spoken to you of sin: he would have told you of departure from a right line; want of moral harmony; discord within: he would have said that the music of your soul was out of tune. Christ came to convince the world of sin. And after Him that deep cloud began to brood upon the hearts of Christendom, which rests upon the conscience which has been called into vitality of action and susceptibility.

For this Greece had no remedy. The universe has no remedy but one. There is no prescription for the sickness of the heart, but that which is written in the Redeemer's blood.

XII.

Preached December 13, 1849.

SECOND ADVENT LECTURE.

THE ROMAN.

Rom. i. 14-16. — "I am debtor both to the Greeks and to the Barbarians, both to the wise and to the unwise. So, as much as in me is, I am ready to preach the Gospel to you that are at Rome also. For I am not ashamed of the Gospel of Christ: for it is the power of God unto salvation to every one that believeth; to the Jew first, and also to the Greek."

The Advent of Christ is the gulf which separates ancient from modern history. The dates B. C. and A. D. are not arbitrary but real division. His coming is the crisis of the world's history. It was the moment from whence light streamed into the realms of darkness, and life descended into the regions of the grave. It was the new birth of worn-out humanity.

Last Thursday we considered the effects of this Advent on Greece. We found the central principle of Grecian life to be worldliness. The Greek saw, sought, and worshipped nothing higher than this life, but only this life itself. Hence Greek religion degenerated into mere Taste, which is perception of the Beautiful. The result on character was threefold: — Restlessness, which sent the Greek through this world with his great human heart unsatisfied, fickle in disposition, and ever inquiring, with insatiable curiosity, after some new thing. Licentiousness; for whatsoever attaches his heart to the outward Beauty, without worshipping chiefly in it that moral Beauty of which all else is but the type and suggestion, necessarily, slowly it may be, but inevitably, sinks down and down into the deepest abyss of sensual existence. Lastly, Unbelief. The Greek, seeing principally this world, lost his hold upon the next. For the law of faith is, that a man can only believe what is already in his spirit. He believes as he is. The Apostle Paul writes in astonishment to these Greeks (of Corinth), "How say some among you there is no resurrection of the dead?" But the thing was explicable. Paul was "dying daily." The outward life decayed: the inner grew and lived with more vitality every day. He *felt* the life to come in which he believed. But the Corinthians, leading an easy, luxurious life — how could it be a reality to them? How could *they* believe in immortality, in whom the immortal scarcely stirred, or only feebly?

To these the apostle felt bound to preach the living Gospel. "I am debtor to the Greeks."

To-day, we turn to the Roman nation, its religion and its life. At the time of which the New Testament speaks, Greece had been nearly a century and a half a province of Rome. In the language of Daniel, the kingdom of brass had given way to the kingdom of iron. The physical might of Rome had subdued Greece, but the mind of Greece had mastered Rome. The Greeks became the teachers of their conquerors. The deities of Greece were incorporated into the national faith of Rome. Greek literature became the education of the Roman youth. Greek philosophy was almost the only philosophy the Roman knew. Rome adopted Grecian arts, and was insensibly moulded by contact with Grecian life. So that the world in name and government was Roman, but in feeling and civilization Greek.

If, therefore, we would understand Roman life, we must contemplate it at an earlier period, when it was free from Greek influence, and purely exhibited its own indiosyncracies.

The nation which we contemplate to-day was a noble one — humanly, one of the noblest that the world has seen. Next to the Jewish, the very highest. We may judge from the fact of St. Paul's twice claiming his Roman citizenship, and feeling the indignation of a Roman citizen at the indignity of chastisement. And this, too, in an age when the name had lost its brightness: when a luxurious, wealthy Greek could purchase his freedom. Claudius Lysias bought it "with a large sum of money." And yet we may conceive what it had been once, when even the faint lustre of its earlier dignity could inspire a foreigner, and that foreigner a Jew, and that Jew a Christian, with such respect.

At the outset, then, we have a rare and high-minded people and their life to think of. They who have imbibed the spirit of its writers from their youth can neither speak nor think of it without enthusiasm. Scarcely can we forbear it even in the pulpit. Nor is this an unchristian feeling, earthly, to be checked: for, in order to elevate Christianity, it is not necessary to vilify heathenism. To exalt revelation, we need not try to show that natural religion has no truths. To exhibit the blessings of the Advent, is is not needful to demonstrate that man was brutalized without it. It is a poor, cowardly system which can only rise by the degradation of all others. Whatever is true belongs to the kingdom of the Truth. The purer the creed — the higher the character — the nobler the men who, without revelation, signally failed at last, the more absolute is the necessity of a Redeemer, and the more are we constrained to refer, gratefully, all blessings to His Advent.

We take three points: — the public and private life of Rome, and its moral and inevitable decay at last.

I. The public life of Rome.

First, I notice the spirit of its religion. The very word shows what that was. *Religion*, a Roman word, means obligation, a blinding power. Very different from the corresponding Greek expression, which implies worship by a sensuous ceremonial (threskeia).

The Roman began, like the Jew, from Law. He started from the idea of Duty. But there was an important difference. The Jew was taught duty or obedience to the Law of a personal, holy God. The Roman obeyed, as his Etruscan ancestors taught him, a Fate or Will; and with very different results. But at present we only observe the lofty character of the early religion which resulted from such a starting-point.

The early history of Rome is wrapped in fable; but the fable itself is worth much, as preserving the spirit of the old life when it does not preserve the facts. Accordingly, the tradition taught that the building of Rome was done in obedience to the intimations of the Will of Heaven. It was rebuilt in a site selected not by human prudence, but by a voice divinely guided. Its first great legislator (Numa) is represented as giving laws, not from a human heart, but after secret communion with the Superhuman. It was the belief of Roman writers that the early faith taught access to God only through the mind; that therefore no images, but only temples, were found in Rome during the first two centuries of her existence. No bloody sacrifices defiled the city. War itself was a religious act; solemnly declared by a minister of religion casting a spear into the enemy's territory. Nay, we even find something in spirit resembling the Jewish sabbath: the command that during the rites of religion no traffic should go on, nor workman's hammer break the consecrated silence, but that men should devoutly contemplate God.

Here was a high, earnest, severe Religion.

Now this resulted in Government, as its highest earthly expression. Duty: and therefore Law on earth, as a copy of the Will of Heaven. Different nations seem, consciously or unconsciously, destined by God to achieve different missions. The Jew had the highest: to reveal to the world holiness. The Oriental stands as a witness to the reality of the Invisible above the visible. The Greek reminded the world of Eternal Beauty; and the destiny of the Roman seems to have been to stamp upon the minds of mankind the ideas of Law, Government, Order.

Beauty was not the object of the Roman contemplation, nor worship; nor was harmony. The taste for them might be taught, superinduced; but it was not natural. It was not indigenous to the soil of his nature. Hence, when Greece was reduced to a Roman province, in 146 B. C., the Roman soldiers took the noblest specimens of Grecian painting and converted them into gambling-tables.

You may distinguish the difference of the two characters from the relics which they have left behind them. The Greek produced a statue or a temple, the expression of a sentiment. The Roman, standing upon visible Fact, dealing with the practical, and living in the actual life of men, has left behind him works of public usefulness: noble roads which intersect empires — mighty aqueducts — bridges — enormous excavations for draining cities, at which we stand astonished: and, above all, that system of Law, the slow result of ages of experience, which has so largely entered into the modern jurisprudence of most European nations.

One of their own writers has distinctly recognised this destiny (Virgil). "It is for others to work brass into breathing shape — others may be more eloquent — or describe the circling movements of the heavens, and tell the rising of the stars. Thy work, O Roman! is to rule the nations: these be thine acts: to impose the conditions of the world's peace: to show mercy to the fallen, and to crush the proud."

In accordance with this, it is a characteristic fact that we find the *institutions* of Rome referred to inspiration. Not a decalogue of private duties; but a code of municipal laws. And, turning to the page of Scripture, whenever the Roman comes prominently forward, we always find him the organ of law, the instrument of public rule and order. Pilate has no idea of condemning unjustly: "Why, what evil had He done?" But he yields at the mention of the source of Law, the Emperor. The Apostle Paul appeals to Cæsar: and even a corrupt Festus respects the appeal: "Unto Cæsar thou shalt go." Nor could even the prisoner's innocence reverse his own appeal: "This man might have been set at liberty if he had not appealed unto Cæsar." The tumult at Ephesus is stilled by a hint of Roman interference: "We are in danger of being called in question for this day's uproar." When the angry crowd at Athens, and the equally angry mob of the Sanhedrim, was about to destroy Paul, again the Roman Claudius Lysias comes "with an army, and rescues him."

It was always the same thing. The Roman seems almost to have existed to exhibit on earth a copy of the Divine order of the universe, the law of the heavenly hierarchies.

II. Private Life.

We observe the sanctity of the domestic ties. Very touching are all the well-known anecdotes. That, for instance, of the noble Roman matron, who felt, all spotless as she was, life-dishonoured, and died by her own hand. The sacredness of home was expressed strongly by the idea of two guardian deities (Lares and Penates) who watched over it. A Roman's own fireside and hearthstone were almost the most sacred spots on earth. There was no battle-cry that came so to his heart as that, "For the altar and the hearth." How firmly this was rooted in the nation's heart is plain from the tradition, that for 170 years no separation took place by law between those who had been once united in wedlock.

There is deep importance in this remark; for it was to this that Rome owed her greatness. The whole fabric of the Commonwealth rose out of the family. The Family was the nucleus round which all the rest agglomerated. First the family: then the clan, made up of the family and its dependents or clients: then the tribe: lastly, the nation. And so the noble structure of the Roman Commonwealth arose, compacted and morticed together, but resting on the foundation of the hearthstone.

Very different is it in the East. A nation is a collection of units, held together by a government. There is a principle of cohesion in them: but only such cohesion as belongs to the column of sand, supported by the whirlwind: when the blast ceases, the atoms fall asunder. When the chief is slain or murdered, the nation is in anarchy — the family does not exist. Polygamy and infanticide, the bane of domestic life, are the destruction, too, of national existence.

There is a solemn lesson in this. Moral decay in the family is the invariable prelude to public corruption. It is a false distinction which we make between public integrity and private honour. The man whom you cannot admit into your family, whose morals are corrupt, cannot be a pure statesman. Whoever studies history will be profoundly convinced that a nation stands or falls with the sanctity of its domestic ties. Rome mixed with Greece, and learned her morals. The Goth was at her gates, but she fell not till she was corrupted and tainted at the heart. The domestic corruption preceded the political. When there was no longer purity on her hearthstones, nor integrity in her senate, then, and not till then, her death-knell was rung.

We will bless God for our English homes. Partly the result of our religion. Partly the result of the climate which God has given us, according to the law of compensation by which physical evil is repaid by moral blessing; so that, its gloom and darkness making life more necessarily spent within doors than it is among continental nations, our life is domestic and theirs is social. When England shall learn domestic maxims from strangers, as Rome from Greece, her ruin is accomplished. And this blessing, too, comes from Christ — who presided at the marriage feast at Cana, who found a home in the family of Nazareth, and consecrated the hearthstone with everlasting inviolability.

Let us break up this private life into particulars.

1. We find manly courage. This too is perserved in a word. Virtue is a Roman word — manhood courage; for courage, manhood, virtue, were one word. Words are fossil thoughts: you trace the ancient feeling in that word — you trace it, too, in the corruption of the word. Among the degenerate descendants of the Romans, *virtue* no longer means manhood: it is simply dilettantism. The decay of life exhibits itself in the debasement even of words.

We dwell on this courage, because it was not merely animal daring. Like everything Roman, it was connected with religion. It was duty: obedience to will: self-surrender to the public good. The Roman legions subdued the world: but it was not their discipline alone; nor their strength; nor their brute daring. It was rather, far, their moral force — a nation whose legendary and historical heroes could thrust their hand into the flame, and see it consumed without a nerve shrinking: or come from captivity on parole, advise their countrymen against peace, and then go back to torture and certain death! or devote themselves by solemn self-sacrifice (like the Decii), who could bid sublime defiance to pain and count dishonour the only evil. The world must bow before such men; for, unconsciously, here was a form of the spirit of the Cross: Self-surrender, unconquerable fidelity to duty, sacrifice for others. And so far as Rome had in her that spirit, and so long as she had it, her career was the career of all those who in any form, even the lowest, take up the Cross; she went forth conquering and to conquer.

2. Deep as Roman greatness was rooted in the courage of her men, it was rooted deeper still in the honour of her women. I take one significant fact, which exhibits national feeling. There was a fire in Rome called Eternal, for ever replenished. It was the type and symbol of the duration of the Republic. This fire was tended by the Vestals: a beautifully significant institution. It implied that the duration of Rome was co-extensive with the preservation of her purity of morals. So long as the dignity of her matrons and her virgins remained unsullied, so long she would last. No longer. Female chastity guarded the Eternal City.

Here we observe something anticipative of Christianity. In the earlier ages after the Advent there were divine honours paid to the Queen of Heaven: and the land was covered over with houses set apart for celibacy. Of course, rude and gross minds can find plenty to sneer at in that institution; and doubtless the form of the truth was mistaken enough, as all mere *forms* of doctrine are. But the heart of truth which lay beneath all that superstition was a precious one. It was this. So long as purity of heart, delicacy of feeling, chastity of life, are found in a nation, so long that nation is great — no longer. Personal purity is the divinest thing in man and woman. It is the most sacred truth which the church of Christ is commissioned to exhibit and proclaim.

Upon these virtues I observe: — The Roman was conspicuous for the virtues of this earth. Honour, fidelity, courage, chastity, all manliness; yet the apostle felt that he had a Gospel to preach to them that were in Rome also. Moral virtues are not religious graces. There are two classes of excellence. There are men whose lives are full of moral principle, and there are others whose feelings are strongly devotional. And, strange to say, each of these is found at times disjoined from the other. Men of almost spotless earthly honour, who scarcely seem to know what reverence for things heavenly and devout aspirations towards God mean. Men who have the religious instinct, pray with fervour, kindle with spiritual raptures, and yet are impure in their feelings, and fail in matters of common truth and honesty. Each of these is but a half man: dwarfed and stunted in his spiritual growth. The "perfect man in Christ Jesus," who has grown to the "measure of the stature of the fulness of Christ," is he who has united these two things: who, to the high Roman virtues which adorn this earth, has added the sublimer feelings which are the investiture of heaven: in whom "justice, mercy, truth," are but the body of which the soul is faith and love.

Yet observe — there are moral virtues, and morality is not religion. Still, beware of depreciating them. Beware of talking contemptuously of "mere morality." If we must choose between two things which ought never to be divided, moral principle and religious sentiment, there is no question which most constitutes the character "which is not far from the kingdom of heaven." Devout feelings are common enough in childhood: religious emotions: religious warmth: instances of which are retailed by the happy parent: common enough, too, in grown men and women — but listen —

those devout feelings, separate from high principle, do not save from immorality: nay, I do believe, are the very stepping-stone towards it. When the sensual is confounded with and mistaken for the spiritual; and merely devout warmth is the rich, rank soil of heart in which moral evil most surely and most rankly grows — you will not easily build Roman virtues upon *that*. But high principle, which is, in other words, the baptism of John, is the very basis on which is most naturally raised the superstructure of religious faith. Happy, thrice happy he who begins with the law and ends with the gospel.

III. The decline of Roman Life.

1. First came corruption of the moral character. The Roman worldliness was of a kind far higher than the Grecian. In his way the Roman really had the world's good at heart. There was a something invisible at which he aimed. Invisible justice — invisible order — invisible right. Still it was only the law on earth: the well-being of this existence. And whatever is only of this earth is destined to decay. The soul of the Roman, bent on this world's affairs, became secularized, then animalized, and so at last, when there was little left to do, pleasure became his aim, as it had been the Grecian's. Then came ruin swiftly. When the emperors lived for their elaborately contrived life of luxury — when the Roman soldier left his country's battles to be fought by mercenaries — the doom of Rome was sealed. Yet, because it was a nobler worldliness, less sensual and less selfish, the struggle with decay was more protracted than in Greece. Lofty spirits rose to stem the tide of corruption; and the death-

throes of Rome were long and terrible. She ran a mighty career of a thousand years.

2. Scepticism and superstition went hand in hand. —An example of the former we have in Pilate's question, "What is truth?" An example of the latter in the superstitious belief of the inhabitants of Lystra, that Paul and Barnabas were "Gods come to them in the likeness of men." And this probably was a tolerably accurate picture of the state of Roman feeling. The lower classes sunk in a debased superstition — the educated classes, too intellectual to believe in it, and having nothing better to put in its stead. Or perhaps there was also a superstition which is only another name for scepticism: infidelity trembling at its self: shrinking from its own shadow. There is a fearful question for which the soul must find an answer: the mystery of its own being and destinies. Men looked into their own souls, and listening, heard only an awful silence there. No response came from the world without. Philosophy had none to give. And then men, terrified at the progress of infidelity, more than half distrusting their own tendencies, took refuge in adding superstition to superstition. They brought in the gods of Greece, and Egypt, and the East: as if multiplying the objects of reverence strengthened the spirit of reverence in the soul; as if every new sacredness was a barrier between them and the dreadful abyss of uncertainty into which they did not dare to look.

This is as true now as then. Superstition is the refuge of a sceptical spirit which has a heart too devout to dare to be sceptical. Men tremble at new theories, new views, the spread of infidelity: and they think to fortify themselves against these by multiplying the sanctities which they reverence. But all this will not do. Superstition cannot do the work of faith, and give repose or peace. It is not by multiplying ceremonies — it is not by speaking of holy things with low, bated breath — it is not by intrenching the soul behind the infallibility of a church, or the infallibility of the words and sentences of a book — it is not by shutting out inquiry, and resenting every investigation as profane, that you can arrest the progress of infidelity. Faith, not superstition, is the remedy. There is a grand fearlessness in faith. He who in his heart of hearts reverences the Good — the True — the Holy; that is, reverences God — does not tremble at the apparent success of attacks upon the outworks of his faith. They may shake those who rested on those outworks — they do not move him, whose soul reposes on the Truth itself. He needs no props or crutches to support his faith. He does not need to multiply the objects of his awe in order to keep dreadful doubt away. Founded on a Rock, Faith can afford to gaze undismayed at the approaches of Infidelity.

3. In Rome, religion degenerated into allegiance to the state. In Greece, as it has been truly said, it ended in taste. In Rome, it closed with the worship of the emperor. Nothing shows the contrast between Greek and Roman feeling more strongly than this. In Greece the poet became the prophet, and the artist was the man divinely inspired. In Rome, the deification of the emperor, as the symbol of Government, was the point towards which, unsuspected, but by a sure and inevitable consecutiveness, the national feeling for ages had been tending.

And the distinction between the Christian and the

Roman tone of feeling is no less strikingly contrasted in the very same allegiance. Sacrament perhaps is the highest word of symbolical life in both. It is a Roman word. In Rome it meant an oath of allegiance to the senate and Roman people. Nothing higher the Roman knew. In the Christian Church it is also the oath of highest fidelity; but its import there is this: "Here we offer and present unto thee, *O Lord*, ourselves, our souls and bodies, to be a lively sacrifice."

In this contrast of the sacramental vows were perceptible the different tendencies of the two starting points of revealed religion and Roman, as remarked before. Judaism began from law or obligation to a holy Person. Roman religion began from obedience to a mere will. Judaism ended in Christianity; whose central principle is joyful surrender to One whose name is Love. The religion of Rome ended, among the nobler, as Cato and the Antonines, in the fatalism of a sublime but loveless Stoicism, whose essential spirit is submission to a Destiny: among the ordinary men, in mere zeal for the state, more or less earthly. It stiffened into Stoicism, or degenerated in public spirit.

4. The last step we notice is the decline of Religion into expediency. It is a startling thing to see men protecting popular superstitions which they despise: taking part with solemn gravity in mummeries which in their heart they laugh at. Yet such, we are told, was the state of things in Rome. It is a trite and often-quoted observation of a great Roman, that one minister of religion could scarcely meet another without a smile upon his countenance, indicating consciousness of a solemn mockery. And an instance of this, I believe,

we have in the Acts of the Apostles. The town-clerk or magistrate of Ephesus stilled the populace by a kind of accommodation to their prejudices, much in the same way in which a nurse would soothe a passionate child. Apparently, as we are told, he belonged to the friends of Paul; and we can scarcely forbear a smile at the solemn gravity with which he assures the people that there could be no doubt that the image fell down from Jupiter: no question throughout all Asia and the world about the greatness of the "great goddess Diana."

For there were cultivated minds which had apprehended some of the truths of Christianity: philosophers who were enlightened far beyond their age. But a line of martyred philosophers had made them cautious. They made a compromise. They enjoyed their own light, kept silence, and left the rest in darkness. The result was destruction of their own moral being; for the law of truth is that it cannot be shut up without becoming a dead thing, and mortifying the whole nature. Not the truth which a man knows, but that which he says and lives, becomes the soul's life. Truth cannot bless except when it is lived for, proclaimed and suffered for.

This was the plan of the enlightened when the Saviour came. And this is the lowest step of a nation's fall, when the few who know the truth refuse to publish it. When governments patronise superstition as a mere engine for governing: when the ministers of religion only half believe the dogmas which they teach, dare not even say to one another what they feel and what they doubt, when they dare not be true to their convictions, for fear of an Ephesian mob.

Therefore it was necessary that One should come who should be True: the Truest of all that are woman-born: whose life was Truth: who from Everlasting had been The Truth. It was necessary that he should come to preach the gospel to the poor, to dare to say to the people some truths which the philosophers dared not say, and other truths of which no philosopher had dreamed. The penalty of that true Life was the Sacrifice which is the world's Atonement. Men saw the Mortal die. But others saw the Immortal rise to take His place at the right hand of Power: and the spirit which has been streaming out ever since from that Life and Death is the world's present Light, and shall be its everlasting Life.

XIII.

Preached December 20, 1849.

THIRD ADVENT LECTURE.

THE BARBARIAN.

ACTS xxviii. 1-7, — "And when they were escaped, then they knew that the island was called Melita. And the barbarous people showed us no little kindness: for they kindled a fire, and received us every one, because of the present rain, and because of the cold. And when Paul had gathered a bundle of sticks and laid them on the fire, there came a viper out of the heat, and fastened on his hand. And when the Barbarians saw the venomous beast hang on his hand, they said among themselves, No doubt this man is a murderer, whom, though he hath escaped the sea, yet vengeance suffereth not to live. And he shook off the beast into the fire, and felt no harm. Howbeit they looked when he should have swollen, or fallen down dead suddenly: but after they had looked a great while, and saw no harm come to him, they changed their minds, and said that he was a god. In the same quarters were possessions of the chief man of the island, whose name was Publius; who received us, and lodged us three days courteously."

OF the four divisions of the world at the time of the Advent, two have already been reviewed. The Greek, seeing the right only on its side of beauty, ended in mere intellectual refinement. The artist took the place of God, and genius stood for Inspiration. The Roman's destiny was different. His was not the kingdom of burnished brass, but the kingdom of iron. He set out with the great idea of Duty and Law: exhibited in consequence the austere simplicity of pure domestic life: in public affairs, Government and Order, stamping upon the world the great idea of Obedience to Law. In the decline of Rome the results of this were manifest. After a mighty career of a thousand years, Rome had run out her course. Among the loftier minds who stood out protesting against her corruption, and daring in a corrupted age to believe in the superiority of Right to enjoyment, grand contempt for pleasure, sublime defiances of pain told out the dying agonies of the iron kingdom, worthy of the heart of steel which beat beneath the Roman's robe. This was Stoicism: the Grecian philosophy which took deepest root, as might have been expected, in the soil of Roman thought. Stoicism was submission to a destiny: hard, rigid, loveless submission. Its language was Must — It must be: and man's highest manliness is to submit to the inevitable. It is right because it must be so. Besides these higher ones, there were others who carried out the idea of Duty in quite another direction. With the mass of the nation, reverence for Law passed into homage to the symbol of Law; loyalty to the government: its highest expression being the sacramental homage to the nation's authority. So that, as I have already said, the Roman spirit stiffened into stoicism, and degenerated into worship of the emperor. This was not accidental; it was the inevitable result of the Idea. It might have taken half the time: or ten times as long: but at last the germ must have ripened into that fruit and no other. The Roman began with obedience to Will.

Law, meaning obedience to a holy God, passes by a natural transition into the gospel: that is, reverential duty to a person becomes the obedience of love at last, which obeys because the beautifulness of obedience is perceived. The Jew began in severity: ended in beauty. The Roman began in severity: ended in rigidity; or else relaxation. To him the Advent came proclaiming the Lord of Love instead of the coercive necessity of a lifeless fate.

To the Greek worshipper of beauty, the Advent came with an announcement of an inner beauty. He who was to them, and all such, "a Root out of a dry ground, with no form or comeliness," with nothing to captivate a refined taste, or gratify an elegant sensibility, lived a life which was divine and beautiful. His religion, as contrasted with the Grecian, supplementing it, and confirming in it what was true, "was the worship of the Lord in the Beauty of Holiness."

The third department is the necessity of the Advent for the *Barbarian* world.

By Barbarian was meant any religion but the Roman or the Greek — a contemptuous term, the spirit of which is common enough in all ages. Just as now every narrow sect monopolizes God, claims for itself an exclusive heaven, contemptuously looks on all the rest of mankind as sitting in outer darkness, and complacently consigns myriads whom God has made, to His uncovenanted mercies, that is, to probable destruction; so, in ancient times, the Jew scornfully designated all nations but his own as Gentiles: and the Roman and Greek, each retaliating in his way, treated all nations but his own under the common epithet of Barbarians.

We shall confine ourselves to-day to a single case of Barbarian life. We shall not enter into the religion of our own ancestors, the Kelts and Teutonic nations, who were barbarians then: nor that of the Scythians or the Africans. One instance will be sufficient.

Twice in his recorded history, St. Paul came in contact with Barbarians — twice he was counted as a god. Once among the semi-barbarians of Lycaonia, at Lystra — once here, at Melita.

There is a little uncertainty about the identification of this Melita. It was a name shared by two islands — Malta, and Melida in the Adriatic. But it seems to be established beyond all reasonable doubt that it was on Malta, not on Melida, that St. Paul was wrecked. The chief objection to this view is, that immediately before the wreck we are told — chap. xxvii. 27 — that they were "driven up and down in Adria." But this is satisfactorily answered by the fact, that the name Adriatic was applied often loosely to all the sea round Sicily. Two great arguments in favour of Malta then remain: After leaving the island, the apostle touched at Syracuse, and so went on to Rhegium and Puteoli. This is the natural direction from Malta to Rome, but not from Melida. Then, besides, "barbarians" will not apply to the inhabitants of Melida. They were Greeks: whereas the natives of Malta, living under Roman government, were originally Carthaginians, who had been themselves a Phœnician colony. The epithet is perfectly correct as applied to them.

It is the Carthaginian or Phœnician religion, then, which moulded the barbarian life, that we examine today. We take three points.

I. Barbarian virtues.
II. Barbarian idea of retribution.
III. Barbarian conception of Deity.

I. Barbarian virtues.

Two errors have been held on the subject of natural goodness. The first, that of those who deny to fallen man any goodness at all; and refuse to admit even kindliness of feeling. In the language of a celebrated and popular expounder of this view, "man in his natural state is one-half beast and one-half devil." This is the effect of a system. No man in his heart believes that. No mother ever gazed upon her child, baptized or unbaptized, and thought so. Men are better than their creed. Their hearts are more than a match for their false theological system. Beneath the black skin of the African there runs a blood as warm as that which is in the blue veins of the Christian. Among the civilized heathen, the instinctive feelings are as kindly and as exquisitely delicate as they were ever found in the bosom of the baptized. Accordingly, we find here these natural barbarian virtues of hospitality and sympathy. The shipwrecked mariners, wet and cold, were received in Melita with a warm, compassionate welcome. The people of the island did not *say*, "Depart in peace, be ye warmed and filled." They gave them those things which were necessary for the body. And a Christian contemplating this, gave this distinct testimony, "The barbarous people showed us no little kindness."

The second error is the opposite one of placing too high a value on these natural virtues. There is a class of writers who talk much of early unsophisticated times. They tell of the days "when wild in woods the noble savage ran." They speak of pastoral simplicity, and the reverence and piety of mountain life. According to them, civilization is the great corrupter. But the truth is, the natural good feelings of human nature are only instincts: no more moral than a long sight or a delicate sense of hearing. The keen feelings of the child are no guarantee of future principle: perhaps rather the reverse. The profuse hospitality of the mountaineer, who rarely sees strangers, and to whom gold is little worth, becomes shrewd and selfish calculation so soon as temptation from passing traffic is placed in his way. You may travel among savages who treat you, as a stranger, with courtesy: but yet feed on the flesh of their enemies. And these Melitans, who "showed no little kindness" to the wrecked crew, belonged to a stock who, in the most civilized days of Carthage, offered human sacrifice, and after every successful battle with the Romans, burnt the chief prisoners alive as a thank-offering to heaven. If we trace them still further back, we find their Phœnician ancestors in the Old Testament tainted with the same practice, and the Hebrews themselves imbibing it from them, so as to be perpetually arraigned by their prophets on the charge of making their sons and daughters "pass through the fire to Baal." They could be kind to strangers: and cruel to enemies.

The Advent of Christ brought a new spirit into the world. "A new commandment give I unto you, that ye love one another." That was not the new part. The Melitans would not have disagreed with that . . . "As I have loved you, that ye love one another." "As I have loved you" . . . . that makes all new. So also 1 John ii. 7, 8. The "old commandment" was old enough. Barbarians felt in their hearts. But the same commandment with "true light" shining on it was different indeed.

"Love your neighbour, hate your enemy." Carthaginians obeyed that. Hear the Law of Love expounded by Himself. Matt. v. 43, 44 — "But I say unto you, Love your enemies, bless them that curse you, do good to them that hate you, and pray for them which despitefully use you and persecute you. For if ye love them which love you, what do ye more than others? Do not even . . . . (the barbarians) . . . the same?"

This is Christianity: that is, the Mind of Christ.

Remark, too, the principle on which this is taught. Matt. v. 45 — "That ye may be the children of your Father which is in heaven: for He maketh His sun to rise on the evil and on the good, and sendeth rain on the just and on the unjust." Not upon merely personal authority; not by a law graven on stone: nor even printed in a book, to be referred to chapter and verse; but on the principle of the imitation of God. His heart interpreted the universe — He read its "open secret," which is open to all who have the heart to feel it, secret to all others. A secret, according to Him, to be gathered from the rain as it fell on the just and the unjust, from the dew of heaven, from the lily, and from the fowls of the air, from the wheat, from every law and every atom. This was His Revelation. He revealed God. He spelled for us the meaning of all this perplexing unintelligible world. He proclaimed its hidden meaning to be Love. So He converted rude barbarian instincts into Christian graces, by expanding their sphere and purifying them of selfishness—causing them to be regulated by principle, and elevating them into a conscious imitation of God in His revealed character.

II. The Barbarian idea of retribution.

The apostle Paul was one of those who are formed to be the leaders of the world. Foremost in persecution — foremost in Christianity, ("nothing behind the chiefest apostles") — foremost in the shipwreck, his voice the calmest, his heart the stoutest, his advice the wisest in the tumult. Foremost, too, when all was over, not as a prisoner, but actively engaged for the general good, it is Paul who is gathering the sticks to make the fire. From those sticks a viper sprung and fastened on his hand, and the first impression of the barbarians was, "No doubt this man is a murderer, whom, though he hath escaped the sea, yet vengeance suffereth not to live."

This is the very basis of all natural religion: the idea of the connection between guilt and retribution. In some form or other it underlies all mythologies. The sleepless, never-dying avengers of wrong — the Nemesis who presides over retribution — the vengeance which suffereth not the murderer to live — the whips and scorpions of the Furies — it seems the first instinct of religion.

In the barbarian conception of it, however, there was something gross, corporeal, and dangerous.

Because they misinterpreted natural laws into vengeance. Yet there is a proneness in man to judge so. We expect that nature will execute the chastisements of the spiritual world. Hence all nature becomes to the imagination leagued against the transgressor. The stars in their courses fight against Sisera. The wall of Siloam falls on guilty men. The sea will not carry the criminal, nor the plank bear him — the viper stings — everything is a minister of wrath. On this conviction nations constructed their trial by ordeal. The guilty man's sword would fail in the duel; and the foot would strike and be burnt by the hot ploughshare. Some idea of this sort lurks in all our minds. We picture to ourselves the spectres of the past haunting the nightly bed of the tyrant. We take for granted that there is an avenger making life miserable.

But experience corrects all this. The tyrant's sleep

is often as sweet and sound as the infant's. The sea will wreck an apostle and bear a murderer trimphantly. The viper stings the innocent turf-cutter. The fang of evil pierces the heel of the noblest as he treads it down. It is the poetry of man's heart, not the reality of the universe, which speaks of the Vengeance which pursues guilt with unrelenting steps to slay. Only in poetry is this form of justice found. Only in poetry does the fire refuse to burn the innocent. Only in poetry can Purity lay her hand on the fawning lion's mane. If we ask where these Melitans got their idea of Retribution, the reply is, out of their own hearts. They felt the eternal connection between wrong-doing and penalty. The penalty they would have executed on murder was death. They naturally threw this idea of theirs into the character of God, and blended together what was theirs and what is His. Valuable as a proof of the instinctive testimony of man's heart to the realities of Retribution. Utterly worthless as a testimony to the form in which Retributive Justice works, because not borne out by the facts of life.

Again, that notion was false, in that it expected vengeance for flagrant crime only. "This man is a murderer." There is a common and superstitious feeling now to that effect, "Murder will out:" as if God had set a black mark on murder — as if, because it is unlikely to escape detection in a country where every man's hand is against the murderer, impunity was not common enough in countries where human life is held cheap. The truth is, we think much of crime, little of sin. There is many a murderer executed whose heart is pure and whose life is white compared with those of many a man who lives a respectable and even honoured life. David was a murderer. The Pharisees had committed no crime; but their heart was rotten at the core. There was in it the sin which has no forgiveness. It is not a Christian but a Barbarian estimate which ranks crime above sin, and takes murder for the chief of sins marked out for Heaven's vengeance.

As information increases, *this* idea of retribution disappears. Natural laws are understood, und retribution vanishes. Then comes Epicureanism or Atheism. "All things come alike to all: there is one end to the righteous and to the sinner; to the clean and to the unclean: to him that sacrificeth, and to him that sacrificeth not." This is the feeling of the voluptuary of Ecclesiastes. If so, then the inference suggests itself to Epicurean indolence. "Let us eat and drink"—it is all the same. Or the sceptical feeling comes thus: "Verily I have cleansed my heart in vain, and washed my hands in innocency." For assuredly there is no vengeance such as this which suffers not the murderer to live, but arms the powers of nature against him. Why do right instead of wrong?

Then the idea of Retribution is gone for those who see no deeper than the outward chance of penalty.

The Advent brought deeper and truer views. It taught what sin is, and what suffering is. It showed the Innocent on the Cross bearing the penalty of the world's sin, but Himself the Son of God, with whom the Father was not angry, but "well pleased."

The penal agonies of sin are chiefly those which are executed within. "Vengeance," said the *Melitans*, "suffereth not the murderer to live." "Whosoever slayeth Cain, " said *God*, "vengeance shall be taken on him sevenfold." Cain, the murderer, lives — *Christ* the holy, dies. Cain is to us the dread type of Hell. To live! *that* is Hell, to live when you fain would die. There is such a thing as being salted with fire, a never annihilating but still consuming torture. You may escape the viper and the wreck. You may by prudence make this world painless, more or less. You cannot escape yourself. Go where you will, you carry with you a soul degraded, its power lost, its finer sensibilities destroyed. Worse than the viper's tooth is the punishment of no longer striving after goodness, or aspiring after the life of God. Just as the man cannot see through the glass on which he breathes, sin darkens the windows of the soul. You cannot look out even to know the glories of the fair world from which your soul excludes itself. There is no punishment equal to the punishment of being base. To sink from sin to sin, from infamy to infamy, that is the fearful retribution which is executed in the spiritual world. You are safe, go where you will, from the viper: as safe as if you were the holiest of God's children. The fang is in your soul.

III. The Barbarian conception of Deity.

When the viper fell off, and Paul was left uninjured, they changed their minds, and said that he was a god.

1. Observe, first, this implied a certain advance in religious notions. There is a stage of worship prior to that of man-worship. Man finds himself helpless among the powers of nature, and worships the forces themselves which he finds around him. This takes different forms. The highest is the worship of that host of heaven from which Job professed himself to be free.

With some it is the adoration of lifeless things: the oak which has been made sacred by the lightning-stroke: the "meteoric stone" which fell down from Jupiter. So the Israelites adored the brazen serpent, with which power had once been in connection. Evidently there can be no holy influence in this. Men worship them by fear, fortify themselves by charms and incantations: do not try to please God by being holy, but defend themselves from danger by jugglery. The Christians of the early ages carried about bits of consecrated bread to protect themselves from shipwreck.

Besides this, men have worshipped brute life: some animal, exhibiting a limited quality, which is reckoned a type of the Divine. The hawk-eyed deities of Egypt, for instance, implied omniscience. Beast-worship was that of Egypt. Israel learned it there, and in an early stage of their history, imitated the highest form which they knew, that of Apis, in their golden calf.

It is quite clear that the Melitans were in a stage beyond this. It is a step when men rise from the worship of lifeless things to that of animals — another when they rise to worship human qualities; for they *are* nearest the Divine. Perhaps a step higher still, when, like the early Romans, they worship a Principle like Destiny, separate from all shape. They were in the stage of worshipping what is human.

2. But in this worship of the human, we have to distinguish that it was the adoration of the Marvellous — not the reverence for the Good. It was not Paul's character to which they yielded homage. It was only to the wonderful mystery of, as they supposed, miraculous escape. So, too, at Lystra. It was the miracle which they chiefly saw.

All that would pass away when they knew that he was a man of like passions with themselves: or when they were informed that it was a Providential escape which might have happened to any ordinary man. When the savage sees the flash of European firearms, he kneels as to a god: but when he has learned its use, his new religion is gone. When the Americans first saw the winged ships of Spain, they thought that the deities spoke in thunder; but when they discovered the secret of their humanity, the worship ceased. And thus science is every day converting the religion of mere wonder into Atheism. The mere worship of the mysterious has a limited existence. As you teach laws, you undermine *that* religion. Men cease to tremble. The Laplander would no longer be awed by the eclipse if he knew how to calculate it with unerring accuracy. The savage's dread of lightning as the bolt of God is over, when he sees the Philosopher draw it from the clouds, and experimentalize on it in his laboratory. The awe created by a pestilence is passed, when it is found to be strictly under the guidance of natural laws. And the Romanist, or the semi-Romanist, whose religion is chiefly a sense of the mysterious, the solemn, the awful, and whose flesh creeps when he sees a miracle in the consecration of the sacraments, ends, as is well known, in infidelity, when enlightenment and reason have struck the ground of false reverence from beneath his feet.

It is upon this indisputable basis that the mightiest system of modern Atheism has been built. The great founder of that system divides all human history into three periods. The first, in which the supernatural is believed in; and a personal Agent is believed in as the cause of all phenomena. The second, in which metaphysical abstractions are assumed as Causes. The third, the Positive stage, in which nothing is expected but the knowledge of sequences by Experience; the Absolute, that lies beneath all phenomena, being for ever unknowable, and a God, if there be a God, undiscoverable by the intellect of man.

This conclusion is irrefragable. Granted that the only basis of religion is awe, a worship of the marvellous — then, verily, there remains nothing for the human race to end in but blank and ghastly Atheism.

Therefore has the Redeemer's Advent taught a deeper truth to man. The Apostle Paul spoke almost slightingly of the marvellous. "Covet earnestly the best gifts: yet show I unto you a more excellent way. Though I speak with the tongues of men and angels, and have not love, I am become as sounding brass, or a tinkling cymbal." Love is diviner that all wondrous powers.

So, too, the Son of God came into this world, depreciating the merely mysterious. "An evil and adulterous generation seeketh after a sign. No sign shall be given to it." "Except ye see signs and wonders, ye will not believe." Nay, His own miracles themselves, so far as the merely wondrous in them was concerned, He was willing, on one occasion at least, to place on the same level with the real or supposed ones of Exorcists among themselves. "If I by Beelzebub cast out devils, by whom do your sons cast them out?" It was not the power, nor the supernatural in them, which proved them divine. It was their peculiar character; their benevolence: their goodness: their love, which manifested Deity.

Herein lies the vast fallacy of the French sceptic. The worship of the supernatural must legitimately end in Atheism as science progresses. Yes, all science removes the Cause of causes further and further back from human ken, — so that the baffled intellect is compelled to confess at last we cannot find It. But "the world by wisdom knew not God." There is a power in the soul, quite separate from the intellect, which sweeps away or recognises the marvellous, by which God is felt. Faith stands serenely far above the reach of the Atheism of Science. It does not rest on the Wonderful, but on the Eternal Wisdom and Goodness of God. The Revelation of the Son was to proclaim a Father, not a Mystery. No science can sweep away the everlasting Love which the *heart* feels, and which the intellect does not even pretend to judge or recognise. And he is safe from the inevitable decay which attends the mere barbarian worship, who has felt, that as faith is the strongest power in the mind of man, so is Love the Divinest principle in the bosom of God: in other words, who adores God known in Christ, rather than trembles before the Unknown: whose homage is yielded to Divine Character rather than Divine Power.

XIV.

Preached December 8, 1849.

THE PRINCIPLE OF THE SPIRITUAL HARVEST.

GAL. vi. 7, 8. — "Be not deceived; God is not mocked: for whatsoever a man soweth, that shall he also reap. For he that soweth to his flesh shall of the flesh reap corruption; but he that soweth to the Spirit shall of the Spirit reap life everlasting."

THERE is a close analogy between the world of nature and the world of spirit. They bear the impress of the same hand; and hence the principles of nature and its laws are the types and shadows of the Invisible. Just as two books, though on different subjects, proceeding from the same pen, manifest indications of the thought of one mind, so the worlds visible and invisible are two books written by the same finger, and governed by the same Idea. Or, rather, they are but one Book, separated into two only by the narrow range of our ken. For it is impossible to study the universe at all without perceiving that it is one system. Begin with what science you will, as soon as you get beyond the rudiments, you are constrained to associate it with another.

You cannot study agriculture long without finding that it absorbs into itself meteorology and chemistry: sciences run into one another till you get the "connection of the sciences;" and you begin to learn that one Divine Idea connects the whole in one system of perfect Order.

It was upon this principle that Christ taught. Truths come forth from His lips not stated simply on authority, but based on the analogy of the universe. His human mind, in perfect harmony with the Divine Mind with which it mixed, discerned the connection of things, and read the Eternal Will in the simplest laws of Nature. For instance, if it were a question whether God would give His Spirit to them that asked, it was not replied to by a truth revealed on His *authority;* the answer was derived from facts lying open to all men's observation. "Behold the fowls of the air," — "behold the lilies of the field," — learn from them the answer to your question. A principle was there. God supplies the wants which He has created. He feeds the ravens ;— He clothes the lilies — He will feed with His Spirit the craving spirits of His children.

It was on this principle of analogy that St. Paul taught in this text. He tells us that there is a law in nature according to which success is proportioned to the labour spent upon the work. In kind and in degree — success is attained in kind; for example, he who has sowed his field with beechmast does not receive a plantation of oaks: a literary education is not the road to distinction in arms, but to success in letters; years spent on agriculture do not qualify a man to be an orator, but they make him a skilful farmer. Success, again, is proportioned to labour in degree: because, ordinarily, as is the amount of seed sown, so is the harvest: he who studies much will know more than he who studies little. In almost all departments it is "the diligent hand which maketh rich."

The keen eye of Paul discerned this principle reaching far beyond what is seen, into the spiritual realm which is unseen, As tare-seed comes up tares, and wheat-seed wheat, and as the crop in both cases is in proportion to two conditions, the labour and the quantity commited to the ground — so in things spiritual, too, whatsoever a man soweth, that shall he also reap. Not something else, but "*that.*" The proportion holds in kind — it holds too in degree, in spiritual things as in natural. "He which soweth sparingly shall reap also sparingly; and he which soweth bountifully shall reap also bountifully." If we could understand and rightly expound that principle, we should be saved from much of the disappointment and surprise which come from extravagant and unreasonable expectations. I shall try first to elucidate the principle which these verses contain, and then examine the two branches of the principle.

I. *The principle* is this, "God is not mocked: for whatsoever a man soweth, that shall he also reap."

There are two kinds of good possible to men: one enjoyed by our animal being, the other felt and appreciated by our spirits. Every man understands more or less the difference between these two; between prosperity and well-doing; between indulgence and nobleness: between comfort and inward peace: between pleasure and striving after perfection: between happiness and blessedness. These are two kinds of Harvest; and the labour necessary for them respectively is of very different kinds. The labour which procures the harvest of the one has no tendency to secure the other.

We will not depreciate the advantages of this world. It is foolish and unreal to do so. Comfort, affluence, success, freedom from care, rank, station — these are in their way real goods; only, the labour bestowed upon them does not procure one single blessing that is spiritual.

On the other hand, the seed which is sown for a spiritual harvest has no tendency whatever to procure temporal well-being. Let us see what are the laws of the sowing and reaping in this department. Christ has declared them: "Blessed are the pure in heart; for they shall see God." "Blessed are they that hunger and thirst after righteousness: for they shall be filled (with righteousness.)" "Blessed are they that mourn: for they shall be comforted." You observe the beatific vision of the Almighty — fulness of righteousness — comfort. There is nothing earthly — it is spiritual results for spiritual labour. It is not said that the pure in heart shall be made rich; nor that they who hunger after goodness shall be filled with bread; nor that they who mourn shall rise in life and obtain distinction. Each department has its own appropriate harvest — reserved exclusively to its own method of sowing.

Everything in this world has its price, and the price buys *that*, not something else. Every harvest demands its own preparation, and that preparation will not produce another sort of harvest. Thus, for example, you cannot have at once the soldier's renown and the quiet of a recluse's life. The soldier pays his price for his glory — sows and reaps. His price is risk of life and limb, nights spent on the hard ground, a weather-beaten constitution. If you will not pay that price, you cannot have what he has — military reputation. You cannot enjoy the stateman's influence together with freedom from public notoriety. If you sensitively shrink from that, you must give up influence; or else pay his price, the price of a thorny pillow, unrest, the chance of being to-day a nation's idol, to-morrow the people's execration. You cannot have the store of information possessed by the student, and enjoy robust health: pay his price, and you have his reward. His price is an emaciated frame, a debilitated constitution, a transparent hand, and the rose taken out of the sunken cheek. To expect these opposite things: a soldier's glory and quiet — a statesman's renown and peace — the student's prize and rude health, would be to mock God, to reap what has not been sowed.

Now the mistakes men make, and the extravagant expectation in which they indulge, are these: — they sow for earth, and expect to win spiritual blessings; or they sow to the Spirit, and then wonder that they have not a harvest of the good things of earth. In each case they complain, What have I done to be treated so?

The unreasonableness of all this appears the moment we have understood the conditions contained in this principle, "Whatsoever a man soweth, *that* shall he also reap."

It is a common thing to hear sentimental wonderings about the unfairness of the distribution of things here. The unprincipled get on in life: the saints are kept back. The riches and rewards of life fall to the lot of the undeserving. The rich man has his good things, and Lazarus his evil things. Whereupon it is taken for granted that there must be a future life to make this fair: that if there were none, the constitution of this world would be unjust. That is, that because a man who has sown to the Spirit does not reap to the flesh here, he will hereafter; that the meed of well-doing must be somewhere in the universe the same kind of recompense which the rewards of the unprincipled were here, comfort, abundance, physical enjoyment, or else all is wrong.

But if you look into it, the balance is perfectly adjusted even here. God has made his world much better than you and I could make it. Everything reaps its own harvest, every act has its own reward. And before you covet the enjoyment which another possesses, you must first calculate the cost at which it was procured.

For instance, the religious tradesman complains that his honesty is a hindrance to his success: that the tide of custom pours into the doors of his less scrupulous neighbours in the same street, while he himself waits for hours idle. My brother! do you think that God is going to reward honour, integrity, high-mindedness, with this world's coin? Do you fancy that He will pay spiritual excellence with plenty of custom? Now, consider the prico that man has paid for his success. Perhaps mental degradation and inward dishonour. His advertisements are all deceptive. His treatment of his workmen tyrannical: his cheap prices made possible by inferior articles. Sow that man's seed, and you will reap that man's harvest. Cheat, lie, advertise, be unscrupulous in your assertions, custom will come to you. But if the price is too dear, let him have his harvest, and take yours; yours is a clear conscience, a pure mind, rectitude within and without — Will you part with that for his? Then why do you complain? He has paid his price, you do not choose to pay it.

Again, it is not an uncommon thing to see a man rise from insignificance to sudden wealth by speculation. Within the last ten or twenty years, England has gazed on many such a phenomenon. In this case, as in spiritual things, the law seems to hold: He that hath, to him shall be given. Tens of thousands soon increase and multiply to hundreds of thousands. His doors are besieged by the rich and great. Royalty banquets at his table, and nobles court his alliance. Whereupon some simple Christian is inclined to complain: "How strange that so much prosperity should be the lot of mere cleverness!" Well, are these really God's chief blessings? Is it for such as these you serve Him? And would these indeed satisfy your soul? Would you have God reward his saintliest with these gauds and gewgaws — all this trash, rank, and wealth, and equipages, and plate, and courtship from the needy great? Call you *that* the heaven of the holy? Compute now what was paid for that? The price that merchant prince paid, perhaps with the blood of his own soul, was shame and guilt. The price he is paying now, is perpetual dread of detection: or worse still, the hardness which can laugh at detection: or one deep lower yet, the low and grovelling soul which can be satisfied with these things as a Paradise, and ask no higher. He has reaped enjoyment — yes, and he has sown, too, the seed of infamy. It is all fair. Count the cost. "He that saveth his life shall lose it." Save your life if you like: but do not complain if you lose your nobler life — yourself: win the whole world: but remember you do it by losing your own soul. Every sin must be paid for: every sensual indulgence is a harvest, the price for which is so much ruin for the soul. "*God is not mocked.*"

Once more, Religious men in every profession are surprised to find that many of its avenues are closed to them. The conscientious churchman complains that his delicate scruples, or his bold truthfulness, stand in the way of his preferment: while another man, who conquers his scruples, or softens the eye of truth, rises, and sits down a mitred peer in Parliament. The honourable lawyer feels that his practice is limited, while the unprincipled practitioner receives all he loses; and the Christian physician feels sore and sad at perceiving that charlatanism succeeds in winning employment; or, if not charlatanism at least, that affability and courtly manners take the place that is due to superior knowledge. Let such men take comfort, and judge fairly. Popularity is one of the things of an earthly harvest, for which quite earthly qualifications are required. I say not always dishonourable qualifications: but a certain flexibility of disposition — a certain courtly willingness to sink obnoxious truths, and adapt ourselves to the prejudices of the minds of others: a certain adroitness at catching the tone of those with whom we are. Without some of these things no man can be popular in any profession. But you have resolved to be a liver — a doer — a champion of the truth. Your ambition is to be pure in the last recesses of the mind. You have your reward: a soul upright and manly — a fearless bearing, that dreads to look no man in the face — a willingness to let men search you through and through, and defy them to see any difference between what you seem and what you are. Now, your price — your price is dislike. The price of being true is the Cross. The warrior of the truth must not expect success. What have you to do with popularity? Sow for it, and you will have it. But if you wish for it, or wish for peace, you have mistaken your calling — you must not be a teacher of the truth — you must not cut prejudice against the grain — you must leave medical, legal, theological truth, to harder and nobler men, who are willing to take the martyr's cross, and win the martyr's crown. This is the mistake men make. They expect both harvests, paying only one price. They would be blessed with goodness and prosperity at once. They would have that on which they bestowed no labour. They take sinful pleasure, and think it very hard that they must pay for it in agony, and worse than agony, souls deteriorated. They would monopolize heaven in their souls, and the world's prizes at the same time. This is to expect to come back, like Joseph's brethren from the land of plenty, with the corn in their sacks, and the money returned, too, in their sacks' mouths. No, no; it will not do. "Be not deceived; God is not mocked." Reap *what* you have sown. If you sow the wind, do not complain if your harvest is the whirlwind. If you sow to the Spirit, be content with a spiritual reward — invisible — within — more life and higher life.

II. Next, the two branches of the application of this principle.

First: He that soweth to the flesh, shall of the flesh reap corruption. There are two kinds of life: one of the flesh — another of the spirit. Amidst the animal and selfish desires of our nature, there is a Voice which clearly speaks of Duty: Right: Perfection. This is the Spirit of Deity in Man — it is the life of God in the soul. This is the evidence of our divine parentage.

But there is a double temptation to live the other life instead of this. First, the desires of our animal nature are *keener* than those of our spiritual. The cry of Passion is louder than the calm voice of Duty. Next, the reward in the case of our sensitive nature is given *sooner*. It takes less time to amass a fortune than to become heavenly-minded. It costs less to indulge an appetite than it does to gain the peace of lulled passion. And hence, when men feel that for the spiritual blessing, the bread must be cast upon the waters which shall not be found until after many days (scepticism whispers "never!"), it is quite intelligible why they choose the visible and palpable instead of the invisible advantage, and plan for an immediate harvest rather than a distant one.

The other life is that of the flesh. The "flesh" includes all the desires of our unrenewed nature — the harmless as well as sinful. Any labour, therefore, which is bounded by present wellbeing is *sowing* to the flesh: whether it be the gratification of an immediate impulse, or the long-contrived plan reaching forward over many years. Sowing to the flesh includes therefore,

1. Those who live in open riot. He sows to the flesh who pampers its unruly animal appetites. Do not think that I speak contemptuously of our animal nature, as if it were not human and sacred. The lowest feelings of our nature become sublime by being made the instruments of our nobler emotion. Love, self-command, will elevate them all: and to ennoble and purify, not to crush them, is the long, slow work of Christian life. Christ, says St Paul, is the Saviour of the *Body*. But if, instead of subduing these to the life of the spirit, a man gives to them the rein and even the spur, the result is not difficult to fore-

see. There are men who do this. They "make provision for the flesh, to fulfil the lusts thereof." They whet the appetites by indulgence. They whip the jaded senses to their work. Whatever the constitutional bias may be, anger, intemperance, epicurism, indolence, desires, there are societies, conversations, scenes, which supply fuel for the flame, as well as opposite ones which cut off the nutriment. Now, to indulge in these, knowing the result, is to foster the desire which brings forth the sin that ends in death. This is "sowing to the flesh."

If there be one to whom these words which I have used, veiled in the proprieties due to delicate reserve, are not without meaning, from this sentence of God's word let him learn his doom. He is looking forward to a harvest wherein he may reap the fruit of his present anticipations. And he *shall* reap it. He shall have his indulgence — he shall enjoy his guilty rapture — he shall have his unhallowed triumph: and the boon companions of his pleasures shall award him the meed of their applause. He has sown the seed: and in fair requital he shall have his harvest. It is all fair. He *shall* enjoy. But tarry awhile: the law hath yet another hold upon him. This deep law of the whole universe goes further. He has sown to the flesh, and of the flesh he has reaped pleasure: he has sown to the flesh, and of the flesh he shall reap corruption. That is, in his case, the ruin of the soul. It is an awful thing to see a soul in ruins: like a temple which once was fair and noble, but now lies overthrown, matted with ivy, weeds, and tangled briers, among which things noisome crawl and live. He shall reap the harvest of disappointment — the harvest of bitter, useless remorse. The crime of sense is avenged by sense, which wears by time. He shall have the worm that gnaws, and the fire that is not quenched. He shall reap the fruit of long indulged desires, which have become tyrannous at last, and constitute him his own tormentor. His harvest is a soul in flames, and the tongue that no drop can cool. Passions that burn, and appetites that crave, when the power of enjoyment is gone. He has sowed to the flesh. "God is not mocked." The man reaps.

2. There is a less gross way of sowing to the flesh. There are men of sagacity and judgment in the affairs of this life, whose penetration is almost intuitive in all things where the step in question involves success or failure here. They are those who are called in the parable the children of this world, wise in their generation. They moralise and speculate about eternity: but do not plan for it. There is no seed sown for an invisible harvest. If they think they have sown for such a harvest, they might test themselves by the question, What would they lose if there were to be no eternity? For the children of God, so far as earth is concerned, "If in this life only they have hope in Christ, then are they of all men most miserable." But *they* — these sagacious, prudent men of this world — they have their reward. What have they ventured, given up, sacrificed, which is all lost for ever, if this world be all? What have they buried like seed in the ground, lost for ever, if there be no eternity?

Now, we do not say these men are absolutely wicked. We distinguish between their sowing to the flesh, and the sowing of those profligates last spoken of. All we say is, there is "corruption" written on their harvest. It was for earth: and with earth it perishes. It may be the labour of the statesman, planning, like the Roman of old, the government and order of the kingdoms of the earth: or that of the astronomer, weighing suns, prescribing rules of return to comets, and dealing with things above earth in space, but unspiritual still: or that of the son of a humbler laboriousness, whose work is merely to provide for a family: or, lastly, the narrower range of the man of pleasure, whose chief care is where he shall spend the next season, in what metropolis, or which watering-place, or how best enjoy the next entertainment. Objects more or less harmless all. But they end. The pyramid crumbles into dust at last. The mighty empire of the eternal city breaks into fragments which disappear. The sowers for earth *have* their harvest here. Success in their schemes — quiet intellectual enjoyment — exemption from pain and loss — the fruits of worldly-wise sagacity. And that is all. "When the breath goeth forth, they return to their dust, and all their thoughts perish." The grave is not to them the gate of paradise, but simply the impressive mockery which the hand of death writes upon that body for which they lived, and with which all is gone. They reap corruption, for all they have toiled for decays!

Ye that lead the life of respectable worldliness! let these considerations arrest your indifference to the gospel. You have sown for earth — Well. And then — what? Hear the gospel. A Saviour whose Sacrifice is the world's life — whose death is the law of life: from whose resurrection streams a Spirit which can change carnal into spiritual men — whose whole existence, reflecting God, was the utterance of the Divine truth and rule of heavenly life, the blessedness of giving — To live so, and to believe so, is to sow to the Spirit.

Lastly — *Sowing to the Spirit.* "He that soweth to the Spirit, shall of the Spirit reap life everlasting."

What is meant by sowing to the Spirit here is plain. "Let us not be weary in well-doing," says the apostle directly after: "for in due season we shall reap if we faint not." *Well-doing:* not faith: but works of goodness, were the sowing that he spoke of.

There is proclaimed here the rewardableness of works. So in many other passages: "Abounding in the work of the Lord, forasmuch as ye know that your labour is not in vain in the Lord." "Laying up a good foundation for the time to come," was the reason alleged for charging rich men to be willing to give — and so all through. There is an irreversible principle. The amount of harvest is proportioned to the seed sown exactly. There are degrees of glory. The man who gives out of his abundance has one blessing. She who gives the mite, all she had, even all her living, has another, quite different. The rectitude of this principle, and what it is, will be plainer from the following considerations.

1. The harvest is Life Eternal. But Eternal Life here does not simply mean a life that lasts for ever. That is the destiny of the *Soul:* all souls, bad as well as good. But the bad do not enter into this "Eternal life." It is not simply the duration, but the quality of the life which constitutes its character of Eternal. A spirit may live for ever, yet not enter into this. And a man may live but for five minutes the life of

Divine benevolence, or desire for perfectness: in those five minutes he has entered into the life which is Eternal, never fluctuates, but is the same unalterably for ever, in the Life of God. *This* is the Reward.

2. The reward is not arbitrary, but natural. God's rewards and God's punishments are all natural. Distinguish between arbitrary and natural. Death is an arbitrary punishment for forgery: it might be changed for transportation. It is not naturally connected. It depends upon the will of the law-maker. But trembling nerves are the direct and natural results of intemperance. They are in the order of nature the results of wrong-doing. The man reaps *what* he has sown. Similarly in rewards. If God gave riches in return for humbleness, that would be an arbitrary connection. He did give such a reward to Solomon. But when He gives Life Eternal, meaning by Life Eternal not duration of existence but heavenly quality of existence, as explained already, it is all natural. The seed sown in the ground contains in itself the future harvest. The harvest is but the development of the germ of life in the seed. A holy act strengthens the inward holiness. It is a seed of life growing into more life. "Whatsoever a man soweth, *that* shall he reap." He that sows much, thereby becomes more conformed to God than he was before — in heart and spirit. That is his reward and harvest. And just as among the apostles, there was one whose spirit, attuned to love, made him emphatically the disciple whom Jesus loved, so shall there be some who, by previous discipline of the Holy Ghost, shall have more of His mind, and understand more of His love, and drink deeper of His joy than others — They that have sowed bountifully.

Every act done in Christ receives its exact and appropriate reward. They that are meek shall inherit the earth. They that are pure shall see God. They that suffer shall reign with Him. They that turn many to righteousness shall shine as the stars for ever. They that receive a righteous man in the name of a righteous man — that is, because he is a righteous man — shall receive a righteous man's reward. Even the cup of cold water, given in the name of Christ, shall not lose its reward.

It will be therefore seen at once, Reward is not the result of merit. It is, in the order of grace, the natural consequence of well-doing. It is life becoming more life. It is the soul developing itself. It is the Holy Spirit of God in man, making itself more felt, and mingling more and more with his soul, felt more consciously with an ever-increasing heaven. You reap what you sow — not something else — but that. An act of love makes the soul more loving. A deed of humbleness deepens humbleness. The thing reaped is the very thing sown, muliplied a hundredfold. You have sown a seed of life — you reap Life everlasting.

XV.

Preached December 31, 1849.

THE LONELINESS OF CHRIST.

JOHN xvi. 31, 32. — "Jesus answered them, Do ye now believe? Behold, the hour cometh, yea is now come, that ye shall be scattered, every man to his own, and shall leave me alone: and yet I am not alone, because the Father is with me."

THERE are two kinds of solitude: the first consisting of insulation in space; the other of isolation of the spirit. The first is simply separation by distance. When we are seen, touched, heard by none, we are said to be alone. And all hearts respond to the truth of that saying, This is not solitude: for sympathy can people our solitude with a crowd. The fisherman on the ocean alone at night is not alone when he remembers the earnest longings which are arising up to heaven at home for his safety — The traveller is not alone when the faces which will greet him on his arrival seem to beam upon him as he trudges on — The solitary student is not alone when he feels that human hearts will respond to the truths which he is preparing to address to them.

The other is loneliness of soul. There are times when hands touch ours, but only send an icy chill of unsympathising indifference to the heart: when eyes gaze into ours, but with a glazed look which cannot read into the bottom of our souls: when words pass from our lips, but only come back as an echo reverberated without reply through a dreary solitude: when the multitude throng and press us, and we cannot say, as Christ said, "Somebody hath *touched* me:" for the contact has been not between soul and soul, but only between form and form.

And there are two kinds of men who feel this last solitude in different ways. The first are the men of self-reliance: self-dependent: who ask no counsel, and crave no sympathy: who act and resolve alone — who can go sternly through duty, and scarcely shrink let what will be crushed in them. Such men command respect: for whoever respects himself, constrains the reverence of others. They are invaluable in all those professions of life in which sensitive feeling would be a superfluity; they make iron commanders: surgeons who do not shrink; and statesmen who do not flinch from their purpose for the dread of unpopularity. But mere self-dependence is weakness: and the conflict is terrible when a human sense of weakness is felt by such men. Jacob was alone when he slept in his way to Padan Aram, the first night that he was away from his father's roof, with the world before him, and all the old broken up: and Elijah was alone in the wilderness when the court had deserted him, and he said, "They have digged down Thine altars, and slain Thy prophets with the sword: and I, even I only, am left, and they seek my life to take it away." But the loneliness of the tender Jacob was very different from that of the stern Elijah. To Jacob the sympathy he yearned for was realized in the form of a simple dream. A ladder raised from earth to heaven figured the possibility of communion between the spirit of man and the Spirit of God. In Elijah's case the storm, and the earthquake, and the fire, did their convulsing work in the soul, before a still, small voice told him that he was not alone. In such a spirit the sense of weakness comes with a burst of agony, and the dreadful conviction of being alone manifests itself with a rending of the heart of rock. It is only so that such souls can be taught that the Father is with them, and that they are not alone.

There is another class of men who live in sympathy. These are affectionate minds which tremble at the thought of being alone: not from want of courage, nor from weakness of intellect comes their dependence upon others, but from the intensity of their affections. It is the trembling spirit of humanity in them. They want not aid, nor even countenance: but only sympathy. And the trial comes to them not in the shape of fierce struggle, but of chill and utter loneliness, when they are called upon to perform a duty on which the world looks coldly, or to embrace a truth which has not found lodgment yet in the breasts of others.

It is to this latter and not to the former class that we must look if we would understand the spirit in which the words of the text were pronounced. The deep Humanity of the Soul of Christ was gifted with those finer sensibilities of affectionate nature which stand in need of sympathy. He not only gave sympathy, but wanted it, too, from others. He who selected the gentle John to be his friend — who found solace in female sympathy, attended by the women who ministered to him out of their substance — who in the Trial hour could not bear even to pray without the human presence, which is the pledge and reminder of God's presence, had nothing in Him of the hard, merely self-dependent character. Even this verse testifies to the same fact. A stern spirit never could have said, "I am not alone: the Father is with Me"— never would have felt the loneliness which needed the balancing truth. These words tell of a struggle: an inward reasoning: a difficulty and a reply: a sense of solitude — "I shall be alone;" and an immediate correction of that; "not alone — the Father is with Me."

There is no thought connected with the Life of Christ more touching, none that seems so peculiarly to characterise His spirit, than the solitariness in which He lived. Those who understood Him best only understood Him half. Those who knew Him best scarcely could be said to *know* Him. On this occasion the disciples thought — Now we do understand — now we do believe. The lonely spirit answered, "*Do* ye now believe? Behold the hour cometh that ye shall be scattered, every man to his own, and shall leave Me alone."

Very impressive is that trait in His history. He was in this world alone.

I. First, then, we meditate on the Loneliness of Christ.

II. On the temper of His solitude.

1. The Loneliness of Christ was caused by the Divine elevation of His character. His infinite superiority severed Him from sympathy — His exquisite affectionateness made that want of sympathy a keen trial.

There is a second-rate greatness which the world can comprehend. If we take two who are brought into direct contrast by Christ Himself, the one the type of human, the other that of Divine excellence, the Son of Man and John the Baptist, this becomes clearly manifest. John's life had a certain rude, rugged goodness, on which was written, in characters which required no magnifying-glass to read, spiritual excellence. The world on the whole accepted him. Pharisees and Sadducees went to his baptism. The people idolized him as a prophet; and if he had not chanced to cross the path of a weak prince and a revengeful woman, we can see no reason why John might not have finished his course with joy, recognised as irreproachable. If we inquire why it was that the world accepted John and rejected Christ, one reply appears to be that the life of the one was finitely simple and one-sided, that of the Other divinely complex. In physical nature, the naturalist finds no difficulty in comprehending the simple structure of the lowest organizations of animal life, where one uniform texture, and one organ performing the office of brain and heart and lungs, at once, leave little to perplex. But when he comes to study the complex anatomy of man, he has the labour of a lifetime before him. It is not difficult to master the constitution of a single country; but when you try to understand the universe, you find infinite appearances of contradiction: law opposed by law: motion balanced by motion; happiness blended with misery: and the power to elicit a divine order and unity out of this complex variety is given to only a few of the gifted of the race. That which the structure of man is to the structure of the limpet: that which the universe is to a single country, the complex and boundless soul of Christ was to the souls of other men. Therefore, to the superficial observer, His life was a mass of inconsistencies and contradictions. All thought themselves qualified to point out the discrepancies. The Pharisees could not comprehend how a holy Teacher could eat with publicans and sinners. His own brethren could not reconcile His assumption of a public office with the privacy which He aimed at keeping. "If thou doest these things, show thyself to the world." Some thought He was "a good man," — others said, "Nay — but He deceiveth the people." And hence it was that He lived to see all that acceptance which had marked the earlier stage of His career, as for instance, at Capernaum, melt away. First, the Pharisees took the alarm: then the Sadducees: then the political party of the Herodians: then the People. That was the most terrible of all: for the enmity of the upper classes is impotent; but when that cry of brute force is stirred from the deeps of society, as deaf to the voice of reason as the ocean in its strength churned into raving foam by the winds, the heart of mere earthly oak quails before that. The apostles, at all events, did quail. One denied: another betrayed: all deserted. They "were scattered, each to his own:" and the Truth Himself was left alone in Pilate's judgment-hall.

Now learn from this a very important distinction. To feel solitary is no uncommon thing. To complain of being alone, without sympathy and misunderstood, is general enough. In every place, in many a family, these victims of diseased sensibility are to be found, and they might find a weakening satisfaction in observing a paralled between their own feelings and those of Jesus. But before that parallel is assumed, be very sure that it is, as in His case, the elevation of your character which severs you from your species. The world has small sympathy for Divine goodness: but it also has little for a great many other qualities which are disagreeable to it. You meet with no response — you are passed by — find yourself unpopular — meet with little communion. — Well? Is that because you are *above* the world, nobler, devising and executing grand plans which they cannot comprehend: vindicating the wronged, proclaiming and living on great principles: offending it by the saintliness of your purity, and the unworldliness of your aspirations? Then yours is the loneliness of Christ. Or is it that you are wrapped up in self — cold, disobliging, sentimental, indifferent about the welfare of others, and very much astonished that they are not deeply interested in you? *You* must not use these words of Christ. They have nothing to do with you.

Let us look at one or two of the occasions on which this loneliness was felt.

The first time was when He was but twelve years old, when His parents found Him in the temple, hearing the doctors and asking them questions. High thoughts were in the Child's soul: expanding views of life: larger views of duty and His own destiny.

There is a moment in every true life — to some it comes very early — when the old routine of duty is not large enough — when the parental roof seems too low, because the Infinite above is arching over the soul — when the old formulas, in creeds, catechisms, and articles, seem to be narrow, and they must either be thrown aside, or else transformed into living and breathing realities — when the earthly father's authority is being superseded by the claims of a Father in heaven.

That is a lonely, lonely moment, when the young soul first feels God — when this earth is recognised as an "awful place, yea, the very gate of heaven." When the dream-ladder is seen planted against the skies, and we wake, and the dream haunts us as a sublime reality.

You may detect the approach of that moment in the young man or the young woman by the awakened spirit of inquiry: by a certain restlessness of look, and an eager earnestness of tone: by the devouring study of all kinds of books: by the waning of your own influence, while the inquirer is asking the truth of the Doctors and Teachers in the vast Temple of the world: by a certain opinionativeness, which is austere and disagreeable enough: but the austerest moment of the fruit's taste is that in which it is passing from greenness into ripeness. If you wait in patience, the sour will become sweet. Rightly looked at, that opinionativeness is more truly anguish: the fearful solitude of feeling the insecurity of all that is human; the discovery that life is real, and forms of social and religious existence hollow. The old moorings are torn away, and the soul is drifting, drifting, drifting, very often without compass, except the guidance of an unseen hand, into the vast infinite of God. Then come the lonely words, and no wonder, "How is it that ye sought me? Wist ye not that I must be about my Father's business?"

2. That solitude was felt by Christ in trial. In the desert: in Pilate's judgment-hall: in the garden, He was alone — and alone must every son of man meet his trial-hour. The individuality of the soul necessitates that. Each man is a new soul in this world: untried, with a boundless Possible before him. No one can predict what he may become, prescribe his duties, or

mark out his obligations. Each man's own nature has its own peculiar rules: and he must take up his life-plan alone, and persevere in it in a perfect privacy with which no stranger intermeddleth. Each man's temptations are made up of a host of peculiarities, internal and external, which no other mind can measure. You are tried alone — alone you pass into the desert — alone you must bear and conquer in the Agony — alone you must be sifted by the world. There are moments known only to a man's own self, when he sits by the poisoned springs of existence, "yearning for a morrow which shall free him from the strife." And there are trials more terrible than that. Not when vicious inclinations are opposed to holy, but when virtue conflicts with virtue, is the real rending of the soul in twain. A temptation, in which the lower nature struggles for mastery, can be met by the whole united force of the spirit. But it is when obedience to a heavenly Father can be only paid by disobedience to an earthly one: or fidelity to duty can be only kept by infidelity to some entangling engagement: or the straight path must be taken over the misery of others: or the counsel of the affectionate friend must be met with a "Get thee behind me, Satan," — Oh! it is then, when human advice is unavailable, that the soul feels what it is to be alone.

Once more — the Redeemer's soul was alone in dying. The hour had come — they were all gone, and He was, as He predicted, left alone. All that is human drops from us in that hour. Human faces flit and fade, and the sounds of the world become confused. "I shall die alone" — yes, and alone you live. The philosopher tells us that no atom in creation touches another atom — they only approach within a certain distance; then the attraction ceases, and an invisible something repels — they only *seem* to touch. No soul touches another soul except at one or two points; and those chiefly external, — a fearful and a lonely thought; but one of the truest of life. Death only realizes that which has been fact all along. In the central deeps of our being we are alone.

II. The spirit or temper of that solitude.

1. Observe its grandeur. I am alone, yet not alone. There is a feeble and sentimental way in which we speak of the Man of sorrows. We turn to the cross, and the agony, and the loneliness, to touch the softer feelings; to arouse compassion. You degrade *that* loneliness by your compassion. Compassion! compassion for Him! Adore if you will — respect and reverence that sublime solitariness with which none but the Father was — but no pity: let it draw out the firmer and manlier graces of the soul. Even tender sympathy seems out of place.

For even in human things, the strength that is in a man can be only learnt when he is thrown upon his own resources and left alone. What a man can do in conjunction with others does not test the man. Tell us what he can do alone. It is one thing to defend the truth when you know that your audience are already prepossessed, and that every argument will meet a willing response: and it is another thing to hold the truth when truth must be supported, if at all, alone — met by cold looks and unsympathising suspicion. It is one thing to rush on to danger with the shouts and the sympathy of numbers: it is another thing when the lonely chieftain of the sinking ship sees the last boatful disengage itself, and folds his arms to go down into the majesty of darkness, crushed, but not subdued.

Such and greater far was the strength and majesty of the Saviour's solitariness. It was not the trial of the lonely hermit. There is a certain gentle and pleasing melancholy in the life which is lived alone. But there are the forms of nature to speak to him, and he has not the positive opposition of mankind if he has the absence of actual sympathy. It is a solemn thing, doubtless, to be apart from men, and to feel eternity rushing by like an arrowy river. But the solitude of Christ was the solitude of a crowd. In that single Human bosom dwelt the Thought which was to be the germ of the world's life: a thought unshared, misunderstood, or rejected. Can you not feel the grandeur of those words, when the Man, reposing on His solitary strength, felt the last shadow of perfect insolation pass across His soul: "My God, my God, why hast *Thou* forsaken me?"

Next, learn from these words self-reliance. "Ye shall leave me alone." Alone then the Son of man was content to be. He threw Himself on his own solitary thought: did not go down to meet the world; but waited, though it might be for ages, till the world should come round to Him. He appealed to the Future: did not aim at seeming consistent; left His contradictions unexplained: I came from the Father: I leave the world, and go to the Father. "Now," said they, "thou speakest no proverb:" that is, enigma. But many a hard and enigmatical saying before He had spoken, and He left them all. A thread runs through all true acts, stringing them together into one harmonious chain:

but it is not for the Son of God to be anxious to prove their consistency with each other.

This is self-reliance — to repose calmly on the thought which is deepest in our bosoms, and be unmoved if the world will not accept it yet. To live on your own convictions against the world, is to overcome the world — to believe that what is truest in you is true for all: to abide by that, and not be over-anxious to be heard or understood, or sympathised with, certain that at last all must acknowledge the same, and that while you stand firm, the world will come round to you: that is independence. It is not difficult to get away into retirement, and there live upon your own convictions: nor is it difficult to mix with men, and follow their convictions: but to enter into the world, and there live out firmly and fearlessly according to your own conscience, that is Christian greatness.

There is a cowardice in this age which is not Christian. We shrink from the consequences of truth. We look round and cling dependently. We ask what men will think; what others will say — whether they will not stare in astonishment. Perhaps they will; but he who is calculating that, will accomplish nothing in this life. The Father — the Father which is with us and in us — what does He think? God's work cannot be done without a spirit of independence. A man is got some way in the Christian life when he has learned to say humbly and yet majestically, "I dare to be alone."

Lastly, — remark the humility of this loneliness. Had the Son of man simply said, I can be alone, He would have said no more than any proud, self-relying man can say. But when He added, "because the

Father is with me," that independence assumed another character, and self-reliance became only another form of reliance upon God. Distinguish between genuine and spurious humility. There is a false humility which says, "It is my own poor thought, and I must not trust it. I must distrust my own reason and judgment, because they are my own. I must not accept the dictates of my own conscience, for is it not my own, and is not trust in self the great fault of our fallen nature?"

Very well. Now, remember something else. There is a Spirit which beareth witness with our spirits — there is a God who "is not far from any one of us" — there is a "Light which lighteth every man which cometh into the world." Do not be unaturally humble. The thought of your mind perchance is the Thought of God. To refuse to follow that may be to disown God. To take the judgment and conscience of other men to live by, where is the humility of that? From whence did their conscience and judgment come? Was the fountain from which they drew exhausted for you? If they refused like you to rely on their own conscience, and you rely upon it, how are you sure that it is more the Mind of God than your own which you have refused to hear?

Look at it in another way. The charm of the words of great men, those grand sayings which are recognised as true as soon as heard, is this, that you recognise them as wisdom which has passed across your own mind. You feel that they are your own thoughts come back to you, else you would not at once admit them: "All that floated across me before, only I could not say it, and did not feel confident enough to assert it: or had not conviction enough to put it into words." Yes, God spoke to you what He did to them: only they believed it, said it, trusted the Word within them, and you did not. Be sure that often when you say, "it is only my own poor thought, and I am alone," — the real correcting thought is this, "alone, but the Father is with me," — therefore I can live that lonely conviction.

There is no danger in this, whatever timid minds may think — no danger of mistake, if the character be a true one. For we are not left in uncertainty in this matter. It is given to us to know our base from our noble hours: to distinguish between the voice which is from above, and that which speaks from below, out of the abyss of our animal and selfish nature. Samuel could distinguish between the impulse, quite a human one, which would have made him select Eliab out of Jesse's sons, and the deeper judgment by which "the *Lord* said, Look not on his countenance, nor on the height of his stature, for I have refused him." Doubtless deep truth of character is required for this: for the whispering voices get mixed together, and we dare not abide by our own thoughts, because we think them our own, and not God's: and this because we only now and then endeavour to know in earnest. It is only given to the habitually true to know the difference. He knew it, because all His blessed life long He could say, "My judgment is just, *because* I seek not my own will, but the will of Him which sent me."

The practical result and inference of all this is a very simple but a very deep one: the deepest of existence. Let life be a life of faith. Do not go timorously about, inquiring what others think, what others believe, and what others say. It seems the easiest, it is the most difficult, thing in life to do this — believe in God. God is near you. Throw yourself fearlessly upon Him. Trembling mortal, there is an unknown might within your soul which will wake when you command it. The day may come when all that is human, man and woman, will fall off from you, as they did from Him. Let His strength be yours. Be independent of them all now. The Father is with you. Look to Him, and He will save you.

XVI.

Preached October 20, 1850.

THE NEW COMMANDMENT OF LOVE TO ONE ANOTHER.

JOHN xiii, 34. — "A new commandment I give unto you, that ye love one another; as I have loved you, that ye also love one another."

THESE words derive impressiveness from having been spoken immediately before the last Supper, and on the eve of the great Sacrifice: the commandment of Love issued appropriately at the time of the Feast of Love, and not long before the great Act of Love. For the love of Christ was no fine *saying:* it cost Him His life to say these words with meaning, "As I have loved you."

There is a difficulty in the attempt to grasp the meaning of this command, arising from the fact that words change their meaning. Our Lord affixed a new significance to the word Love: it had been in use, of course, before, but the new sense in which He used it made it a new word.

His law is not adequately represented by the word Love: because love is, by conventional usage, appropriated to one species of human affection, which, in the commoner men, is the most selfish of all our feelings: in the best, too exclusive and individual to represent that Charity which is universal.

Nor is Charity a perfect symbol of His meaning: for charity by use is identified with another form of love which is but a portion of it, almsgiving: and too saturated with that meaning to be entirely disengaged from it, even when we use it most accurately.

Benevolence or Philanthropy, in derivation, come

nearer to the idea: but yet you feel at once that these words fall short: they are too tame and cool; too merely passive, as states of feeling rather than forms of life.

We have no sufficient word. There is therefore no help for it, but patiently to strive to master the meaning of this mighty word Love, in the only light that is left us, the light of the Saviour's life: "As I have loved you:" that alone expounds it.

We will dispossess our minds of all preconceived notions; remove all low associations, all partial and conventional ones. If we would understand this law, it must be ever a "new" commandment, ever receiving fresh light and meaning from His life.

Take, I. The novelty of the law — "That ye love one another."

II. The Spirit or measure of it — "As I have loved you."

I. Its novelty. A "new commandment:" yet that law was old. See 1 John II. 7, 8.

1. It was new as a historical fact. We talk of the apostolic mission as a matter of course; we say that the apostles were ordered to go and plant churches, and so we dismiss the great fact. But we forget that the command was rather the result of a spirit working from within, than of an injunction working from without. That spirit was Love.

And when that new spirit was in the world, see how straightway it created a new thing. Men before that had travelled into foreign countries: the naturalist to collect specimens: the historian to accumulate facts: the philosopher to hive up wisdom, or else he had stayed in his cell or grove to paint *pictures* of beautiful love. But the spectacle of an Apostle Paul crossing oceans not to conquer kingdoms, not to hive up knowledge, but to impart life: not to accumulate stores for self, but to give, and to spend himself — was new in the history of the world. The celestial fire had touched the hearts of men, and their hearts flamed: and it caught, and spread, and would not stop. On they went, that glorious band of brothers, in their strange enterprise, over oceans, and through forests, penetrating into the dungeon, and to the throne — to the hut of the savage feeding on human flesh, and to the shore lined with the skin-clad inhabitants of these far Isles of Britain. Read the account given by Tertullian of the marvellous rapidity with which the Christians increased and swarmed, and you are reminded of one of those vast armies of ants which move across a country in irresistible myriads, drowned by thousands in rivers, cut off by fire, consumed by man and beast, and yet fresh hordes succeeding interminably to supply their place.

A new voice was heard: a new yearning upon earth; man pining at being severed from his brother, and longing to burst the false distinctions which had kept the best hearts from each other so long — an infant cry of life — the cry of the young Church of God. And all this from Judea — the narrowest, most bigoted, most intolerant nation on the face of the earth.

Now I say that this was historically a new thing.

2. It was new in extent. It was, in literal words, an old Commandment given before both to Jew and Gentile. To the Jew, as, for instance, in Lev. xix. 18. To the Gentile, in the recognition which was so often made of the beauty of the law in its partial applica-

tion, as in the case of friendship, patriotism, domestic attachment, and so on.

But the difference lay in the extent in which these words "one another" were understood. By them, or rather by "neighbour," the Jew meant his countrymen; and narrowed that down again to his friends among his countrymen — so that the well-known Rabbinical gloss upon these words, current in the days of Christ, was, "Thou shalt love thy neighbour and hate thine enemy." And what the Gentile understood by the extent of the law of love, we may learn from the well-known words of their best and wisest, who thanked heaven that he was born a man, and not a brute — a Greek, and not a barbarian: as if to be a barbarian were identical with being a brute.

Now, listen to Christ's exposition of the word neighbour. "Ye have heard that it was said, Thou shalt love thy neighbour and hate thine enemy. But I say unto you, Love your enemies." And he went further, — As a specimen of a neighbour he specially selected one of that nation whom, as a theologian and a patriot, every Jew had been taught to hate. And just as the application of electricity to the innumerable wants of human life and to new ends, is reckoned a new discovery and invention of modern times (though the fact has been familiar for ages to the Indian child in the forest of the far west, and applied by him for ages to his childish sports), so the extension of this grand principle of Love to all the possible cases of life, and to all possible persons — even though the principle was known and applied long before, in love to friends, country, and relations — is truly and properly a new commandment, a discovery, a gospel, a revelation.

3. It was new in being made the central principle of a system. Never had obedience before been trusted to a principle: it had always been hedged round by a law. The religion of Christ is not law, but a spirit —not a creed, but a life. To the one motive of Love God has entrusted the whole work of winning the souls of His redeemed. The heart of man was made for love: pants and pines for it: — only in the love of Christ, and not in restrictions, can his soul expand. Now it was reserved for One to pierce, with the glance of intuition, down into the springs of human action, and to proclaim the simplicity of its machinery. "Love," said the apostle after him — "Love is the fulfilling of the law."

We are told that in the new commandment the old perishes: that under the law of love, man is free from the law of works. Let us see now.

Take any commandment — for example the sixth, the seventh, the eighth. I may abstain from murder and theft, deterred by law: because law has annexed to them certain penalties. But I may also rise into the spirit of Charity: then I am free from the law: the law was not made for a righteous man; the law no more binds or restrains me, now that I love my neighbour, than the dyke built to keep in the sea at high tide restrains it when that sea has sunk to low water-mark.

Or the seventh. You may keep that law from dread of discovery — or you may learn a higher Love: and then you *cannot* injure a human soul: you cannot degrade a human spirit. Charity has made the old commandment superfluous. In the strong language of St. John, you *cannot* sin because you are born of God.

It was the proclamation of this, the great living principle of human obedience, not with the pedantry of a philosopher, nor the exaggeration of an orator, but in the simple reality of life, which made this commandment of Christ a new commandment.

II. The spirit or measure of the law, — "*as* I have loved you."

Broadly, the love of Christ was the spirit of giving all He had to give. "Greater love hath no man than this, that a man lay down his life for his friend." Christ's love was not a sentiment; it was a self-giving. To that His adversaries bore testimony: — "He saved others; himself He cannot save." Often as we have read these words, did it ever strike us, and if not, does it not bring a flash of surprise when we perceive it, that these words, meant as taunt, were really the noblest panegyric, a testimony higher and more adequate far than even that of the centurion? "He saved others; Himself He cannot save." The first clause contained the answer to the second — "Himself He cannot save!" How *could* He, having saved others? How can any keep what he gives? How can any live for self, when he is living for others? Unconsciously, those enemies were enunciating the very principle of Christianity, the grand law of all existence, that only by losing self you can save others; that only by giving life you can bless. Love gives itself. The mother spends herself in giving life to her child; the soldier dies for his country; nay, even the artist produces nothing destined for immortality, nothing that will *live*, except so far as he has forgotten himself, and merged his very being in his work.

"He saved others; Himself He cannot save." That was the love of Christ. Now to descend to particulars.

That spirit of self-giving manifests itself in the shape of considerate kindliness. Take three cases: — First, that in which He fed the people with bread. "I have compassion on the multitude, because they continue with me now three days, and have nothing to eat." There was a tenderness which, not absorbed in His own great designs, considered a number of small particulars of their state, imagined, provided; and this for the satisfaction of the lowest wants. Again, to the disciples: "Come ye yourselves apart into a desert place, and rest awhile." He would not overwork them in the sublimest service. He did not grudge from duty their interval of relaxation; He even tenderly enforced it. Lastly, His dying words: "Behold thy mother! Woman, behold thy son!" Short sentences. He was too exhausted to say more. But in that hour of death-torture, He could think of her desolate state when He was gone, and with delicate, thoughtful attention provide for her well-being.

There are people who would do great acts; but because they wait for great opportunities, life passes, and the acts of love are not done at all. Observe, this considerateness of Christ was shown in little things. And such are the parts of human life. Opportunities for doing *greatly* seldom occur — life is made up of infinitesimals. If you compute the sum of happiness in any given day, you will find that it was composed of small attentions, kind looks, which made the heart swell, and stirred into health that sour, rancid film of misanthropy which is apt to coagulate on the stream of our inward life, as surely as we live in heart apart from our fellow-creatures. Doubtless, the memory of each one of us will furnish him with the picture of some member of a family whose very presence seemed to shed happiness: A daughter, perhaps, whose light step even in the distance irradiated every one's countenance. What was the secret of such an one's power? what had she done? Absolutely nothing; but radiant smiles, beaming good humour, the tact of divining what every one felt, and every one wanted, told that she had got out of self and learned to think for others; so that at one time it showed itself in deprecating the quarrel, which lowering brows and raised tones already showed to be impending, by sweet words; and another, by smoothing an invalid's pillow; at another, by soothing a sobbing child; at another, by humouring and softening a father who had returned weary and ill-tempered from the irritating cares of business. None but she saw those things. None but a loving heart *could* see them.

That was the secret of her heavenly power. Call you those things homely trifles, too homely for a sermon? By reference to the character of Christ, they rise into something quite sublime. For *that* is loving as He loved. And remark, too, these trifles prepared for larger deeds. The one who will be found in trial capable of great acts of love, is ever the one who is always doing considerate small ones. The Soul which poured itself out to death upon the cross for the human race, was the Spirit of Him who thought of the wants of the people, contrived for the rest of the disciples, and was thoughtful for a mother.

Once again, — It was a love never foiled by the unworthiness of those on whom it had been once bestowed. It was a love which faults, desertion, denial, unfaithfulness, could not chill, even though they wrung His heart. He had chosen: and He trusted. Even in ordinary manhood, that is a finely-tempered heart, one of no ordinary mould, which can say, "It ever was my way, and shall be still, when I do trust a man to trust him wholly." And yet there was everything to shake His trust in humanity. The Pharisees called Him Good Master, and were circumventing Him all the while. The people shouted hosannas, and three days afterwards were shrieking for His blood. One disciple who had dipped in the same dish, and been trusted with His inmost counsels, betrayed and deceived Him; another was ashamed of Him; three fell asleep while He was preparing for death; all forsook Him. Yet nothing is more surprising than that unshaken, I had well-nigh said, *obstinate*, trust with which He clung to His hopes of our nature, and believed in the face of demonstration.

As we mix in life, there comes, especially to sensitive natures, a temptation to distrust. In young life, we throw ourselves with unbounded and glorious confidence on such as we think well of — an error soon corrected: for we soon find out — too soon — that men and women are not what they seem. Then comes disappointment; and the danger is a reaction of desolating and universal mistrust. For if we look on the doings of man with a merely worldly eye, and pierce below the surface of character, we are apt to feel bitter scorn and disgust for our fellow-creatures. We have lived to see human hollowness: the ashes of the Dead Sea shore: the falseness of what seemed so fair; the mouldering beneath the whited sepulchre: and no wonder if we are tempted to think "friendship *all* a cheat — smiles hypocrisy — words deceit;" and they who are what is called *knowing* in life contract by degrees, as the result of their experience, a hollow distrust of men, and learn to sneer at apparently good motives. That demoniacal sneer which we have seen, ay perhaps felt, curling the lip at times, "Doth Job serve God for nought?"

The only preservation from this withering of the heart is Love. Love is its own perennial fount of strength. The strength of affection is a proof not of the worthiness of the object, but of the largeness of the soul which loves. Love descends, not ascends. The might of a river depends not on the quality of the soil through which it passes, but on the inexhaustibleness and depth of the spring from which it proceeds. The greater mind cleaves to the smaller with more force than the other to it. A parent loves the child more than the child the parent; and partly because the parent's heart is larger, not because the child is worthier. The Saviour loved His disciples infinitely more than His disciples loved Him, because His heart was infinitely larger. Love trusts on — ever hopes and expects better things, and this, a trust springing from itself and out of its own deeps alone.

And more than this. It is this *trusting* love that makes men what they are trusted to be, so realizing itself. Would you make men *trustworthy?* Trust them. Would you make them true? Believe them. This was the real force of that sublime battle-cry which no Englishman hears without emotion. When the crews of the fleet of Britain knew that they were *expected* to do their duty, they *did* their duty. They felt in that spirit-stirring sentence that they were trusted: and the simultaneous cheer that rose from every ship was a forerunner of victory — the battle was half-won already. They went to serve a country which expected from them great things: and they *did* great things. Those pregnant words raised an enthusiasm for the chieftain who had thrown himself upon his men in trust, which a double line of hostile ships could not appal, nor decks drenched in blood extinguish.

And it is on this principle that Christ wins the hearts of his redeemed. He trusted the doubting Thomas; and Thomas arose with a faith worthy "of his Lord and his God." He would not suffer even the lie of Peter to shake His conviction that Peter might love him yet; and Peter answered nobly to that sublime forgiveness. His last prayer was in extenuation and hope for the race who had rejected Him — and the kingdoms of the world are become His own. He has loved us, God knows why — I do not — and we, all unworthy though we be, respond faintly to that love, and try to be what He would have us.

Therefore, come what may, hold fast to love. Though men should rend your heart, let them not embitter or harden it. We win by tenderness: we conquer by forgiveness. Oh, strive to enter into something of that large celestial Charity which is meek, enduring, unretaliating, and which even the overbearing world cannot withstand for ever. Learn the new commandment of the Son of God. Not to love merely, but to love *as He loved.* Go forth in this spirit to your life-duties: go forth, children of the Cross, to carry everything before you, and win victories for God by the conquering power of a love like His.

XVII.

Preached June 15, 1851.

THE MESSAGE OF THE CHURCH TO MEN OF WEALTH.*

1 SAM. xxv. 10, 11. — "And Nabal answered David's servants, and said Who is David? and who is the son of Jesse? There be many servants now a days that break away every man from his master. Shall I then take my bread, and my water, and my flesh that I have killed for my shearers, and give it unto men whom I know not whence they be?"

I have selected this passage for our subject this evening, because it is one of the earliest cases recorded in the Bible in which the interests of the employer and the employed, the man of wealth and the man of work, stood, or seemed to stand, in antagonism to each other.

It was a period in which an old system of things was breaking up; and the new one was not yet established. The patriarchal relationship of tutelage and dependence was gone, and monarchy was not yet in firm existence. Saul was on the throne; but his rule was irregular and disputed. Many things were slowly growing up into custom which had not yet the force of law; and the first steps by which custom passes into law from precetend to precetend are often steps at every one of which struggle and resistance must take place.

The history of the chapter is briefly this. Nabal, the wealthy sheep-master, fed his flocks in the pastures of Carmel. David was leader of a band of men who

* This subject was continued on the following Sunday. By accident the continuation was omitted from the first edition of Vol. I., and inserted, at the beginning of Vol. II. It has been thought better to continue that arrangement, merely drawing attention to the fact, that the conclusion of the subject is to be sought in Vol. II.

got their living by the sword on the same hills: outlaws whose excesses he in some degree restrained, and over whom he retained a leader's influence. A rude irregular honour was not unknown among those fierce men. They honourably abstained from injuring Nabal's flocks. They did more: they protected them from all harm against the marauders of the neighbourhood. By the confession of Nabal's own herdsmen, "they were a wall unto them both by night and day, all the time they were with them keeping their flocks."

And thus a kind of Right grew up: irregular enough, but sufficient to establish a claim on Nabal for remuneration of those services: a new claim, not admitted by him: reckoned by him an exaction, which could be enforced by no law; only by that law which is above all statute-law, deciding according to emergencies; an indefinable instinctive sense of Fairness and Justice. But as there was no law, and each man was to himself a law, and the sole arbiter of his own rights, what help was there but that disputes should rise between the wealthy proprietors and their self-constituted champions, with exaction and tyranny on the one side, churlishness and parsimony on the other? Hence a fruitful and ever-fresh source of struggle: the one class struggling to take as much, and the other to give as little as possible. In modern language, the Rights of Labour were in conflict with the Rights of Property.

The story proceeds thus: — David presented a demand, moderate and courteous enough (v. 6, 7, 8). It was refused by Nabal, and added to the refusal were those insulting taunts of low birth and outcast condition which are worse than injury, and sting, making men's blood run fire. One court of appeal was left. There remained nothing but the trial by Force. "Gird ye on," said David, "every man his sword."

Now, observe the fearful, hopeless character of this struggle. The question had come to this: whether David with his ferocious, needy six hundred mountaineers united by the sense of wrong, or Nabal with his well-fed and trained hirelings bound by interest not love to his cause, were stronger? Which was the more powerful, want whetted by insult, or selfishness pampered by abundance; they who wished to keep by force, or they who wished to take? An awful and uncertain spectacle, but the spectacle which is exhibited in every country where Rights are keenly felt and Duties lightly — where insolent demand is met by insulting defiance. Wherever classes are held apart by rivalry and selfishness instead of drawn together by the Law of Love — wherever there has not been established a kingdom of heaven, but only a kingdom of the world — there exist the forces of inevitable collision.

I. The causes of this false social state.

II. The message of the Church to the man of wealth.

I. False basis on which social superiority was held to rest.

Throughout, Nabal's conduct was built upon the assumption of his own superiority. He was a man of wealth. David was dependent on his own daily efforts. Was not that enough to settle the question of superiority and inferiority? It was enough on both sides for a long time, till the falsehood of the assumption became palpable and intolerable. But palpable and intolerable it did become at last.

A social falsehood will be borne long, even with considerable inconvenience, until it forces itself obtrusively on men's attention, and can be endured no longer. The exact point at which *this* social falsehood, that wealth constitutes superiority and has a right to the subordination of inferiors, becomes intolerable, varies according to several circumstances.

The evils of poverty are comparative — they depend on climate. In warm climates, where little food, no fuel, and scanty shelter are required, the sting is scarcely felt till poverty becomes starvation. They depend on contrast. Far above the point where poverty becomes actual famine, it may become unbearable if contrasted strongly with the unnecessary luxury and abundance enjoyed by the classes above. Where all suffer equally, as men and officers suffer in an Arctic voyage, men bear hardship with cheerfulness: but where the suffering weighs heavily on some, and the luxury of enjoyment is out of all proportion monopolised by a few, the point of reaction is reached long before penury has become actual want: or, again, when wealth or rank assumes an insulting domineering character — when contemptuous names for the poor are invented, and current among the more unfeeling of a wealthy class: then the falsehood of superiority can be tolerated no longer; for we do not envy honours which are meekly borne, nor wealth which is unostentatious.

Now it was this which brought matters to a crisis. David had borne poverty long — nay, he and his men had long endured the contrast between their own cavern-homes and beds upon the rock, and Nabal's comforts.

But when Nabal added to this those pungent biting sneers, which sink into poor men's hearts and rankle; which are not forgotten, but come out fresh in the day of retribution, — "Who is David? and who is the son of Jesse? There be many servants now a days that break away every man from his master," then David began to measure himself with Nabal; — Not a wiser man — nor a better — nor even a stronger, Who is this Nabal? Intellectually, a fool — morally, a profligate, drowning reason in excess of wine at the annual sheep shearing. A tyrant over his slaves — overbearing to men who only ask of him their rights. Then rose the question, which Nabal had better not have forced men to answer for themselves. By what right does this possessor of wealth lord it over men who are inferior in no one particular?

Now observe two things.

1. An apparent inconsistency in David's conduct. David had received injury after injury from Saul, and had only forgiven. One injury from Nabal, and David is striding over the hills to revenge his wrong with naked steel. How came this reverence and irreverence to mix together.

We reply: Saul had a claim of Authority on David's allegiance: Nabal only one of rank. Between these the Bible makes a vast difference. It says, The *powers* which be are ordained of God. But *upper* and *lower*, as belonging to difference in property, are fictitious terms: true, if character corresponds with titular superiority; false, if it does not. And such was the difference manifested in the life of the Son of God. To lawful authority, whether Roman or Jewish, even priestly, He paid deference: but to the titled mark of conventional distinction, none. Rabbi, Rabbi, was no Divine authority. It was not power, a delegated attribute of God: it was only a name. In Saul, therefore, David reverenced one his superior in authority; but in Nabal he only had one surpassing him in wealth. And David refused, somewhat too rudely, to acknowledge the bad, great man as his superior: would pay him no reverence, respect, or allegiance whatever. Let us mark that distinction well, so often confused — kings, masters, parents: here is a power ordained of God. Honour it. But wealth, name, title, distinctions, always fictitious, often false and vicious, if you claim homage for these, separate from worth, you confound two things essentially different. Try that by the test of His Life. Name the text where Christ claimed reverence for wealth or rank. On the Mount did the Son of Man bow the knee to the majesty of wealth and wrong, or was His Sonship shown in that He would not bow down to that as if of God?

2. This great falsehood respecting superior and inferior rested on a truth. There had been a superiority in the wealthy class once. In the patriarchal system wealth and rule had gone together. The father of the family and tribe was the one in whom proprietorship was centred. But the patriarchal system had passed away. Men like Nabal succeeded to the patriarch's wealth, and expected the subordination which had been yielded to patriarchal character and position: and this when every particular of relationship was altered. Once the patriarch was the protector of his dependants. Now David's class was independent, and the protectors rather than the protected: at all events able to defend themselves. Once the rich man was ruler in virtue of pa-

ternal relationship. Now wealth was severed from rule and relationship: a man might be rich, yet neither a ruler, nor a protector, nor a kinsman. And the fallacy of Nabal's expectation consisted in this, that he demanded for wealth that reverence which had once been due to men who happened to be wealthy.

It is a fallacy in which we are perpetually entangled. We expect reverence for that which was once a symbol of what was reverenced, but is reverenced no longer. Here, in England, it is common to complain that there is no longer any respect of inferiors towards superiors: that servants were once devoted and grateful, tenants submissive, subjects enthusiastically loyal. But we forget that servants were once protected by their masters: and tenants safe from wrong only through the guardianship of their powerful lords: that thence a personal gratitude grew up: that now they are protected by the law from wrong by a different social system altogether: and that the individual bond of gratitude subsists no longer. We expect that to masters and employers the same reverence and devotedness shall be rendered which were due to them under other circumstances, and for different reasons: as if wealth and rank had ever been the claim to reverence, and not merely the accidents and accompaniments of the claim: as if anything less sacred than holy ties could purchase sacred feelings: as if the homage of free manhood could be due to gold and name: as if to the mere Nabal-fool, who is labelled as worth so much, and whose signature carries with it so much coin, the holiest and most ennobling sensations of the soul, reverence and loyalty, were due by God's appointment.

No. That patriarchal system has passed for ever.

No sentimental wailings for the past, no fond regrets for the virtues of a bygone age, no melancholy, poetical, retrospective antiquarianism can restore it. In church and state the past *is* past: and you can no more bring back the blind reverence than the rude virtues of those days. The day has come in which if feudal loyalty or patriarchal reverence are to be commanded, they must be won by patriarchal virtues or feudal real superiorities.

II. Cause of this unhealthy social state: A false conception respecting Rights.

It would be unjust to Nabal to represent this as an act of wilful oppression and conscious injustice. He did what appeared to him fair between man and man. He paid his labourers. Why should he pay anything beyond stipulated wages?

David's demand appeared an extravagant and insolent one, provoking unfeigned astonishment and indignation. It was an invasion of his rights. It was a dictation with respect to the employment of that which was his own. "Shall I take my bread, and my water, and my flesh that I have killed for my shearers, and give it unto men whom I know not whence they be?"

Recollect, too, there was something to be said for Nabal. This view of the irresponsible right of property was not *his* invention. It was the view probably entertained by all his class. It had descended to him from his parents. They were prescriptive and admitted rights on which he stood. And however false or unjust a prescriptive right may be, however baseless when examined, there is much excuse for those who have inherited and not invented it; for it is hard to see through the falsehood of any system by which we profit, and which is upheld by general consent, especially when good men, too, uphold it. Rare, indeed, is that pure-heartedness which sees with eagle glance through conventionalisms — This is a wrong, and I and my own class are the doers of it.

On the other hand, David and his needy followers were not slow to perceive that they had their rights over that property of Nabal's.

Men on whom wrongs press are the first to feel them, and their cries of pain and indignation are the appointed means of God to direct to their wrongs the attention of society. Very often the fierce and maddened shriek of suffering is the first intimation that a wrong exists at all.

There was no law in Israel to establish David's claims. This guardianship of Nabal's flocks was partly a self-constituted thing. No bargain had been made: no sum of reward expressly stipulated. But there is a Law besides, and above all written law, which gives to written laws their authority, and from which, so often as they diverge, it is woe to the framers of the law; for their law must perish, and the Eternal Law unseen will get itself acknowledged as a truth from heaven, or a truth from hell — a truth begirt with fire and sword, if they will not read it except so.

In point of fact, David had a right to a share of Nabal's profits. The harvest was in part David's harvest, for without David it never could have been reaped. The sheep were in part David's sheep, for without David not a sheep would have been spared by the marauders of the hills. Not a sheaf of corn was carried to Nabal's barn, nor a night passed in repose by Nabal's shepherds, but what told of the share of David in the saving of that sheaf, and the procurement of that repose (not the less real because it was past and unseen). The right which the soldier has by law to his pay, was the right which David had by unwritten law; a right resting on the fact that his services were indispensable for the harvest.

Here, then, is one of the earliest instances of the Rights of Labour coming into collision with the Rights of Property: rights shadowy, undefined, perpetually shifting their boundaries, varying with every case, altering with every age, incapable of being adjusted except rudely by law, and leaving always something which the most subtle and elaborate law cannot define, and which in any moment may grow up into a wrong.

Now, when it comes to this, Rights against Rights, there is no determination of the question but by overwhelming numbers or blood. David's remedy was a short, sharp, decisive one. "Gird ye on every man his sword." And it is difficult, for the sake of humanity, to say to which side in such a quarrel we should wish well. If the rich man succeeds in civil war, he will bind the chain of degradation more severely and more surely for years, or ages, on the crushed serf. If the champions of popular rights succeed by the sword, you may then await, in awe, the reign of tyranny, licentiousness, and lawlessness. For the victory of the lawless, with the memory of past wrongs to avenge, is almost more sanguinary than the victory of those who have had power long, and whose power has been defied.

3. We find another cause in circumstances. Want and unjust exclusion precipitated David and his men

into this rebellion. It is common enough to lay too much weight on circumstances. Nothing can be more false than the popular theory that ameliorated outward condition is the panacea for the evils of Society. The gospel principle begins from within and works outwards. The world's principle begins with the outward condition, and expects to influence inwardly. To expect that by changing the world without, in order to suit the world within, by taking away all difficulties and removing all tempations, instead of hardening the man within against the force of outward temptation — to adapt the lot to the man, instead of moulding the spirit to the lot, is to reverse the gospel method of procedure. Nevertheless, even that favourite speculation of theorists, that perfect circumstances will produce perfect character, contains a truth. Circumstances of outward condition are not the sole efficients in the production of character, but they are efficients which must not be ignored. Favourable condition will not produce excellence: but the want of it often hinders excellence. It is true that vice leads to poverty: all the moralizers tell us that; but it is also true that poverty leads to vice. There are some in this world to whom, speaking humanly, social injustice and social inequalities have made goodness impossible. Take, for instance, the case of these bandits on Mount Carmel. Some of them were outlawed by their own crimes, but others doubtless by debts not wilfully contracted — one at least, David, by a most unjust and unrighteous persecution. And these men, excluded, needy, exasperated by a sense of wrong, untaught — outcasts, could you gravely expect from them obedience, patience, meekness, religious resignation? Yes, my brethren, that is exactly the marvellous impossibility people do most inconsistently expect; and there are no bounds to their astonishment if they do not get what they expect: — Superhuman honesty from starving men, to whom life by hopelessness has become a gambler's desperate chance! — chivalrous loyalty and high forbearance from creatures to whom the order of society has presented itself only as an unjust system of partiality! We forget that forbearance and obedience are the very last and highest lessons learned by the spirit in its most careful training, By those unhallowed conventionalisms through which we, like heathens, and not like Christians, crush the small offender and court the great one — that damnable cowardice by which we banish the seduced and half admire the seducer — by which, in defiance of all manliness and all generosity, we punish the weak and tempted, and let the tempter go free: — by all these we make men and women outcasts, and then expect from them the sublimest graces of reverence and resignation!

II. The message of the Church to the man of wealth.

The message of the Church contains those principles of Life which, carried out, would, and hereafter will, realize the Divine Order of Society. The revealed Message does not create the facts of our humanity — it simply makes them known. The Gospel did not make God our Father — it authoritatively reveals that He is so. It did not create a new duty of loving one another — it revealed the old duty which existed from eternity, and must exist as long as Humanity is Humanity. It was no "new commandment," but an old commandment which had been heard from the beginning. The Church of God is that living body of men who are called by Him out of the world, not to be the inventors of a new social system, but to exhibit in the world by word and life, chiefly by life, what Humanity is, was, and will be, in the Idea of God. Now, so far as the social economy is concerned, the revelations of the Church will coincide with the discoveries of a Scientific Political Economy. Political Economy discovers slowly the facts of the immutable laws of social well-being. But the living principles of those laws, which cause them to be obeyed, Christianity has revealed to loving hearts long before. The Spirit discovers them to the spirit. For instance, Political Economy, gazing on such a fact as this of civil war, would arrive at the same principles which the Church arrives at. She too would say, Not selfishness, but love. Only that she arrives at these principles by experience, not intuition: by terrible lessons, not revelation: by revolutions, wars, and famines, not by spiritual impulses of charity.

And so because these principles were eternally true in humanity, we find in the conduct of Abigail towards David in this early age, not explicitly, but implicitly, the very principles which the Church of Christ has given to the world; and more, the very principles which a sound economy would sanction. In her reply to David we have the anticipation by a loving heart of those duties which selfish prudence must have taught at last.

1. The spiritual dignity of man as man. Recollect David was the poor man, but Abigail, the high-born lady, admits his worth: "The Lord will certainly make my lord a sure house; because my lord fighteth the

battles of the Lord, and evil hath not been found in thee all thy days." Here is a truth revealed to that age. Nabal's day, and the day of such as Nabal, is past — another power is rising above the horizon. David's cause is God's cause. Worth does not mean what a man is worth — you must find some better definition than that.

Now this is the very truth revealed in the Incarnation. David, Israel's model king; the king by the grace of God, not by the conventional rules of human choice, is a shepherd's son. Christ, the King who is to reign over our regenerated humanity, is humbly born — the poor woman's Son. That is the Church's message to the man of wealth, and a message which it seems has to be learned afresh in every age. It was new to Nabal. It was new to the men of the age of Christ. In His day, they were offended in Him, because He was humbly born. "Is not this the carpenter's son?" It is the offence now. They who retain those superstitious ideas of the eternal superiority of rank and wealth, have the first principles of the Gospel yet to learn. How can they believe in the Son of Mary? They may honour Him with the lip, they deny Him in His brethren. Whoever helps to keep alive that ancient lie of upper and lower, resting the distinction not on official authority or personal worth, but on wealth and title, is doing his part to hinder the establishment of the Redeemer's kingdom.

Now the Church of Christ proclaims that truth in baptism. She speaks of a kingdom here in which all are, as spirits, equal. She reveals a fact. She does not affect to create the fact. She says — not hypothetically, "This child *may* be the child of God if prevenient grace has taken place, or if hereafter he shall have certain feelings and experiences:" nor, " Hereby I create this child magically by supernatural power in one moment, what it was not a moment before:" but she says, authoritatively, "I pronounce this child the child of God: the brother of Christ the First-born — the son of Him who has taught us by His Son to call Him *our* Father, not *my* Father. Whatever that child may become hereafter in fact, he is now by right of creation and redemption the child of God. Rich or poor, titled or untitled, he shares the spiritual nature of the second Adam — the Lord from Heaven."

2. The second truth expressed by Abigail was the Law of Sacrifice. She did not heal the grievance with smooth words. Starving men are not to be pacified by professions of good will. She brought her two hundred loaves, and her two skins of wine, her five sheep ready dressed, &c. A princely provision!

You might have said this was waste — half would have been enough. But the truth is, liberality is a most real economy. She could not stand there calculating the smallest possible expense at which the affront might be wiped out. True economy is to pay liberally and fairly for faithful service. The largest charity is the best economy. Nabal had had a faithful servant. He should have counted no expense too great to retain his services, instead of cheapening and depreciating them. But we wrong Abigail if we call this economy or calculation. In fact, had it been done on economical principles, it would have failed. Ten times this sum from Nabal would not have arrested revenge. For Nabal it was too late. Concessions extracted by fear only provoke exaction further. The poor know well what is given because it must be given, and what is conceded from a sense of justice. They *feel* only what is real. David's men and David felt that these were not the gifts of a sordid calculation, but the offerings of a generous heart. And it won them — their gratitude — their enthusiasm — their unfeigned homage.

This is the attractive power of that great Law, whose highest Expression was the Cross. "I, if I be lifted up, will draw all men unto Me." Say what you will, it is not interest, but the sight of noble qualities, and true sacrifice, which commands the devotion of the world. Yea, — even the bandit and the outcast will bend before that as before a Divine thing. In one form or another it draws all men — it commands all men.

Now this the Church proclaims as part of its special message to the rich. It says that the Divine Death was a Sacrifice. It declares that death to be the law of every life which is to be like His. It says that the Law, which alone can interpret the mystery of life, is the self-sacrifice of Christ. It proclaims the law of His life to have been this: "For their sakes I devote (sanctify) Myself, that they also may be devoted through the Truth." In other words, the Self-sacrifice of the Redeemer was to be the living principle and law of the self-devotion of His people. It asserts that to be the principle which alone can make any human life a true life. "I fill up that which is behind of the afflictions of Christ in my flesh, for His body's sake, which is the church." We have petrified *that* Sacrifice into a dead theological dogma, about the exact efficacy of which we dispute metaphysically, and charge each other with heresy. That atonement will become a living fact only when we humbly recognise in it the eternal fact that sacrifice is the Law of life. The very mockers at the crucifixion unwittingly declared the principle: "He saved others: Himself he cannot save." Of course — How could He save Himself who had to save others? You can only save others when you have ceased to think of saving your own soul — you can only truly bless when you have done with the pursuit of personal happiness. Did you ever hear of a soldier who saved his country by making it his chief work to secure himself? And was the Captain of our salvation to become the Saviour by contravening that universal law of Sacrifice, or by obeying it?

Brother men, the early Church gave expression to that principle of sacrifice in a very touching way. They had all things in common. "Neither said any of them that aught of the things which he possessed was his own." They failed, not because they declared that, but because men began to think that the duty of sharing was compulsory. They proclaimed principles which were unnatural, inasmuch as they set aside all personal feelings, which are part of our nature too. They virtually compelled private property to cease, because he who retained private property when all were giving up was degraded, and hence became a hypocrite and liar, like Ananias. But let us not lose the truth which they expressed in an exaggerated way: "Neither said any of them that aught of the things which he possessed was his own." Property is sacred. It is *private* property; if it were not, it could not be sacrificed. If it were to be shared equally by the idle and the industrious, there could be no love in giving. Property is the rich man's own. Nabal is right in saying, My bread — my water — my flesh. But there is a higher Right which says, It is not yours. And that voice speaks to every rich man in one way or another, according as he is selfish or unselfish: coming as a voice of terror or a voice of blessing. It came to Nabal with a double curse, turning his heart into stone with the vision of the danger and the armed ranks of David's avengers; and laying on David's soul the sin of intended murder. It came to the heart of Abigail with a double blessing: blessing her who gave and him who took. To the spirit of the Cross alone we look as the Remedy for social evils. When the people of this great country, especially the rich, shall have been touched with the spirit of the Cross to a largeness of sacrifice of which they have not dreamed as yet, there will be an atonement between the Rights of Labour and the Rights of Property.

3. The last part of the Church's message to the man of wealth touches the matter of rightful influence.

Very remarkable is the demeanour of David towards Nabal, as contrasted with his demeanour towards Abigail. In the one case, defiance, and a haughty self-assertion of equality — in the other, deference, respect, and the most eloquent benediction. It was not, therefore, against the wealthy class, but against individuals of the class, that the wrath of these men burned.

See, then, the folly and the falsehood of the sentimental regret that there is no longer any reverence felt towards superiors. There *is* reverence to superiors, if only it can be shown that they are superiors. Reverence is deeply rooted in the heart of humanity — you cannot tear it out. Civilization — science — progress — only change its direction: they do not weaken its force. If it no longer bows before crucifixes and candles, priests and relics, it is not extinguished towards what is truly sacred and what is priestly in man. The fiercest revolt against false authority is only a step towards submission to rightful authority. Emancipation from false lords only sets the heart free to honour true ones. The freeborn David will not do homage to Nabal. Well, now go and mourn over the degenerate age which no longer feels respect for that which is above it. But behold — David has found a something nobler than himself. Feminine charity — sacrifice and justice — and in gratitude and profoundest respect he bows to that. The state of society which is coming is not one of protection and dependence: nor one of mysterious authority, and blind obedience to it — nor one in which any class shall be privileged by Divine right, and another remain in perpetual tutelage; but it is one in which unselfish services and personal qualities will command, by Divine right, gratitude and admiration, and secure a true and spiritual leadership.

Oh! let not the rich misread the signs of the times, or mistake their brethren: they have less and less respect for titles and riches: for vestments and ecclesiastical pretensions: but they have a real respect for superior knowledge and superior goodness: they listen like children to those whom they believe to know a subject better than themselves. Let those who know it say, whether there is not something inexpressibly touching and even humbling in the large, hearty, manly, English reverence and love which the working men show towards those who love and serve them truly, and save them from themselves and from doing wrong. See how David's feelings gush forth — "Blessed be the Lord God of Israel which sent thee this day to meet me: and blessed be thy advice, and blessed be thou which hast kept me this day from coming to shed blood, and from avenging myself with mine own hand."

The rich and great may have that love if they will.

To conclude. Doubtless, David was wrong: he had no right even to redress wrongs thus: patience was his divinely appointed duty; and doubtless in such circumstances we should be very ready to preach submission and to blame David. Alas! we, the clergy of the Church of England, have been only too ready to do this: for three long centuries we have taught submission to the powers that be, as if that were the only text in Scripture bearing on the relations between the ruler and the ruled. Rarely have we dared to demand of the powers that be, justice; of the wealthy man and the titled, duties. We have produced folios of slavish flattery upon the Divine Right of Power. Shame on us! we have not denounced the wrongs done to weakness: and yet for one text in the Bible which requires submission and patience from the poor, you will find a hundred which denounce the vices of the rich — in the writings of the noble old Jewish prophets, *that*, and almost that only — *that* in the Old Testament, with a deep roll of words that sound like Sinai thunders: — and *that* in the New Testament in words less impassioned and more calmly terrible from the apostles and their Master: — and woe to us in the great day of God, if we have been the sycophants of the rich instead of the Redressers of the poor man's wrongs: woe to us if we have been tutoring David into respect to his superior, Nabal, and forgotten that David's cause, not Nabal's, is the cause of God.

XVIII.

Preached July 13, 1851.

FREEDOM BY THE TRUTH.

JOHN viii. 32. — "And ye shall know the truth, and the truth shall make you free."

IF these words were the only record we possessed of the Saviour's teaching, it may be that they would be insufficient to prove His personal Deity, but they would be enough to demonstrate the Divine Character of His mission.

Observe the greatness of the aim, and the wisdom of the means.

The aim was to make all men free. He saw around Him servitude in every form — man in slavery to man, and race to race: His own countrymen in bondage to the Romans — slaves both of Jewish and Roman masters, frightfully oppressed: men trembling before priestcraft: and those who were politically and ecclesiastically free in worse bondage still, the rich and rulers slaves to their own passions.

Conscious of His inward Deity and of His Father's intentions, He, without hurry, without the excitement which would mark the mere earthly Liberator, calmly said, "Ye shall be free."

See, next, the peculiar wisdom of the means.

The craving for liberty was not new — it lies deep in human nature. Nor was the promise of satisfying it new. Empirics, charlatans, demagogues, and men who were not charlatans nor demagogues, had promised in vain.

1. First they had tried by force. Wherever force has been used on the side of freedom we honour it; the names which we pronounce in boyhood with enthusiasm are those of the liberators of nations and the vindicators of liberty. Israel had had such: Joshua — the Judges — Judas Maccabæus. Had the Son of God willed so to come, even on human data the success was certain. I waive the truth of His inward Deity; of His miraculous power: of his power to summon to His will more than twelve legions of angels. I only notice now that men's hearts were full of Him: ripe for revolt: and that at a single word of His, thrice three hundred thousand swords would have started from their scabbards.

But had He so come, one nation might have gained liberty; not the race of man: moreover, the liberty would only have been independence of a foreign conqueror.

Therefore as a conquering king He did not come.

2. Again, it might have been attempted by legislative enactment. Perhaps only once has this been done successfully, and by a single effort. When the names of conquerors shall have been forgotten, and modern civilization shall have become obsolete — when England's shall be ancient history, one act of hers will be remembered as a record of her greatness, that act by which in costly sacrifice she emancipated her slaves.

But one thing England could not do. She could give freedom — she could not fit for freedom, not make it lasting. The stroke of a monarch's pen will do the one — the discipline of ages is needed for the other. Give to-morrow a constitution to some feeble eastern nation, or a horde of savages, and in half a century, they will be subjected again.

Therefore the Son of Man did not come to free the world by legislation.

3. It might be done by civilization. Civilization does free — intellect equalizes. Every step of civilization is a victory over some lower instinct. But civilization contains within itself the elements of a fresh servitude. Man conquers the powers of nature and becomes in turn their slave. The workman is in bondage to the machinery which does his will: his hours, his wages, his personal habits determined by it. The rich man fills his house with luxuries, and cannot do without them. A highly civilized community is a very spectacle of servitude. Man is there a slave to dress, to hours, to manners, to conventions, to etiquette. Things contrived to make his life more easy become his masters.

Therefore Jesus did not talk of the progress of the species nor the growth of civilization, He did not trust the world's hope of liberty to a right division of property. But he freed the inner man, that so the outer might become free too. "Ye shall know the truth, and the *truth* shall make you free."

I. The truth that liberates.
II. The liberty which truth gives.

The truth which Christ taught was chiefly on these three points — God: Man: Immortality.

1. God. Blot out the thought of God, a Living Person, and life becomes mean, existence unmeaning,

the universe dark, and resolve is left without a stay, aspiration and duty without a support.

The Son exhibited God as Love: and so that fearful bondage of the mind to the necessity of Fate was broken. A living Lord had made the world; and its dark and unintelligible mystery meant good, not evil. He manifested Him as a Spirit; and if so, the only worship that could please Him must be a spirit's worship. Not by sacrifices is God pleased: nor by droned litanies and liturgies: nor by fawning and flattery: nor is His wrath bought off by blood. Thus was the chain of superstition rent asunder; for superstition is wrong views of God; exaggerated or inadequate; and wrong conceptions of the way to please Him.

And so when the woman of Samaria brought the conversation to that old ecclesiastical question about consecrated buildings, whether on Mount Gerizim or on Mount Moriah, God was the more acceptably adored, He cut the whole conversation short by the enunciation of a single truth: "God is a Spirit, and they that worship Him must worship Him in spirit and in truth."

2. Truth respecting man.

We are a mystery to ourselves. Go to any place where the nations have brought together their wealth and their inventions, and before the victories of mind you stand in reverence. Then stop to look at the passing crowds who have attained that civilization. Think of their low aims, their mean lives, their conformation only a little higher than that of brute creatures, and a painful sense of degradation steals upon you. So great, and yet so mean! And so of individuals. There is not one here whose feelings have not been deeper than we can fathom — nor one who would venture to tell out to his brother man the mean, base thoughts that have crossed his heart during the last hour. Now this riddle He solved — He looked on man as fallen, but magnificent in his ruin. We, catching that thought from Him, speak as He spoke. But none that were born of woman ever felt this or lived this like him. Beneath the vilest outside He saw this — A human soul, capable of endless growth: and thence He treated with what for want of a better term we may call respect, all who approached Him; not because they were titled Rabbis, or rich Pharisees, but because they were men.

Here was a germ for freedom. It is not the shackle on the wrist that constitutes the slave — but the loss of self-respect — to be treated as degraded till he feels degraded — to be subjected to the lash till he believes that he deserves the lash; and liberty is to suspect and yet reverence self: to suspect the tendency which leaves us ever on the brink of fall: to reverence that within us which is allied to God, redeemed by God the Son, and made a temple of the Holy Ghost.

Perhaps we have seen an insect or reptile imprisoned in wood or stone. How it got there is unknown — how the particles of wood in years, or of stone in ages, grew round it, is a mystery, but not a greater mystery than the question of how man became incarcerated in evil. At last the day of emancipation came. The axe stroke was given: and the light came in, and the warmth: and the gauze wings expanded, and the eye looked bright: and the living Thing stepped forth, and you saw that there was not its home. Its home was the free air of heaven.

Christ taught that truth of the human soul. It is not in its right place. It never is in its right place in the dark prison-house of sin. Its home is freedom, and the breath of God's life.

3. Truth respecting immortality.

He taught that this life is not all: that it is only a miserable state of human infancy. He taught that in words: by His life, and by His Resurrection.

This, again, was freedom. If there be a faith that cramps and enslaves the soul, it is the idea that this life is all. If there be one that expands and elevates, it is the thought of immortality: and this, observe, is something quite distinct from the selfish desire of happiness. It is not to enjoy, but to *be* that we long for. To enter into more and higher life: a craving which we can only part with when we sink below humanity, and forfeit it.

This was the martyr's strength. They were tortured, not accepting deliverance, that they might attain a better Resurrection. In that hope, and the knowledge of that truth, they were free from the fear of pain and death.

II. The nature of the liberty which truth gives.

1. Political freedom.

It was our work, last Sunday, to show that Christianity does not directly interfere with political questions. But we should have only half done our work, if we had not also learned that, mediately and indirectly, it must influence them. Christ's gospel did not promise political freedom, yet it gave it: more surely than conqueror, reformer, or patriot, that gospel will bring about a true liberty at last.

This, not by theories nor by schemes of constitutions, but by the revelations of Truths. God a Spirit: man His child; redeemed and sanctified. Before that spiritual equality, all distinctions between peer and peasant, monarch and labourer, privileged and unprivileged, vanish. A better man, or a wiser man than I, is in my presence, and I feel it a mockery to be reminded that I am his superior in rank.

Let us hold that truth; let us never weary of proclaiming it: and the truth shall make us free at last.

2. Mental independence.

Slavery is that which cramps powers. The worst slavery is that which cramps the noblest powers. Worse therefore than he who manacles the hands and feet, is he who puts fetters on the mind, and pretends to demand than men shall think, and believe, and feel thus and thus, because others so believed, and thought, and felt before.

In Judæa life was become a set of forms, and religion a congeries of traditions. One living word from the lips of Christ, and the mind of the world was free.

Later, a mountain mass of superstition had gathered round the Church, atom by atom, and grain by grain. Men said that the soul was saved by doing and believing what the priesthood taught. Then the heroes of the Reformation spoke. They said the soul of man is saved by the grace of God: a much more credible hypothesis. Once more the mind of the world was free: and free by Truth.

There is a tendency in the masses always to think — not what is true, but — what is respectable, correct, orthodox: Is that authorized? we ask. It comes partly from cowardice, partly from indolence: from habit: from imitation: from the uncertainty and darkness of all moral truths, and the dread of timid minds to plunge into the investigation of them. Now, truth known and believed respecting God and man, frees from this, by warning of individual responsibility. But responsibility is personal. It cannot be delegated to another, and thrown off upon a church. Before God, face to face, each soul must stand, to give account.

Do not, however, confound mental independence with mental pride. It may, it ought to co-exist with the deepest humility. For that mind alone is free which, conscious ever of its own feebleness, feeling hourly its own liability to err, turning thankfully to light from whatever side it may come, does yet refuse to give up that right, with which God has invested it of judging or to abrogate its own responsibility, and so, humbly, and even awfully, resolves to have an opinion, a judgment, a decision of its own.

3. Superiority to temptation.

It is not enough to define the liberty which Christ promises as freedom from sin. Many circumstances will exempt from sin which do not yet confer that liberty "where the Spirit of the Lord is." Childhood, paralysis, ill health, the impotence of old age, may remove the capacity and even the desire of transgression: but the child, the paralytic, the old man, are not free through the Truth.

Therefore, to this definition we must add, that one whom Christ liberates is free by his own will. It is not that he would and cannot: but that he can, and will not. Christian liberty is right will, sustained by love, and made firm by faith in Christ.

This may be seen by considering the opposite of liberty — moral bondage. Go to the intemperate man in the morning, when his head aches, his hand trembles, his throat burns, and his whole frame is relaxed and unstrung: he is ashamed, hates his sin, would not do it. Go to him at night, when the power of habit is on him like a spell, and he obeys the mastery of his craving. He can use the language of Rom. vii.: "That which he would, he does not; but the evil that he hates, that does he." Observe, he is not in possession of a true self. It is not he, but sin which dwelleth in him, that does it. A power which is not himself, which is not he, commands him against himself. And that is Slavery.

This is a gross case, but in every more refined instance the slavery is just as real. Wherever a man would and cannot, there is servitude. He may be unable to control his expenditure, to rouse his indolence, to check his imagination. Well — he is not free. He may boast, as the Jews did, that he is Abraham's son, or any other great man's son: that he belongs to a free country: that he never was in bondage to any man; but free in the freedom of the Son he is not.

4. Superiority to fear.

Fear enslaves, courage liberates — and that always. Whatever a man intensely dreads, that brings him into bondage, if it be above the fear of God, and the reverence of duty. The apprehension of pain, the fear of death, the dread of the world's laugh, of poverty, or the loss of reputation, enslave alike.

From such fear Christ frees, and through the power of the truths I have spoken of. He who lives in the habitual contemplation of immortality cannot be in bondage to time, or enslaved by transitory temptations. I do not say he *will* not, "he *cannot* sin," saith the Scripture, while that faith is living. He who feels his soul's dignity, knowing what he is and who, redeemed by God the Son, and freed by God the Spirit, cannot cringe, nor pollute himself, nor be mean. He who aspires to gaze undazzled on the intolerable brightness of that One before whom Israel veiled their faces, will scarcely quail before any earthly fear.

This is not picture-painting. This is not declamation. These are things that have been. There have been men on this earth of God's, of whom it was simply true that it was easier to turn the sun from its course than them from the paths of honour. There have been men like John the Baptist, who could speak the truth which had made their own spirits free, with the axe above their neck. There have been men, redeemed in their inmost being by Christ, on whom tyrants and mobs have done their worst, and when, like Stephen, the stones crashed in upon their brain, or when their flesh hissed and crackled in the flames, were calmly superior to it all. The power of evil had laid its shackles on the flesh: but the mind, and the soul, and the heart were free.

We conclude with two inferences:

1. To cultivate the love of truth. I do not mean veracity: that is another thing. Veracity is the correspondence between a proposition and a man's belief. Truth is the correspondence of the proposition with fact. The love of truth is the love of realities: the determination to rest upon facts, and not on semblances. Take an illustration of the way in which the habit of cultivating truth is got. Two boys see a misshapen,

hideous object in the dark. One goes up to the cause of his terror, examines it, learns what it is; he knows the truth, and the truth has made him free. The other leaves it in mystery and unexplained vagueness, and is a slave for life to superstitious and indefinite terrors. Romance, prettiness, "dim religious light," awe and mystery — these are not the atmosphere of Christ's gospel of liberty. Base the heart on facts. The truth alone can make you free.

2. See what a Christian is. Our society is divided into two classes. Those who are daring, inquisitive, but restrained by no reverence, and kept back by little religion. Those who may be called religious: but, with all their excellences, we cannot help feeling that the elements of their character are feminine rather than masculine, and that they have no grasp or manly breadth, that they hold on feeling rather than on truth.

Now, see what a Christian is, drawn by the hand of Christ. He is a man on whose clear and open brow God has set the stamp of truth: one whose very eye beams bright with honour; in whose very look and bearing you may see freedom, manliness, veracity: a brave man — a noble man — frank, generous, true; with, it may be, many faults: — whose freedom may take the form of impetuosity or rashness, but the form of meanness never. Young Men! if you have been deterred from religion by its apparent feebleness and narrowness, remember — It is a manly thing to be a Christian.

XIX.

Preached at the Autumn Assizes held at Lewes, 1852.

THE KINGDOM OF THE TRUTH.

JOHN xviii. 37. — "Pilate therefore said unto him, Art thou a king then? Jesus answered, Thou sayest that I am a king. To this end was I born, and for this cause came I into the world, that I should bear witness unto the truth. Every one that is of the truth heareth my voice."

THE Church is the kingdom of God on earth, and the whole fabric of the Christian Religion rests on the monarchy of Christ. The Hebrew prisoner who stood before the Roman Judge claimed to be the King of men: and eighteen centuries have only verified his claim. There is not a man bearing the Christian name, who does not in one form or another acknowledge Him to be the Sovereign of his soul.

The question therefore at once suggests itself — On what title does this claim rest?

Besides the title on which the Messiah grounded His pretensions to be the Ruler of a kingdom, three are conceivable. The title of force: the title of prescriptive authority: or the title of incontrovertible reasoning.

Had the Messiah founded His kingdom upon the basis of Force, He would simply have been a rival of the Cæsars. The imperial power of Rome rested on that Principle. This was all that Pilate meant at first by the question, "Art thou a king?" As a Roman he had no other conception of rule. Right well had Rome fulfilled her mission as the iron kingdom which was to command by strength, and give to the world the principles of Law. But that kingdom was wasting when these words were spoken. For seven hundred years had the empire been building itself up. It gave way at last, and was crumbled into fragments by its own ponderous massiveness. To use the language of the prophet Daniel, miry clay had mixed with the kingdom of iron, and the softer nations which had been absorbed into it broke down its once invincible strength; by corrupting and enervating its citizens: the conquerors of the world dropped the sword from a grasp grown nerveless. The Empire of strength was passing away; for no kingdom founded on force is destined to permanence. "They that take the sword shall perish with the sword."

Before Pontius Pilate Christ distinctly disclaimed this Right of Force as the foundation of his sovereignty. "If my kingdom were of this world, then would my servants fight: but now is my kingdom not from hence." (v. 36.)

The next conceivable basis of a universal kingdom is prescriptive authority. The scribes and priests who waited outside for their victim conceived of such a kingdom. They *had* indeed already an ecclesiastical kingdom which dated back far beyond the origin of Rome. They claimed to rule on a title such as this — "It is written." But neither on this title did the Saviour found His claim. He spoke lightly of institutions which were venerable from age. He contravened opinions which were grey with the hoar of ages. It may be, that at times He *defended* Himself on the authority of Moses, by showing that what He taught was not in opposition to Moses; but it is observable that He never rested His claims as a Teacher, or as the Messiah, on that foundation. The scribes fell back on this — "It has been said;" or, "It is written." Christ taught, as the men of His day remarked, on an authority very different from that of the scribes. Not even on His own authority — He did not claim that His words should be recognised because He said them: but because they were true. "If I say the truth, why do ye not believe me?" Prescription — personal authority — these were not the basis of His kingdom.

One more possible title remains. He might have claimed to rule over men on the ground of incontrovertible demonstration of His principles. This was the ground taken by every philosopher who was the founder of a sect. Apparently, after the failure of his first guess, Pilate thought in the second surmise that this was what Jesus meant by calling Himself a king. When he heard of a kingdom, he thought he had before him a rival of Cæsar: but when Truth was named, he seems to have fancied that he was called to try a rival of the philosophers: some new candidate for a system: some new pretender of a truth which was to dethrone its rival system.

This seems to be implied in the bitter question, "What is Truth?" For the history of opinion in those days was like the history of opinion in our own: religions against religions, philosophies against philosophies: religion and philosophy opposed to one another: the opinion of to-day dethroned by the opinion of to-morrow: the heterodoxy of this age reckoned the orthodoxy of the succeeding one. And Pilate, feeling the vainness and the presumption of these pretensions, having lived to see failure after failure of systems which pretended to teach That which is, smiled bitterly at the enthusiast who again asserted confidently His claims to have discovered the undiscoverable. There broke from his lips a bitter, half-sarcastic, half-sad exclamation of hopeless scepticism, "What is Truth?"

And, indeed, had the Redeemer claimed this — to overthrow the doctrine of the Porch and of the Academy, and to enthrone Christianity as a Philosophy of Life upon their ruins, by argument, that sceptical cry would have been not ill-timed.

In these three ways have men attempted the Propagation of the Gospel. By force, when the Church ruled by persecution — by prescriptive authority, when she claimed infallibility, or any modification of infallibility in the Popery of Rome or the Popery of the pulpit — by Reasoning, in the age of "evidences," when she only asked to have her proofs brought forward and calmly heard, pledged herself to rule the world by the conviction of the understanding, and laid the foundations of rationalism deep and broad. Let us hear the claim of the King Himself. He rested His royal rights on His testimony to the Truth. "Thou sayest, for I am a King (a more correct translation); to this end was I born, to bear witness to the Truth." The mode in which the subjects of the kingdom were brought beneath His sway was by assimilation. "Every one that is of the Truth, heareth My voice." These, then, are our points.

I. The basis of the kingly rule of Christ.
II. The qualifications of the subjects of the kingdom.

I. The basis of the kingly rule of Christ.

Christ is a king in virtue of His being a witness to the truth. "Thou sayest right, To this end was I born, and for this cause came I into the world, that I should bear witness unto the truth."

Truth is used here in a sense equivalent to reality — for "truth" substitute reality, and it will become more intelligible. For "the truth" is an ambiguous expression, limited in its application, meaning often nothing more than a theological creed, or a few dogmas of a creed which this or that party have agreed to call "the truth." It would indeed fritter down the majesty of the Redeemer's life, to say that He was a witness for the truth of any number of theological dogmas. Himself — His Life, were a witness to Truth in the sense of Reality. The realities of life — the realities of the universe — to these His every act and word bore testimony. He was as much a witness to the truth of the purity of domestic life as to the truth of the doctrine of the Incarnation: to the truth of Goodness being identical with Greatness as much as to the doctrine of the Trinity — and more — His mind corresponded with Reality as the dial with the sun.

Again, in being a witness to Reality, we are to understand something very much deeper than the statement that He spoke truly. There is a wide difference between truthfulness and mere veracity. Veracity implies a correspondence between words and thoughts: truthfulness, a correspondence between thoughts and realities. To be veracious, it is only necessary that a man give utterance to his convictions: to be true, it is needful that his convictions have affinity with Fact.

Let us take some illustrations of this distinction. The Prophet tells of men who put sweet for bitter, and bitter for sweet: who called good evil, and evil good; yet these were veracious men; for to them evil *was* good, and bitter *was* sweet: — There was a correspondence between their opinions and their words: this was veracity. But there was no correspondence between their opinions and eternal Fact: this was untruthfulness. They spoke their opinions truly, but their opinions were not true. The Pharisees in the time of Christ were men of veracity. What they thought they said. They thought that Christ was an impostor. They believed that to tithe mint, anise, and cummin, was as acceptable to God as to be just, and merciful, and true. It was their conviction that they were immeasurably better than publicans and profligates: yet veracious as they were, the title perpetually affixed to them is, "Ye hypocrites. The life they led being a false life, is called, in the phraseology of the Apostle John, a lie.

If a man speak a careless slander against another, believing it, he has not sinned against veracity: but the carelessness which has led him into so grave an error effectually bars his claim to clear truthfulness. He is a veracious witness, but not a true one. Or a man may have taken up second-hand, indolently, religious views: may believe them: defend them vehemently, — Is he a man of truth? Has he bowed before the majesty of truth with that patient, reverential humbleness which is the mark of those who love her?

Imagination has pictured to itself a domain in which every one who enters should be compelled to speak only what he thought, and pleased itself by calling such domain the Palace of Truth. A palace of veracity, if you will; but no temple of the truth: — a place where every one would be at liberty to utter his own crude unrealities — to bring forth his delusions, mistakes, half-formed hasty judgments: where the depraved ear would reckon discord harmony: and the depraved eye mistake colour: the depraved moral taste take Herod or Tiberius for a king, and shout, beneath the Redeemer's Cross, "Himself He cannot save." A temple of the truth? Nay, only a palace echoing with veracious falsehoods: a Babel of confused sounds, in which egotism would rival egotism, and truth would be each man's own lie. Far, far more is implied here than that the Son of Man spoke veraciously, in saying that He was a Witness to the Truth.

Again, when it is said that He was a Witness to the Truth, it is implied that His very Being, here, *manifested* to the world Divine realities. Human nature is but meant to be a witness to the Divine; the true Humanity is a manifestation — or reflection of God. And that is Divine Humanity, in which the Humanity is a perfect representation of the Divine. "We behold," says the Apostle Paul, "in Christ, as in a glass, the glory of the Lord." And, to borrow and carry on the metaphor, the difference between Christ and other men is this; they are imperfect reflections, He a perfect one, of God.

There are mirrors which are concave, which magnify the thing that they reflect: there are mirrors convex, which diminish it. And we, in like manner, represent the Divine in a false, distorted way. Fragments of truth torn out of connection: snatches of harmony joined without unity. We exaggerate and diminish till all becomes untrue. We bring forth our own fancies, our own idiosyncrasies, our own imaginations: and the image of God can be no longer recognised.

In One alone has the Divine been so blended with the Human, that, as the ocean mirrors every star and every tint of blue upon the sky, so was the earthly Life of Christ the Life of God on earth.

Now, observe, that the perfection of humanity consists in faithful imitation of, or witness borne to, the Mind and Life of God. Whoever has studied and understood the Life of Christ will have remarked, not without surprise, that the whole principle of His existence was the habit of unceasing imitation. Listen to a few instances of this.

"The Son can do nothing of Himself, but that which He seeth the Father do." "The words which I speak I speak not of myself, but the Father which is with me, He doeth the works." Do we remember the strange and startling principle on which He defends His infraction of the literal, legal Sabbath? "My Father worketh hitherto, and I work." God the Father works all the Sabbath-day. So may Man, His Son. Do we recollect the ground on which He enforces forgiveness of injuries? A strange ground surely, which would never have occurred except to One whose life was habitual imitation. "Love your enemies: do good to them that hate you, and pray for them which despitefully use you and persecute you: that ye may be the children of (that is, resemble) your Father. . . for He sendeth His rain upon the just and upon the unjust."

This, then, is Man's: this was the Son of Man's relation to the Truth. Man is but a learner — a devout recipient of a revelation — here to listen with open ear devoutly for that which he shall hear; to gaze and watch for that which He shall see. Man can do no more. He cannot create Truth: he can only bear witness to it: he has no proud right of private judgment: he can only listen and report that which is in the universe. If he does not repeat and witness to that, he speaketh of his own, and forthwith ceaseth to be true. He is a liar and the *father* of it, because he creates it. Each man in his vocation is in the world to do this; — as truly as it was said by Christ, may it be said by each of us, even by those from whose trades and professions it seems most alien, "To this end was I born, and for this cause came I into the world, to bear witness to the Truth."

The architect is here to be a witness. He succeeds only so far as he is a witness, and a true one. The lines and curves, the acanthus on his column, the proportions, all are successful and beautiful, only so far as they are true: the report of an eye which has lain open to God's world. If he build his lighthouse to resist the storm, the law of imitation bids him build it after the shape of the spreading oak which has defied the tempest. If man construct the ship which is to cleave the waters, calculation or imitation builds it on the model upon which the Eternal Wisdom has already constructed the fish's form. The artist is a witness to the truth; or he will never attain the beautiful. So is the agriculturist; or he will never reap a harvest. So is the statesman, building up a nation's polity on the principles which time has proved true, or else all his work crumbles down in revolution: for national revolution is only the Divine Rejection stamped on the social falsehood — which cannot stand. In every department of life man must work truly — as a witness. He is born for that, nothing else: and nothing else can he do. Man the Son can do nothing of Himself, but that which He seeth God the Father do.

This was the Saviour's title to be a King; and His kingdom formed itself upon this law: "Every one that is of the Truth heareth my voice;" that Eternal law which makes truth assimilate all that is congenial to itself. Truth is like Life: whatever lives absorbs into itself all that is congenial. The leaf that trembles in the wind assimilates the light of heaven to make its colour, and the sap of the parent stem — innumerable influences from heaven, and earth, and air, to make up its beautiful being.

So grew the Church of Christ: round Him as a centre, attracted by the truth: all that had in it harmony with His Divine Life and words, grew to Him (by gradual accretions): clung to Him as the iron to the magnet. All that were of His Spirit believed: all that had in them the Spirit of Sacrifice were attracted to His Cross. "I, if I be lifted up, will draw all men unto me."

He taught not by elaborate trains of argument, like a scribe or a phiosopher: He uttered His truths rather as detached intuitions, recognised by intuition, to be judged only by being felt. For instance, "Blessed are the pure in heart: for they shall see God." "It is more blessed to give than to receive." "Blessed are ye when men shall revile you, and persecute you." Prove that — by force — by authority — by argument — you cannot. It suffices that a man reply, "It is not so to me: it is more blessed to receive than it is to give." You have no reply: if he be not of the truth, you cannot make him hear Christ's voice. The truth of Christ is true to the unselfish: a falsehood to the selfish. They that are of the truth, like Him, hear His voice: and it you ask the Christian's proof of the truth of such things, he has no other than this, — It is true to me, as any other intuitive truth is true — equals are equal, because my mind is so constituted that they seem so perforce. Purity is good, because my heart is so made that it feels it to be good.

Brother men, — the truer you are, the humbler, the nobler, the more will you feel Christ to be your King. You may be very little able to prove the King's Divine genealogy, or to appreciate those claims to your allegiance which arise out of His Eternal generation: but He will be your Sovereign and your Lord by that affinity of character which compels you to acknowledge His words and life to be Divine. "He that receiveth His testimony hath set to his seal that God is true."

II. We pass to the consideration of the qualification of the subjects of the Empire of the truth. Who are they that are of the Truth?

1. The first qualification is to *be* true: "He that *is* of the truth heareth My Voice." Truth lies in character. Christ did not simply *speak* truth: He *was* truth: true through and through; for truth is a thing, not of words, but of Life and Being. None but a Spirit can be true.

For example. The friends of Job spoke words of truth. Scarcely a maxim which they uttered could be impugned: cold, hard, theological verities: but verities out of place, in that place cruel and untrue. Job spoke many words not strictly accurate — hasty, impetuous, blundering, wrong; but the whirlwind came, and, before the Voice of God the veracious falsehoods were swept into endless nothingness: the *true* man, wrong, perplexed, in verbal error, stood firm: he was true though his sentences were not: turned to the truth as the sunflower to the sun: as the darkened plant imprisoned in the vault turns towards the light, struggling to solve the fearful enigma of his existence.

Job was a servant of the truth, being true in character.

2. The next qualification is integrity. But by integrity I do not mean simply sincerity or honesty; integrity rather according to the meaning of the word as its derivation interprets it — entireness — wholeness — soundness; that which Christ means when He says, "If thine eye be single or sound, thy whole body shall be full of light."

This integrity extends through the entireness or wholeness of the character. It is found in small matters as well as great; for the allegiance of the soul to truth is tested by small things rather than by those which are more important. There is many a man who would lose his life rather than perjure himself in a court of justice, whose life is yet a tissue of small insincerities. We think that we hate falsehood when we are only hating the consequences of falsehood. We resent hypocrisy, and treachery, and calumny, not because they are untrue, but because they harm us. We hate the false calumny, but we are half pleased with the false praise. It is evidently not the element of untruth here that is displeasing, but the element of harmfulness. Now he is a man of integrity who hates untruth *as* untruth: who resents the smooth and polished falsehood of society which does no harm: who turns in indignation from the glittering whitened lie of sepulchral Pharisaism which injures no one. Integrity recoils from deceptions which men would almost smile to hear called deception. To a moral, pure mind, the artifices in every department of life are painful: the stained wood which passes for a more firm and costly material in a building, and deceives the eye by seeming what it is not, marble: the painting which is intended to be taken for a reality: the gilding which is meant to pass for gold; and the glass which is worn to look like jewels; for there is a moral feeling and a truthfulness in architecture, in painting, and in dress, as well as in the market-place, and in the senate, and in the judgment-hall.

"These are trifles." Yes, these are trifles — but it is just these trifles which go to the formation of character. He that is habituated to deceptions and artificialities in trifles, will try in vain to be true in matters of importance: for truth is a thing of habit rather than of will. You cannot in any given case, by any sudden and single effort, will to be true, if the habit of your life has been insincerity. And it is a fearful question, and a difficult one, how all these things, the atmosphere which we breathe of our daily life, may sap the very foundations of the power of becoming a servant of the truth. Life becomes fictitious: and it passes into religion, till our very religion bases itself upon a figment too. We are not righteous, but we expect God to make believe that we are righteous, in virtue of some peculiar doctrines which we hold; and so our very righteousness becomes the fictitious righteousness of the Scribes and Pharisees, instead of the righteousness which is by faith, the righteousness of those who are the children of the kingdom of the truth.

3. Once more. He alone is qualified to be the subject of the King who *does* the truth. Christianity joins

two things inseparably together: acting truly, and perceiving truly. Every day the eternal nature of that principle becomes more certain. If any man will do His will, he shall know of the doctrine whether it be of God.

It is a perilous thing to separate feeling from acting; to have learnt to feel rightly without acting rightly. It is a danger to which, in a refined and polished age, we are peculiarly exposed. The romance, the poem, and the sermon, teach us how to feel. Our feelings are delicately correct. But the danger is this: — feeling is given to lead to action; if feeling be suffered to awake without passing into duty, the character becomes untrue. When the emergency for real action comes, the feeling is, as usual, produced: but accustomed as it is to rise in fictitious circumstances without action, neither will it lead on to action in the real ones. "We pity wretchedness and shun the wretched." We utter sentiments, just, honourable, refined, lofty — but somehow, when a truth presents itself in the shape of a duty, we are unable to perform it. And so such characters become by degrees like the artificial pleasure-grounds of bad taste, in which the waterfall does not fall, and the grotto offers only the refreshment of an imaginary shade, and the green hill does not strike the skies, and the tree does not grow. Their lives are a sugared crust of sweetness trembling over black depths of hollowness: more truly still, "whited sepulchres" — fair without to look upon, "within full of all uncleanness."

It is perilous again to separate thinking rightly from acting rightly. He is already half false who speculates on truth and does not do it. Truth is given, not to be contemplated, but to be done. Life is an action — not a thought. And the penalty paid by him who speculates on truth, is that by degrees the very truth he holds becomes to him a falsehood.

There is no truthfulness, therefore, except in the witness borne to God by doing His will — to live the truths we hold, or else they will be not truths at all. It was thus that He witnessed to the truth. He lived it. He spoke no touching truths for sentiment to dwell on, or thought to speculate upon. Truth with Him was a matter of life and death. He perilled His life upon the words He said. If He were true, the life of men was a painted life, and the woes he denounced unflinchingly would fall upon the Pharisees. But if *they* were true, or even strong, His portion in this life was the Cross.

Who is a true man? He who does the truth; and never holds a principle on which he is not prepared in any hour to act, and in any hour to risk the consequences of holding it.

I make in conclusion one remark. The kingly character of truth is exhibited strikingly in the calmness of the bearing of the Son of Man before His judge. Veracity is not necessarily dignified. There is a vulgar effrontery — a spirit of defiance which taunts, and braves, and challenges condemnation. It marks the man who is conscious of sincerity, but of nothing higher — whose confidence is in himself and his own honesty, and who is absorbed in the feeling, "I speak the truth and am a martyr." Again, the man of mere veracity is often violent, for what he says rests upon his own assertion; and vehemence of assertion is the only addition he can make to it. Such was the violence of Paul before Ananias. He was indignant at the injustice of being smitten contrary to the law; and the powerlessness of his position, the hopelessness of redress, joined to a conviction of the truth of what he said, produced that vehemence.

It has been often remarked that there is a great difference between theological and scientific controversy. Theologians are proverbially vituperative: because it is a question of veracity: the truth of their views, their moral perceptions, their intellectual acumen. There exists no test but argument on which they can fall back. If argument fails, all fails. But the man of science stands calmly on the facts of the universe. He is based upon reality. All the opposition and controversy in the world cannot alter facts, nor prevent the facts being manifest at last. He can be calm because he is a witness for the Truth.

In the same way, but in a sense far deeper and more sacred, the Son of Man stood *calm*, rooted in the Truth. There was none of the egotism of self-conscious veracity in those placid, confident, dignified replies. This was not the feeling — "I hold the truth," — but "I am witness to the truth." They might spit upon Him — kill Him — crucify Him — give His ashes to the winds — they could not alter the Truth by which He stood. Was not that His own feeling? "Heaven and earth shall pass away, but My words shall not pass away."

There was the kingly dignity of One who, in Life and Death, stood firm on Truth as on a Rock.

In the name of Christ, I respectfully commend these thoughts for the special consideration of the present week, to those who will be pledged by oath to witness to the whole truth they know, and nothing but the truth: to those who, permitted by the merciful spirit of English jurisprudence, to watch that their client, if condemned, shall be condemned only according to the law — are yet not justified by the spirit of the life of Christ in falsifying or obscuring facts; and who, owing a high duty to a client, owe one yet higher to the Truth: and, lastly, to those whom the severe intellectual, and much more, moral training of the English bar has qualified for the high office of disentangling truth from the mazes of conflicting testimony.

From the trial-hour of Christ — from the Cross of the Son of God — there arises the principle to which all His life bore witness, that the first lesson of Christian life is this, Be true — and the second this, Be true — and the third this, Be true.

XX.

Preached November 7, 1852.

THE SCEPTICISM OF PILATE.

JOHN xviii. 38. — "Pilate said unto him, What is truth?"

THE lesson which we are to draw from this verse must depend upon the view we take of the spirit in which the words were spoken. Some of the best commentators conceive them to have been words of mockery: and such in the great Lord Bacon's view. "'What is truth?' said jesting Pilate, and would not wait for a reply."

In all deference to such authority, we cannot believe that this sentence was spoken in jest. In Pilate's whole conduct there is no trace of such a tone. It betrays throughout much of uncertainty, nothing of lightness. He was cruelly tormented with the perplexity of efforts to save his prisoner. He risked his own reputation. He pronounced Him, almost with vehemence, innocent. He even felt awe, and was afraid of Him. In such a frame of mind, mockery was impossible.

Let us try to comprehend the character of the man who asked this question. His character will help us to judge the tone in which he asked. And his character, the character of his mind and life, are clear enough from the few things recorded of him. He first hears what the people have to say; then asks the opinion of the priests — then comes back to Jesus — goes again to the priests and people — lends his ear — listens to the ferocity on the one hand, and feels the beauty on the other, balancing between them; and then he becomes bewildered, as a man of the world is apt to do who has had no groundwork of religious education, and hears superficial discussions on religious matters, and superficial charges, and superficial slanders, till he knows not what to think. What *could* come out of such procedure? Nothing but that cheerlessness of soul to which certainty respecting anything and everything here on earth seems unattainable. This is the exact mental state which we call scepticism.

Out of that mood, when he heard the enthusiast before him speak of a Kingdom of the Truth, there broke a sad, bitter, sarcastic sigh, "What is Truth?" Who knows anything about it? Another discoverer of the undiscoverable! *Jesting* Pilate! with Pilate the matter was beyond a jest. It was not a question put for the sake of information: for he went immediately out, and did not stay for information. It was not put for the sake of ridicule, for he went out to say, "I find no fault in Him." Sarcasm there was perhaps: but it was that mournful, bitter sarcasm which hides inward unrest in sneering words: that sad irony whose very laugh rings of inward wretchedness.

We shall pursue, from this question of Pilate, two lines of thought.

I. The causes of Pilate's scepticism.

II. The way appointed for discovering what is Truth.

I. The causes — and among these I name,

1st, Indecision of character.

Pilate's whole behaviour was a melancholy exhibition. He was a thing set up for the world's pity. See how he acts: he first throws the blame on the priests

— and then acknowledges that all responsibility is his own: washes his hands before the multitude, saying, "I am innocent of the blood of this just person. See ye to it." And then — "Knowest thou not that *I* have power to crucify thee, and power to release thee?" He pronounces Jesus innocent; and then, with wondrous inconsistency, delivers Him to be scourged: yields Him up to be crucified, and then tries every underhand expedient to save Him.

What is there in all this but vacillation of character lying at the root of unsettledness of opinion? Here is a man knowing the right and doing the wrong — not willing to do an act of manifest injustice if he can avoid it, but hesitating to prevent it, for fear of a charge against himself — pitiably vacillating because his hands were tied by the consciousness of past guilt and personal danger. How could such a man be certain about anything? What could a mind, wavering, unstable, like a feather on the wind, know or believe of solid, stable truth, which altereth not, but remaineth like a rock amidst the vicissitudes of the ages and the changeful fashions of the minds of men? "A double-minded man is unstable in all his ways." "He that is *of* the truth, heareth the voice of truth." To the untrue man all things are untrue. To the vacillating man, who cannot know his own mind, all things seem alterable, changeful, unfixed; just as to the man tossed at sea, all things motionless in themselves seem to move round, upwards, downwards, or around, according to his own movements.

2nd, Falseness to his own convictions.

Pilate had a conviction that Jesus was innocent. Instead of acting at once on that, he went and parleyed.

He argued and debated till the practical force of the conviction was unsettled.

Now let us distinguish: I do not say that a man is never to re-examine a question once settled. A great Christian writer, whose works are very popular, has advised that when a view has once been arrived at as true, it should be as it were laid on the shelf, and never again looked on as an open question: but surely this is false. A young man of twenty-three, with such light as he has, forms his views: is he never to have more light? Is he never to open again the questions which his immature mind has decided on once? Is he never in manhood, with manhood's data and manhood's experience, to modify, or even reverse, what once seemed the very Truth itself? Nay, my brethren — the weak pride of consistency, the cowardice which dares not say I have been wrong all my life, the false anxiety which is fostered to be true to our principles rather than to make sure that our principles are true, all this would leave in Romanism the man who is born a Romanist. It is not so: the best and bravest have struggled from error into truth: they listened to their honest doubts, and tore up their old beliefs by the very roots.

Distinguish however. A man may unsettle the verdict of his intellect: it is at his peril that he tampers with the convictions of his conscience. Every opinion and view must remain an open question, freely to be tried with fresh light. But there are Eternal Truths of Right and Wrong, such as the plain moralities and instinctive decencies of social life, upon which it is perilous to argue. There are plain cases of immediate duty where it is only safe to act at once.

Now Pilate was false to his *conscience*. His conviction was that Jesus was innocent. It was not a matter of speculation or probability at all, nor a matter in which fresh evidence was even expected, but a case sifted and examined thoroughly. The Pharisees are persecuting a guiltless man. His claims to royalty are not the civil crime which they would make out. Every charge has fallen to the ground. The clear mind of the Roman Procurator saw that, as in sunlight, and he did not try to invalidate that judicial conviction. He tried to get rid of the clear duty which resulted from it. Now it is a habit such as this which creates the temper of scepticism.

I address men of a speculative turn of mind. There is boundless danger in all inquiry which is merely curious. When a man brings a clear and practised intellect to try questions, by the answer to which he does not mean to rule his conduct, let him not marvel if he feels, as life goes on, a sense of desolation; existence a burden, and all uncertain. It is the law of his human nature which binds; for truth is for the heart rather than the intellect. If it is not *done* it becomes unreal — as gloomily unreal and as dreamily impalpable as it was to Pilate.

3rd. The third cause of Pilate's scepticism was the taint of the worldly temper of his day. Pilate had been a public man. He knew life: had mixed much with the world's business, and the world's politics: had come across a multiplicity of opinions, and gained a smattering of them all. He knew how many philosophies and religions pretended to an exclusive possession of Truth; and how the pretensions of each were overthrown by another. And his incredulity was but a specimen of the scepticism fashionable in his day. The polished scepticism of a polished, educated Roman, a sagacious man of the world, too much behind the scenes of public life to trust professions of goodness or disinterestedness, or to believe in enthusiasm and a sublime life. And his merciful language, and his desire to save Jesus, was precisely the liberalism current in our day as in his — an utter disbelief in the truths of a world unseen, but at the same time an easy, careless toleration, a half-benevolent, half-indolent unwillingness to molest the poor dreamers who chose to believe in such superstitions.

This is the superficial liberalism which is contracted in public life. Public men contract a rapid way of discussing and dismissing the deepest questions: never going deep: satisfied with the brilliant flippancy which treats religious beliefs as phases of human delusion, seeing the hollowness of the characters around them, and believing that all is hollow: and yet not without their moments of superstition, as when Pilate was afraid, hearing of a Son of God, and connecting it doubtless with the heathen tales of gods who had walked this earth in visible flesh and blood; which he had laughed at, and which he now for one moment suspected might be true: not without their moments of horrible insecurity, when the question, "What is Truth?" is not a brilliant sarcasm, but a sarcasm on themselves, on human life, on human nature, wrung out of the loneliest and darkest bewilderment that can agonize a human soul.

To such a character Jesus would not explain His Truth. He gave no reply: He held His peace. God's Truth is too sacred to be expounded to superficial worldliness in its transient fit of earnestness.

4th, Lastly, I assign, as a cause of scepticism, that priestly bigotry which forbids inquiry and makes doubt a crime.

The priests of that day had much to answer for. Consider for a moment the state of things. One — of whom *they* only knew that He was a man of unblemished life — came forward to proclaim the Truth. But it was new: they had never heard such views before: they were quite sure *they* had never taught such, nor sanctioned such: and so they settled that the thing was heresy. He had no accredited ordination. "We know that God spake to Moses: as for this fellow we know not whence He is." Then they proceeded to bind that decision upon others. A man was heard to say, "Why, what evil hath He done?" Small offence enough; but it savoured of a dangerous candour towards a suspected man; and in the priestly estimate, candour is the next step to heresy. "Thou wast altogether born in sin, and dost Thou teach us? and they cast him out of the synagogue." And so again with Pilate: they stifled his soul's rising convictions with threats and penalties. "If thou let this man go, thou art not Cæsar's friend."

This was what they were always doing: they forbade all inquiry, and made doubt of their decision a crime.

Now, the results of this priestcraft were twofold. The first result was seen in the fanaticism of the people, who cried for blood: the second, in the scepticism of Pilate.

And these are the two results which come from all claims to infallibility, and all prohibition of inquiry. They make bigots of the feeble-minded who cannot think: cowardly bigots, who at the bidding of their priests or ministers swell the ferocious cry which forces a government, or a judge, or a bishop, to persecute some opinion which they fear and hate; turning private opinion into civil crime: and they make sceptics of the acute intellects which, like Pilate, see through their fallacies, and like Pilate, too, dare not publish their misgivings.

And it matters not in what form that claim to infallibility is made: whether in the clear, consistent way in which Rome asserts it, or whether in the inconsistent way in which churchmen make it for the church, or religious bodies for their favourite opinions: wherever penalties attach to a conscientious conviction, be they the penalties of the rack and flame, or the penalties of being suspected, and avoided, and slandered, and the slur of heresy affixed to the name, till all men count him dangerous lest they too should be put out of the synogogue — and let every man who is engaged in persecuting any opinion ponder it: these two things must follow — you make fanatics, and you make sceptics; believers you cannot make.

Therefore do we stand by the central protest and truth of Protestantism. There is infallibility nowhere on this earth: not in Rome; not in councils or convocations; not in the Church of England; not in priests; not in ourselves. The soul is thrown in the grandeur of a sublime solitariness on God. Woe to the spirit that stifles its convictions, when priests threaten and the mob which they have maddened cries heresy, and insinuates disloyalty: "Thou art not Cæsar's friend."

II. The mode appointed for discovering the reply to the question, "What is Truth?"

Observe — I do not make our second division that which might seem the natural one — what Truth is. I am not about to be guilty of the presumption of answering the question which Jesus did not answer. Some persons hearing the text might think it to be the duty of any man who took it as a text to preach upon, to lay down what Truth is: and if a minister were so to treat it, he might give you the fragment of Truth which his own poor mind could grasp: and he might call it as the phrase is, *The* Truth, or *The* Gospel: and he might require his hearers to receive it on peril of salvation. And then he would have done as the priests did; and they who lean on other minds would have gone away bigoted: and they who *think* would have smiled, sadly, bitterly, or sarcastically; and gone home to doubt still more, "What *is* truth, and is it to be found?"

No, my brethren; The Truth cannot be compressed into a sermon. The reply to Pilate's question cannot be contained in any verbal form. Think you, that if Christ Himself could have answered that question in a certain number of sentences, He would have spent thirty years of life in witnessing to it? Some men would compress into the limits of one reply, or one discourse, the Truth which it took Christ thirty years to teach, and which He left unfinished for the Spirit to complete.

One word. The Truth is infinite as the firmament above you. In childhood, both seem near and measurable: but with years they grow and grow; and seem further off, and further and grander, and deeper, and vaster, as God Himself; till you smile to remember how you thought you could touch the sky, and blush to recollect the proud and self-sufficient way in which you used to talk of knowing or preaching "The Truth."

And once again: the truth is made up of principles: an inward Life, not any mere formula of words. God's Character: Spiritual worship: the Divine Life in the Soul. How shall I put that into sentences ten or ten thousand? "The words which I speak unto you, they are Truth, and they are *Life*." How could Pilate's question be answered except by a Life? The Truth, then, which Pilate wanted — which you want, and I want — is not the boundless verities, but truth of inward life. Truth for me: Truth enough to guide me in this darkling world: enough to teach me how to live and how to die.

Now — the appointed ways to teach this Truth. They are three: Independence — Humbleness — Action.

First, Independence. Let no man start as if independence savoured of presumption. Protestant independence, they tell us, is pride and self-reliance: but in truth it is nothing more than a deep sense of personal responsibility; a determination to trust in God rather than in man to teach: in God and God's light in the soul. You choose a guide among precipices and glaciers: but you walk for yourself: judge his opinion, though more experienced than your own: overrule it if needs be: use your own strength: rely on your own nerves. That is independence.

You select your own physician, deciding upon the respective claims of men, the most ignorant of whom knows more of the matter than you. You prudently hesitate at times to follow the advice of the one you trust most, yet that is only independence without a particle of presumption.

And so precisely in matters of religious Truth. No man cares for your health as you do: therefore you rely blindly upon none. No man has the keeping of your own soul, or cares for it as you do. For yourself, therefore, you inquire and think, and you refuse to delegate that work to bishop, priest, or church. Call they that presumption? Oh! the man who knows the awful feeling of being alone, and struggling for Truth as for life and death — he knows the difference between independence and presumption.

Second, Humbleness. There is no infallibility in man — if so, none in us. *We* may err: that one thought is enough to keep a man humble.

There are two kinds of temper contrary to this spirit. The first is a disputing, captious temper. Disagreement is refreshing when two men lovingly desire to compare their views to find out the truth. Controversy is wretched when it is an attempt to prove one another wrong. Therefore Christ would not *argue* with Pilate. Religious controversy does only harm. It destroys the humble inquiry after truth: it throws all the energies into an attempt to prove ourselves right. — The next temper contrary is a hopeless spirit. Pilate's question breathed of hopelessness. He felt that Jesus was unjustly condemned, but he thought Him in views as hopelessly wrong as the rest — all wrong. What was truth? Who knew anything about it? He spoke too bitterly — too hopelessly — too disappointedly to get an answer. In that despairing spirit no man gets at truth: "*The meek* will He guide in judgment. . . ."

Lastly, Action. This was Christ's rule — "If any man will *do* His will. . . ." A blessed rule: a plain and simple rule. Here we are in a world of mystery, where all is difficult, and very much dark — where a hundred jarring creeds declare themselves to be The Truth, and all are plausible. How shall a man decide? Let him *do* the right that lies before him: much is uncertain — some things at least are clear. Whatever else may be wrong, it *must* be right to be pure — to be just and tender, and merciful and honest. It *must* be right to love, and to deny one's-self. Let him do the Will, and he shall know. Observe — men begin the other way. They say, if I could but believe, then I would make my life true. If I could but be sure what is truth, then I would set to work to live in earnest. No — God says, Act — make the life true, and then you will be able to believe. Live in earnest, and you will know the answer to "What is Truth?"

Infer the blessedness of belief. Young men are prone to consider scepticism a proof of strong-mindedness — a something to be proud of. Let Pilate be a specimen — and a wretched one he is. He had clear-mindedness enough to be dissatisfied with all the views he knew: enough to see through and scorn the squabbles and superstitions of priests and bigots. All well: if from doubt of falsehood he had gone on to a belief in a higher truth. But doubt, when it left him doubting — why — the noblest opportunity man ever had — that of saving the Saviour, he missed: he became a thing for the people to despise, and after ages to pity. And that is scepticism. Call you that a manly thing?

To believe is to be happy: to doubt is to be wretched. But I will not urge that. Seventy years — and the most fevered brain will be still enough. We will not say much of the wretchedness of doubt. To believe is to be *strong*. Doubt cramps energy. Belief is power: only so far as a man believes strongly, mightily, can he act cheerfully, or do anything that is worth the doing.

I speak to those who have learned to hold cheap the threats wherewith priests and people would terrify into acquiescence — to those who are beyond the appeal of fear, and can only yield, if at all, to higher motives. Young men! the only manly thing, the only strong thing, is Faith. It is not so far as a man doubts, but so far as he believes, that he can achieve or perfect anything. "All things are possible to *him that believeth.*"

XXI.

(Preached on the first day of Public Mourning for the Queen Dowager, 1849.)

THE ISRAELITE'S GRAVE IN A FOREIGN LAND.*

GEN. l. 24-26. — "And Joseph said unto his brethren, I die: and God will surely visit you, and bring you out of this land unto the land which he sware to Abraham, to Isaac, and to Jacob. And Joseph took an oath of the children of Israel, saying, God will surely visit you, and ye shall carry up my bones from hence. So Joseph died, being an hundred and ten years old: and they embalmed him, and he was put in a coffin in Egypt."

THERE is a moment when a man's life is re-lived on earth. It is in that hour in which the coffin lid is shut down, just before the funeral, when earth has seen the last of him for ever. Then the whole life is,

* *This Sermon was formerly published by the Author in a separate form, and the following Preface to that publication explains so well the circumstances under which all the other Sermons have been preserved, that it has been thought best to reprint the preface here.*

"For the publication of the common-place observations contained in the following pages, the common-place excuse may, perhaps, suffice, that printing was the simplest way of multiplying copies for a few friends who desired them. Perhaps, too, the uncommonness of the occasion may justify the writer in giving to an ephemeral discourse an existence somewhat less transient than the minutes spent in listening to it.

"The Sermon is published as nearly as possible as it was spoken. It was written out concisely for a friend on the day of its delivery, with no intention of publication. Afterwards, it seemed better to leave it in that state, with only a few corrections, and the addition of a few sentences, than to attempt to re-write it after an interval too great to recal what had been said. This will account for the abruptness and want of finish which pervades the composition.

"The writer takes this opportunity of disowning certain sermons which have been published in his name. They would not have been worth notice, had not the innumerable blunders of thought and expression which they contain been read and accepted by several as his. For this reason he feels it due to himself to state that they are published without his sanction, and against his request, and that he is not responsible for either the language or the ideas."

as it were, lived over again in the conversation which turns upon the memory of the departed. The history of threescore years and ten is soon recapitulated: not, of course, the innumerable incidents and acts which they contained, but the central governing principle of the whole. Feverish curiosity sometimes spends itself upon the last hours; and a few correct sentences, implying faith after the orthodox phraseology, would convey to some greater hope than a whole life breathing the Spirit of Christ, separate from such sentences. But it is not thus the Bible speaks. It tells us very little of the closing scene, but a great deal of the general tenor of a life. In truth, the closing scene is worth very little. The felon, who, up to the last fortnight, has shown his impenitence by the plea of not guilty, in the short compass of that fortnight makes a confession, as a matter of course exhibits the externals of penitence, and receives the last Supper. But it would be credulity, indeed, to be easily persuaded that the eternal state of such a one is affected by it. A life of holiness sometimes mysteriously terminates in darkness; but it is not the bitterest cries of forsakenness — so often the result of physical exhaustion — nor even blank despair, that shall shake our deep conviction that he whose faith shone brightly through life, is now safe in the Everlasting arms. The dying scene is worth little — little, at least, to us — except so far as it is in harmony with the rest of life.

It is for this reason that the public estimate, pronounced upon the departed, is generally a fair criterion of worth. There are, of course, exceptional cases — cases in which the sphere of action has been too limited for the fair development of the character, and nothing but the light of the Judgment day can reveal it in its true aspect — cases in which party spirit has defaced a name, and years are wanted to wash away the mask of false colour which has concealed the genuine features — cases in which the champion of truth expires amidst the execrations of his contemporaries, and after-ages build his sepulchre. These, however, are exceptions. For the most part, when all is over, general opinion is not far from truth. Misrepresentation and envy have no provocatives left them. What the departed was is tolerably well-known in the circle in which he moved. The epitaph may be falsified by the partiality of relations; but the broad judgment of society reverses that, rectifies it, and pronounces with perhaps a rude, but on the whole, fair approximation to the truth.

These remarks apply to the history of the man whose final scene is recorded in the text. The verdict of the Egyptian world was worth much. Joseph had gone to Egypt some years before, a foreigner; had lived there in obscurity; had been exposed to calumny; by his quiet, consistent goodness, had risen, step by step, first to respect, then to trust, command, and veneration; was embalmed after death in the affections, as well as with the burial rights, of the Egyptians; and his honoured form reposed at last amidst the burial place of the Pharaohs.

In this respect the text branches into a twofold division. The life of Joseph; and the death which was in accordance with that life.

1. The history of Joseph, as of every man, has two sides — its outward circumstances and its inner life.

The outward circumstances were chequered with

misfortune. Severed from his home in very early years, sold into slavery, cast into prison — at first, grief seemed to have marked him for her own. And this is human life. Part of its lot is misery. There are two inadequate ways of accounting for this mystery of sorrow. One, originating in a zeal for God's justice, represents it as invariably the chastisement of sin, or at the least, as correction for fault. But, plainly, it is not always such. Joseph's griefs were the consequences, not of fault, but of rectitude. The integrity which, on some unknown occasion, made it his duty to carry his brethren's "evil report" to their father, was the occasion of his slavery. The purity of his life was the cause of his imprisonment. Fault is only a part of the history of this great matter of sorrow. Another theory, created by zeal for God's love, represents sorrow as the exception, and happiness as the rule of life. We are made for enjoyment, it is said, and on the whole there is more enjoyment than wretchedness. The common idea of Love being that which identifies it with a simple wish to confer happiness, no wonder that a feeble attempt is made to vindicate God, by a reduction of the apparent amount of pain. Unquestionably, however, love is very different from a desire to shield from pain. Eternal Love gives to painlessness a very subordinate place in comparison of excellence of character. It does not hesitate to secure man's spiritual dignity at the expense of the sacrifice of his well-being. The solution will not do. Let us look the truth in the face. You cannot hide it from yourself. "Man is born to sorrow as the sparks fly upwards." Sorrow is not an accident, occurring now and then; it is the very woof which is woven into the warp of life. God has created the nerves to agonize, and the heart to bleed; and before a man dies, almost every nerve has thrilled with pain, and every affection has been wounded. The account of life which represents it as probation is inadequate: so is that which regards it chiefly as a system of rewards and punishments. The truest account of this mysterious existence seems to be that it is intended for the development of the soul's life, for which sorrow is indispensable. Every son of man who would attain the true end of his being, must be baptized with fire. It is the law of our humanity, as that of Christ, that we must be perfected through suffering. And he who has not discerned the Divine Sacredness of Sorrow, and the profound meaning which is concealed in pain, has yet to learn what life is. The Cross, manifested as the Necessity of the Highest Life, alone interprets it.

2. Besides this, obloquy was part of Joseph's portion. His brethren, even his father, counted him a vain dreamer, full of proud imaginings. He languished long in a dungeon with a stain upon his character. He was subjected to almost all the bitterness which changes the milk of kindly feelings into gall: to Potiphar's fickleness, to slander, to fraternal envy, to the ingratitude of friendship in the neglect of the chief butler who left his prison, and straightway forgot his benefactor. Out of all which a simple lesson arises, "Cease ye from man, whose breath is in his nostrils." Yet that may be over-stated. Nothing chills the heart like universal distrust. Nothing freezes the genial current of the soul so much as doubts of human nature. Human goodness is no dream. Surely we have met unselfishness, and love, and honour among men. Surely we

have seen, and not in dreams, pure benevolence beaming from human countenances. Surely we have met with integrity that the world's wealth could not bribe; and attachment which might bear the test of any sacrifice. It is not so much the depravity as the frailty of men, that makes it impossible to count on them. Was it not excusable in Jacob, and even natural, if he attributed to vanity his son's relation of the dream in which the sun, and the moon, and the eleven stars, bowed down before him? Was it not excusable if Potiphar distrusted his tried servant's word, when his guilt appeared so indisputably substantiated? Was not even the chief butler's forgetfulness intelligible, when you remember his absorbing interest in his own danger, and the multiplied duties of his office? The world is not to be too severely blamed, if it misrepresents us. It is hard to reach the truth: very hard to sift a slander. Men who believe such rumours, especially in courtly life, may be ignorant, hasty, imperfect, but are not necessarily treacherous. Yet, even while you keep this in mind, that the heart may not be soured, remember, your dearest friend may fail you in the crisis; a truth of experience was wrapped up in the old fable, and the thing you have fostered in your bosom may wound you to the quick; the one you have trusted may become your Accuser, and throw his own blame with dastard meanness upon you. That was the experience of Joseph. Was not that His fate who trusted Judas? There is One, and but One, whose Love is as a rock, which will not fail you when you cling. It is a fearful, solitary feeling, that lonely truth of life; yet not without a certain strength and grandeur in it. The life that is the deepest and the truest will feel most vividly both its desolation and its majesty. We live and die alone. God and our own souls — we fall back upon them at last. "Behold, the hour cometh, yea is now come, that ye shall be scattered, every man to his own, and shall leave Me alone; and yet I am not alone, because the Father is with Me."

3. Success, besides, marked the career of Joseph. Let us not take half views of men and things. The woof of life is dark; that we granted: but it is shot through a web of brightness. Accordingly, in Joseph's case, even in his worst days, you find a kind of balance, to be weighed against his sorrows. The doctrine of compensation is found through all. Amidst the schemings of his brothers' envy he had his father's love. In his slavery he had some recompense in feeling that he was gradually winning his master's confidence. In his dungeon he possessed the consciousness of innocence, and the grateful respect of his fellow-prisoners. In that beautiful hymn which some of you read last Sunday,* you may remember that a parallel is drawn between human life and the aspects of the weather. The morning rainbow, glittering among the dangerous vapours of the west, predicts that the day will not unclouded pass away. The evening rainbow declares that the storms are past, and that serene weather is setting in. Such is the life of all whom God disciplines. The morning or the evening brightness is the portion of a life, the rest of which is storm. Rarely are the manful struggles of principle in the first years of life suffered to be in vain. Joseph saw the early clouds which darkened the morning of his existence, pass away: and the rainbow of heavenly peace arched over

* Keble's Christian Year. Twenty-fifth Sunday after Trinity.

the calmness of his later years. "The Lord was with Joseph, and he was a prosperous man." And it is for this special purpose it is written, "And Joseph saw Ephraim's children of the third generation; the children also of Machir, the son of Manasseh, were brought up upon Joseph's knees." Long life, an honoured old age, a quiet grave; these were the blessings reckoned desirable in Jewish modes of thought: and they are mentioned as evidences of happiness.

And this, too, is Life. The sorrows of the past stand out most vividly in our recollections: because they are the keenest of our sensations. At the end of a long existence we should probably describe it thus, "Few and evil have the days of the years of thy servant been." But the innumerable infinitesimals of happiness that from moment to moment made life sweet and pleasant are forgotten; and very richly has our Father mixed the materials of these with the homeliest actions and domesticities of existence. See two men meeting together in the streets; mere acquaintances. They will not be five minutes together before a smile will overspread their countenances, or a merry laugh ring of, at the lowest, amusement. This has God done. God created the smile and the laugh, as well as the sigh and the tear. The aspect of this life in stern; very stern. It is a very superficial account of it which slurs over its grave mystery, and refuses to hear its low, deep undertone of anguish. But there is enough, from hour to hour, of bright, sunny happiness, to remind us that its Creator's highest name is Love.

Now turn to the spirit of Joseph's inner life. First of all, that life was forgiveness. You cannot but have remarked that, conversant as his experience was with human treachery, no expressions of bitterness escape from him. No sentimental wailing over the cruelty of relations, the falseness of friendship, or the ingratitude of the world. No rancorous outburst of misanthropy: no sarcastic scepticism of man's integrity or woman's honour. He meets all bravely, with calm, meek, and dignified forbearance. If ever man had cause for such doubts, he had; yet his heart was never soured. At last, after his father's death, his brothers, apprehending his resentful recollections of their early cruelty, come to deprecate his revenge. Very touching is his reply. "Fear not: for am I in the place of God? But as for you, ye thought evil against me: but God meant it unto good, to bring to pass, as it is this day, to save much people alive. Now therefore, fear ye not: I will nourish you and your little ones."

This is the Christian spirit before the Christian times. Christ was in Joseph's heart, though not definitely in Joseph's creed. The Eternal Word whispered in the souls of men before it spoke articulately aloud in the Incarnation. It was the Divine Thought before it became the Divine Expression.* It was the Light that lighteth every man that cometh into the world, before It blazed into the Day-spring from on high which visited us. The Mind of Christ, the Spirit of the years yet future, blended itself with life before He came; for His words were the Eternal Verities of our Humanity. In all ages Love is the truth of life. Men cannot injure us except so far as they exasperate us to forget ourselves. No man is really dishonoured except by his own act. Calumny, injustice, ingratitude —

* Λόγος ἐνδιάθετος — προφορικός.

the only harm these can do us is by making us bitter, or rancorous, or gloomy: by shutting our hearts, or souring our affections. We rob them of their power if they only leave us more sweet and forgiving than before. And this is the only true victory. We win by love. Love transmutes all curses, and forces them to rain down in blessings. Out of the jealousy of his brothers Joseph extracted the spirit of forgiveness. Out of Potiphar's weak injustice, and out of the machinations of disappointed Passion, he created an opportunity of learning meekness. Our enemies become unconsciously our best friends, when their slanders deepen in us heavenlier graces. Let them do their worst; they only give us the God-like victory of forgiving them.

2. Distinguished from the outward circumstances, we find simplicity of character: partly in the willingness to acknowledge his shepherd father in Egypt, where the pastoral life was an abomination; partly in that incidental notice which we have of the feast at which he entertained his brethren, where the Egyptians sat at a table by themselves, and Joseph by himself. So that, elevated as he was, his heart remained Hebrew still. He had contracted a splendid alliance, by marrying into one of the noblest families in Egypt, that of Potipherah the priest of On. And yet he had not forgotten his country, nor sought to be naturalized there. His heart was in that far land where he had fed his father's flocks, in his simple, genial boyhood. The divining cup of Egyptian silver was on his table; but he remembered the days when the only splendour he knew was that coat of many colours which was made for him by his father. He bore a simple, un-

sophisticated heart amidst the pomp of an Egyptian court.

There is a great mistake made on the subject of simplicity. There is one simplicity of circumstances: another simplicity of heart. These two must not be confounded. It is common to talk of the humble poor man, and the proud rich man. Let not these ideas be inseparably blended together. There is many a man who sits down to a meal of bread and milk on a wooden table, whose heart is as proud as the proudest whose birth is royal. There is many a one whose voice is heard in the public meeting, loudly descanting on regal tyranny and aristocratic insolence, who in his own narrow circle is as much a tyrant as any oppressor who ever disgraced the throne. And there is many a man who sits down to daily pomp, to whom gold and silver are but as brass and tin, and who bears in the midst of it all a meek, simple spirit, and a "heart refrained as a weaned child." Many a man who lives surrounded with homage, and hearing the applause and flattery of men perpetually, on whose heart these things fall flat and dead, without raising one single emotion of fluttered vanity.

The world cannot understand this. They cannot believe that Joseph can be humble, while he is conscious of such elevation above the crowd of men, not even dreaming of it. They cannot understand how carelessly these outsides of life can be worn, and how they fall off like the unregarded and habitual dress of daily life. They cannot know how the spirit of the Cross can crucify the world, make grandeur painful, and calm the soul with a vision of the Eternal Beauty. They cannot dream how His life and death, once felt as the grandest, write mockery on all else, and fill the soul with an ambition which is above the world. It is not the unjewelled finger: nor the affectation of an almost quakerish simplicity of attire: nor the pedestrian mode of travelling: nor the scanty meal, that constitute humility. It is that simple, inner life of real greatness, which is indifferent to magnificence, and surrounded by it all, lives far away in the distant country of a Father's Home, with the Cross borne silently and self-sacrificingly in the heart of hearts.

3. One characteristic of Joseph's inner life remains — benevolence. It was manifested in the generosity with which he entertained his brethren, and in the discriminating tenderness with which he provided his best beloved brother's feast with extraordinary delicacies. These were traits of thoughtfulness. But farther still. The prophetic insight of Joseph enabled him to foresee the approach of famine. He took measures accordingly; and when the famine came, the royal storehouses were opened, and every man in Egypt owed his life to the benevolent providence of the Hebrew stranger. It was productive of a great social revolution. It brought, by degrees, all the land of Egypt into the power of the Crown, so that a kind of feudal system was established, every man holding in direct tenancy from the Crown. Hence the nation became compacted into a new unity, and power was concentrated in the hands of government, partly by the pecuniary revenue thus added, and partly by the lustre of goodness which Joseph had thrown round the royal acts. For acts like these are the real bulwarks of a throne. One such man as Joseph does more to strengthen the Crown than all the speculations, solemn

or trifling, which were ever written on the "Divine right of kings." There *is* a right divine which requires no elaborate theory to make it felt.

II. The death of Joseph was in accordance with his life.

1. The funeral was a homage paid to goodness. Little is said in the text of Joseph's funeral. To know what it was, we must turn to the earlier part of the chapter, where that of Jacob is mentioned. A mourning of seventy days; a funeral whose imposing greatness astonished the Canaanites. They said, "This is a grievous mourning to the Egyptians." Seventy days were the time, or nearly so, fixed by custom for a royal funeral; and Jacob was so honoured, not for his own sake, but because he was Joseph's father. We cannot suppose that Joseph's own obsequies were on a scale less grand.

Now, weigh what is implied in this. This was not the homage paid to talent, nor to wealth, nor to birth. Joseph was a foreign slave, raised to eminence by the simple power of goodness. Every man in Egypt felt, at his death, that he had lost a friend. There were thousands whose tears would fall when they recounted the preservation of lives dear to them in the years of famine, and felt that they owed those lives to Joseph. Grateful Egypt mourned the Good Foreigner; and, for once, the honours of this world were given to the graces of another.

2. We collect from this, besides, a hint of the resurrection of the body. The Egyptian mode of sepulture was embalming; and the Hebrews, too, attached much importance to the body after death. Joseph

commanded his countrymen to preserve his bones to take away with them. In this we detect that unmistakeable human craving, not only for immortality, but immortality associated with a form. No doubt, the Egyptian feeling was carried out absurdly. They tried to redeem from the worm the very aspect that had been worn, the very features they had loved; and there was a kind of feeling, that while that mummy lasted, the man had not yet perished from earth. They expected that, in process of years, it would again be animated by its spirit.

Now, Christianity does not disappoint, but rather meets, that feeling. It grants all that the materialist, and all that the spiritualist, have a right to ask. It grants to the materialist, by doctrine of the resurrection of the body, that future life shall be associated with a material form. Leaving untouched all the questions which may be raised about the identity of the atoms that have been buried, it simply pronounces that the spirit shall have a body. It grants to the spiritualist all he ought to wish, that the spirit shall be free from evil. For it is a mistake of ultra-spiritualism, to connect degradation with the thought of a risen body; or to suppose that a mind, unbound by the limitations of space, is a more spiritual idea of resurrection than the other. The opposite to spirituality is not materialism, but sin. The form of matter does not degrade. For what is this world itself but the form of Deity, whereby the manifoldness of His mind and Beauty manifests, and wherein it clothes itself? It is idle to say that spirit can exist apart from form. We do not know that it can. Perhaps even the Eternal Himself is more closely bound to His works than our philosophical systems have conceived. Perhaps matter is only a mode of thought. At all events, all that we know or can know of mind, exists in union with form. The resurrection of the body is the Christian verity, which meets and satisfies those cravings of the ancient Egyptian mind, that expressed themselves in the process of embalming, and the religious reverence felt for the very bones of the departed by the Hebrews.

Finally, in the last Will and Testament of Joseph, we find faith. He commanded his brethren, and through them, his nation, to carry his bones with them when they migrated to Canaan. In the Epistle to the Hebrews, that is reckoned an evidence of faith. "By faith Joseph gave commandment concerning his bones." How did he know that his people would ever quit Egypt? We reply, by faith. Not faith in a written word, for Joseph had no Bible; rather, faith in that conviction of his own heart, which is itself the substantial evidence of faith. For religious faith ever dreams of something higher, more beautiful, more perfect, than the state of things with which it feels itself surrounded. Ever, a day future lies before it: the evidence for which is its own hope. Abraham, by that creative faith, saw the day of Christ, and was glad. Joseph saw his family in prosperity, even in affluence; but he felt that this was not their rest. A higher life than that of affluence — a nobler destiny than that of stagnant rest, there must be for them in the future; else all the anticipations of a purer earth, and a holier world, which imagination bodied forth within his soul, were empty dreams, not the intuitions of God's Spirit. It was this Idea of perfection, which was "the substance of things hoped for," that carried him far beyond the period of his own death, and made him feel himself partaker of his nation's blessed future.

And that is the evidence of immortality. When the coffin is lowered into the grave, and the dull, heavy sound of earth falling on it is heard, there are some to whom that sound seems but an echo of their worst anticipations; seems but to reverberate the idea of decay for ever, in the words, "Earth to earth, ashes to ashes, dust to dust." There are others, to whom it sounds pregnant with the expectations of immortality, the "sure and certain hope of a resurrection to eternal life." The difference between these two feelings is measured by the difference of lives. They whose life is low and earthly, how can they believe in aught beyond the grave, when nothing of that life which is eternal has yet stirred within them? They who have lived as Joseph lived, just in proportion to their purity and their unselfishness, must believe it. They cannot but believe it. The eternal existence is already pulsing in their veins; the life of trust and high hope, and sublime longings after perfection, with which the decay of the frame has nothing at all to do. That is gone — yes — but it was not that life in which they lived, and when it finished, what had that ruin to do with the destruction of the Immortal?

For what is our proof of immortality? Not the analogies of nature; the resurrection of nature from a winter grave, or the emancipation of the butterfly. Not even the testimony to the fact of risen dead; for who does not know how shadowy and unsubstantial these intellectual proofs become in unspiritual frames of mind? No, the life of the spirit is the evidence.

Heaven begun is the living proof that makes the heaven to come credible. "Christ in you *is* the hope of glory." It is the eagle eye of faith which penetrates the grave, and sees far into the tranquil things of death. He alone can believe in immortality, who feels the resurrection in him already.

There is a special application to be made of this subject to our hearts. It is not often that the pulpit can be used for a funeral eulogium. Where Christ is to be exalted in solitary pre-eminence, it is but rarely that the praise of man may be heard. Rank, Royalty itself could not command from the lips of a minister of the King of kings one syllable of adulatory, undeserved, or unfelt homage. But there are cases in which to loftiness of birth is added dignity of character; and then we gladly relax the rule, to pay a willing tribute to the majesty of Goodness. There is one to whom your thoughts must have reverted often during the history which we have been going through, suggesting a parallel, all the more delicately felt from the absence of direct allusion. That royal Lady, for whose loss the marvellous uniformity of the unbroken funeral hue which pervades this congregation, tells eloquently of general mourning, came to this land a few years ago, like Joseph, a foreigner. Like Joseph, the earlier years of her sojourn were spent in comparative obscurity. Like Joseph, she had her share of calumny, though in a different form. There are many here who can remember that in that year when our political feuds had attained the acme of rancour, the irreverent lip of party Slander dared to breathe its rank venom upon the name of one of the gentlest that ever adorned a throne. There are some who know how that unpopularity was met: with meekness — with Christian forgiveness — with quiet dignity — with that composure which is the highest result and evidence of strength. Like Joseph, she passed through the temptations of a court with unsullied spotlessness — like Joseph, the domestic and social relationships were sustained with beautiful fidelity — like Joseph, she lived down opposition, outlived calumny — like Joseph, she used the noble income entrusted to her, in acts of almost unexampled munificence — like Joseph, her life was chequered with sorrow, and when the clouds of earlier difficulties had cleared away, the rainbow sign of peace, even in the midst of broken health, spanned the calmness of her evening years — like Joseph, she will have a regal burial, and her ashes will repose with the dust of England's princes, amidst the mourning of the nation in which she found a home.

The homage which is given to her is not the homage yielded to rank, or wealth, or genius. There will be silver on her coffin, and magnificence in the pageantry which attends her to the grave;* but it is not in these that the glory of her funeral lies. These were the privileges of the most profligate of her ancestors as well as her. These are the world's rewards for those whom she delights to honour. There will be something in her funeral, beside which these things are mean. There is a grandeur in a nation's tears; and they will be shed in unfeigned reverence over the remains of all that was most queenly, and all that was most womanly. No

* This anticipation has not been realized. In one of the most touching and unaffected documents that ever went right home to English hearts, the Queen of a British Sovereign requested to be borne to the grave as the wife of a sailor.

political fervour mixes with her obsequies. She stood identified with no party politics. No peculiar religious party mourns its patroness. Of all our jarring religious sects, in the Church, and out of it, not one dares to claim her as its own. Her spirit soared above these things. It is known that she scarcely recognised them. All was lost in the sublimer name of Christian. It is a *Christian* who has passed from this earth away, to take her place in the general Assembly and Church of the first-born: to stand before God, the Judge of all, among the spirits of the just made perfect.

One word more. Honouring the Queen, profoundly reverencing the Woman, let not contemplation stop there. Do not bury thought in the human and finite. Mildly as her lustre shone on earth, remember it was but one feeble ray of the Light that is Uncreated. All that she had she received. If we honour her, it is to adore Him who made her what she was. Of His fulness she had received, and grace for grace. What she was she became through adoring faith in Christ. It is an elevating thing to gaze on human excellence, because through it the Highest becomes conceivable. It is a spirit-stirring thing to see saintly Goodness asserting its celestial origin by turning pale the lustre of the highest earthly rank. For in this universal mourning our noble country has not bowed the knee in reverence to the majesty which is of time. Every heart in England has felt that the Sovereign was merged in the servant of Christ. "The King's daughter was all glorious within." Here was *Christian* goodness. Her eyes had beheld the King in His Beauty, and therefore her life was beautiful, and feminine, and meek, and simple. It was all derived beauty. She had robed herself in

Christ. "Reflecting back, as from a burnished mirror, the glory of the Lord, she was changed into the same image, from glory to glory, even as by the Spirit of the Lord." *

* 2 Cor. iii. 18. This appears to be the true force and rendering of the metaphor.

Subjoined are the directions given by her late Majesty for her own funeral. The reader will be glad to have them preserved in a form less inconvenient than the columns of a newspaper. Should he be one who feels it a relief to miss, for once, the worn-out conventionalisms of religious expression, and come in contact with something fresh and living, he will find more in these quiet lines than in ten sermons; more to make a very happy tear start; more of the simplicity and the beauty of the life in God; more to cool the feverishness of his heart, and still its worldliness into silence; more of that deep rest into which the meek and humble enter; more that will make him long to be simple and inartificial, and real, as Christ was, desiring only, in life and death, and judgment, to be found in HIM.

[COPY.]

"I die in all humility, knowing well that we are all alike before the Throne of God, and request, therefore, that my mortal remains be conveyed to the grave without any pomp or state. They are to be moved to St. George's Chapel, Windsor, where I request to have as private and quiet a funeral as possible.

"I particularly desire not to be laid out in state, and the funeral to take place by daylight, no procession, the coffin to be carried by sailors to the chapel.

"All those of my friends and relations, to a limited number, who wish to attend, may do so. My nephew, Prince Edward of Saxe Weimar, Lords Howe and Denbigh, the Hon. William Ashley, Mr. Wood, Sir Andrew

Barnard, and Sir D. Davis, with my dressers, and those of my ladies who may wish to attend.

"I die in peace, and wish to be carried to the tomb in peace, and free from the vanities and the pomp of this world.

"I request not to be dissected, nor embalmed; and desire to give as little trouble as possible.

(Signed) "ADELAIDE R.

"November, 1849."

THE END.

PRINTING OFFICE OF THE PUBLISHER.

COLLECTION

OF

BRITISH AUTHORS.

VOL. 557.

SERMONS

BY THE LATE

REV. FREDERICK W. ROBERTSON, M.A.

IN THREE VOLUMES.

VOL. II.

SERMONS,

PREACHED AT

TRINITY CHAPEL, BRIGHTON,

BY THE LATE

REV. FREDERICK W. ROBERTSON, M.A.,

THE INCUMBENT.

COPYRIGHT EDITION.

IN THREE VOLUMES.

VOL. II.

LEIPZIG

BERNHARD TAUCHNITZ

1861.

CONTENTS

OF VOLUME II.

SERMON I.

Preached June 22, 1851.

CHRIST'S JUDGMENT RESPECTING INHERITANCE.

*** This Sermon should have followed next after Sermon XVII. in Volume I. (The Message of the Church to Men of Wealth), to which it is the sequel, completing the argument.

SERMON II.

Preached January 6, 1850.

THE STAR IN THE EAST.

SERMON III.

Preached February 10, 1850.

THE HEALING OF JAIRUS' DAUGHTER.

SERMON IV.

Preached March 10, 1850.

BAPTISM.

SERMON V.

Preached March 17, 1850.

BAPTISM.

SERMON VI.

Preached October 13, 1850.

ELIJAH.

SERMON VII.

Preached January 12, 1851.

NOTES ON PSALM LI.

SERMON VIII.

Preached March 2, 1851.

OBEDIENCE THE ORGAN OF SPIRITUAL KNOWLEDGE.

SERMON IX.

Preached March 30, 1851.

RELIGIOUS DEPRESSION.

SERMON X.

Preached April 6, 1851.

FAITH OF THE CENTURION.

SERMON XI.

Preached July 27, 1851.

THE RESTORATION OF THE ERRING.

SERMON XII.

Preached Christmas Day, 1851.

CHRIST THE SON.

SERMON XVII.

Preached January 16, 1853.

THE SANCTIFICATION OF CHRIST.

SERMON XVIII.

Preached January 23, 1853.

THE FIRST MIRACLE.

I. THE GLORY OF THE VIRGIN MOTHER.

SERMON XIX.

Preached January 30, 1853.

THE FIRST MIRACLE.

II. THE GLORY OF THE DIVINE SON.

SERMON XX.

Preached March 20, 1853.

THE GOOD SHEPHERD.

SERMON XXI.

Preached Easter Day, March 27, 1853.

THE DOUBT OF THOMAS.

SERMON XXII.

Preached May 8, 1853.

THE IRREPARABLE PAST.

SERMONS.

I.

Preached June 29, 1851.

CHRIST'S JUDGMENT RESPECTING INHERITANCE.*

LUKE xii. 13-15.—"And one of the Company said unto him, Master, speak to my brother, that he divide the inheritance with me. And he said unto him, Man, who made me a judge or a divider over you? And he said unto them, Take heed, and beware of covetousness: for a man's life consisteth not in the abundance of the things which he possesseth."

THE Son of God was misunderstood and misinterpreted in His day. With this fact we are familiar; but we are not at all familiar with the consideration that it was very natural that He should be so mistaken.

He went about Galilee and Judea proclaiming the downfall of every injustice, the exposure and confutation of every lie. He denounced the lawyers who refused education to the people in order that they might retain the key of knowledge in their own hands. He reiterated Woe! woe! woe! to the Scribes and Pharisees, who revered the past and systematically persecuted every new prophet and every brave man who rose up to vindicate the Spirit of the past against the *institutions* of the past. He spoke parables which bore hard on the men of wealth. That, for instance, of the rich man

* This Sermon was preached the Sunday after that on which "The Message of the Church to Men of Wealth" was preached, and it was intended as a further illustration of that subject. It was accidentally omitted from the First Volume.

who was clothed in purple and fine linen, and fared sumptuously every day: who died, and in hell lift up his eyes being in torments. That of the wealthy proprietor who prospered in the world; who pulled down his barns to build greater; who all the while was in the sight of God a fool; who in front of judgment and eternity was found unready. He stripped the so-called religious party of that day of their respectability, convicted them, to their own astonishment, of hypocrisy, and called them "whited sepulchres." He said God was against them: that Jerusalem's day was come, and that she must fall.

And now consider candidly: — suppose that all this had taken place in this country; that an unknown stranger, with no ordination, with no visible authority, basing his authority upon his truth, and his agreement with the mind of God the Father, had appeared in this England, uttering half the severe things He spoke against the selfishness of wealth, against ecclesiastical authorities, against the clergy, against the popular religious party: suppose that such an one should say that our whole social life is corrupt and false — suppose that instead of "thou blind Pharisee," the word had been "thou blind Churchman!"

Should *we* have fallen at the feet of such an one, and said, Lo! this is a message from Almighty God, and He who brings it is a Son of God; perhaps what He says Himself, His only Son — God — of God?

Or should we not have rather said, This is dangerous teaching, and revolutionary in its tendencies, and He who teaches it is an incendiary, a mad, democratical, dangerous fanatic?

That was exactly what they did say of your Redeemer in His day; nor does it seem at all wonderful that they did.

The sober, respectable inhabitants of Jerusalem, very comfortable themselves, and utterly unable to conceive why things should not go on as they had been going on for a hundred years — not smarting from the misery and the moral degradation of the lazars with whom He associated, and under whose burdens his loving spirit groaned — thought it excessively dangerous to risk the subversion of their quiet enjoyment by such outcries. They said, prudent men! if He is permitted to go on this way, the Romans will come and take away our place and nation. The Priests and Pharisees, against whom He had spoken specially, were fiercer still. They felt there was no time to be lost.

But still more, His own friends and followers misunderstood Him.

They heard him speak of a Kingdom of Justice and Righteousness in which every man should receive the due reward of his deeds. They heard Him say that this kingdom was not far off, but actually among them, hindered only by their sins and dulness from immediate appearance. Men's souls were stirred and agitated. They were ripe for anything, and any spark would have produced explosion. They thought the next call would be to take the matter into their own hands.

Accordingly, on one occasion, St. John and St. James asked permission to call down fire from heaven upon a village of the Samaritans which would not receive their message. On another occasion, on a single figurative mention of a sword, they began to gird themselves for the struggle: "Lord," said one, "behold here are two swords." Again, as soon as He entered Jerusalem for the last time, the populace heralded His way with shouts, thinking that the long-delayed hour of retribution was come at last. They saw the Conqueror before them who was to vindicate their wrongs. In imagination they already felt their feet upon the necks of their enemies.

And because their hopes were disappointed, and He was not the Demagogue they wanted, therefore they turned against Him. Not the Pharisees but the people whom He had come to save, the outcast, and the publican, and the slave, and the maid-servant; they whose cause He had so often pleaded, and whose emancipation He had prepared. It was the *People* who cried, "Crucify Him, crucify Him!"

This will become intelligible to us if we can get at the spirit of this passage.

Among those who heard Him lay down the laws of the Kingdom of God, — Justice, Fairness, Charity, there was one who had been defrauded, as it seems, by his brother, of his just share of the patrimony. He thought that the One who stood before him was exactly what he wanted: — A redresser of wrongs — a champion of the oppressed — a divider and arbiter between factions — a referee of lawsuits — one who would spend His life in the unerring decision of all misunderstandings.

To his astonishment the Son of Man refused to interfere in his quarrel, or take part in it at all. "Man, who made me a judge or a divider between you?"

We ask attention to two things.

I. The Saviour's refusal to interfere.

II. The source to which He traced the appeal for interference.

I. The Saviour's refusal to interfere.

1. He implied that it was not His *part* to interfere. "Who made me a Judge or a Divider?"

It is a common saying that religion has nothing to do with politics, and particularly there is a strong feeling current against all interference with politics by the ministers of religion. This notion rests on a basis which is partly wrong, partly right.

To say that religion has nothing to do with politics is to assert that which is simply false. It were as wise to say that the atmosphere has nothing to do with the principles of architecture. Directly, nothing — indirectly, much. Some kinds of stone are so friable, that though they will last for centuries in a dry climate, they will crumble away in a few years in a damp one. There are some temperatures in which a form of building is indispensable which in another would be unbearable. The shape of doors, windows, apartments, all depend upon the air that is to be admitted or excluded. Nay, it is for the very sake of procuring a habitable atmosphere within certain limits that architecture exists at all. The atmospheric laws are distinct from the laws of architecture; but there is not an architectural question into which atmospheric considerations do not enter as conditions of the question.

That which the air is to architecture, religion is to politics. It is the vital air of every question. Directly, it determines nothing — indirectly, it conditions every problem that can arise. The kingdoms of this world must become the kingdoms of our Lord and of His Christ. How, if His Spirit is not to mingle with political and social truths?

Nevertheless, in the popular idea that religion as such must not be mixed with politics, there is a profound truth. Here, for instance, the Saviour will not meddle with the question. He stands aloof, sublime and dignified. It was no part of His to take from the oppressor and give to the oppressed, much less to encourage the oppressed to take from the oppressor himself. It was His part to forbid oppression. It was a Judge's part to decide what oppression was. It was not His office to determine the boundaries of civil right, nor to lay down the rules of the descent of property. Of course there was a spiritual and moral principle involved in this question. But He would not suffer His sublime mission to degenerate into the mere task of deciding casuistry.

He asserted principles of love, unselfishness, order, which would decide all questions: but the questions themselves He would not decide. He would lay down the great political principle, "Render unto Cæsar the things that be Cæsar's, and unto God the things which are God's." But He would not determine whether this particular tax was due to Cæsar or not.

So, too, He would say, Justice, like Mercy and Truth, is one of the weightier matters of the law: but He would not decide whether in this definite case this or that brother had justice on his side. It was for themselves to determine that, and in that determination lay their responsibility.

And thus religion deals with men, not cases: with human hearts, not casuistry.

Christianity determines general principles, out of which, no doubt, the best government would surely spring: but what the best government is it does not determine — whether Monarchy or a Republic, an Aristocracy or a Democracy.

It lays down a great social law; "Masters, give unto your servants that which is just and equal." But it is not its part to declare how much is just and equal. It has no fixed scale of wages according to which masters must give. *That* it leaves to each master and each age of society.

It binds up men in a holy brotherhood. But what are the best institutions and surest means for arriving at this brotherhood it has not said. In particular, it has not pronounced whether competition or co-operation will secure it.

And hence it comes to pass that Christianity is the Eternal Religion, which can never become obsolete. If it sets itself to determine the temporary and the local, the justice of this tax, or the exact wrongs of that conventional maxim, it would soon become obsolete: — it would be the religion of one century, not of all. As it is, it commits itself to nothing except eternal *principles*.

It is not sent into this world to establish monarchy, or secure the franchise: to establish socialism, or to frown it into annihilation: but to establish a Charity, and a Moderation, and a sense of Duty, and a love of Right, which will modify human life according to any circumstances that can possibly arise.

2. In this refusal, again, it was implied that His

kingdom was one founded on Spiritual disposition, not one of outward Law and Jurisprudence.

That this lawsuit should have been decided by the brothers themselves, in love, with mutual fairness, would have been much: that it should be determined by authoritative arbitration, was, spiritually speaking, nothing. The right disposition of their hearts, and the right division of their property thence resulting, was Christ's kingdom. The apportionment of their property by another's division had nothing to do with His kingdom.

Suppose that both were wrong: one oppressive, the other covetous. Then, that the oppressor should become generous, and the covetous liberal, were a great gain. But to take from one selfish brother in order to give to another selfish brother, what spiritual gain would there have been in this?

Suppose, again, that the retainer of the inheritance was in the wrong, and that the petitioner had justice on his side — that he was a humble, meek man, and his petition only one of right. Well, to take the property from the unjust and give it to Christ's servant, might be, and was, the duty of a Judge. But it was not Christ's part, nor any gain to the cause of Christ. He does not reward His servants with inheritances, with lands, houses, gold. The kingdom of God is not meat and drink, but righteousness, and peace, and joy in the Holy Ghost. Christ triumphs by wrongs meekly borne, even more than by wrongs legally righted. What we call poetical justice is not His kingdom.

To apply this to the question of the day. The great problem which lies before Europe for solution is, or will be this: Whether the present possessors of the soil have an exclusive right to do what they will with their own, or whether a larger claim may be put in by the workman for a share in the profits? Whether Capital has hitherto given to Labour its just part, or not? Labour is at present making an appeal, like that of this petitioner, to the Church, to the Bible, to God. "Master, speak unto my brother, that he divide the inheritance with me."

Now in the *mere* setting of that question to rest, Christianity is not interested. That landlords should become more liberal, and employers more merciful: that tenants should be more honourable, and workmen more unselfish; that would be indeed a glorious thing — a triumph of Christ's cause; and any arrangement of the inheritance *thence* resulting would be a real coming of the Kingdom of God. But whether the soil of the country and its capital shall remain the property of the rich, or become more available for the poor, — the rich and the poor remaining as selfish as before, — whether the selfish rich shall be able to keep, or the selfish poor to take, is a matter, religiously speaking, of profound indifference. Which of the brothers shall have the inheritance, the monopolist or the covetous? Either — neither — who cares? Fifty years hence what will it matter? But a hundred thousand years hence it *will* matter whether they settled the question by mutual generosity and forbearance.

3. I remark a third thing. He refused to be the friend of one, because he was the friend of both. He never was the champion of a class, because He was the champion of Humanity.

We may take for granted that the petitioner was an injured man — one at all events who thought himself injured: and Christ had often taught the spirit which would have made his brother right him: but He refused to take his part against his brother, just because he *was* his brother, Christ's servant, and one of God's family, as well as he.

And this was His spirit always. The Pharisees thought to commit Him to a side when they asked whether it was lawful to give tribute to Cæsar or not. But He would take no side as the Christ; neither the part of the government against the tax-payers; nor the part of the tax-payers against the government.

Now it is a common thing to hear of the rights of man; a glorious and a true saying: but, as commonly used, the expression only means the rights of a section or class of men. And it is very worthy of remark, that in these social quarrels both sides appeal to Christ and to the Bible as the champions of their rights, precisely in the same way in which this man appealed to Him. One class appeal to the Bible, as if it were the great Arbiter which decrees that the poor shall be humble and the subject submissive: and the other class appeal to the same Book triumphantly, as if it were exclusively on their side, its peculiar blessedness consisting in this, that it commands the rich to divide the inheritance, and the ruler to impose nothing that is unjust.

In either of these cases Christianity is degraded, and the Bible misused. They are not, as they have been made, O shame! for centuries, the servile defenders of Rank and Wealth, nor are they the pliant advocates of discontent and rebellion.

The Bible takes neither the part of the poor against the rich exclusively, nor that of the rich against the poor: and this because it proclaims a real, deep, true, and not a revolutionary brotherhood.

The brotherhood of which we hear so much is often only a one-sided brotherhood. It demands that the rich shall treat the poor as brothers. It has a right to do so. It is a brave and a just demand: but it forgets that the obligation is mutual; that in spite of his many faults, the rich man is the poor man's brother, and that the poor man is bound to recognize him and feel for him as a brother.

It requires that every candid allowance shall be made for the vices of the poorer classes, in virtue of the circumstances which, so to speak, seem to make such vices inevitable: for their harlotry, their drunkenness, their uncleanness, their insubordination. Let it enforce that demand: it may and must do it in the name of Christ. He was mercifully and mournfully gentle to those who through terrible temptation and social injustice had sunk; and sunk into misery at least as much as into sin. But, then, let it not be forgotten that some sympathy must be also due on the same score of circumstances to the rich man. Wealth has its temptations: so has power. The vices of the rich are his forgetfulness of responsibility, his indolence, his extravagance, his ignorance of wretchedness. These must be looked upon, not certainly with weak excuses, but with a brother's eye by the poor man, if he will assert a brotherhood. It is not just to attribute all to circumstances in the one case, and nothing in the other. It is not brotherhood to say that the labourer does wrong because he is tempted; and the man of wealth because he is intrinsically bad.

II. The Source to which he traced this appeal for a division.

Now it is almost certain that the reflection which arose to the lips of Christ is not the one which would have presented itself to us under similar circumstances. We should probably have sneered at the state of the law in which a lawsuit could obtain no prompt decision, and injury get no redress: Or we should have remarked upon the evils of the system of primogeniture, and asked whether it were just that one brother should have all, and the others none: Or we might, perhaps, have denounced the injustice of permitting privileged classes at all.

He did nothing of this kind: He did not sneer at the law, nor inveigh against the system, nor denounce the privileged classes. He went deeper: to the very root of the matter. "Take heed and beware of covetousness." It was covetousness which caused the unjust brother to withhold: it was covetousness which made the defrauded brother indignantly complain to a stranger. It is covetousness which is at the bottom of all lawsuits, all social grievances, all political factions. So St. James traces the genealogy. "From whence come wars and fightings among you? Come they not hence, even from your lusts which reign in your flesh?"

Covetousness: the covetousness of all. Of the oppressed as well as of the oppressor; for the cry "Divide" has its root in covetousness just as truly as "I will not." There are no innocent classes: no devils who oppress, and angels who are oppressed. The guilt of a false social state must be equally divided.

We will consider somewhat more deeply this covetousness. In the original the word is a very expressive one. It means the desire of having more — not of having more because there is not enough; but simply a craving after more. More when a man has not enough. More when he has. More, More, ever More. Give. Give. Divide. Divide.

This craving is not universal. Individuals and whole nations are without it. There are some nations, the condition of whose further civilization is, that the desire of accumulation be increased. They are too indolent or too unambitious to be covetous. Energy is awakened when wants are immediate, pressing, present; but ceases with the gratification.

There are other nations in which the craving is excessive, even to disease. Pre-eminent among these is England. This desire of accumulation is the source of all our greatness and all our baseness. It is at once our glory and our shame. It is the cause of our commerce, of our navy, of our military triumphs, of our enormous wealth, and our marvellous inventions. And it is the cause of our factions and animosities, of our squalid pauperism, and the worse than heathen degradation of the masses of our population.

That which makes this the more marvellous is, that of all the nations on the earth, none are so incapable of enjoyment as we. God has not given to us that delicate development which He has given to other races. Our sense of harmony is dull and rare, our perception of beauty is not keen. An English holiday is rude and boisterous: if protracted, it ends in ennui and self-dissatisfaction. We cannot enjoy. Work, the law of human nature, is the very need of an English nature. That cold shade of Puritanism which passed over us, sullenly eclipsing all grace and enjoyment, was but the shadow of our own melancholy unenjoying national character.

And yet, we go on accumulating as if we could enjoy more by having more. To quit the class in which they are and rise into that above, is the yearly, daily, hourly effort of millions in this land. And this were well if this word "above" implied a reality: if it meant higher intellectually, morally, or even physically. But the truth is, it is only higher fictitiously. The middle classes already have every real enjoyment which the wealthiest can have. The only thing they have not is the ostentation of the means of enjoyment. More would enable them to multiply equipages, houses, books. It could not enable them to enjoy them more.

Thus, then, we have reached the root of the matter. Our national craving is, in the proper meaning of the term, covetousness. Not the desire of enjoying more, but the desire of having more. And if there be a country, a society, a people, to whom this warning is specially applicable, that country is England, that society our own, that people are we. "Take heed and beware of covetousness."

The true remedy for this covetousness He then proceeds to give. "A man's life consisteth not in the abundance of the things which he possesses."

Now, observe the distinction between His view and the world's view of humanity. To the question, What is a man worth? the world replies by enumerating what he has. In reply to the same question, the Son of Man replies by estimating what he is. Not what he has, but what he is, *that*, through time and through eternity, is his real and proper life. He declared the presence of the soul: He announced the dignity of the spiritual man: He revealed the being that we are. Not that which is supported by meat and drink, but that whose very life is in Truth, Integrity, Honour, Purity. "Skin for skin" was the satanic version of this matter; "All that a man hath will he give for his *life.*" "What shall it profit a man," was the Saviour's announcement, "if he shall gain the whole world and lose his own *soul?*"

For the oppressed and the defrauded this was the true consolation and compensation. The true consolation. This man had lost so much loss. Well; how is he consoled? By the thought of retaliation? By the promise of revenge? By the assurance that he shall have what he ought by right to have? Nay, but thus — *as it were:* Thou hast lost so much, but thyself remains. "A man's life consisteth not in the abundance of the things that he possesses."

Most assuredly Christianity proclaims laws which will eventually give to each man his rights. I do not deny this. But I say that the hope of these rights is not the message, nor the promise, nor the consolation of Christianity. Rather they consist in the assertion of the true Life, instead of all other hopes: of the substitution of blessedness which is inward character, for happiness which is outward satisfaction of desire. For the broken-hearted, the peace which the world cannot give. For the poor, the life which destitution cannot take away. For the persecuted, the thought that they are the children of their Father which is in Heaven.

A very striking instance of this is found in the consolation offered by St. Paul to slaves. How did he reconcile them to their lot? By promising that Christianity would produce the abolition of the slave-trade?

No; though this *was* to be effected by Christianity; but by assuring them that, though slaves, they might be inly free; Christ's freedmen. Art thou called, being a slave? *Care not for it.*

This, too, was the real compensation offered by Christianity for injuries.

The other brother had the inheritance: and to win the inheritance he had laid upon his soul the guilt of injustice. His advantage was the property: the price he paid for that advantage was a hard heart. The injured brother had *no inheritance*, but instead he had, or might have had, innocence, and the conscious joy of knowing that he was not the injurer. Herein lay the balance.

Now there is great inconsistency between the complaints and claims that are commonly made on these subjects. There are outcries against the insolence of power and the hard-hearted selfishness of wealth. Only too often these cries have a foundation of justice. But be it remembered that these are precisely the cost at which the advantages, such as they are, are purchased. The price which the man in authority has paid for power is the temptation to be insolent. He has yielded to the temptation, and bought his advantage dear. The price which the rich man pays for his wealth is the temptation to be selfish. They have paid in spirituals for what they have gained in temporals. Now, if you are crying for a share in that wealth, and a participation in that power, you must be content to run the risk of becoming as hard and selfish and overbearing as the man whom you denounce. Blame their sins if you will, or despise their advantages; but do not think that you can covet their advantages, and keep clear of their temptations. God is on the side of the poor, and the persecuted, and the mourners — a light in darkness, and a life in death. But the poverty, and the persecution, and the darkness are the condition on which they feel God's presence. They must not expect to have the enjoyment of wealth and the spiritual blessings annexed to poverty at the same time. If you will be rich, you must be content to pay the price of falling into temptation, and a snare, and many foolish and hurtful lusts, which drown men in perdition; and if that price be too high to pay, then you must be content with the quiet valleys of existence, where alone it is well with us: kept out of the inheritance, but having instead God for your portion, your all-sufficient and everlasting portion. Peace, and quietness, and rest with Christ.

II.

Preached January 6, 1850.

THE STAR IN THE EAST.

MATT. ii. 1, 2. — "Now when Jesus was born in Bethlehem of Judea, in the days of Herod the king, behold there came wise men from the east to Jerusalem, saying, Where is he that is born King of the Jews? for we have seen his star in the east, and are come to worship him."

OUR subject is the Manifestation of Christ to the Gentiles. The King of the Jews has become the Sovereign of the world: a fact, one would think, which must cause a secret complacency in the heart of all Jews. For that which is most deeply working in modern life and thought is the Mind of Christ. His name has passed over our institutions, and much more has His spirit penetrated into our social and domestic existence. In other words, a Hebrew mind is now, and has been for centuries, ruling Europe.

But the gospel which He proclaimed was not limited to the Hebrews: it was a gospel for the nations. By the death of Christ, God had struck His deathblow at the root of the hereditary principle. "We be the seed of Abraham" was the proud pretension of the Israelite: and he was told that spiritual dignity rests not upon spiritual descent, but upon spiritual character. New tribes were adopted into the Christian union: and it became clear that there was no distinction of race in the spiritual family. The Jewish rite of circumcision, a symbol of exclusiveness, cutting off one nation from all others, was exchanged for Baptism, the symbol of universality, proclaiming the nearness of all to God, His Paternity over the human race, and the Sonship of all who chose to claim their privileges.

This was a Gospel for the World: and nation after nation accepted it. Churches were formed; the Kingdom which is the domain of Love grew; the Roman empire crumbled into fragments; but every fragment was found pregnant with life. It brake not as some ancient temple might break, its broken pieces lying in lifeless ruin, overgrown with weeds: rather as one of those mysterious animals break, of which, if you rend them asunder, every separate portion forms itself into a new and complete existence. Rome gave way; but every portion became a Christian kingdom, alive with the mind of Christ, and developing the Christian idea after its own peculiar nature.

The portion of Scripture selected for the text and for the gospel of the day, has an important bearing on this great Epiphany. The "wise men" belonged to a creed of very hoary and venerable antiquity; a system, too, which had in it the elements of strong vitality. For seven centuries after, the Mahometan sword scarcely availed to extirpate it — indeed could not. They whom the Mahometan called fire-worshippers, clung to their creed with vigour and tenacity indestructible, in spite of all his efforts.

"Here, then, in this act of homage to the Messiah, were the representatives of the highest then existing influences of the world, doing homage to the Lord of a mightier influence, and reverently bending before the dawn of the Star of a new and brighter Day. It was the first distinct turning of the Gentile mind to Christ; the first instinctive craving after a something higher than Gentilism could ever satisfy.

In this light our thoughts arrange themselves thus:

I. The expectation of the Gentiles.

II. The Manifestation or Epiphany.

I. The expectation: "Where is He that is born King of the Jews? for we have seen his star in the east, and are come to worship Him."

Observe, 1. The craving for Eternal Life. The "wise men" were "Magians," that is, Persian priests. The name, however, was extended to all the eastern philosophers who professed that religion, or even that philosophy. The Magians were chiefly distinguished by being worshippers of the stars, or students of astronomy.

Now astronomy is a science which arises from man's need of religion; other sciences spring out of wants bounded by this life. For instance, anatomy presupposes disease. There would be no prying into our animal frame, no anatomy, were there not a malady to stimulate the inquiry. Navigation arises from the necessity of traversing the seas to appropriate the produce of other countries. Charts, and maps, and soundings are made, because of a felt earthly want. But in astronomy the first impulse of mankind came not from the craving of the intellect, but from the necessities of the soul.

If you search down into the constitution of your being till you come to the lowest deep of all, underlying all other wants you will find a craving for what is infinite: a something that desires perfection: a wish that nothing but the thought of that which is eternal can satisfy. To the untutored mind nowhere was that want so called into consciousness, perhaps, as beneath the mighty skies of tho East. Serene and beautiful are the nights in Persia, and many a wise man in earlier days, full of deep thoughts, went out into the fields, like Isaac, to meditate at eventide. God has so made us that the very act of looking *up* produces in us perceptions of the sublime. And then those skies in their calm depths mirroring that which is boundless in space and illimitable in time, with a silence profound as death and a motion gliding on for ever, as if symbolizing eternity of life — no wonder if men associated with them their highest thoughts, and conceived them to be the home of Deity. No wonder if an Eternal Destiny seemed to sit enthroned there. No wonder if they seemed to have in their mystic motion an invisible sympathy with human life and its mysterious destinies. No wonder if he who best could read their laws was reckoned best able to interpret the duties of this life, and all that connects man with that which is invisible. No wonder if in those devout days of young thought, science was only another name for religion, and the Priest of the great temple of the universe was also the Priest in the temple made with hands. Astronomy was the religion of the world's youth.

The Magians were led by the star to Christ; their astronomy was the very pathway to their Saviour.

Upon this I make one or two remarks.

1. The folly of depreciating human wisdom. Of all vanities the worst is the vanity of ignorance. It is common enough to hear learning decried, as if it were an opposite of religion. If that means that science is not religion, and that the man who can calculate the motions of the stars may never have bowed his soul to Christ, it contains a truth. But if it means, as it often

does, that learning is a positive incumbrance and hindrance to religion, then it is as much as to say that the God of nature is not the God of grace; that the more you study the Creator's works, the further you remove from Himself: nay, we must go further to be consistent, and hold, as most uncultivated and rude nations do, that the state of idiocy is nearest to that of inspiration.

There are expressions of St. Paul often quoted as sanctioning this idea. He tells his converts to beware "lest any man spoil you through philosophy." Whereupon we take for granted that modern philosophy is a kind of antagonist to Christianity. This is one instance out of many of the way in which an ambiguous word misunderstood, becomes the source of infinite error. Let us hear St. Paul. He bids Timothy "beware of profane and old wives' fables." He speaks of "endless genealogies" — "worshipping of angels" — "intruding into those things which men have not seen." This was the philosophy of those days: a system of wild fancies spun out of the brain — somewhat like what we might now call demonolatry; but as different from philosophy as any two things can differ.

They forget, too, another thing. Philosophy has become Christian; science has knelt to Christ. There is a deep significance in that homage of the Magians. For it in fact was but a specimen and type of that which science has been doing ever since. The mind of Christ has not only entered into the Temple, and made it the house of prayer: it has entered into the temple of science, and purified the spirit of philosophy. This is its spirit now, as expounded by its chief interpreter, "Man, the interpreter of Nature, knows nothing, and can do nothing, except that which Nature teaches him." What is this but science bending before the Child, becoming childlike, and, instead of projecting its own fancies upon God's world, listening reverently to hear what it has to teach him? In a similar spirit, too, spoke the greatest of philosophers, in words quoted in every child's book: "I am but a child, picking up pebbles on the shore of the great sea of Truth."

Oh! be sure all the universe tells of Christ and leads to Christ. Rightly those ancient Magians deemed, in believing that God was worshipped truly in that august temple. The stars preach the mind of Christ. Not as of old, when a mystic star guided their feet to Bethlehem: but now, to the mind of the astronomer, they tell of Eternal Order and Harmony: they speak of changeless Law where no caprice reigns. You may calculate the star's return; and to the day, and hour, and minute it will be there. This is the fidelity of God. These mute masses obey the law impressed upon them by their Creator's Hand, unconsciously: and that law is the law of their own nature. To understand the laws of our nature, and consciously and reverently to obey them, that is the mind of Christ, the sublimest spirit of the Gospel.

I remark again, — This universe may be studied in an irreverent spirit. In Dan. ii. 48, we find the reverence which was paid to science. Daniel among the Chaldees was made chief of the wise men, that is, the first of the Magians: and King Nebuchadnezzar bowed before him, with incense and oblations. In later days we find that spirit changed. Another king, Herod, commands the wise men to use their science for the purpose of letting him know where the Child was. In earlier times they honoured the priest of nature: in later times they made use of him.

Only by a few is science studied now in the sublime and reverent spirit of old days. A vulgar demand for utility has taken the place of that lowly prostration with which the world listened to the discoveries of truth. The discovery of some new and mighty agent, by which the east and west are brought together in a moment, awakens chiefly the emotion of delight in us that correspondence and travelling will be quickened. The merchant congratulates himself upon the speedier arrival of the news which will give him the start of his rivals, and enable him to outrace his competitors in the competition of wealth. Yet what is this but the utilitarian spirit of Herod, seeing nothing more solemn in a mysterious star than the means whereby he might crush his supposed Rival?

There is a spirit which believes that "godliness is gain," and aims at being godly for the sake of advantage — which is honest, because honesty is the best policy — which says, Do right, and you will be the better, that is, the richer for it. There is a spirit which seeks for wisdom simply as a means to an earthly end — and that often a mean one. This is a spirit rebuked by the nobler reverence of the earlier days of Magianism. Knowledge for its own pure sake. God for His own sake. Truth for the sake of truth. This was the reason for which, in earlier days, men read the aspect of the heavens.

2. Next, in this craving of the Gentiles, we meet with traces of the yearning of the human soul for light. The Magian system was called the system of Lihgt about seven centuries B.C. A great reformer (Zoroaster)

had appeared, who either restored the system to its purity, or created out of it a new system. He said that Light its Eternal — that the Lord of the Universe is Light; but because there was an eternal Light, there was also an eternal possibility of the absence of Light. Light and Darkness therefore were the eternal principles of the universe — not equal principles, but one the negation of the other. He taught that the soul of man needs light — a light external to itself, as well as in itself. As the eye cannot see in darkness, and is useless, so is there a capacity in the soul for light; but it is not itself light; it needs the Everlasting light from outside itself.

Hence the stars became worshipped as the symbols of this light. But by degrees these stars began to stand in the place of the Light Himself. This was the state of things in the days of these Magians.

Magianism was now midway between its glory and its decline. For its glory we must go back to the days of Daniel, when a monarch felt it his privilege to do honour to the priest of Light — when that priest was the sole medium of communication between Deity and man, and through him alone "Oromasdes" made his revelations known — when the law given by the Magian, revealed by the eternal stars, was "the law of the Medes and Persians which altereth not." For its lowest degradation we must pass over about half a century from the time we are now considering, till we find ourselves in Samaria, in the presence of Simon the Magian. He gave himself out for the great power of God. He prostituted such powers and knowledge as he possessed to the object of making gain. Half-dupe, half-impostor, in him the noble system of light had sunk to petty charlatanism: Magianism had degenerated into Magic.

Midway between these two periods, or rather nearer to the latter, stood the Magian of the text. There is a time in the history of every superstition when it is respectable, even deserving reverence, when men believed it – when it is in fact associated with the highest feelings that are in man, and the channel even for God's manifestation to the soul. And there is a time when it becomes less and less credible, when clearer science is superseding its pretensions: and then is the period in which one class of men, like Simon, keep up the imposture: the priests who will not let the old superstition die, but go on, half-impostors, half-deceived by the strong delusion wherewith they believe their own lie. Another class, like Herod, the wise men of the world, who patronize it for their own purposes, and make use of it as an engine of state. Another still, who turn from side to side, feeling with horror the old, and all that they held dear, crumbling away beneath them — the ancient lights going out, more than half suspecting the falsehood of all the rest, and with an earnestness amounting almost to agony, leaving their own homes and inquiring for fresh light.

Such was the posture of these Magians. You cannot enter into their questions or sympathize with their wants unless you realize all this. For that desire for light is one of the most impassioned of our nobler natures. That noble prayer of the ancient world (ἐν δὲ φάει καὶ ὄλεσσον) "Give light, and let us die:" can we not feel it? Light — light. O if the result were the immediate realization of the old fable, and the blasting of the daring spirit in the moment of Revelation of its

God — yet give us light. The wish for light; the expectation of the manifestation of God, is the mystery which lies beneath the history of the whole ancient world.

II. The Epiphany itself.

First, they found a king. There is something very significant in the fact of that king being discovered as a child. The royal child was the answer to their desires. There are two kinds of monarchy, rule, or command. One is that of hereditary title; the other is that of Divine Right. There are kings of men's making, and kings of God's making. The secret of that command which men obey involuntarily, is submission of the Ruler himself to law. And this is the secret of the Royalty of the Humanity of Christ. No principle through all His Life is more striking, none characterizes it so peculiarly, as His submission to another Will. "I came not to do Mine own will, but the will of Him that sent Me." "The words which I speak, I speak not of myself." His commands are not arbitrary. They are not laws given on authority only — they are the eternal laws of our humanity, to which He Himself submitted: obedience to which alone can make our being attain its end. This is the secret of His kingship — "He became obedient . . . wherefore God also hath highly exalted Him."

And this is the secret of all influence and all command. Obedience to a law above you, subjugates minds to you who never would have yielded to mere will. "Rule thyself, thou rulest all."

2. Next, observe the adoration of the Magians — very touching and full of deep truth. The wisest of

the world bending before the *Child.* Remember the history of Magianism. It began with awe, entering into this world beneath the serene skies of the east: in Wonder and Worship. It passed into priestcraft and scepticism. It ended in Wonder and Adoration as it had begun; only with a truer and nobler meaning.

This is but a representation of human life. "Heaven lies around us in our infancy." The child looks on this world of God's as *one*, not many — all beautiful — wonderful — God's — the creation of a Father's hand. The man dissects — breaks it into fragments — loses love and worship in speculation and reasoning — becomes more manly, more independent, and less irradiated with a sense of the presence of the Lord of all; till at last, after many a devious wandering, if he be one whom the Star of God is leading blind by a way he knows not, he begins to see all as one again, and God in all. Back comes the Childlike spirit once more in the Christianity of old age. We kneel before the Child — we feel that to adore is greater than to reason — that to love, and worship, and believe, bring the soul nearer heaven than scientific analysis. The Child is nearer God than we.

And this, too, is one of the deep sayings of Christ — "Except ye be converted and become as little children, ye shall in no case enter into the kingdom of heaven."

3. Lastly, In that Epiphany we have to remark the Magians' joy. They had seen the star in the east. They followed it — it seemed to go out in dim obscurity. They went about inquiring: asked Herod, who could tell them nothing: asked the scribes, who only gave them a vague direction. At last the star shone out once more, clear before them in their path.

"When they saw the star, they rejoiced with exceeding great joy."

Perhaps the hearts of some of us can interpret that. There are some who have seen the star that shone in earlier days go out; quench itself in black vapours or sour smoke. There are some who have followed many a star that turned out to be but an ignis fatuus, one of those bright exhalations which hover over marshes and churchyards, and only lead to the chambers of the dead, or the cold damp pits of disappointment: and, O the blessing of "exceeding joy," after following in vain — after inquiring of the great men and learning nothing — of the religious men and finding little — to see the Star at last resting over "the place where the young Child lies" — after groping the way alone, to see the star stand still — to find that Religion is a thing far simpler that we thought — that God is near us — that to kneel and adore is the noblest posture of the soul. For, whoever will follow with fidelity his *own* star, God will guide him aright. He spoke to the Magians by the star; to the shepherds by the melody of the heavenly host; to Joseph by a dream; to Simeon by an inward revelation. "Gold, and frankincense, and myrrh," — these, and ten times these, were poor and cheap to give for that blessed certainty that the star of God is on before us.

Two practical hints in conclusion.

1. A hint of immortality. That star is now looking down on the wise men's graves; and if there be no life to come, then this is the confusion — that mass of inert matter is pursuing its way through space, and the minds that watched it, calculated its movements, were led by it through aspiring wishes to holy adorations —

those minds, more precious than a thousand stars, have dropped out of God's universe. And then God cares for mere material masses more than for spirits, which are the emanation and copy of Himself. Impossible. "God is not the God of the dead, but of the living." God is the Father of our *Spirits*. Eternity and immeasurableness belong to Thought alone. You may measure the cycles of that star by years and miles: — Can you bring any measurement which belongs to time or space by which you can compute the length or breadth or the duration of one pure thought, one aspiration, one moment of love? This is eternity. Nothing but thought can be immortal.

2. Learn, finally, the truth of the Epiphany by heart. To the Jew it chiefly meant that the Gentile, too, could become the child of God. But to us? — Is that doctrine obsolete? Nay, it requires to be reiterated in this age as much as in any other. There is a spirit in all our hearts whereby we would monopolize God, conceiving Him an unapproachable Being; whereby we may terrify other men outside our own pale, instead of the Father that is near to all, whom we have to approach, and whom to adore is blessedness.

This is our Judaism: we do not believe in the Epiphany. We do not believe that God is the Father of the world — we do not actually credit that He has a star for the Persian priest, and celestial melody for the Hebrew shepherd, and an unsyllabled voice for all the humble and inquiring spirits in His world. Therefore remember, Christ has broken down the middle wall of partition — He has revealed *Our* Father, proclaimed that there is no distinction in the spiritual family, and established a real Brotherhood on earth.

III.

Preached February 10, 1850.

THE HEALING OF JAIRUS' DAUGHTER.

MATT. ix. 23-25. — "And when Jesus came into the ruler's house, and saw the minstrels and the people making a noise, He said unto them, Give place; for the maid is not dead, but sleepeth. And they laughed him to scorn. But when the people were put forth, He went in, and took her by the hand, and the maid arose."

THIS is one of a pair of miracles, the full instruction from neither of which can be gained unless taken in connection with the other.

On his way to heal the daughter of Jairus, the Son of Man was accosted by another sufferer, afflicted twelve years with an issue of blood. Humanly speaking, there were many causes which might have led to the rejection of her request. The case was urgent: a matter of life and death: delay might be fatal: a few minutes might make all the difference between living and dying. Yet Jesus not only performed the miracle, but refused to perform it in a hurried way: paused to converse: to inquire who had touched Him: to perfect the lesson of the whole. On His way to perform one act of Love, He turned aside to give His attention to another.

The practical lesson is this: There are many who are so occupied by one set of duties as to have no time for others: some whose life-business is the suppression of the slave-trade — the amelioration of the state of prisons — the reformation of public abuses. Right, except so far as they are monopolized by these, and feel themselves discharged from other obligations. The minister's work is spiritual; the physician's temporal. But if the former neglect physical needs, or the latter shrink from spiritual opportunities on the plea that the cure of bodies, not of souls, is his work, so far they refuse to imitate their Master.

He had an ear open for every tone of wail: a heart ready to respond to every species of need. Specially the Redeemer of the soul, He was yet as emphatically the "Saviour of the body." He "taught the people:" but He did not neglect to multiply the loaves and fishes. The peculiar need of the woman: the father's cry of anguish: the infant's cry of helplessness: the wail of oppression, and the shriek of pain, — all were heard by Him, and none in vain.

Therein lies the difference between Christian love and the impulse of mere inclination. We hear of men being "interested" in a cause: it has some peculiar charm for them individually: the wants of the heathen; or the destitution of the soldier and sailor; or the conversion of the Jews, according to men's associations, or fancies, or peculiar bias, may engage their attention, and monopolize their sympathy. I am far from saying these are wrong: I only say that so far as they only *interest*, and monopolize interest, the source from which they spring is only human, and not the highest. The difference between such beneficence and that which is the result of Christian love, is marked by partiality in one case, universality in the other. Love is universal. It is interested in all that is human: not merely in the concerns of its own family, nation, sect, or circle of associations. Humanity is the sphere of its activity.

Here, too, we find the Son of Man the pattern of our humanity. His bosom was to mankind what the Ocean is to the world. The Ocean has its own mighty tide; but it receives and responds to, in exact proportion, the tidal influences of every estuary, and river, and small creek which pours into its bosom. So in Christ; His bosom heaved with the tides of our humanity: but every separate sorrow, pain, and joy gave its pulsation, and received back influence from the sea of His being.

Looking at this matter somewhat more closely, it will be plain that the delay was only apparent — seemingly there was delay, and fatal delay: while He yet spake, there came news of the child's death. But just so far as the resurrection of the dead is a mightier miracle than the healing of the sick, just so far did the delay enhance and illustrate, instead of dimming the glory of His mission.

But more definitely still. The miracles of Jesus were not merely arbitrary acts: they were subject to the laws of the spiritual world. It was, we may humbly say, impossible to convey a spiritual blessing to one who was not spiritually susceptible. A certain inward character, a certain relation *(rapport)* to the Redeemer, was required to make the mercy efficacious. Hence in one place we read, "He could not do many miracles there because of their unbelief." And His perpetual question was, "Believest thou that I am able to do this?"

Now Jairus beheld this miracle. He saw the woman's modest touch approaching the hem of the Saviour's garment. He saw the abashed look with which she shrunk from public gaze and exposure. He heard the language of Omniscience, "Somebody hath touched Me." He heard the great principle enunciated, that the only touch which reaches God is that of Faith.

The multitude may throng and press: but heart to heart, soul to soul, mind to mind, only so do we come in actual contact with God. And remembering this, it is a matter not of probability, but of certainty, that the soul of Jairus was actually made more capable of a blessing than before: that he must have walked with a more hopeful step: that he must have heard the announcement, "Thy daughter is dead," with less dismay: that the words, "Fear not, only believe," must have come to him with deeper meaning, and been received with more implicit trust, than if Jesus had not paused to heal the woman, but hurried on.

And this is the principle of the spiritual kingdom. In matters worldly, the more occupations, duties, a man has, the more certain is he of doing all imperfectly. In the things of God, it is reversed. The more duties you perform, the more you are fitted for doing others: what you lose in time, you gain in strength. You do not love God the less but the more, for loving man. You do not weaken your affection for your family by cultivating attachments beyond its pale, but deepen and intensify it. Respect for the alien, tenderness for the heretic, do not interfere with, but rather strengthen, attachment to your own country and your own church. He who is most liberal in the case of a foreign famine or a distant mission, will be found to have only learned more liberal love towards the poor and the unspiritualized of his own land: so false is the querulous complaint that money is drained away by such calls, to the disadvantage of more near and juster claims.

You do not injure one cause of mercy by turning aside to listen to the call of another.

I. The uses of adversity.

II. The principles of a Miracle.

I. The simplest and most obvious use of sorrow is to remind of God. Jairus and the woman, like many others, came to Christ from a sense of want. It would seem that a certain shock is needed to bring us in contact with reality. We are not conscious of our breathing till obstruction makes it felt. We are not aware of the possession of a heart till some disease, some sudden joy or sorrow, rouses it into extraordinary action. And we are not conscious of the mighty cravings of our half Divine humanity; we are not aware of the God within us, till some chasm yawns which must be filled, or till the rending asunder of our affections forces us to become fearfully conscious of a need.

And this, too, is the reply to a rebellious question which our hearts are putting perpetually: Why am I treated so? Why is my health or my child taken from me? What have I done to deserve this? So Job passionately complained that God had set him up as a mark to empty His quiver on.

The reply is, that gifts are granted to elicit our affections: they are resumed to elicit them still more: for we never know the value of a blessing till it is gone. Health, children — we must lose them before we know the love which they contain.

However, we are not prepared to say that a charge might not with some plausibility be brought against the love of God, were no intimation ever given that God means to resume His blessings. That man may fairly complain of his adopted father, who has been educated as his own son, and after contracting habits of extravagance, looking forward to a certain line of life, cultivating certain tastes, is informed that he is only adopted: that he must part with these temporary advantages, and sink into a lower sphere. It would be a poor excuse to say that all he had before was so much gain, and unmerited. It is enough to reply that false hopes were raised, and knowingly.

Nay, the laws of countries sanction this. After a certain period, a title to property cannot be interfered with: if a right of way or road has existed, in the venerable language of the law, after a custom "whereof the memory of man runneth not to the contrary," no private right, however dignified, can overthrow the public claim. I do not say that a bitter feeling might not have some show of justice if such were the case with God's blessings.

But the truth is this: God confers His gifts with distinct reminders that they are His. He gives us for a season, spirits taken out of His universe: brings them into temporary contact with us: and we call them father, mother, sister, child, friend. But just as in some places, on one day in the year, the way or path is closed in order to remind the public that they pass by sufferance and not by right, in order that no lapse of time may establish "adverse possession," so does God give warning to us. Every ache and pain: every wrinkle you see stamping itself on a parent's brow: every accident which reveals the uncertain tenure of life and possessions: every funeral-bell that tolls — are only God's reminders that we are tenants at will and not by right — pensioners on the bounty of an hour. He is closing up the right of way, warning fairly that what we have, is lent, not given: His, not ours. His mercies are so much gain. The resumption of them is no injustice. Job learned that, too, by heart, "The Lord gave, and the Lord hath taken away: blessed be the name of the Lord."

Again, observe the misuse of sorrow. When he came to the house, He found the minstrels and people making a noise. In the East, not content with natural grief, they use artificial means to deepen and prolong it. Men and women make it a separate profession to act as mourners, to exhibit for hire the customary symbols and wail of grief, partly to soothe and partly to rivet sorrow deeply, by expression of it.

The South and North differ greatly from each other in this respect. The nations of the North restrain their grief — affect the tearless eye, and the stern look. The expressive South, and all the nations whose origin is from thence, are demonstrative in grief. They beat their breasts, tear their hair, throw dust upon their heads. It would be unwise were either to blame or ridicule the other, so long as each is true to Nature. Unwise for the nations of the South to deny the reality of the grief which is repressed and silent. Unjust in the denizen of the North were he to scorn the violence of Southern grief, or call its uncontrollable demonstrations unmanly. Much must be allowed for temperament.

These two opposite tendencies, however, indicate the two extremes into which men may fall in this matter of sorrow. There are two ways in which we may defeat the purposes of God in grief — by forgetting it, or by over-indulging it.

The world's way is to forget. It prescribes gaiety as the remedy for woe: banishes all objects which recall the past: makes it the etiquette of feeling, even amongst near relations, to abstain from the mention of the names of the lost: gets rid of the mourning weeds as soon as possible — the worst of all remedies for grief. Sorrow, the discipline of the Cross, is the school for all that is highest in us. Self-knowledge, true power, all that dignifies humanity, are precluded the moment you try to merely banish grief. It is a touching truth that the Saviour refused the anodyne on the cross that would have deadened pain. He would not steep his senses in oblivion. He would not suffer one drop to trickle down the side of His Father's cup of anguish untasted.

The other way it to nurse sorrow: nay, even our best affections may tempt us to this. It seems treason to those we have loved to be happy now. We sit beneath the cypress; we school ourselves to gloom. Romance magnifies the fidelity of the broken heart: we refuse to be comforted.

Now all this must be done by effort, generally speaking. For God has so constituted both our hearts and the world, that it is hard to prolong grief beyond a time. Say what we will, the heart has in it a surprising, nay, a startling elasticity. It cannot sustain unalterable melancholy: and beside our very pathway plants grow, healing and full of balm. It is a sullen heart that can withstand the slow but sure influences of the morning sun, the summer sky, the trees and flowers, and the soothing power of human sympathy.

We are meant to sorrow; "but not as those without hope." The rule seems to consist in being simply natural. The great thing which Christ did was to call men back to simplicity and nature; not to perverted but original nature. He counted it no derogation of His manhood to be seen to weep. He thought it no shame to mingle with merry crowds. He opened His heart wide to all the genial and all the mournful impressions of this manifold life of ours. And this is what we have to do; be natural. Let God, that is, let the influences of God, freely play unthwarted upon the soul. Let there be no unnatural repression, no control of feeling by mere effort. Let there be no artificial and prolonged grief, no "minstrels making a noise." Let great Nature have her way. Or rather, feel that you are in a Father's world, and live in it with Him, frankly, in a free, fearless, childlike, and natural spirit. Then grief will do its work healthily. The heart will bleed, and stanch when it has bled enough. Do not stop the bleeding: but, also, do not open the wound afresh.

II. We come to the principles on which a miracle rests.

1. I observe that the perception of it was confined to a few. Peter, James, John, and the parents of the child, were the only ones present. The rest were excluded. To behold wonders, certain inward qualifications, a certain state of heart, a certain susceptibility are required. Those who were shut out were rendered incapable by disqualifications. Absence of spiritual susceptibility in the case of those who "laughed Him to scorn" — unbelief, in those who came with courteous scepticism, saying, "Trouble not the Master:" in other words, He is not master of impossibilities — unreality in the professional mourners — the most helpless of all disqualifications. Their whole life was acting: they

had caught the tone of condolence and sympathy as a trick. Before minds such as these the wonders of creation may be spread in vain. Grief and joy alike are powerless to break through the crust of artificial semblance which envelopes them. Such beings see no miracles. They gaze on all with dead, dim eyes — wrapped in conventionalisms, their life a drama in which they are but actors, modulating their tones and simulating feelings according to a received standard. How can such be ever witnesses of the supernatural, or enter into the presence of the wonderful? Two classes alone were admitted. They who, like Peter, James, and John, lived the life of courage, moral purity, and love, and they who, like the parents, had had the film removed from their eyes by grief. For there is a way which God has of forcing the spiritual upon men's attention. When you shut down the lid upon the coffin of a child, or one as dearly loved, there is an awful want, a horrible sense of insecurity, which sweeps away the glittering mist of time from the edge of the abyss, and you gaze on the phantom wonders of the unseen. Yes — real anguish qualifies for an entrance into the solemn chamber where all is miracle.

In another way, and for another reason, the numbers of those who witness a miracle must be limited. Jairus had his daughter restored to life: the woman was miraculously healed. But if every anxious parent and every sick sufferer could have the wonder repeated in his or her case, the wonder itself would cease. This is the preposterousness of the sceptic's demand. Let *me* see a miracle, on an appointed day and hour, and I will believe. Let us examine this.

A miracle is commonly defined to be a contravention of the laws of nature. More properly speaking, it is only a higher operation of those same laws, in a form hitherto unseen. A miracle is perhaps no more a suspension or contradiction of the laws of nature than a hurricane or a thunderstorm. They who first travelled to tropical latitudes came back with anecdotes of supernatural convulsions of the elements. In truth, it was only that they had never personally witnessed such effects: but the hurricane which swept the waves flat, and the lightning which illuminated all the heaven or played upon the bayonets or masts in lambent flames, were but effects of the very same laws of electricity and meteorology which were in operation at home. A miracle is perhaps no more in contravention of the laws of the universe than the direct interposition of a whole nation in cases of emergency to uphold what is right in opposition to what is established, is an opposition to the laws of the realm. For instance, the whole people of Israel reversed the unjust decree of Saul which had sentenced Jonathan to death. But law is the expression only of a people's will. Ordinarily we see that expression mediately made through judges, office-bearers, kings: and so long as we see it in this mediate form, we are by habit satisfied that all is legal. There are cases, however, in which, not an indirect, but a direct expression of a nation's will is demanded. Extraordinary cases; and because extraordinary, they who can only see what is legal in what is customary, conventional, and in the routine of written precedents, get bewildered, and reckon the anomalous act illegal or rebellious. In reality, it is only the source of earthly law, the nation, pronouncing the law without the intervention of the subordinate agents.

This will help us to understand the nature of a miracle. What we call laws are simply the subordinate expressions of a Will. There must be a Will before there can be a law. Certain antecedents are followed by certain consequents. When we see this succession, we are satisfied, and call it natural. But there are emergencies in which it may be necessary for the Will to assert Itself, and become not the mediate, but the immediate antecedent to the consequent. No subordinate agent interposes; simply the First cause comes in contact with a result. The audible expression of Will is followed immediately by something which is generally preceded by some lower antecedent, which we call a cause. In this case, you will observe, there has been no contravention of the laws of Nature — there has only been an immediate connection between the First cause and the last result. A miracle is the manifestation to man of the voluntariness of Power.

Now, bearing this in mind, let it be supposed that every one had a right to demand a miracle; that the occurrence of miracles was unlimited; that as often as you had an ache, or trembled for the loss of a relation, you had but to pray, and receive your wish.

Clearly in this case, first of all, the constitution of the universe would be reversed. The will of man would be substituted for the will of God. Caprice and chance would regulate all: — God would be dethroned: God would be degraded to the rank of one of those beings of supernatural power with whom eastern romance abounds, who are subordinated by a spell to the will of a mortal, who is armed with their powers and uses them as vassals: God would be merely the genius who would be chained by the spell of prayer to obey the behests of man. Man would arm himself with the powers of Deity, and God would be his slave.

Further still: This unlimited extension of miracles would annihilate miracles themselves. For suppose that miracles were universal: that prayer was directly followed by a reply: that we could all heal the sick and raise the dead: this then would become the common order of things. It would be what we now call nature. It would cease to be extraordinary, and the infidel would be as unsatisfied as ever. He would see only the antecedent, prayer, and the invariable consequent, a reply to prayer; exactly what he sees now in the process of causation. And then, just as now, he would say, What more do you want? These are the laws of the universe: Why interpose the complex and cumbrous machinery of a God, the awkward hypothesis of a Will, to account for laws?

Miracles, then, are necessarily limited. The non-limitation of miracles would annihilate the miraculous.

Lastly, It is the intention of a miracle to manifest the Divine in the common and ordinary.

For instance, in a boat on the sea of Tiberias, the Redeemer rose and rebuked the storm. Was that miracle merely a proof of His divine mission? Are we merely to gather from it, that then and there on a certain day, in a certain obscure corner of the world, Divine power was at work? It is conceivable that a man might credit that miracle: that he might be exceedingly indignant with the rationalist who resolves it into a natural phenomenon — and it is conceivable that that very man might tremble in a storm. To what purpose is that miracle announced to him? He believes in God existing in the past, but not in the present: he believes in a Divine presence in the supernatural, but discredits it in the natural; he recognises God in the marvellous, but does not feel Him in the wonderful of every day: unless it has taught him that the waves and winds *now* are in the hollow of the hand of God, the miracle has lost its meaning.

Here again, as in many other cases, Christ healed sickness and raised the dead to life. Are we merely to insert this among the "Evidences of Christianity," and then, with lawyer-like sagacity, having laid down the rules of Evidence, say to the infidel, "Behold our credentials: we call upon you to believe our Christianity." This were a poor reason to account for the putting forth of Almighty Power. More truly and more deeply, these miracles were vivid manifestations to the senses that Christ is the Saviour of the body: that now, as then, the issues of life and death are in His hands: that our daily existence is a perpetual miracle. The extraordinary was simply a manifestation of God's power in the ordinary. Nay, the ordinary marvels are greater than the extraordinary, for these are subordinate to them; merely indications and handmaids guiding us to perceive and recognise a constant Presence, and reminding us that in every-day existence the miraculous and the God-like rule us.

IV.

Preached March 10, 1850.

BAPTISM.

GAL. iii. 26-29. — "For ye are all the children of God by faith in Christ Jesus. For as many of you as have been baptized into Christ have put on Christ. There is neither Jew nor Greek, there is neither bond nor free, there is neither male nor female: for ye are all one in Christ Jesus. And if ye be Christ's, then are ye Abraham's seed, and heirs according to the promise."

WHEREVER opposite views are held with warmth by religious-minded men, we may take for granted that there is some higher truth which embraces both. All high truth is the union of two contradictories. Thus predestination and freewill are opposites: and the truth does not lie between these two, but in a higher reconciling truth which leaves both true. So with the opposing views of baptism. Men of equal spirituality are ready to sacrifice all to assert, and to deny, the doctrine of baptismal regeneration. And the truth, I believe, will be found, not in some middle, moderate, timid doctrine, which skilfully avoids extremes, but in a truth larger than either of these opposite views, which is the basis of both, and which really is that for which each party tenaciously clings to its own view as to a matter of life and death.

The present occasion (the decision of the Privy Council) only requires us to examine three views.

I. That of Rome.

II. That of modern Calvinism.

III. That of (as I believe) Scripture and the Church of England.

I. The doctrine of Rome respecting baptism. We will take her own authorities.

1. "If any one say that the sin of Adam . . . . is taken away, either by the powers of human nature or by any other remedy than the merit of the One Mediator, our Lord Jesus Christ . . . . . or denies that the merit of Jesus Christ, duly conferred by the sacrament of baptism in the church form, is applied to adults as well as to children — let him be accursed." Sess. V. 4.

"If any one deny that the imputation of original sin is remitted by the grace of our Lord Jesus Christ, which is conferred in baptism, or even asserts that the whole of that which has the true and proper character of sin, is not taken away, but only not imputed — let him be accursed." Sess. V. 5.

"If any one say that grace is not given by sacraments of this kind always and to all, so far as God's part is concerned, but only at times, and to some, although they be duly received — let him be accursed."

"If any one say that by the sacraments of the New Covenant themselves, grace is not conferred by the efficacy of the rite (opus operatum), but that faith alone is sufficient for obtaining grace — let him be accursed."

"If any one say that in three sacraments, *i. e.* baptism, confirmation, and orders, a character is not impressed upon the soul, *i. e.* a certain spiritual and indelible mark (for which reason they cannot be repeated) — let him be accursed." Sess. VII. cap. 7-9.

"By baptism, putting on Christ, we are made a new creation in Him, obtaining plenary and entire remission of all sins."

It is scarcely possible to misrepresent the doctrine

so plainly propounded. Christ's merits are instrumentally applied by baptism: original sin is removed by a change of nature: a new character is imparted to the soul: a germinal principle or seed of life is miraculously given; and all this, in virtue not of any condition in the recipient, nor of any condition except that of the due performance of the rite.

This view is held with varieties, and modifications of many kinds, by an increasingly large number of the members of the church of England; but we do not concern ourselves with these timid modifications, which painfully attempt to draw some subtle hair's-breadth distinction between themselves and the above doctrine. The true, honest, and only honest representation of this view is that put forward undisguisedly by Rome.

When it is objected to the Romanist that there is no evidence in the life of the baptized child different from that given by the unbaptized, sufficient to make credible a change so enormous, he replies, as in the case of the other sacrament — The miracle is invisible. You cannot see the bread and wine become flesh and blood: but the flesh and blood are there, whether you see them or not. You cannot see the effects of regeneration: but they are there, hidden, whether visible to you or not. In other words, Christ has declared that it is with every one born of the Spirit as with the wind: "*Thou hearest the sound thereof.*" But the Romanist distinctly holds that you *cannot* hear the sound: that the wind hath blown, but there is no sound: that the Spirit hath descended, and there are no fruits whereby the tree is known.

In examining this view, at the outset we deprecate those vituperative and ferocious expressions which are used so commonly against the church of Rome — unbecoming in private conversation, disgraceful on the platform, they are still more unpardonable in the pulpit. I am not advocating that feeble softness of mind which cannot speak strongly because it cannot feel strongly. I know the value, and in their place, the need of strong words. I know that the Redeemer used them: stronger and keener never fell from the lips of man. I am aware that our Reformers used coarse and vehement language; but we do not imbibe the Reformers' spirit by the mere adoption of the Reformers' language — nay, paradoxical as it may seem, the use of their language even proves a degeneracy from their spirit. You will find harsh and gross expressions enough in the Homilies; but remember that when they spoke thus, Rome was in the ascendancy; she had the power of fire and sword: and the men who spoke so were candidates for martyrdom, by the expressions that they used. Every one might be called upon by fire and steel to prove the quality of what was in him, and account for the high pretension of his words. I grant the grossness. But when they spoke of the harlotries of Rome, and spoke of her adulteries, and fornications, and lies, which she had put in full cup to the lips of nations, it was the sublime defiance of freehearted men against oppression in high places, and falsehood dominant. But now, when Rome is no longer dominant, and the only persecutions that we hear of are the petty persecutions of Protestants among themselves, to use language such as this is not the spirit of a daring Reformer, but only the pusillanimous shriek of a cruel cowardice, which keeps down the enemy whose rising it is afraid of.

We will do justice to this doctrine of Rome. It has this merit at least, that it recognises the character of a church: it admits it to be a society, and not an association. An association is an arbitrary union. Men form associations for temporary reasons: and, arbitrarily made, they can be arbitrarily dissolved. Society, on the contrary, is made not by will, but facts. Brotherhood — sonship — families — nations, are nature's work: real facts. Rome acknowledges this. It permits no arbitrary drawing of the lines of that which calls itself the church. A large, broad, mighty field: the Christian world: all baptized: nay, expressly, even those who are baptized by heretics. It shares the spirit, instead of monopolizing it.

Practically, therefore, in the matter of education, we should teach children on the basis on which Rome works. We say as Rome says, You are the child of God: Baptism declares you such. Rome says as Paul says, "As many of you as are baptized into Christ have put on Christ."

Consequently, we distinguish between this doctrine as held by spiritual and as held by unspiritual men. Spirituality often neutralizes error in views. Men are better often than their creeds. The Calvinist ought to be an Antinomian — he is not. So, in holy-minded men, this doctrine of baptismal regeneration loses its perniciousness — nay, even becomes, in erroneous form, a precious, blessed truth.

It is quite another thing, however, held by unspiritual men. Our objections to this doctrine are,

1. Because it assumes baptism to be not the testimony to a fact, but the fact itself. Baptism *proclaims* the child of God. The Romanist says it *creates* him. Then

and there a mysterious change takes place, inward, spiritual, effected by an external rite. This makes baptism not a sacrament, but an event.

2. Because it is materialism of the grossest kind. The order of Christian life is from within to that which is without — from the spiritual truth to the material expression of it. The Roman order is from the outward to the creation of the inward. This is magic. The Jewish cabalists believed that the pronunciation of certain magical words, engraved on the seal of Solomon, would perform marvels. The whole Eastern world fancied that such spells could transform one being into another — a brute into a man, or a man into a brute. Books containing such trash were burnt at Ephesus in the dawn of Christianity. But here, in the midday of Christianity, we have belief in such spells, given, it is true that it is said, by God, whereby the demoniacal nature can be exorcised, the Divine implanted in its stead, and the evil heart transformed unconsciously into a pure spirit.

Now this is degrading God. Observe the results: A child is to be baptized on a given day; but when that day arrives, the child is unwell, and the ceremony must be postponed another week or month. Again a delay takes place — the day is damp or cold. At last the time arrives: the service is read; it may require, if read slowly, five minutes more than ordinarily. Then and there, when that reading is slowly accomplished, the mystery is achieved. And all this time, while the child is ill, while the weather is bad, while the reader procrastinates — I say it solemnly — the Eternal Spirit who rules this universe must wait patiently, and come down, obedient to a mortal's spell, at the very second that it suits his convenience. God must wait attendance on the caprice of a careless parent, ten thousand accidents, nay, the leisure of an indolent or an immoral priest. Will you dare insult the Majesty on high by such a mockery as this result?

3. We object, because this view makes Christian life a struggle for something that is lost, instead of a progress to something that lies before. Let no one fancy that Rome's doctrine on this matter makes salvation an easy thing. The Spirit of God is given — the germ is implanted; but it may be crushed — injured — destroyed. And her doctrine is, that venial sins after baptism are removed by absolutions and attendance on the ordinances: whereas for mortal sins there is — not no hope — but no certainty ever after, until the judgment-day. Vicious men may make light of such teaching, and get periodic peace from absolution, to go and sin again: but to a spiritual Romanist this doctrine is no encouragement for laxity. Now, observe, after sin life becomes the effort to get back to where you were years ago. It is the sad longing glance at the Eden from which you have been expelled, which is guarded now by a fiery sword in this world for ever. And, therefore, whoever is familiar with the writings of some of the earliest leaders of the present movement Romewards, writings that rank among the most touching and beautiful of English compositions, will remember the marked tone of sadness which pervades them, their high sad longings after the baptismal purity that is gone: their mournful contemplations of a soul that once glistened with baptismal dew, now "seamed and scarred" with the indelible marks of sin. The true Christian life is ever onwards, full of trust and hope: a life wherein

even past sin is no bar to saintliness, but the step by which you ascend to higher vantage ground of holiness. The "indelible grace of baptism" — how can it teach that?

The Second view is that held by what we, for the sake of avoiding personalities, call modern Calvinism. It draws a distinction between the visible and the invisible church. It holds that baptism admits all into the former, but into the latter only a special few. Baptismal regeneration, as applied to the first, is merely a change of state — though what is meant by a *change of state* it were hard to say, or to determine wherein an unbaptized person admitted to all the ordinances would differ in *state* from a person baptized. The real benefit of baptism, however, only belongs to the elect. With respect to others, to predicate of them regeneration, in the highest sense, is at best an ecclesiastical fiction, said, "in the judgment of charity."

This view maintains that you are not God's child until you become such *consciously*. Not until evidence of a regenerate life is given — not until signs of a converted soul are shown, is it right to speak of being God's child, except in this judgment of charity. Now we remark,

1. This judgment of charity ends at the baptismal font. It is never heard of in after-life. It is like the charitable judgment of the English law, which presumes, or is said to presume, a man innocent till proved guilty: valuable enough as a legal fiction; nevertheless, it does not prevent a man barring his windows, guarding his purse, keenly watching against the dealings of those around him who are presumed innocent. Similarly, the so-called "judgment of charity" terminates

with infancy. They who speak of the church's language, in which children are called children of God, as being quite right, but only in "the judgment of charity," are exactly the persons who do not in after-life charitably presume that all their neighbours are Christians. "He is not a Christian." "She is one of the world:" or "one of the unregenerate." Such is the language applied to those who are in baptism reckoned children of God. They *could* not consistently apply to all adults the language applied in this text: "As many of you as have been baptized into Christ, have put on Christ. Ye are *all* the children of God by faith in Christ Jesus."

2. Next, I observe that this view is identical with the Roman one in this respect, that it *creates* the fact instead of testifying to it. Only, instead of baptism, it substitutes certain views, feelings, and impressions, and asserts that these *make* the man into a child of God. The Romanist says Baptism, the Calvinist says Faith, makes *that* true, which was *not* true before. It is not a fact that God is that person's Father, till in the one case Baptism, in the other Faith, have made him such.

3. Observe the pernicious results of this teaching in the matter of Education. Here again I draw the distinction between the practical consequences which legitimately ought to be, and those which actually are deduced from it. Happily men are better than their views. Hear the man speaking out of his theological system, and then hear him speaking out of the abundance of his heart. Hear the religious mother when the system is in view, and all are indiscriminately, except a certain few, corrupt, vile, with nothing good

in them, heirs of ruin. But hear her talk unguardedly of her own children. They have the frailties, weaknesses, common faults of childhood; but they have no vice in them: there is nothing base or degraded in her children! When the embraces of her child are round her neck, it will require more eloquence than you possess, to convince her that she is nursing a little demon in her lap. The heart of the mother is more than a match for the creed of the Calvinist.

There are some, however, who do not shrink from consistency, and develope their doctrine in all its consequences. The children follow out their instructions with fearful fidelity. Taught that they are not the children of God till certain feelings have been developed in them, they become by degrees bewildered, or else lose their footing on reality. They hear of certain mystic joys and sorrows; and unless they fictitiously adopt the language they hear, they are painfully conscious that they know nothing of them as yet. They hear of a depression for sin which they certainly have never experienced — a joy in God, making His service and His house the gate of heaven; and they know that it is excessively irksome to them — a confidence, trust, and assurance, of which they know nothing — till they take for granted what has been told them, that they are *not* God's children. Taught that they are as yet of the world, they live as the world — they carry out their education, which has dealt with them as children of the devil, to be converted: and children of the devil they become.

Of these two views, the last is by far the most certain to undermine Christianity in every Protestant country. The first at least assumes God's badge an universal one; and in education is so far right, practically: only wrong in the decision of the question how the child was created a child of God. But the second assumes a false, partial, party-badge — election, views, feelings. No wonder that the children of such religionists proverbially turn out ill.

III. We pass to the doctrine of the Bible and (I believe) of the Church.

Christ came to reveal a Name — the Father. He abolished the exclusive "my," and He taught to pray "our Father." He proclaimed God the Father — man the Son: revealed that the Son of Man is also the Son of God. Man — as man, God's child. He came to redeem the world from that ignorance of the relationship which had left them in heart aliens and unregenerate. Human nature, therefore, became, viewed in Christ, a holy thing and divine. The Revelation is a common humanity, sanctified in God. The appearance of the Son of God is the sanctification of the human race.

The development of this startled men. Sons of God! Yes; ye Jews have monopolized it too long. Is that Samaritan, heretic and alien, a child of God? Yes. The Samaritan: but not these outcasts of society? Yes; these outcasts of society. He went into the publican's house, and proclaimed that "he, too, was a son of Abraham." He suffered the sinful penitent to flood His feet with tears. He saw there the Eternal Light unquenched — the eye, long dimmed and darkened, which yet still could read the Eternal Mind. She, too, is God's erring, but forgiven, beloved, and "much-loving" child. One step further. He will not dare to say — the Gentiles? — the Gentiles who bow down to stocks and stones? Yes, the Gentiles too. He spake to them a parable. He told of a younger son who had lived long away from his Father's home. But his forgetfulness of his father could not abrogate the fact of his being His son, and as soon as he recognised the relationship, all the blessings of it were his own.

Now this is the Revelation. Man is God's child, and the sin of the man consists in perpetually living as if it were false. It is the sin of the heathen — and what is your mission to him but to tell him that he is God's child, and not living up to his privilege? It is the sin of the baptized Christian — waiting for feelings for a claim on God. It was the false life which the Jews had led: precisely this, that they were living coerced by law. Christ had come to redeem them from the law that they might receive the *adoption* of sons. But they were sons already, if they only knew it. "*Because* ye are sons, God hath sent forth the Spirit of His Son into your hearts, whereby ye cry Abba, Father:" To be a son of God is one thing: to know that you are and call Him Father, is another — and that is regeneration.

Now there was wanted a permanent and authoritative pledge, revealing and confirming this: for, to mankind in the mass, invisible truths become real only when they have been made visible. All spiritual facts must have an existence in form for the human mind to rest on. This pledge is baptism. Baptism is a visible witness to the world of that which the world is for ever forgetting. A common humanity united in God. Baptism authoritatively reveals and pledges to the individual that which is true of the race. Baptism takes the child and addresses it by name. Paul — no longer Saul — you are a child of God. Remember it henceforth. It is now revealed to you, and recognised by you, and to recognise God as the Father is to be regenerate (John i. 12). *You*, Paul, are now regenerate — you will have foes to fight — the world, the flesh, and the devil: but remember, they only keep you out of an inheritance which is your own; not an inheritance which you have to win, by some new feeling or merit in yourself. It *is* yours; you *are* the child of God — you *are* a member of Christ — you *are* an inheritor of the kingdom of heaven.

Observe, then, baptism does not *create* a child of God. It authoritatively declares him so. It does not make the fact: it only reveals it. If baptism made it a fact then and there for the first time, baptism would be magic. Nay, faith does not create a child of God any more than baptism, nor does it make a fact. It only appropriates that which is a fact already. For otherwise see what inextricable confusion you fall into. You ask a man to believe, and thereby be created a child of God. Believe what? That God is his Father. But God is not his Father. He is *not* a child of God, you say, till he believes. Then you ask him to believe a lie.

Herein lies the error, in basis identical, of the Romanist and the Calvinist. Faith is to one what baptism is to the other, the creator of a fact; whereas they both *rest* upon a fact, which is a fact whether they exist or not — before they exist; nay, without whose previous existence both of them are unmeaning and false.

The Catechism, however, says: In baptism . . . I was *made* a child of God. Yes; coronation makes a sovereign; but, paradoxical as it may seem, it can only *make* one a sovereign who is a sovereign already. Crown a pretender, that coronation will not create the king. Coronation is the authoritative act of the nation *declaring* a fact which was fact before. And ever after, coronation is the event to which all dates back — and the crown is the expression used for all royal acts: the crown pardons, the prerogatives of the crown, &c.

Similarly with baptism. Baptism makes a child of God in the sense in which coronation makes a king. And baptism naturally stands in Scripture for the title of regeneration and the moment of it. Only what coronation is in an earthly way, an authoritative manifestation of an invisible earthly truth, baptism is in a heavenly way. God's authoritative declaration in material form of a spiritual reality. In other words, no bare sign, but a Divine Sacrament.

Now for the blessings of this view.

1. It prevents exclusiveness and spiritual pride, and all condemnation and contempt of others: for it admits those who have no spiritual capacity or consciousness to be God's children. It proclaims a kingdom, not for a few favourites, but for mankind. It protests against the idea that Sonship depends on feelings. It asserts it as a broad, grand, universal, blessed fact. It bids you pray with a meaning of added majesty in the words, *Our* Father. Take care. Do not say of others that they are unregenerate, of the world. Do not make a distinction within the church of Christians and not-Christians. If you do, what do you more than the Pharisees of old? That wretched beggar that holds

his hat at the crossing of the street is God's child as well as you, if he only knew it. You know it — he does not: that is the difference: but the immortal is in him too, and the Eternal Word speaks in him. That daughter of dissipation whom you despise, spending night after night in frivolity, she, too, has a Father in heaven. "My Father and *your* Father, my God and *your* God." She has forgotten Him, and, like the prodigal, is trying to live on the husks of the world — the empty husks which will not satisfy — the degrading husks which the swine did eat. But whether she will or not, her baptism is valid, and proclaims a fact — which may be, alas! the worse for her, if she will not have it the better.

2. This doctrine protests against the notion of our being separate units in the Divine life. The church of Calvinism is merely a collection of atoms, a sand-heap piled together with no cohesion among themselves; or a mass of steel filings cleaving separately to a magnet, but not to each other. Baptism proclaims a church. Humanity joined in Christ to God. Do not say that the separating work of baptism, drawing a distinction between the church and the world, negatives this. Do not say, that because the church is separated from the world, therefore the world are not God's children. Rather that very separation proves it. You baptize a separate body in order to realize that which is true of the collective race, as in this text, "There is neither Jew nor Greek." In all things it is the same. If you would sanctify all time, you set apart a sabbath — not to show that other days are not intended to be sacred, but for the very purpose of making them sacred. If you would have a "nation of priests," you set apart

a priesthood; not as if the priestly functions of instruction and assisting to approach God were exclusively in that body, but in order, by concentration, to bring out to greater perfection the priestly character which is shared by the whole, and then thereby make the whole more truly "priests to God to offer spiritual sacrifices." In the same way, if God would baptize humanity, He baptizes a separate church, in order that that church may baptize the race. The church is God's ideal of humanity realized.

Lastly, This doctrine of baptism sanctifies materialism. The Romanist was feeling his way to a great fact, when he said that there are other things of sacramental efficacy besides these two — Baptism and the Supper of the Lord. The things of earth are pledges and sacraments of things in heaven. It is not for nothing that God has selected for His sacrament the commonest of all acts, a meal, and the most abundant of all materials — water. Think you that He means to say that only through two channels His Spirit streams into the soul? Or is it not much more in unison with His dealings to say, that these two are set apart to signify to us the sacramental character of all nature? Just as a miracle was intended not to reveal God working there, at *that* deathbed and in *that* storm, but to call attention to His presence in *every* death and *every* storm. Go out at this spring season of the year: see the mighty preparations for life that Nature is making: feel the swelling sense of gratefulness, and the persuasive expanding consciousness of love for all Being; and then say, whether this whole Form which we call Nature is not the great Sacrament of God, the revelation of His existence, and the channel of His communications to the spirit?

V.

Preached March 17, 1850.

BAPTISM.

1 Peter iii. 21. — "The like figure whereunto even baptism doth also now save us."

Last Sunday we considered the subject of baptism in reference to the Romish and modern Calvinistic views. The truth seemed to lie not in a middle course between the two extremes, but in a truth deeper than either of them. For there are various modifications of the Romish view which soften down its repulsive features. There are some who hold that the guilt of original sin is pardoned, but the tendencies of an evil nature remain. Others who attribute a milder meaning to "Regeneration," understanding by it a change of state instead of a change of nature. Others who acknowledge a certain mysterious benefit imparted by baptism, but decline determining how much grace is given, or what the exact nature of the blessing is. Others who acknowledge that it is in certain cases the moment when regeneration takes place, but hold that it is conditional, occurring sometimes, not always, and following upon the condition of what they call "prevenient grace." We do not touch upon these views. They are simply modifications of the Romish view; and as such, more offensive than the view itself: for they contain that which is in it most objectionable, and special evils of their own besides.

We admitted the merits of the two views. We are grateful to the Romanist for the testimony which he bears to the truth of the extent of Christ's salvation: for the privilege which he gives of calling all the baptized, children of God, — for the protest which his doctrine makes against all party monopoly of God, — for the protest against ultra-spiritualism, in acknowledging that material things are the types and channels of the Almighty Presence.

We are grateful to the Calvinist for his strong protest against formalism: for his assertion of the necessity of an inward change, — for the distinction which he has drawn between being in the *state* of sons and having the *nature* of sons of God.

The error in these two systems, contrary as they are, appeared to us to be identically one and the same, — that of pretending to create a fact instead of witnessing to it. The Calvinist maintains, that on a certain day and hour, under the ministry of the word, under the preaching of some one who "proclaims the gospel," he was born again, and God became his Father: and the Romanist declares, that on a certain day, at a certain moment by an earthly clock, by the hands of a priest apostolically ordained, the evil nature was expelled from him, and a new fact in the world was created — he attained the right of calling God his Father.

Now if baptism makes God our Father, baptism is incantation: if faith makes him so, faith rests upon a falsehood.

For the Romanist does no more than the red Indian and the black negro pretend to do: exorcise the devil, and infuse God. The only question then becomes, Which is the true enchanter, and which is the impostor? for the juggler does, by the power of imagination, often cure the sick man: but the mysterious effects of baptism never are visible, and never can be tested in this world.

On the other hand, Faith would rest upon a falsehood: for if faith is to give the right of calling God a Father, how can you believe that which is not true the very moment before belief? God is not your Father. If you believe He is, your belief is false.

The truth which underlies these two views, on which all that is true in them rests, and in which all that is false is absorbed, is the Paternity of God. This is the Revelation of the Redeemer. This is authoritatively declared by baptism, appropriated personally by faith: but a truth independent both of baptism and faith; which would still be true if there were neither a baptism nor a faith in the world. They are the *witnesses* of the Fact — not the creators of it.

Here, however, two difficulties arise. If this be so, do we not make light of Original Sin? And do we not reduce baptism into a superfluous ceremony?

Before we enter upon these questions, I must vindicate myself from the appearance of presumption. Where the wisest and holiest have held opposite views, it seems immodest to speak with unfaltering certainty and decisive tone. Hesitation, guarded statements, caution, it would seem, would be far more in place. Now, to speak decidedly is not necessarily to speak presumptuously. There are questions involving great research, and questions relating to truths beyond our ken, where guarded and uncertain tones are only a duty. There are others, where the decision has become conviction, a kind of intuition, the result of years of thought, which has been the day to a man's darkness, "the fountain-light of all his seeing," which has interpreted him to himself, made all clear where all was perplexed before, been the key to the riddle of truths that seemed contradictory, become part of his very being, and for which more than once he has held himself cheerfully prepared to sacrifice all that is commonly held dear. With respect to convictions such as these, of course, the arguments by which they are enforced may be faulty, the illustrations inadequate, the power of making them intelligible very feeble: nay, the views themselves may be wrong: but to pretend to speak with hesitation or uncertainty respecting such convictions, would be not modesty, but affectation.

For let us remember in what spirit we are to enter on this inquiry. Not in the spirit of mere cautious orthodoxy, endeavouring to find a safe mean between two extremes — inquiring what is the view held by the sound, and judicious, and respectable men, who were never found guilty of any enthusiasm, and under the shelter of whose opinion we may be secure from the charge of anything unsound. Nor in the spirit of the lawyer, patiently examining documents, weighing evidence, and deciding whether upon sufficient testimony there is such a thing as "prevenient grace" or not. Nor, once more, in the spirit of superstition. The superstitious mother of the lower classes baptizes her child in all haste because she believes it has a mystic influence on its health, or because she fancies that it confers the name without which it would not be summoned at the day of judgment. And the superstitious mother of the upper classes baptizes her child, too, in all haste, because, though she does not precisely know what the mystic effect of baptism is, she thinks it best to be on the safer side, lest her child should die, and its eternity should be decided by the omission. And we go to preach to the heathen, while there are men and women in our Christian England so bewildered with systems and sermons, so profoundly in the dark respecting the Father of our Lord Jesus Christ, so utterly unable to repose in Eternal Love and Justice, that they must guard their child *from* Him by a ceremony, and have the shadow of a shade of doubt whether or not, for omission of theirs, that child's Creator and Father may curse its soul for all eternity!

We are to enter upon this question as a real one of life and death: as men who feel in their bosoms sin and death, and who want to determine no theological nicety, but this: Whether we have a right to claim to be Sons of God or not? And if so, on what grounds? In virtue of a ceremony? or in virtue of a certain set of feelings? or in virtue of an Eternal Fact — the fact of God's Paternity?

I reply to two objections.

I. The apparent denial of original sin.

II. The apparent result that baptism is nothing.

I. The text selected is a strong and distinct one. It proclaims the value of baptism. "Baptism *saves* us." But it declares that it can only be said figuratively: "The like figure whereunto even baptism doth also now save us."

Now the first reply I make is, that in truth the Romish view seems to make lighter of original sin than this. Methinks original sin must be a trifling thing if a little water and a few human words can do away with it. A trifling thing if, after it is done away, there is no distinguishable difference between the baptized and unbaptized; if the unbaptized Quaker is just as likely to exhibit the fruits of goodness as the baptized son of the Church of England. We have got out of the land of reality into the domain of figments and speculations. A fictitious guilt is done away with by a fictitious pardon; neither the appearance nor the disappearance being visible.

Original sin is an awful fact. It is not the guilt of an ancestor imputed to an innocent descendant: but it is the tendencies of that ancestor living in his offspring and incurring guilt. Original sin can be forgiven only so far as original sin is removed. It is not Adam's: it is yours: and it must cease to be yours, or else what is "taking away original sin?"

Now he who would deny original sin must contradict all experience in the transmission of qualities. The very hound transmits his peculiarities learnt by education, and the Spanish horse his paces, taught by art, to his offspring, as a part of their nature. If it were not so in man, there could be no history of man as a species: no tracing out the tendencies of a race or nation: nothing but the unconnected repetitions of isolated individuals, and their lives. It is plain that the first man must have exerted on his race an influence quite peculiar: that his acts must have biassed their acts. And this bias or tendency is what we call original sin.

Now original sin is just this denial of God's Paternity, refusing to live as His children, and saying we are not His children. To live as His child is the true life: to live as not His child is the false life. What was the Jews' crime? Was it not this: "He came unto

His own, and His own received Him not:" that they *were* His own, and in act denied it, preferring to the claim of spiritual relationship, the claim of union by circumcision or hereditary descent? What was the crime of the Gentiles? Was it not this: that "when they knew God, they glorified Him not as God, neither were thankful?" For what were they to be thankful? For being His enemies? Were they not His children, His sheep of another fold? Was not the whole falsehood of their life the worship of demons and nothings instead of Him? Did not the parable represent them as the younger son, a wanderer from home, but still a *son?*

From this state Christ redeemed. He revealed God not as the Mechanic of the universe: not the Judge: but as the Father, and as the Spirit who is in man, "lighting every man," moving in man his infinite desires and infinite affections. This was the Revelation. The reception of that revelation is Regeneration. "He came unto His own, and His own received Him not; but to as many as *received* Him to them gave He power to become the Sons of God, even to as many as believed on His Name." They *were* His own — yet they wanted power to become His own.

Draw a distinction, therefore, between being the child of God and realizing it. The fact is one thing; the feeling of the fact, and the life which results from that feeling, is another. Redemption is the taking of us out of the life of falsehood into the life of truth and fact. "Of His own will begat He us by the word of Truth." But, remember, it is a truth: true whether you believe it or not: true whether you are baptized or not.

There are two ways in which that Revelation may be accepted. 1. By a public recognition called baptism. 2. By faith. In two ways, therefore, may it be said that man is saved. "We are saved by faith." But it is also true, figuratively, "Baptism saves us."

II. If baptism is only the public recognition and symbol of a fact, is not baptism degraded and made superfluous?

1. Baptism is given as a something to rest upon: nay, as a something without which redemption would soon become unreal: which converts a doctrine into a reality: which realizes visibly what is invisible.

For our nature is such, that immaterial truths are unreal to us until they are embodied in material form. Form almost gives them reality and being. For instance, Time is an eternal fact. But Time only exists to our conceptions as an actuality by measurements of materialism. When God created the sun, and moon, and stars, to serve for "signs and for seasons, and for days and years," He was actually, so far as man was concerned, creating time. Our minds would be only floating in an eternal Now, if it were not for symbolical successions which represent the processes of thought. The clock in the house is almost a fresh creation. It realizes. The gliding heavens, and the seasons, and the ticking clock, what is time to us without them? Nothing.

God's character, again, nay, God Himself, *to us* would be nothing if it were not for the creation, which is the great symbol and sacrament of His presence. If there were no light — no sunshine — no sea — no national and domestic life — no material witness of

His being, God would be to us as good as lost. The Creation *gives* us God: for ever real in Himself, by Creation He becomes a Fact to *us*.

It is in virtue, again, of this necessity in man for an outward symbol to realize an invisible Idea, that a bit of torn and blackened rag hanging from a fortress or the tafferel of a ship, is a kind of life to iron-hearted men. Why is it that in the heat of battle there is one spot where the sabres flash most rapidly, and the pistols' ring is quicker, and men and officers close in most densely, and all are gathered round one man, round whose body that tattered silk is wound, and held with the tenacity of a death-struggle? Are they only children fighting for a bit of rag? That flag is everything to them: their regiment — their country — their honour — their life: Yet it is *only* a symbol! Are symbols nothing?

In the same way, baptism is a fact for man to rest upon: a doctrine realized to flesh and blood. A something in eternity which has no place in time brought down to such time expressions as "then and there."

2. Again, baptism is the token of a church: the token of an universal church. Observe the importance of its being the sacrament of an universal church instead of the symbol of a sect. Not episcopacy, not justification by faith, nor any party-badge; but "one baptism." How blessed, on the strength of this, to be able to say to the baptized dissenter, You are my brother: you anathematize my church — link popery and prelacy together — malign me; but the same sign is on our brow, and the same Father was named over our baptism. Or to say to a baptized Romanist, You are my brother too — in doctrinal error perhaps — in error of

life it may be too: but my brother — our enemies the same — our struggle the same — our hopes and warfare the very same. Or to the very outcast, — And you, my poor degraded friend, are my brother still — sunk, oblivious of your high calling; but still whatever keeps you away from heaven, keeps you from your own. You may live the false life till it is too late: but still, you only exclude yourself from your home. Of course this is very offensive. What! the Romanist my brother! the synagogue of Satan the house of God! the Spirit of God dwelling with the church of Rome! the believer in transubstantiation my brother and God's child! Yes, even so; and it is just your forgetfulness of what baptism is and means, that accounts for that indignation of yours. Do you remember what the elder brother in the parable was doing? He went away sulky and gloomy, because one, not half so good as himself, was recognised as his Father's child.

3. Baptism is seen to be no mere superfluity when you remember that it is an authoritative symbol. Draw the distinction between an arbitrary symbol and an authoritative one — for this difference is everything.

I take once again the illustration of the coronation act. Coronation places the crown on the brow of one who *is* sovereign. It does not make the fact; it witnesses it. Is coronation therefore nothing? An arbitrary symbolical act agreed on by a few friends of the sovereign would be nothing: but an act which is the solemn ratification of a country is everything. It realizes a fact scarcely till then felt to be real. Yet the fact was fact before — otherwise the coronation would be invalid. Even when the third William was crowned, there was the symbol of a previous fact — the nation's decree that he should be king: and accordingly, ever after, all is dated back to that. You talk of crown-prerogatives. You say in your loyalty you "would bow to the crown, though it hung upon a bush." Yet it is only a symbol! You only say it "in a figure." But that figure contains within it the royalty of England.

In a figure, the Bible speaks of baptism as you speak of coronation, as identical with that which it proclaims. It calls it regeneration. It says baptism saves. A grand figure — because it rests upon eternal fact. Call you that nothing?

We look to the Bible to corroborate this. In the Acts of the Apostles, Cornelius is baptized. On what grounds? To manufacture him into a child of God? or because he *was* the child of God? Did his baptism create the fact? or was the fact prior to his baptism, and the ground on which his baptism was valid? The history is this: St. Peter could not believe that a Gentile could be a child of God. But miraculous phenomena manifested to his astonishment that this Gentile actually *was* God's child — whereupon the argument of Peter was very natural. He has the spirit, therefore baptism is superfluous. Nay! he has the spirit, therefore give him the *symbol* of the spirit. Let it be revealed to others what he is. He *is* heir to the inheritance, therefore give him the title-deeds. He *is* of royal lineage — put the crown upon his head. He *is* a child of God — baptize him. "Who shall forbid water, seeing these have received the Holy Ghost as well as we?"

One illustration more from the marriage ceremony; and I select this for two reasons: because it is the type in Scripture of the union between Christ and His church, and because the church of Rome has called it a sacrament.

A deep truth is in that error. Rome calls it a sacrament, because it is the authoritative symbol of an invisible fact. That invisible fact is the agreement of two human beings to be one. We deny it to be a sacrament, because, though it is the symbol of an invisible fact, it is not the symbol of a spiritual fact — nor an eternal fact: no spiritual truth, but only a changeful human covenant.

Now observe the difference between an arbitrary or conventional, and an authoritative ceremony of marriage-union. There are conventional acknowledgments of that agreement, ceremonies peculiar to certain districts, private pledges, betrothals. In the sight of God those are valid: they cannot be lightly broken without sin. You cannot in the courts of heaven distinguish between an oath to God, and a word pledged to man. He said, "Let your yea be yea, and your nay, nay." Such an engagement cannot be infringed without penalty: the penalty of frivolized hearts, and that habit of changefulness of attachment which is the worst of penalties. But now, additional to that, will any one say that the marriage-ceremony is superfluous — that the ring he gives his wife is nothing? It is everything. It is the authoritative ratification by a country and before God of that which before was for all purposes of earth unreal. Authoritative — therein lies the difference. Just in that authoritativeness lies the question whether the ceremony is nothing or everything.

And yet remember, the ceremony itself does not pretend to create the fact. It only claims to realize the fact. It admits the fact existing previously. It bases itself upon a fact. Forasmuch as two persons have consented together — and forasmuch as a token and pledge of that in the shape of a ring has been given, therefore, only therefore, the appointed minister *pronounces* that they are what betrothal had made them already in the sight of God.

Exactly so, the *authoritativeness* is the all in all which converts baptism from a mere ceremony into a sacrament. Baptism is not merely a conventional arrangement, exceedingly convenient, agreed on by men to remind themselves and one another that they are God's children — but valid as a legal, eternal Truth, a condensed, embodied Fact.

Is this making baptism nothing? I should rather say baptism is everything. Baptism saves us.

One word now practically. I address myself to any one who is conscious of fault, sin-laden, struggling with the terrible question whether he has a right to claim God as his father or not, bewildered on the one side by Romanism — on the other by Calvinism. My brother! let not either of these rob you of your privileges. Let not Rome send you to the fearful questioning as to whether the mystic seed infused at a certain moment by an act of man remains in you still, or whether it has been so impaired by sin that henceforth there is nothing but penance, tears, and uncertainty until the grave. Let not Calvinism send you with terrible self-inspection to the more dreadful task of searching your own soul for the warrant of your redemption, and deciding whether you have or not the feelings and the faith which give you a right to be one of God's elect. Better make up your mind at once you have not — you have no feelings that entitle you to that. Take your stand upon the broader, sublimer basis of God's Paternity. God created the world — God redeemed the world. Baptism proclaims separately, personally, by name, to you — God created you — God redeemed you. Baptism is your warrant, you *are* His child. And now, because you are His child, live as a child of God: be redeemed from the life of evil which is false to your nature into the Life of Light and Goodness, which is the Truth of your Being. Scorn all that is mean: hate all that is false: struggle with all that is impure. Love whatsoever "things are true, whatsoever things are just, whatsoever things are honest, whatsoever things are lovely, whatsoever things are of good report?" certain that God is on your side, and that whatever keeps you from Him, keeps you from your own Father. Live the simple, lofty life which befits an heir of immortality.

VI.

Preached October 13, 1850.

ELIJAH.

1 Kings xix. 4. — "But he himself went a day's journey into the wilderness, and came and sat down under a juniper-tree: and he requested for himself that he might die; and said, It is enough: now, O Lord, take away my life: for I am not better than my fathers."

It has been observed of the holy men of Scripture, that their most signal failures took place in those points of character for which they were remarkable in excellence. Moses was the meekest of men — but it was Moses who "spake unadvisedly with his lips." St. John was the apostle of charity; yet he is the very type to us of religious intolerance, in his desire to call down fire from heaven. St. Peter is proverbially the apostle of impetuous intrepidity: yet twice he proved a craven. If there were anything for which Elijah is remarkable, we should say it was superiority to human weakness. Like the Baptist, he dared to arraign and rebuke his sovereign: like the commander who cuts down the bridge behind him, leaving himself no alternative but death or victory, he taunted his adversaries, the priests of Baal on Mount Carmel; making them gnash their teeth and cut themselves with knives, but at the same time ensuring for himself a terrible end, in case of failure, from his exasperated foes. And again, in his last hour, when he was on his way to a strange and unprecedented departure from this world — when the whirlwind and flame-chariot were ready, he asked for no human companionship. The bravest men are pardoned if one lingering feeling of human weakness clings to them at the last, and they desire a human eye resting on them — a human hand in theirs — a human presence. But Elijah would have rejected all. In harmony with the rest of his lonely severe character, he desired to meet his Creator alone. Now it was this man — so stern, so iron, so independent, so above all human weakness, of whom it was recorded that in his trial hour he gave way to a fit of petulance and querulous despondency to which there is scarcely found a parallel. Religious despondency, therefore, is our subject.

I. The causes of Elijah's despondency.

II. God's treatment of it.

The causes of Elijah's despondency.

1. Relaxation of physical strength.

On the reception of Jezebel's message, Elijah flies for his life — toils on the whole day — sits down under a juniper-tree, faint, hungry, and travel-worn; the gale of an Oriental evening, damp and heavy with languid sweetness, breathing on his face. The prophet and the man give way. He longs to die: you cannot mistake the presence of causes in part purely physical.

We are fearfully and wonderfully made. Of that constitution, which in our ignorance we call union of soul and body, we know little respecting what is cause and what is effect. We would fain believe that the mind has power over the body, but it is just as true that the body rules the mind. Causes apparently the most trivial: a heated room — want of exercise — a sunless day — a northern aspect — will make all the difference between happiness and unhappiness, between faith and doubt, between courage and indecision. To our fancy there is something humiliating in being thus at the mercy of our animal organism. We would fain find nobler causes for our emotions. We talk of the hiding of God's countenance, and the fiery darts of Satan. But the picture given here is true. The body is the channel of our noblest emotions as well as our sublimest sorrows.

Two practical results follow. First, instead of vilifying the body, complaining that our nobler part is chained down to a base partner, it is worth recollecting that the body too is the gift of God, in its way Divine: "the temple of the Holy Ghost;" and that to keep the body in temperance, soberness, and chastity, to guard it from pernicious influence, and to obey the laws of health, are just as much religious as they are moral duties; just as much obligatory on the Christian as they are on a member of a Sanitary Committee. Next, there are persons melancholy by constitution, in whom the tendency is incurable; you cannot exorcise the phantom of despondency. But it is something to know that it is a phantom, and not to treat it as a reality — something taught by Elijah's history, if we only learn from it to be patient, and wait humbly the time and good pleasure of God.

Second Cause — Want of sympathy. "I, even I only, am left." Lay the stress on *only*. The loneliness of his position was shocking to Elijah. Surprising this: for Elijah wanted no sympathy in a far harder trial on Mount Carmel. It was in a tone of triumph that he proclaimed that he was the single, solitary prophet of the Lord, while Baal's prophets were 450 men.

Observe, however, the difference. There was in

that case an opposition which could be grappled with: here nothing against which mere manhood was availing. The excitement was passed — the chivalrous look of the thing gone. To die as a martyr: yes, that were easy, in grand failure — but to die as a felon — to be hunted, caught, taken back to an ignominious death, flesh and blood recoiled from that.

And Elijah began to feel that popularity is not love. The world will support you when you have constrained its votes by a manifestation of power: and shrink from you when power and greatness are no longer on your side. "I, even I only, am left."

This trial is most distinctly realized by men of Elijah's stamp and placed under Elijah's circumstances. It is the penalty paid by superior mental and moral qualities, that such men must make up their minds to live without sympathy. Their feelings will be misunderstood, and their projects uncomprehended. They must be content to live alone. It is sad to hear such appeal from the present to the judgment of the future. Poor consolation! Elijah has been judged at that bar. We are his posterity: our reverence this day is the judgment of posterity on him. But to Elijah what is that now? Elijah is in that quiet country where the voice of praise and the voice of blame are alike unheard. Elijah lived and died alone: once only the bitterness of it found expression. But what is posthumous justice to the heart that ached *then*?

What greater minds like Elijah's have felt intensely, all we have felt in our own degree. Not one of us but what has felt his heart aching for want of sympathy. We have had our lonely hours, our days of disappointment, and our moments of hopelessness —

times when our highest feelings have been misunderstood, and our purest met with ridicule.

Days when our heavy secret was lying unshared, like ice upon the heart. And then the spirit gives way: we have wished that all were over — that we could lie down tired, and rest like the children, from life — that the hour was come when we could put down the extinguisher on the lamp, and feel the last grand rush of darkness on the spirit.

Now, the final cause of this capacity for depression — the reason for which it is granted us, is that it may make God necessary. In such moments it is felt that sympathy beyond human is needful. Alone, the world against him, Elijah turns to God. "It is enough: now, *O Lord*."

3. Want of occupation.

As long as Elijah had a prophet's work to do, severe as that work was, all went on healthily: but his occupation was gone. To-morrow and the day after, what has he left on earth to do? The misery of having nothing to do proceeds from causes voluntary or involuntary in their nature. Multitudes of our race, by circumstances over which they have no control, in single life or widowhood — in straitened circumstances, are compelled to endure lonely days, and still more lonely nights and evenings. They who have felt the hours hang so heavy, can comprehend part of Elijah's sadness.

This misery, however, is sometimes voluntarily incurred. In artificial civilization certain persons exempt themselves from the necessity of work. They eat the bread which has been procured by the sweat of the brow of others — they skim the surface of the thought which has been ploughed by the sweat of the brain of others. They are reckoned the favoured ones of fortune, and envied: Are they blessed? The law of life is, in the sweat of thy brow thou shalt eat bread. No man can evade that law with impunity. Like all God's laws it is its own executioner. It has strange penalties annexed to it — would you know them? Go to the park, or the esplanade, or the solitude after the night of dissipation, and read the penalties of being useless, in the sad, jaded, listless countenances — nay, in the very trifles which must be contrived to create excitement artificially. Yet these very eyes could, dull as they are, beam with intelligence: on many of those brows is stamped the mark of possible nobility. The fact is, that the capacity of ennui is one of the signatures of man's immortality. It is his very greatness which makes inaction misery. If God had made us only to be insects, with no nobler care incumbent on us than the preservation of our lives, or the pursuit of happiness, we might be content to flutter from sweetness to sweetness, and from bud to flower. But if men with souls live only to eat and drink and be amused, is it any wonder if life be darkened with despondency?

Fourth Cause — Disappointment in the expectation of success. On Carmel the great object for which Elijah had lived seemed on the point of being realized. Baal's prophets were slain — Jehovah acknowledged with one voice: false worship put down. Elijah's life-aim — the transformation of Israel into a kingdom of God, was all but accomplished. In a single day all this bright picture was annihilated.

Man is to desire success, but success rarely comes.

The wisest has written upon life its sad epitaph. "All is vanity," *i.e.* nothingness.

The tradesman sees the noble fortune for which he lived, every coin of which is the representative of so much time and labour spent, squandered by a spendthrift son. The purest statesmen find themselves at last neglected, and rewarded by defeat. Almost never can a man look back on life and say that its anticipations have been realized. For the most part life is disappointment, and the moments in which this is keenly realized are moments like this of Elijah's.

II. God's treatment of it.

1. First he recruited his servant's exhausted strength. Read the history. Miraculous meals are given — then Elijah sleeps, wakes, and eats: on the strength of that goes forty days' journey. In other words, like a wise physician, God administers food, rest, and exercise, and then, and not till then, proceeds to expostulate — for before, Elijah's mind was unfit for reasoning.

Persons come to the ministers of God in seasons of despondency; they pervert with marvellous ingenuity all the consolation which is given them: turning wholesome food into poison. Then we begin to perceive the wisdom of God's simple homely treatment of Elijah, and discover that there are spiritual cases which are cases for the physician rather than the divine.

2. Next Jehovah calmed his stormy mind by the healing influences of Nature. He commanded the hurricane to sweep the sky, and the earthquake to shake the ground. He lighted up the heavens till they were one mass of fire. All this expressed and reflected Elijah's feelings. The mode in which Nature soothes

us is by finding meeter and nobler utterance for our feelings than we can find in words — by expressing and exalting them. In expression there is relief. Elijah's spirit rose with the spirit of the storm. Stern wild defiance — strange joy — all by turns were imaged there. Observe, "*God* was not in the wind," nor in the fire, nor in the earthquake. It was Elijah's stormy self reflected in the moods of the tempest, and giving them their character.

Then came a calmer hour. Elijah rose in reverence — felt tenderer sensations in his bosom. He opened his heart to gentler influences, till at last out of the manifold voices of Nature there seemed to speak, not the stormy passions of the man, but the "still small voice" of the harmony and the peace of God.

There are some spirits which must go through a discipline analogous to that sustained by Elijah. The storm-struggle must precede the still small voice. There are minds which must be convulsed with doubt before they can repose in faith. There are hearts which must be broken with disappointment before they can rise into hope. There are dispositions which, like Job, must have all things taken from them, before they can find all things again in God. Blessed is the man who, when the tempest has spent its fury, recognises his Father's voice in its under-tone, and bares his head and bows his knee, as Elijah did. To such spirits, generally those of a stern rugged cast, it seems as if God had said, "In the still sunshine and ordinary ways of life you cannot meet Me, but like Job, in the desolation of the tempest you shall see My Form, and hear My Voice, and know that your Redeemer liveth."

3. Besides, God made him feel the earnestness of

life. What *doest* thou here, Elijah? Life is for doing. A prophet's life for nobler doing — and the prophet was not doing but moaning.

Such a voice repeats itself to all of us, rousing us from our lethargy, or our despondency, or our protracted leisure, "What doest thou here?" here in this short life. There is work to be done — evil put down — God's Church purified — good men encouraged — doubting men directed — a country saved — time going — life a dream — eternity long — one chance, and but one for ever. What *doest thou* here?

Then he went on further, "Arise, go on thy way." That speaks to us: on thy way. Be up and doing — fill up every hour, leaving no crevice or craving for a remorse, or a repentance to creep through afterwards. Let not the mind brood on self: save it from speculation, from those stagnant moments in which the awful teachings of the spirit grope into the unfathomable unknown, and the heart torments itself with questions which are insoluble except to an active life. For the awful Future becomes intelligible only in the light of a felt and active Present. Go, return on thy way if thou art desponding — *on thy way* health of spirit will return.

4. He completed the cure by the assurance of victory. "Yet have I left me seven thousand in Israel who have not bowed the knee to Baal." So, then, Elijah's life had been no failure after all. Seven thousand at least in Israel had been braced and encouraged by his example, and silently blessed him perhaps for the courage which they felt. In God's world for those that are in earnest there is no failure. No work truly done — no word earnestly spoken — no sacrifice

freely made, was ever made in vain. Never did the cup of cold water given for Christ's sake lose its reward.

We turn naturally from this scene to a still darker hour and more august agony. If ever failure seemed to rest on a noble life, it was when the Son of Man, deserted by His friends, heard the cry which proclaimed that the Pharisees had successfully drawn the net round their Divine Victim. Yet from that very hour of defeat and death there went forth the world's life — from that very moment of apparent failure there proceeded forth into the ages the spirit of the conquering Cross. Surely if the Cross says anything, it says that apparent defeat is real victory, and that there is a heaven for those who have *nobly and truly* failed on earth.

Distinguish, therefore, between the Real and the Apparent. Elijah's apparent success was in the shouts of Mount Carmel. His real success was in the unostentatious, unsurmised obedience of the seven thousand who had taken his God for their God.

A lesson for all. For teachers who lay their heads down at night sickening over their thankless task. Remember the power of *indirect* influences: those which distil from a life, not from a sudden, brilliant effort. The former never fail: the latter often. There is good done of which we can never predicate the when or where. Not in the flushing of a pupil's cheek: or the glistening of an attentive eye: not in the shining results of an examination does your real success lie. It lies in that invisible influence on character which He alone can read who counted the seven thousand nameless ones in Israel.

For ministers again — what is ministerial success?

Crowded churches — full aisles — attentive congregations — the approval of the religious world — much impression produced? Elijah thought so: and when he found out his mistake, and discovered that the applause on Carmel subsided into hideous stillness; his heart well-nigh broke with disappointment. Ministerial success lies in altered lives and obedient humble hearts: unseen work recognised in the judgment-day.

A public man's success? That which can be measured by feast-days and the number of journals which espouse his cause? Deeper, deeper far must he work who works for Eternity. In the eye of That, nothing stands but gold — real work — all else perishes.

Get below appearances, below glitter and show. Plant your foot upon reality. Not in the jubilee of the myriads on Carmel, but in the humble silence of the hearts of the seven thousand, lay the proof that Elijah had not lived in vain.

VII.

Preached January 12, 1851.

NOTES ON PSALM LI.

Written by David, after a double crime: — Uriah put in the fore-front of the battle — the wife of the murdered man taken, &c.

A DARKER guilt you will scarcely find — kingly power abused — worst passions yielded to. Yet this psalm breathes from a spirit touched with the finest sensibilities of spiritual feeling.

Two sides of our mysterious twofold being here. Something in us near to hell: something strangely near to God. "Half beast — half devil?" No: rather half diabolical — half divine: half demon — half God. This man mixing with the world's sins in such sort that we shudder. But he draws near the Majesty of God, and becomes softened, purified, melted.

Good to observe this that we rightly estimate: generously of fallen humanity; moderately of highest saintship.

In our best estate and in our purest moments there is a something of the Devil in us which, if it could be known, would make men shrink from us. The germs of the worst crimes are in us all. In our deepest degradation there remains something sacred, undefiled, the pledge and gift of our better nature: a germ of indestructible life, like the grains of wheat among the cerements of a mummy surviving through three thousand years; which *may* be planted, and live, and grow again.

It is this truth of human feeling which makes the Psalms, more than any other portion of the Old Testament, the link of union between distant ages. The historical books need a rich store of knowledge before they can be a modern book of life: but the Psalms are the records of individual experience. Personal religion is the same in all ages. The deeps of our humanity remain unruffled by the storms of ages which change the surface. This psalm, written three thousand years ago, might have been written yesterday: describes the vicissitudes of spiritual life in an Englishman as truly as of a Jew. "Not of an age but for all time."

I. Scripture estimate of sin.

II. Spiritual restoration.

I. Scripture estimate of sin.

1. Personal accountability. "My sin" — strange, but true. It is hard to believe the sin we do our own. One lays the blame on circumstances: another on those who tempted: a third on Adam, Satan, or his own nature, as if it were not himself. "The fathers have eaten a sour grape, and the children's teeth are set on edge."

In this psalm there is no such self-exculpation. Personal accountability is recognised throughout. No source of evil suggested or conceived but his own guilty will: no shifting of responsibility: no pleading of a passionate nature, or of royal exposure as peculiar. "I have sinned." "I acknowledge *my* transgression: *my* sin is ever before me."

One passage only seems at first to breathe a different tone, "In sin did my mother conceive me." By some interpreted as referring to hereditary sin:

alleged as a proof of the doctrine of transmitted guilt, as if David traced the cause of his act to his maternal character.

True as the doctrine is that physical and moral qualities are transmissible, you do not find that doctrine here. It is not in excuse, but in exaggeration of his fault that David speaks. He lays on himself the blame of a tainted nature, instead of that of a single fault: not a murder only, but of a murderous nature. "Conceived in sin." From his first moments up till then, he saw sin — sin — sin: nothing but sin.

Learn the individual character of sin — its personal origin, and personal identity. There can be no transference of it. It is individual and incommunicable. My sin cannot be your sin, nor yours mine.

Conscience, when it is healthy, ever speaks thus: "my transgression." It was not the guilt of them that tempted you: they have theirs; but each as a separate agent, his own degree of guilt. Yours is your own: the violation of your own and not another's sense of duty; solitary, awful, unshared, adhering to you alone of all the spirits of the universe.

Perilous to refer the evil in us to any source out of and beyond ourselves. In this way penitence becomes impossible: fictitious.

2. Estimated as hateful to God. "Against thee, thee only, have I sinned, and done this evil in thy sight; that thou mightest be justified when thou speakest, and be clear when thou judgest." The simple judgment of the conscience. But another estimate, born of the intellect, comes in collision with this religion and bewilders it. Look over life, and you will find it hard

to believe that sin is *against* God: that it is not rather *for* Him.

Undeniable, that out of evil comes good: that evil is the resistance in battle, with which good is created and becomes possible. Physical evil, for example, Hunger, an evil, is the parent of industry, human works, all that man has done: it beautifies life. The storm fire burns up the forest, and slays man and beast; but purifies the air of contagion. Lately, the tragic death of eleven fishermen elicited the sympathy and charities of thousands.

Even moral evil is also generative of good. Peter's cowardice enabled him to be a comforter: "when he was converted, to strengthen his brethren." David's crime was a vantage ground, from which he rose through penitence nearer to God. Through it this psalm has blessed ages. But if the sin had not been done!

Now, contemplating this, we begin to perceive that evil is God's instrument. "If evil be in the city the Lord hath done it." Then the contemplative intellectualist looks over this scene of things, and complacently approves of evil as God's contrivance, as much as good is: a temporary necessity, worthy of His wisdom to create. And then, can He truly hate that which He has made? Can His agent be His enemy? Is it not shortsightedness to be angry with it? Not the antagonist of God surely, but His creature and faithful servant this evil. Sin cannot be "against God."

Thus arises a horrible contradiction between the instincts of the conscience and the judgment of the understanding. Judas must have been, says the intellect, God's agent as much as Paul. "Why doth He yet find fault? for who had resisted His will? Do not evil men perform His will? Why should I blame sin in another or myself seeing it is necessary? Why not say at once, Crime and Virtue are the same?"

Thoughts such as these, at some time or another, I doubt not haunt and perplex us all. Conscience is overborne by the intellect. Some time during every life the impossibility of reconciling these two verdicts is felt, and the perplexity confuses action. Men sin with a secret peradventure behind. "Perhaps evil is not so bad after all — perhaps good — who knows?"

Remember, therefore, in matters practical, Conscience not intellect is our guide. Unsophisticated conscience ever speaks this language of the Bible.

We cannot help believing that our sentiments towards Right and Wrong are a reflection of God's. That we call just and true, we cannot but think is just and true in His sight. That which seems base and vile to us, we are compelled to think is so to Him: and this in proportion as we act up to duty. In that proportion we feel that His sentiments coincide with ours.

In such moments, when the God within us speaks most peremptorily and distinctly, we feel that the language of this psalm is true: and that no other language expresses the truth. Sin is not *for* God — cannot be: but "against God." An opposition to His will, a contradiction to His nature: not a coincidence with it. He abhors it — will banish it, and annihilate it.

In these days, when French sentimentalism, theological dreams, and political speculations, are unsettling the old landmarks with fearful rapidity, if we do not hold fast, and that simply and firmly, that first principle, that right is right, and wrong wrong, all our moral judgments will become confused, and the penitence of the noblest hearts an absurdity. For what can be more absurd than knowingly to reproach ourselves for that which God intended?

3. Sin estimated as separation from God. Two views of sin: The first reckoning it evil, because consequences of pain are annexed: the second, evil, because a contradiction of our own nature and God's will.

In this psalm the first is ignored: the second, implied throughout. "Take not thy Holy Spirit from me." "Have mercy upon me," does not mean, Save me from torture. You cannot read the psalm and think so. It is not the trembling of a craven spirit in anticipation of torture, but the agonies of a noble one in the horror of *being* evil.

If the first view were true, then, if God were by an act of will to reverse the consequences, and annex pain to goodness and joy to crime, to lie and injure would become Duty as much as before they were sins. But penalties do not change good into evil. Good is for ever good; evil for ever evil. God Himself could not alter that by a command. Eternal hell could not make Truth wrong: nor everlasting pleasure ennoble sensuality.

Do you fancy that men like David, shuddering in sight of evil, dreaded a material hell? I venture to say, into true penitence the idea of punishment never enters. If it did it would be almost a relief: but, oh! those moments in which a selfish act has appeared more hideous than any pain which the fancy of a Dante could devise! when the idea of the strife of self-will in battle with the loving will of God prolonged for ever, has painted itself to the imagination as the real Infinite Hell! when self-concentration and the extinction of love in the soul has been felt as the real damnation of the Devil-nature!

And recollect how sparingly Christianity appeals to the prudential motives. Use them it does, because they are motives, but rarely. Retribution is a truth: and Christianity, true to nature, warns of retribution. But, except to rouse men sunk in forgetfulness, or faltering with truth, it almost never appeals to it: and never with the hope of eliciting from such motives as the hope of heaven or the fear of hell, high goodness.

To do good for reward, the Son of Man declares to be the sinner's religion. "If ye lend to them who lend to you, what thank have ye?" and He distinctly proclaims that alone to be spiritually good, "the righteousness of God," which "does good, hoping for nothing in return;" adding, as the only motive, "that ye may be the children of (*i. e.*, resemble) your Father which is in Heaven: for He maketh His sun to shine on the evil and the good, and sendeth rain on the just and on the unjust."

II. Restoration.

First step — Sacrifice of a broken spirit.

Observe the accurate and even Christian perception of the real meaning of sacrifice by the ancient spiritually-minded Jews.

Sacrifice has its origin in two feelings: one human; one divine or inspired.

True feeling: something to be given to God: surrendered: that God must be worshipped with our best.

Human: added to this — mixed up with it, is the fancy that this sacrifice pleases God because of the loss or pain which it inflicts. Then men attribute to God their own revengeful feelings: think that the philosophy of sacrifice consists in the necessity of punishing: call it justice to let the blow fall somewhere — no matter where: blood must flow. Hence heathen sacrifices were offered to *appease* the Deity, to buy off His wrath — the purer the offering the better: — to glut His fury. Instances illustrating the feeling: Iphigenia: Zaleucus — two eyes given to the law: barbarian rude notions of justness mixed up with a father's instincts. Polycrates and Amasis: seal sacrificed to avert the anger of heaven — supposed to be jealous of mortal prosperity. These notions mixed with Judaism: nay, are mixed up now with Christian conceptions of Christ's sacrifice.

Jewish sacrifices therefore presented two thoughts — to the spiritual, true notions; to the unspiritual, false: and expressed these feelings for each. But men like David felt that what lay beneath all sacrifice as its ground and meaning, was surrender to God's will: that a man's best is himself: and to sacrifice this is the true sacrifice. By degrees they came to see that the sacrifice was but a form — typical: and that it might be superseded.

Compare this psalm with Psalm L.

They were taught this chiefly through sin and

suffering. Conscience, truly wounded, could not be appeased by these sacrifices which were offered year by year continually. The selfish coward, who saw in sin nothing terrible but the penalty, could be satisfied of course. Believing that the animal bore his punishment, he had nothing more to dread. But they who felt sin to be estrangement from God, who were not thinking of punishment; what relief could be given to them by being told that the *penalty* of their sins was borne by another being? They felt that only by surrender to God could conscience be at rest.

Learn then — God does not wish pain, but goodness: not suffering, but you — yourself — your heart.

Even in the sacrifice of Christ, God wished only this. It was precious not because it was pain: but because the pain, the blood, the death, were the last and highest evidence of entire surrender. — Satisfaction? Yes, the blood of Christ satisfied. Why? Because God can glut His vengeance in innocent blood more sweetly than in guilty? Because, like the barbarian Zaleucus, so long as the whole penalty is paid, He cares not by whom? Or was it because for the first time He saw human nature a copy of the Divine nature: the will of Man the Son perfectly coincident with the will of God the Father: the Love of Deity for the first time exhibited by man: obedience entire, "unto death, even the death of the cross?" Was that the sacrifice which He saw in His beloved Son wherewith He was well pleased? Was that the sacrifice of Him who, through the Eternal Spirit, offered Himself without spot to God: the sacrifice once offered which hath perfected for ever them that are sanctified?

2. Last step — Spirit of liberty. Thy free spirit — literally, princely. But the translation is right. A princely is a free spirit: unconstrained. Hence, St. James, "the royal law of liberty."

Two classes of motives may guide to acts of seeming goodness: — 1. Prudential. 2. Generous.

The agent of the Temperance Society appeals to prudential motives when he demonstrates the evils of intoxication: enlists the aid of anatomy: contrasts the domestic happiness and circumstantial comfort of the temperate home with that of the intemperate.

An appeal to the desire of happiness and fear of misery. A motive, doubtless: and of unquestionable potency. All I say is, that from this class of motives comes nothing of the highest stamp.

Prudential motives will move men: but compare the rush of population from east to west for gold with a similar rush in the time of the Crusades. A dream — a fancy; but an appeal to generous and unselfish emotions: to enthusiasm which has in it no reflex consideration of personal greed: in the one case, simply a transfer of population, with vices and habits unchanged: in the other, a sacrifice of home, country, all.

Tell men that salvation is personal happiness, and damnation personal misery, and that goodness consists in seeking the one and avoiding the other, and you will get religionists: but poor, stunted, dwarfish: — asking, with painful self-consciousness, Am I saved? Am I lost? Prudential considerations about a distant happiness, conflicting with passionate impulses to secure a near and present one: men moving in shackles — "letting I dare not wait upon I would."

Tell men that God is Love: that Right is Right, and Wrong Wrong: let them cease to admire philanthropy, and begin to love men: cease to pant for heaven, and begin to love God: then the spirit of liberty begins.

When fear has done its work — whose office is not to create holiness, but to arrest conscience — and self-abasement has set in in earnest; then the Free Spirit of God begins to breathe upon the soul like a gale from a healthier climate, refreshing it with a more generous and a purer love. Prudence is no longer left in painful and hopeless struggle with desire: Love bursts the shackles of the soul, and we are free.

VIII.

Preached March 2, 1851.

OBEDIENCE THE ORGAN OF SPIRITUAL KNOWLEDGE.

JOHN vii. 17.—"If any man will do his will, he shall know of the doctrine, whether it be of God, or whether I speak of myself."

THE first thing we have to do is to put ourselves in possession of the history of these words.

Jesus taught in the temple during the Feast of Tabernacles. The Jews marvelled at His spiritual wisdom. The cause of wonder was the want of scholastic education: "How knoweth this man letters, never having learned?" They had no conception of any source of wisdom beyond learning.

He Himself gave a different account of the matter. "My doctrine is not mine, but His that sent me." And how He came possessed of it, speaking humanly, He taught (chap. v. 30): "My judgment is just, because I seek not mine own will, but the will of the Father which hath sent me."

That principle whereby He attained spiritual judgment or wisdom, He extends to all. "If *any* man will do his will, he shall know of the doctrine, whether it be of God, or whether I speak of myself." Here, then, manifestly, there are two opinions respecting the origin of spiritual knowledge:

1. The popular one of the Jews: relying on a cultivated understanding.

2. The principle of Christ, which relied on trained affections and habits of obedience.

What is Truth? Study, said the Jews. Act, said Christ, and you shall know. A very precious principle to hold by in these days; and a very pregnant one of thought to us, who during the next few days must be engaged in the contemplation of crime, and to whom the question will suggest itself, How can men's lives be made true.

Religious controversy is fast settling into a conflict between two great extreme parties. Those who believe everything, and those who believe nothing: the disciples of credulity, and the disciples of scepticism.

The first rely on authority.

Foremost among these, and the only self-consistent ones, are the adherents of the Church of Rome — and into this body, by logical consistency, ought to merge all — Dissenters, Churchmen, Bible, Christians — all who receive their opinions because their sect, their church, or their documents assert them, not because they are true eternally in themselves.

The second class rely solely on a cultivated understanding. This is the root principle of Rationalism. Enlighten, they say, and sin will disappear. Enlighten, and we shall know all that can be known of God. Sin is an error of the understanding, not a crime of the will. Illuminate the understanding, show man that sin is folly, and sin will disappear. Political Economy will teach public virtue: knowledge of anatomy will arrest the indulgence of the passions. Show the drunkard the inflamed tissues of the brain, and he will be sobered by fear and reason.

Only enlighten, and spiritual truths will be tested. When the anatomist shall have hit on a right method of dissection, and appropriated sensation to this filament of the brain, and the religious sentiment to that fibre, we shall know whether there be a soul or not, and whether consciousness will survive physical dissolution. When the chemist shall have discovered the principle of life, and found cause behind cause, we shall know whether the last cause of all is a Personal Will or a lifeless Force.

Concerning whom I only remark now, that these disciples of scepticism become easily disciples of credulity. It is instructive to see how they who sneer at Christian mysteries as old wives' fables, bow in abject reverence before Egyptian mysteries of three thousand years' antiquity; and how they who have cast off a God, believe in the veriest imposture, and have blind faith in the most vulgar juggling. Scepticism and credulity meet. Nor is it difficult to explain. Distrusting everything, they doubt their own conclusions and their own mental powers; and that for which they cannot account presents itself to them as supernatural and mysterious. Wonder makes them more credulous than those they sneer at.

In opposition to both these systems, stands the Christianity of Christ.

1. Christ never taught on personal authority. "My doctrine is not mine." He taught "not as the scribes." They dogmatized: "because it was written" — stickled for maxims, and lost principles. His authority was the authority of Truth, not of personality: He commanded men to believe, not because He said it; but He said it because it was true. Hence John XII. 47, 48, "If any man hear my words and believe not, I judge him not — the word that I have spoken, the same shall judge him in the last day."

2. He never taught that cultivation of the understanding would do all: but exactly the reverse. And

so taught His apostles. St. Paul taught, "The world by wisdom knew not God." His master said, not that clear intellect will give you a right heart, but that a right heart and a pure life will clarify the intellect. Not, Become a man of letters and learning, and you will attain spiritual freedom: but, Do rightly, and you will judge justly: Obey and you will know. "My judgment is just, because I seek not mine own will but the will of the Father which sent me." "If any man will do His will, he shall know of the doctrine, whether it be of God, or whether I speak of myself."

I. The knowledge of the Truth, or Christian knowledge.

II. The condition on which it is attainable.

Christian knowledge — "he shall know." Its object — "the doctrine." Its degree — certainty — "shall *know*."

Doctrine is now, in our modern times, a word of limited meaning; being simply opposed to practical. For instance, the Sermon on the Mount would be called practical: St. Paul's epistles doctrinal. But in Scripture, doctrine means broadly, teaching: anything that is taught is doctrine. Christ's doctrine embraces the whole range of His teaching — every principle and every precept. Let us select three departments of "doctrine" in which the principle of the text will be found true. "If any man will do His will, he shall know of the doctrine, whether it be of God, or whether I speak of myself."

1. It holds good in speculative truth. If any man will do God's will, he shall know what is truth and

what is error. Let us see how wilfulness and selfishness hinder impartiality. How comes it that men are almost always sure to arrive at the conclusions reached by their own party? Surely because fear, interest, vanity, or the desire of being reckoned sound and judicious, or party spirit, bias them. Personal prospects: personal antipathies: these determine most men's creed. How will you remove this hindrance? By increased cultivation of mind? Why the Romanist is as accomplished as the Protestant; and learning is found in the Church and out of it. You are not sure that that high mental cultivation will lead a man either to Protestantism or to the Church of England. Surely, then, by removing self-will, and so only, can the hindrance to right opinions be removed. Take away the last trace of interested feeling, and the way is cleared for men to come to an approximation towards unity, even in judgment on points speculative; and so he that will do God's will shall know of the doctrine.

2. In practical truths the principle is true. It is more true to say that our opinions depend upon our lives and habits, than to say that our lives depend upon our opinions, which is only now and then true. The fact is, men think in a certain mode on these matters, because their life is of a certain character, and their opinions are only invented afterwards as a defence for their life.

For instances, St. Paul speaks of a maxim among the Corinthians, "Let us eat and drink, *for* to-morrow we die." They excused their voluptuousness on the ground of its consistency with their sceptical creed. Life was short. Death came to-morrow. There was no hereafter. Therefore it was quite consistent to live for pleasure. But who does not see that the creed was the result, and not the cause of the life? Who does not see that *first* they ate and drank, and *then* believed tomorrow we die? "Getting and spending we lay waste our powers." Eating and drinking we lose sight of the life to come. When the immortal is overborne and smothered in the life of the flesh, how *can* men believe in life to come? Then disbelieving, they mistook the cause for the effect. Their moral habits and creed were in perfect consistency: yet it was the life that formed the creed, not the creed that formed the life. Because they were sensualists, immortality had become incredible.

Again, slavery is defended, philosophically. The negro, on his skull and skeleton, they say, has God's intention of his servitude written: he is the inferior animal, therefore it is right to enslave him. Did this doctrine precede the slave-trade? Did man arrive at it, and then, in consequence, conscientiously proceed with human traffic? Or was it invented to defend a practice existing already — the offspring of self-interest? Did not men first make slaves, and then search about for reasons to make their conduct plausible to themselves?

So, too, a belief in predestination is sometimes alleged in excuse of crime. But a man who suffers his will to be overpowered, naturally comes to believe that he is the sport of fate: feeling powerless, he believes that God's decree has made him so. But let him but put forth one act of loving will, and then, as the nightmare of a dream is annihilated by an effort, so the incubus of a belief in tyrannous destiny is dissipated the moment a man wills to do the Will of God.

Observe, how he knows the doctrine, directly he does the Will.

There is another thing said respecting this knowledge of Truth. It respects the degree of certainty — "he shall *know*," not he shall have an opinion. There is a wide distinction between supposing and knowing — between fancy and conviction — between opinion and belief. Whatever rests on authority remains only supposition. You have an opinion, when you know what others think. You *know* when you feel. In matters practical you know only so far as you can do. Read a work on the "Evidences of Christianity," and it may become highly probable that Christianity, &c., are true. That is an opinion. Feel God: Do His will, till the Absolute Imperative within you speaks as with a living voice — Thou shalt, and thou shalt not; and then you do not think, you *know* that there is a God. That is a conviction and a belief.

Have we never seen how a child, simple and near to God, cuts asunder a web of sophistry with a single direct question? How, before its steady look and simple argument, some fashionable utterer of a conventional falsehood has been abashed? How a believing Christian scatters the forces of scepticism, as a morning ray, touching the mist on the mountain side, makes it vanish into thin air? And there are few more glorious moments of our humanity than those in which Faith does battle against intellectual proof: when, for example, after reading a sceptical book, or hearing a cold-blooded materialist's demonstration, in which God, the soul, and life to come, are proved impossible — up rises the heart in all the giant might of its immortality to do battle with the understanding, and with the simple argument, "I *feel* them in my best and highest moments to be true," annihilates the sophistries of logic.

These moments of profound faith do not come once for all: they vary with the degree and habit of obedience. There is a plant which blossoms once in a hundred years. Like it the soul blossoms only now and then in a space of years: but these moments are the glory and the heavenly glimpses of our purest humanity.

II. The condition on which knowledge of truth is attainable. "If any man will do His will, he shall know of the doctrine, whether it be of God, or whether I speak of myself."

This universe is governed by laws. At the bottom of everything here there is a law. Things are in this way and not that: we call that a law or condition. All departments have their own laws. By submission to them, you make them your own. Obey the laws of the body: such laws as say, Be temperate and chaste: or of the mind: such laws as say, Fix the attention; strengthen by exercise: and then their prizes are yours — health, strength, pliability of muscle, tenaciousness of memory, nimbleness of imagination, &c. Obey the laws of your spiritual being, and it has its prizes too. For instance, the condition or law of a peaceful life is submission to the law of meekness: "Blessed are the meek, for they shall inherit the earth." The condition of the Beatific vision is a pure heart and life: "Blessed are the pure in heart, for they shall see God." To the impure God is simply invisible. The condition annexed to a sense of God's presence — in other words, that without which a sense of God's presence cannot be — is obedience to the laws of love: "If we love one another,

God dwelleth in us, and His love is perfected in us." The condition of spiritual wisdom, and certainty in truth is obedience to the will of God, surrender of private will: "If any man will do His will, he shall know of the doctrine, whether it be of God, or whether I speak of myself."

In every department of knowledge, therefore, there is an appointed "organ," or instrument for discovery of its specific truth, and for appropriating its specific blessings. In the world of sense, the empirical intellect: in that world the Baconian philosopher is supreme. His Novum Organon is experience: he knows by experiment of touch, sight, &c. The religious man may not contravene his assertions — he is lord in his own province. But in the spiritual world, the "organ" of the scientific man — sensible experience — is powerless. If the chemist, geologist, physiologist, come back from their spheres and say, we find in the laws of affinity, in the deposits of past ages, in the structure of the human frame, no trace nor token of a God, I simply reply, I never expected you would. Obedience and self-surrender is the sole organ by which we gain a knowledge of that which cannot be seen nor felt. "Eye hath not seen, nor ear heard." . . . . And just as by copying perpetually a master-painter's works we get at last an instinctive and infallible power of recognising his touch, so by copying and doing God's will, we recognise what is His — we know of the teaching whether it be of God, or whether it be an arbitrary invention of a human self.

2. Observe the universality of the law. "If *any* man will do His will, he shall know of the doctrine, whether it be of God, or whether I speak of myself."

The law was true of the Man Christ Jesus Himself. He tells us it is true of all other men.

In God's universe there are no favourites of heaven who may transgress the laws of the universe with impunity — none who can take fire in the hand and not be burnt — no enemies of heaven who if they sow corn will reap nothing but tares. The law is just and true to all: "Whatsoever a man soweth, that shall he also reap."

In God's spiritual universe there are no favourites of heaven who can attain knowledge and spiritual wisdom apart from obedience. There are none reprobate by an eternal decree, who can surrender self, and in all things submit to God, and yet fail of spiritual convictions. It is not therefore a rare, partial condescension of God, arbitrary and causeless, which gives knowledge of the Truth to some, and shuts it out from others; but a vast, universal, glorious law. The light lighteth every man that cometh into the world. "If any man will do His will, he shall know."

See the beauty of this Divine arrangement. If the certainty of truth depended upon the proof of miracles, prophecy, or the discoveries of science; then Truth would be in the reach chiefly of those who can weigh evidence, investigate history, and languages, study by experiment; whereas as it is, "The *meek* will He guide in judgment, and the meek will He teach His way." "Thus saith the high and lofty One that inhabiteth eternity, whose name is Holy; I dwell in the high and holy place, with him also that is of a contrite and humble spirit." The humblest and the weakest may know more of God, of moral evil and of good, by a single act of charity, or a prayer of self-surrender, than all the sages can teach: ay, or all the theologians can dogmatize upon.

They know nothing perhaps, these humble ones, of evidence, but they are sure that Christ is their Redeemer. They cannot tell what "matter" is, but they know that *they* are Spirits. They know nothing of the "argument from design," but they feel God. The truths of God are spiritually discerned. They have never learned letters, but they have reached the Truth of Life.

3. Annexed to this condition, or a part of it, is earnestness. "If any man *will* do His will." Now that word "will" is not the will of the future tense, but will meaning volition. If any man wills, resolves, has the mind to do the will of God. So then it is not a chance fitful obedience that leads us to the Truth: nor an obedience paid while happiness lasts and no longer — but an obedience rendered in entireness and in earnest. It is not written, If any man does his will — but if any man has the spirit and desire. If we are in earnest we shall persevere like the Syrophenician woman, even though the ear of the universe seem deaf, and Christ Himself appear to bid us back. If we are not in earnest, difficulties will discourage us. Because will is wanting, we shall be asking still in ignorance and doubt, What is truth?

All this will seem to many time misspent. They go to Church because it is the custom: all Christians believe it is the established religion. But there are hours, and they come to us all at some period of life or other, when the hand of Mystery seems to lie heavy on the soul — when some life-shock scatters existence, leaves it a blank and dreary waste henceforth for ever, and there appears nothing of hope in all the expanse which stretches out, except that merciful gate of death which opens at the end — hours when the sense of misplaced or ill-requited affection, the feeling of personal worthlessness, the uncertainty and meanness of all human aims, and a doubt of all human goodness, unfix the soul from all its old moorings, — and leave it drifting — drifting over the fast Infinitude, with an awful sense of solitariness. Then the man whose faith rested on outward Authority and not on inward life, will find it give way: the authority of the Priest: the authority of the Church: or merely the authority of a document proved by miracles and backed by prophecy: the soul — conscious life hereafter — God — will be an awful desolate Perhaps. Well! in such moments you doubt all — whether Christianity be true: whether Christ was man, or God, or a beautiful fable. You ask bitterly, like Pontius Pilate, What is Truth? In such an hour what remains? I reply, Obedience. Leave those thoughts for the present. Act — be merciful and gentle — honest: force yourself to abound in little services: try to do good to others: be true to the Duty that you know. *That* must be right whatever else is uncertain. And by all the laws of the human heart, by the word of God, you shall not be left to doubt. Do that much of the will of God which is plain to you, "You shall know of the doctrine, whether it be of God."

IX.

Preached March 30, 1851.

RELIGIOUS DEPRESSION.

PSALM xlii. 1-3. — "As the hart panteth after the water-brooks, so panteth my soul after thee, O God. My soul thirsteth for God, for the living God: when shall I come and appear before God? My tears have been my meat day and night, while they continually say unto me, Where is thy God?"

THE value of the public reading of the Psalms is, that they express for us indirectly those deeper feelings which there would be a sense of indelicacy in expressing directly.

Example of Joseph: asking after his father, and blessing his brothers, as it were under the personality of another.

There are feelings of which we do not speak to each other: they are too sacred and too delicate. Such are most of our feelings to God. If we do speak of them, they lose their fragance: become coarse: nay, there is even a sense of indelicacy and exposure.

Now the Psalms afford precisely the right relief for this feeling: wrapped up in the forms of poetry (metaphor, &c.), that which might seem exaggerated is excused by those who do not feel it: while they who do can read them, applying them, without the suspicion of uttering *their own* feelings. Hence their soothing power, and hence, while other portions of Scripture may become obsolete, they remain the most precious parts of the Old Testament. For the heart of man is the same in all ages.

This forty-second Psalm contains the utterance of a sorrow of which men rarely speak. There is a grief worse than lack of bread or loss of friends: man in former times called it spiritual desertion. But at times the utterances of this solitary grief are as it were overheard, as in this Psalm. Read verse 6-7. And in a more august agony, "My God, my God, why hast thou forsaken me."

I. Causes of David's despondency.

II. The consolation.

I. Causes of David's despondency.

1. The thirst for God. "My soul thirsteth for God, for the living God: when shall I come and appear before God?"

There is a desire in the human heart best described as the cravings of infinitude. We are so made that nothing which has limits satisfies.

Hence the sense of freedom and relief which comes from all that suggests the idea of boundlessness: the deep sky — the dark night — the endless circle — the illimitable ocean.

Hence, too, our dissatisfaction with all that is or can be done. There never was the beauty yet than which we could not conceive something more beautiful. None so good as to be faultless in our eyes. No deed done by us, but we feel we have it in us to do a better. The heavens are not clean in our sight: and the angels are charged with folly.

Therefore to never rest is the price paid for our greatness. Could we rest, we must become smaller in soul. Whoever is satisfied with what he does has reached his culminating point, he will progress no more. Man's destiny is to be not dissatisfied, but for ever unsatisfied.

Infinite goodness — a beauty beyond what eye hath seen or heart imagined, a justice which shall have no flaw, and a righteousness which shall have no blemish — to crave for that, is to be "athirst for God."

2. The temporary loss of the sense of God's personality. "My soul is athirst for the living God."

Let us search our own experience. What we want is, we shall find, not infinitude, but a boundless *One;* not to feel that love is the *law* of this universe, but to feel One whose name is Love.

For else, if in this world of order there be no One in whose bosom that order is centred, and of whose Being it is the expression: in this world of manifold contrivance, no Personal Affection which gave to the skies their trembling tenderness, and to the snow its purity: then order, affection, contrivance, wisdom, are only horrible abstractions, and we are in the dreary universe alone.

Foremost in the declaration of this truth was the Jewish religion. It proclaimed — not "Let us meditate on the Adorable light, it shall guide our intellects," — which is the most sacred verse of the Hindoo Sacred books: but "Thus saith the Lord, I am that I am." In that word I am, is declared Personality; and it contains, too, in the expression, thus *saith*, the real idea of a Revelation, viz. the voluntary approach of the Creator to the creature.

Accordingly, these Jewish Psalms are remarkable for that personal tenderness towards God — those outbursts of passionate, individual attachment which are in every page. A person, asking and giving heart for heart — inspiring love, because feeling it — that was the Israelite's Jehovah.

Now distinguish this from the God of the philosopher and the God of the mere theologian.

The God of the mere theologian is scarcely a living God — He did live; but for some eighteen hundred years we are credibly informed that no trace of His life has been seen. The canon is closed. The proofs that He was are in the things that He has made, and the books of men to whom He spake; but He inspires and works wonders no more. According to the theologians, He gives us proofs of design instead of God: doctrines instead of the life indeed.

Different, too, from the God of the philosopher. The tendency of philosophy has been to throw back the personal Being further and still further from the time when every branch and stream was believed a living Power, to the period when "Principles" were substituted for this belief: then "Laws:" and the philosopher's God is a law into which all other laws are resolvable.

Quite differently to this speaks the Bible of God. Not as a Law: but as the Life of all that is — the Being who feels and is felt — is loved and loves again — feels my heart throb into His — counts the hairs of my head: feeds the ravens, and clothes the lilies: hears my prayers and interprets them through a Spirit which has affinity with my spirit.

It is a dark moment when the sense of that personality is lost: more terrible than the doubt of immortality. For of the two — eternity without a personal God, or God for seventy years without immortality — no one after David's heart would hesitate, "Give me God for life, to know and be known by Him." No thought is more hideous than that of an eternity without Him. "My soul is athirst for God." The desire of immortality is second to the desire for God.

3. The taunts of scoffers. "As the hart panteth after the water-brooks, so panteth my soul after thee, O God." Now the hart here spoken of is the hart hunted, at bay, the big tears rolling from his eyes, and the moisture standing black upon his side. Let us see what the persecution was. "Where is now thy God?" ver. 3. This is ever the way in religious perplexity: the unsympathizing world taunts or misunderstands. In spiritual grief they ask, why is he not like others? In bereavement they call your deep sorrow unbelief. In misfortune they comfort you, like Job's friends, by calling it a visitation. Or like the barbarians at Melita, when the viper fastened on Paul's hand: no doubt they call you an infidel, though your soul be crying after God. Specially in that dark and awful hour, when *He* called on God, "Eloi, Eloi:" they said, "Let be: let us see whether Elias will come to save Him."

Now this is sharp to bear. It is easy to say Christian fortitude should be superior to it. But in darkness to have no sympathy: when the soul gropes for God, to have the hand of man relax its grasp! Forest-flies, small as they are, drive the noble war-horse mad: therefore David says, "as a sword in my bones," ver. 10. Now, observe, this feeling of forsakenness is no proof of being forsaken. Mourning after an absent God is an evidence of love as strong as rejoicing in a present one. Nay, further, a man may be more decisively the servant of God and goodness while doubting His existence, and in the anguish of his soul crying for light, than while resting in a common creed, and coldly serving Him. There has been One at least whose apparent forsakenness, and whose seeming doubt, bears the stamp of the majesty of Faith. "My God, my God, why hast thou forsaken me?"

II. David's consolation.

1. And first, in hope (see v. 5.): distinguish between the *feelings* of faith that God is present, and the *hope* of faith that He will be so.

There are times when a dense cloud veils the sunlight: you cannot see the sun, nor feel him. Sensitive temperaments feel depression: and that unaccountably and irresistibly. No effort can make you *feel*. Then you hope. Behind the cloud the sun is: from thence he will come: the day drags through, the darkest and longest night ends at last. Thus we bear the darkness and the otherwise intolerable cold, and many a sleepless night. It does not shine now — but it will. So too, spiritually.

There are hours in which physical derangement darkens the windows of the soul; days in which shattered nerves make life simply endurance; months and years in which intellectual difficulties, pressing for solution, shut out God. Then faith must be replaced by hope. "What I do thou knowest not now; but thou shalt know hereafter." Clouds and darkness are round about Him: *but* Righteousness and Truth are the habitation of His throne. "My soul, hope thou in God: for I shall yet praise Him, who is the health of my countenance and my God."

2. This hope was *in God.*

The mistake we make is to look for a source of comfort in ourselves: self-contemplation instead of gazing upon God. In other words, we look for comfort precisely where comfort never can be.

For, first, it is impossible to derive consolation from our own feelings, because of their mutability: to-day we are well, and our spiritual experience, partaking of these circumstances, is bright: but to-morrow some outward circumstances change — the sun does not shine, or the wind is chill, and we are low, gloomy, and sad. Then if our hopes were unreasonably elevated, they will now be unreasonably depressed; and so our experience becomes flux and reflux, ebb and flow; like the sea, that emblem of instability.

Next, it is impossible to get comfort from our own acts; for though acts are the test of character, yet in a low state no man can judge justly of his own acts. They assume a darkness of hue which is reflected on them by the eye that contemplates them. It would be well for all men to remember that sinners cannot judge of sin — least of all can we estimate our own sin.

Besides, we lose time in remorse. I have sinned — well — by the grace of God I must endeavour to do better for the future. But if I mourn for it overmuch all to-day, refusing to be comforted, to-morrow I shall have to mourn the wasted to-day; and that again will be the subject of another fit of remorse.

In the wilderness, had the children of Israel, instead of gazing on the serpent, looked down on their own wounds to watch the process of the granulation of the flesh, and see how deep the wound was, and whether it was healing slowly or fast, cure would have been impossible: their only chance was to look off the wounds. Just so, when giving up this hopeless and sickening work of self-inspection, and turning from ourselves in Christian self-oblivion, we gaze on God, then first the chance of consolation dawns.

He is not affected by our mutability: our changes do not alter Him. When we are restless, He remains serene and calm: when we are low, selfish, mean, or dispirited, He is still the unalterable I AM. The same yesterday, to-day, and for ever, in whom is no variableness, neither shadow of turning. What God is in Himself, not what we may chance to feel Him in this or that moment to be, that is our hope. "My soul, hope thou *in God.*"

X.

Preached April 6, 1851.

FAITH OF THE CENTURION.

MATT. viii. 10. — "When Jesus heard it, he marvelled, and said to them that followed, Verily I say unto you, I have not found so great faith, no, not in Israel."

THAT upon which the Son of God fastened as worthy of admiration was not the centurion's benevolence, nor his perseverance, but his faith. And so speaks the whole New Testament; giving a special dignity to faith. By faith we are justified. By faith man removes mountains of difficulty. As the Divinest attribute in the heart of God is Love, and the mightiest, because the most human, principle in the breast of man is faith: Love is heaven, faith is that which appropriates heaven.

Faith is a theological term rarely used in other matters. Hence its meaning is obscured. But faith is no strange, new, peculiar power, supernaturally infused by Christianity; but the same principle by which we live from day to day, one of the commonest in our daily life.

We trust our senses; and that though they often deceive us. We trust men; a battle must often be risked on the intelligence of a spy. A merchant commits his ships with all his fortunes on board to a hired captain, whose temptations are enormous. Without this principle society could not hold together for a day. It would be a sandheap.

Such, too, is religious faith; we trust on probabilities; and this though probabilities often are against us. We cannot prove God's existence. The balance of probabilities, scientifically speaking, are nearly equal for a living Person or a lifeless Cause: Immortality, &c., in the same way. But faith throws its own convictions into the scale and decides the preponderance.

Faith, then, is that which, when probabilities are equal, ventures on God's side and on the side of right, on the guarantee of a something within which makes the thing seem true because loved.

So defined by St. Paul: "Faith is the substance of things hoped for, the evidence of things unseen." The hope is the ground.

I. The faith which was commended.

II. The causes of the commendation.

I. The faith which was commended.

First evidence of its existence — His tenderness to his servant.

Of course this good act might have existed separate from religion. Romans were benevolent to their domestics, ages before the law had been enacted regulating the relationship between patron and client.

But we are forbidden to view it so, when we remember that he was a proselyte. Morality is not religion, but it is ennobled and made more delicate by religion.

How? By instinct you may be kind to dependants. But if it be only by instinct, it is but the same kind of tenderness you show to your hound or horse. Disbelief in God, and Right, and Immortality, degrades the man you are kind to, to the level of the beast you feel for. Both are mortal, and for both your kindness is finite and poor.

But the moment Faith comes, dealing as it does with things infinite, it throws something of its own infinitude on the persons loved by the man of faith, upon his affections, and his acts: it raises them.

Consequently you find the centurion "building Synagogues," "caring for our (*i. e.* the Jewish) nation," as the Repository of the Truth — tending his servants. And this last, observe, approximated his moral goodness to the Christian standard: for therein does Christianity differ from mere religiousness, that it is not a worship of the high, but a lifting up of the low — not hero-worship, but Divine condescension.

Thus, then, was his kindliness and evidence of his faith.

Second proof. His humility: "Lord, I am not worthy that thou shouldest come under my roof."

Now Christ does not call this humility, though it was humility. He says, I have not found so great *faith*. Let us see why. How is humbleness the result of, or rather identical with, Faith?

Faith is trust. Trust is dependence on another; the spirit which is opposite to independence or trust in self. Hence where the spirit of proud independence is, faith is not.

Now observe how this differs from our ordinary and modern modes of thinking. The first thing taught a young man is that he must be independent. Quite right in the Christian sense of the word, to owe no man anything: to resolve to get his own living and not be beholden to charity, which fosters idleness: to depend on his own exertions, and not on patronage or connection. But what is commonly meant by independence is to rejoice at being bound by no ties to other human beings; to owe no allegiance to any will except our own: to be insolated and unconnected by any feeling of intercommunion or dependence; a spirit whose very life is jealousy and suspicion: which in politics is revolutionism, and in religion atheism. This is the opposite of Christianity, and the opposite of the Christian freedom whose name it usurps. For true freedom is to be emancipated from all false lords, in order to owe allegiance to all true lords: to be free from the slavery of all lusts, so as voluntarily to serve God and Right. Faith alone frees.

And this was the freedom of the Centurion: that he *chose* his master. He was not fawning on the Emperor at Rome: nor courting the immoral ruler at Cæsarea, who had titles and places to give away: but he bent in lowliest homage of heart before the Holy One. His freedom was the freedom of uncoerced and voluntary dependence; the freedom and humility of Faith,

3. His belief in an invisible, living will. "Speak the word only." Remark how different this is from a reliance on the influence of the senses. He asked not the presence of Christ, but simply an exertion of His will. He looked not like a physician to the operation of unerring laws: or the result of the contact of matter with matter. He believed in Him who is the Life indeed. He felt that the Cause of Causes is a Person: Hence he could trust the Living Will out of sight. This is the highest form of faith.

Here, however, I observe:

The Centurion learned this through his own profession. "I am a man under authority, having soldiers under me." The argument ran thus. I by the command of will obtain the obedience of my dependants

Thou by will the obedience of Thine: sickness and health are Thy servants.

Evidently he looked upon this universe with a soldier's eye: he could not look otherwise. To him this world was a mighty camp of Living Forces in which authority was paramount. Trained in obedience to military law, accustomed to render prompt submission to those above him, and to exact it from those below him, he read Law everywhere: and Law to him meant nothing, unless it meant the expression of a Personal Will. It was this training through which Faith took its *form*.

The Apostle Paul tells us that the invisible things of God from the Creation of the world are clearly seen; and, we may add, from *every part* of the creation of the world — "The heavens declare the glory of God;" but so also does the buttercup and the raindrop.

The invisible things of God from life are clearly seen — and, we may add, from every department of life. There is no profession, no trade, no human occupation which does not in its own way educate for God.

The soldier through Law read a personal will; and he might from the same profession, in the unity of an army, made a living and organised unity by the variety of its parts, have read the principle of God's and the Church's unity, through the opportunities that profession affords for self-control, for generous deeds. When the Gospel was first announced on earth, it was proclaimed to the shepherds and Magians in a manner appropriate to their modes of life.

Shepherds, like sailors, are accustomed to hear a supernatural Power in the sounds of the air, in the moaning of the night-winds, in the sighing of the storm; to see a more than mortal life in the clouds that wreathe around the headland. Such men, brought up among the sights and sounds of nature, are proverbially superstitious. No wonder therefore that the intimation came to them, as it were, on the winds in the melodies of the air: "a multitude of the heavenly host praising God, and saying, Glory to God in the highest, and on earth peace, good-will toward men."

But the Magians being astrologers, accustomed to read the secrets of Life and Death in the clear star-lit skies of Persia, are conducted by a meteor.

Each in his own way: each in his own profession: each through that little spot of the universe given to him. For not only is God everywhere, but all of God is in every point. Not His wisdom here, and His goodness there: the whole truth may be read, if we had eyes, and heart, and time enough, in the laws of a daisy's growth. God's Beauty, His Love, His Unity: nay, if you observe how each atom exists not for itself alone, but for the sake of every other atom in the universe, in that atom or daisy you may read the law of the Cross itself. The crawling of a spider before now has taught perseverance, and led to a crown. The little moss, brought close to a traveller's eye in an African desert, who had lain down to die, roused him to faith in that Love which had so curiously arranged the minute fibres of a thing so small, to be seen once and but once by a human eye, and carried him like Elijah of old in the strength of that heavenly repast, a journey of forty days and forty nights to the sources of the Nile; yet who could have suspected divinity in a spider, or theology in a moss?

II. The causes of Christ's astonishment.

The reasons why he marvelled may be reduced under two heads.

1. The Centurion was a Gentile; therefore unlikely to know revealed truth.

2. A soldier, and therefore exposed to a recklessness, and idleness, and sensuality, which are the temptations of that profession. But he turned his loss to glorious gain.

The Saviour's comment therefore contained the advantage of disadvantages, and the disadvantage of advantages. The former, "Many shall come from the east and the west, and shall sit down with Abraham, and Isaac, and Jacob, in the kingdom of heaven." The latter, "The children of the kingdom shall be cast out into outer darkness; there shall be weeping and gnashing of teeth."

There are spirits which are crushed by difficulties; others would gain strength from them. The greatest men have been those who have cut their way to success through difficulties. And such have been the greatest triumphs of art and science: such too of religion. Moses, Elijah, Abraham, the Baptist, the giants of both Testaments, were not men nurtured in the hothouse of religious advantages. Many a man would have done good if he had not a superabundance of the means of doing it. Many a spiritual giant is buried under mountains of gold.

Understand therefore the real amount of advantage which there is in religious privileges. Necessary especially for the feeble, as crutches are necessary; but, like crutches, they often enfeeble the strong. For every advantage which facilitates performance and supersedes toil, a corresponding price is paid in loss. Civilization gives us telescopes and microscopes; but it takes away the unerring acuteness with which the savage reads the track of man and beast upon the ground at his feet: it gives us scientific surgery, and impairs the health which made surgery superfluous.

So, ask you where the place of religious might is? Not the place of religious privileges — not where prayers are daily, and sacraments monthly — not where sermons are so abundant as to pall upon the pampered taste: but on the hill-side with the Covenanter: in the wilderness with John the Baptist: in our own dependencies where the liturgy is rarely heard, and Christian friends meet at the end of months: — there, amidst manifold disadvantages, when the soul is thrown upon itself, a few kindred spirits, and God: grow up those heroes of faith, like the Centurion, whose firm conviction wins admiration even from the Son of God Himself.

Lastly, See how this incident testifies to the perfect Humanity of Christ. The Saviour "marvelled:" — that wonder was no fictitious semblance of admiration. It was a real genuine wonder. He had not expected to find such faith. The Son of God increased in wisdom as well as stature. He knew more at thirty than at twenty. There were things He knew at twenty which He had not known before. In the last year of His life, He went to the fig-tree expecting to find fruit, and was disappointed. In all matters of Eternal truth: principles, which are not measured by more or less true: His knowledge was absolute: but it would seem that in matters of earthly fact, which are modified by time and space, His knowledge was like ours, more or less dependent upon experience.

Now we forget this — we are shocked at the thought of the partial ignorance of Christ, as if it were irreverence to think it: we shrink from believing that He really felt the force of temptation; or that the Forsakenness on the Cross and the momentary doubt have parallels in our human life. In other words, we make that Divine Life a mere mimic representation of griefs that were not real, and surprises that were feigned, and sorrows that were theatrical.

But thus we lose the Saviour. For it is well to know that He was Divine: but if we lose that truth, we should still have a God in heaven. But if there has been on this earth no real, perfect human life, no Love that never cooled, no Faith that never failed, which may shine as a loadstar across the darkness of our experience, a Light to light amidst all convictions of our own meanness and all suspicions of others' littleness — why, we may have a Religion, but we have not a Christianity. For if we lose Him as a Brother, we cannot feel Him as a Saviour.

XI.

Preached July 27, 1851.

THE RESTORATION OF THE ERRING.

GAL. vi. 1, 2. — "Brethren, if a man be overtaken in a fault, ye which are spiritual restore such an one in the spirit of meekness; considering thyself, lest thou also be tempted. Bear ye one another's burdens, and so fulfil the law of Christ."

It would be a blessed thing for our Christian society if we could contemplate sin from the same point of view from which Christ and His Apostles saw it. But in this matter society is ever oscillating between two extremes, undue laxity and undue severity.

In one age of the Church, the days of Donatism for instance, men refuse the grace of repentance to those who have erred: holding that baptismal privileges once forfeited cannot be got back: that for a single distinct lapse there is no restoration.

In another age, the Church, having found out its error, and discovered the danger of setting up an impossible standard, begins to confer periodical absolutions and plenary indulgences, until sin, easily forgiven, is as easily committed.

And so too with societies and legislatures. In one period puritanism is dominant and morals severe. There are no small faults. The statute-book is defiled with the red mark of blood, set opposite innumerable misdemeanours. In an age still earlier, the destruction of a wild animal is punished like the murder of a man. Then in another period we have such a medley of sentiments and sickliness that we have lost all our bearings, and cannot tell what is vice and what is goodness. Charity and toleration degenerate into that feeble dreaminess which refuses to be roused by stern views of life.

This contrast, too, may exist in the same age, nay, in the same individual. One man gifted with talent, or privileged by rank, outrages all decency: the world smiles, calls it eccentricity, forgives, and is very merciful and tolerant. Then some one unshielded by these advantages, endorsed neither by wealth nor birth, sins — not to one-tenth, nor one ten-thousandth part of the same extent: society is seized with a virtuous indignation — rises up in wrath — asks what is to become of the morals of the community if these things are committed; and protects its proprieties by a rigorous exclusion of the offender, cutting off the bridge behind him against his return for ever.

Now the Divine Character of the New Testament is shown in nothing more signally than in the stable ground from which it views this matter, in comparison with the shifting and uncertain standing-point from whence the world sees it. It says, never retracting nor bating, "The wages of sin is death." It speaks sternly with no weak sentiment, "Go, and sin no more, lest a worse thing happen unto thee." But then it accepts every excuse, admits every palliation: looks upon this world of temptation and these frail human hearts of ours, not from the cell of a monk or the study of a recluse, but in a large, real way: accepts the existence of sin as a fact, without affecting to be shocked or startled: assumes that it must needs be that offences come, and deals with them in a large noble way, as the results of a disease which must be met, which should be, and which can be, cured.

I. The Christian view of other men's sin.

II. The Christian power of restoration.

I. The first thing noticeable in the apostle's view of sin is, that he looks upon it as if it might be sometimes the result of a surprise. "If a man be overtaken in a fault." In the original, anticipated, taken suddenly in front. As if circumstances had been beforehand with the man: as if sin, supposed to be left far behind, had on a sudden got in front, tripped him up, or led him into ambush.

All sins are not of this character. There are some which are in accordance with the general bent of our disposition: and the opportunity of committing them was only the first occasion for manifesting what was in the heart: so that if they had not been committed then, they probably would or must have been at some other time, and looking back to them we have no right to lay the blame on circumstances — we are to accept the penalty as a severe warning meant to show what was in our hearts.

There are other sins of a different character. It seems as if it were not in us to commit them. They were so to speak unnatural to us: you were going quietly on your way, thinking no evil, suddenly temptation, for which you were not prepared, presented itself, and before you knew where you were, you were in the dust, fallen.

As, for instance, when a question is suddenly put to a man which never ought to have been put, touching a secret of his own or another's. Had he the presence of mind or adroitness, he might turn it aside, or refuse to reply. But being unprepared and accosted suddenly, he says hastily that which is irreconcileable with strict truth; then to substantiate and make it look probable, misrepresents or invents something else: and so he has woven round himself a mesh which will entangle his conscience through many a weary day and many a sleepless night.

It is shocking, doubtless, to allow ourselves even to admit that this is possible: yet no one knowing human nature from men and not from books, will deny that this might befall even a brave and true man. St. Peter was both: yet this was his history. In a crowd, suddenly, the question was put directly, "This man also was with Jesus of Nazareth." Then a prevarication — a lie: and yet another. This was a sin of surprise. He was overtaken in a fault.

Every one of us admits the truth of this in his own case. Looking back to past life, he feels that the errors which have most terribly determined his destiny were the result of mistake. Inexperience, a hasty promise, excess of trust, incaution, nay, even a generous devotion, have been fearfully, and as it seems to us, inadequately chastised. There may be some undue tenderness to ourselves when we thus palliate the past: still a great part of such extenuation is only justice.

Now the Bible simply requires that we should judge others by the same rule by which we judge ourselves. The law of Christ demands that what we plead in our own case, we should admit in the case of others. Believe that in this or that case which you judge so harshly, the heart in its deeps did not consent to sin, nor by preference love what is hateful: simply admit that such an one may have been overtaken in a fault. This is the large law of Charity.

1. Again, the apostle considers fault as that which has left a burden on the erring spirit. "Bear ye one another's burdens."

For we cannot say to the laws of God I was overtaken. We live under stern and unrelenting laws, which permit no excuse and never hear of a surprise. They never send a man who has failed once, back to try a second chance. There is no room for a mistake; you play against them for your life; and they exact the penalty inexorably, "Every man must bear his own burden." Every law has its own appropriate penalty: and the wonder of it is that often the severest penalty seems set against the smallest transgression: we suffer more for our vices than our crimes: we pay dearer for our imprudences than even for our deliberate wickedness.

Let us examine this a little more closely. One burden laid on fault, is that chain of entanglement which seems to drag down to fresh sins. One step necessitates many others. One fault leads to another, and crime to crime. The soul gravitates downward beneath its burden. It was profound knowledge indeed which prophetically refused to limit Peter's sin to once. "Verily I say unto thee ... thou shalt deny Me thrice."

We will try to describe that sense of burden. A fault has the power sometimes of distorting life till all seems hideous and unnatural. A man who has left his proper nature, and seems compelled to say and do things unnatural and in false show, who has thus become untrue to himself, — to him life and the whole universe becomes untrue. He can grasp nothing — he does not stand on fact — he is living as in a dream — himself a dream. All is ghastly, unreal, spectral. A burden is on him as of a nightmare. He moves about in nothingness and shadows as if he were not. His own existence swiftly passing, might seem a phantom life, were it not for the corroding pang of anguish in his soul, for that at least is real!

2. Add to this, the burden of the heart weighing on itself.

It has been truly said that the human heart is like the millstone, which, if there be wheat beneath it, will grind to purposes of health; if not, will grind still, at the will of the wild wind, but on itself. So does the heart wear out itself, against its own thought. One fixed idea — one remembrance, and no other — one stationary, wearing anguish. This is remorse, passing into despair; itself the goad to fresh and wilder crimes.

The worst of such a burden is that it keeps down the soul from good. Many an ethereal spirit, which might have climbed the heights of holiness and breathed the rare and difficult air of the mountain top, where the heavenliest spirituality alone can live, is weighed down by such a burden to the level of the lowest. If you know such an one, mark his history — without restoration, his career is done. That soul will not grow henceforth.

3. The burden of a secret.

Some here know the weight of an uncommunicated sin. They know how it lies like ice upon the heart. They know how dreadful a thing the sense of hypocrisy is; the knowledge of inward depravity, while all without looks pure as snow to men.

How heavy this weight may be, we gather from these indications. First, from this strange, psychological fact. A man with a guilty secret will tell out the tale of his crimes as under the personality of another: a mysterious necessity seems to force him to give it utterance. As in the old fable of him who breathed out his weighty secret to the reeds: a remarkable instance of this is afforded in the case of that murderer, who, from the richness of his gifts and the enormity of his crime, is almost an historical personage, who, having become a teacher of youth, was in the habit of narrating to his pupils the anecdote of his crime, with all the circumstantial particularity of fact; but all the while, under the guise of a pretended dream. Such men tread for ever on the very verge of a confession: they seem to take a fearful pleasure in talking of the guilt, as if the heart could not bear its own burden, but must give it *outness*.

Again, it is evidenced by the attempt to get relief in profuse and general acknowledgments of guilt. They adopt the language of religion: they call themselves vile dust and miserable sinners. The world takes generally what they mean particularly. But they get no relief, they only deceive themselves; for they have turned the truth itself into a falsehood, using true words which they know convey a false impression, and getting praise for humility instead of punishment for guilt. They have used all the effort, and suffered all the pang, which it would have cost them to get real relief; and they have not got it: and the burden unacknowledged remains a burden still.

The third indication we have of the heaviness of this burden is the commonness of the longing for confession. None but a minister of the gospel can estimate this: he only, who looking round his congregation, can point to person after person whose wild tale of guilt or sorrow he is cognisant of; who can remember how often similar griefs were trembling upon lips which did not unburden themselves: whose heart being the receptacle of the anguish of many, can judge what is in human hearts: he alone can estimate how much there is of sin and crime lying with the weight and agony of concealment on the spirits of our brethren.

The fourth burden is an intuitive consciousness of the hidden sins of others' hearts.

To two states of soul it is given to detect the presence of evil: states the opposite of each other — innocence and guilt.

It was predicted of the Saviour while yet a child, that by Him the thoughts of many hearts should be revealed: the fulfilment of this was the history of His life. He went through the world, by His innate purity detecting the presence of evil, as He detected the touch of her who touched His garment in the crowd.

Men, supposed spotless before, fell down before Him crying, "Depart from me, for I am a sinful man, O Lord!" This in a lower degree is true of all innocence; you would think that one who can deeply read the human heart and track its windings must be himself deeply experienced in evil. But it is not so; at least not always. Purity can detect the presence of the evil which it does not understand: just as the dove, which has never seen a hawk, trembles at its presence: and just as a horse rears uneasily when the wild beast unknown and new to it is near, so innocence understands, yet understands not the meaning of, the unholy look, the guilty tone, the sinful manner. It shudders and shrinks from it by a power given to it, like that which God has conferred on the unreasoning mimosa. Sin gives the same power, but differently. Innocence apprehends the approach of evil, by the instinctive tact of contrast. Guilt by the instinctive consciousness of similarity. It is the profound truth contained in the history of the Fall. The eyes are opened: the knowledge of good and evil has come. The soul knows its own nakedness: but it knows also the nakedness of all other souls which have sinned after the similitude of its own sin.

Very marvellous is that tost power of guilt: it is vain to think of eluding its fine capacity of penetration. Intimations of evil are perceived and noted, when to other eyes all seems pure. The dropping of an eye — the shunning of a subject — the tremulousness of a tone — the peculiarity of a subterfuge, will tell the tale. These are tendencies like mine, and here is a spirit conscious as my own is conscious.

This dreadful burden the scriptures call the knowledge of good and evil: can we not all remember the salient sense of happiness, which we had when all was innocent? when crime was the tale of some far distant hemisphere, and the guilt we heard of was not suspected in the hearts of the beings around us: and can we not recollect too, how by our own sin, or the cognisance of other's sin, there came a something which hung the heavens with shame and guilt, and all around seemed laden with evil? This is the worst burden that comes from transgression: loss of faith in human goodness: the being sentenced to go through life haunted with a presence from which we cannot escape: the presence of Evil in the hearts of all that we approach.

II. The Christian power of restoration: "Ye which are spiritual, restore such an one."

First, then, restoration is possible. That is a Christian fact. Moralists have taught us what sin is: they have explained how it twines itself into habit: they have shown us its ineffaceable character. It was reserved for Christianity to speak of restoration. Christ, and Christ only, has revealed that he who has erred may be restored, and made pure and clean and whole again.

Next, however, observe that this restoration is accomplished by men. Causatively, of course, and immediately, restoration is the work of Christ and of God the Spirit. Mediately and instrumentally, it is the work of men. "*Brethren*.... restore such an one." God has given to man the power of elevating his brother man. He has conferred on His Church the power of the keys to bind and loose, "Whosesoever sins ye remit, they are remitted; and whosesoever sins ye retain, they are retained." It is therefore in the power of man, by his conduct, to restore his brother, or to hinder his restoration. He may loose him from his sins, or retain their power upon his soul.

Now the words of the text confine us to two modes in which this is done: by sympathy and by forgiveness. "Bear ye one another's burdens."

By sympathy: we Protestants have one unvarying sneer ready for the system of the Romish confessional. They confess, we say, for the sake of absolution, that absolved they may sin again. A shallow, superficial sneer, as all sneers are. In that craving of the heart which gives the system of the Confessional its dangerous power, there is something far more profound than any sneer can fathom. It is not the desire to sin again that makes men long to unburden their consciences; but it is the yearning to be true, which lies at the bottom, even of the most depraved hearts, to appear what they are and to lead a false life no longer: and besides this, the desire of sympathy. For this comes out of that dreadful sense of loneliness which is the result of sinning; — the heart severed from God, feels severed from all other hearts; goes alone, as if it had neither part nor lot with other men; itself a shadow among shadows. And its craving is for sympathy: it wants some human heart to know what it feels. Thousands upon thousands of laden hearts around us are crying, Come and bear my burden with me: and observe here, the apostle says, "Bear ye *one another's* burdens." Nor let the priest bear the burdens of all: that were most unjust. Why should the priest's heart be the common receptacle of all the crimes and wickedness of a congregation. "Bear ye *one another's* burdens."

Again, by forgiveness. There is a truth in the doctrine of absolution. God has given to man the power to absolve his brother, and so restore him to himself. The forgiveness of man is an echo and an earnest of God's forgiveness. He whom society has restored realizes the possibility of restoration to God's favour. Even the mercifulness of one good man sounds like a voice of pardon from heaven: just as the power and the exclusion of men sound like a knell of hopelessness, and do actually bind the sin upon the soul. The man whom society will not forgive nor restore is driven into recklessness. This is the true Christian doctrine of absolution, as expounded by the Apostle Paul, 2 Cor. II. 7-10. The degrading power of severity, the restoring power of pardon, vested in the Christian community, the voice of the minister being but their voice.

Now then let us inquire into the Christianity of our society. Restoration is the essential work of Christianity. The Gospel is the declaration of God's sympathy and God's pardon. In these two particulars, then, what is our right to be called a Christian community?

Suppose that a man is overtaken in a fault. What does he or what shall he do? Shall he retain it unacknowledged, or go through life a false man? God forbid. Shall he then acknowledge it to his brethren, that they by sympathy and merciful caution may restore him? Well, but is it not certain that it is exactly from those to whom the name of brethren most peculiarly belongs that he will not receive assistance? Can a man in mental doubt go to the members of the same religious communion, or does he not know that they precisely are the ones who will frown upon his doubts, and proclaim his sins? Or will a clergyman unburden his mind to his brethren in the ministry? Are they not in their official rigour the least capable of largely understanding him? If a woman be overtaken in a fault, will she tell it to a sister-woman? Or does she not feel instinctively, that her sister-woman is ever the most harsh, the most severe, and the most ferocious judge?

Well, you sneer at the confessional; you complain that mistaken ministers of the Church of England are restoring it amongst us. But who are they that are forcing on the confessional? who drive laden and broken hearts to pour out their long pent up sorrows into any ear that will receive them? I say it is we: we by our uncharitableness; we by our want of sympathy and unmerciful behaviour; we by the unchristian way in which we break down the bridge behind the penitent, and say, On, on in sin — there is no returning.

Finally, the apostle tells us the spirit in which this is to be done, and assigns a motive for the doing it. The mode is "in the spirit of meekness." For Satan cannot cast out Satan. Sin cannot drive out sin. For instance, my anger cannot drive out another man's covetousness: my petulance or sneer cannot expel another's extravagance. The meekness of Christ alone has power. The charity which desires another's goodness above his well-being; that alone succeeds in the work of restoration.

The motive is, "considering thyself, lest thou also be tempted." For sin is the result of inclination, or weakness combined with opportunity. It is therefore in a degree the offspring of circumstances. Go to the hulks, the jail, the penitentiary, the penal colony, statistics will almost mark out for you beforehand the classes which have furnished the inmates, and the exact proportion of the delinquency of each class. You will not find the wealthy there, nor the noble — nor those guarded by the fences of social life; but the poor, and the uneducated, and the frail, and the defenceless. Can you gravely surmise that this regular tabulation depends upon the superior virtue of one class compared with others? Or must you admit that the majority at least of those who have not fallen are safe because they were not tempted? Well, then, when St. Paul says, "considering thyself, lest thou also be tempted," it is as if he had written — Proud Pharisee of a man, complacent in thine integrity, who thankest God that thou art not as other men are, extortioners, unjust, &c., hast thou gone through the terrible ordeal and come off with unscathed virtue? Or art thou in all these points simply untried? Proud Pharisee of a woman, who passest by an erring sister with an haughty look of conscious superiority, dost thou know what temptation is, with strong feeling and mastering opportunity? Shall the rich-cut crystal which stands on the table of the wealthy man, protected from dust and injury, boast that it has escaped the flaws, and the cracks, and the fractures which the earthen jar has sustained, exposed and subjected to rough and general uses? O man or woman! thou who wouldst be a Pharisee, consider, O consider thyself, lest thou also be tempted.

XII.

Preached Christmas Day, 1851.

CHRIST THE SON.

HEB. i. 1. — "God, who at sundry times, and in divers manners, spake in time past unto the fathers by the prophets, hath in these last days spoken unto us by his Son."

Two critical remarks.

1. "Sundry times" — more literally, sundry portions — sections, not of time, but of the matter of the revelation. God gave His revelation in parts, piecemeal, as you teach a child to spell a word — letter by letter, syllable by syllable — adding all at last together. God had a Word to spell — His own Name. By degrees He did it. At last it came entire. The Word was made Flesh.

2. "His Son," more correctly, "a Son" — for this is the very argument. Not that God now spoke by Christ, but that whereas once by prophets, now by a Son. The Filial dispensation was the last.

This epistle was addressed to Christians on the verge of apostasy. See those passages: "It is impossible for those who were once enlightened, and have tasted of the heavenly gift, and were made partakers of the Holy Ghost, and have tasted the good word of God, and the powers of the world to come, if they shall fall away, to renew them again unto repentance; seeing they crucify to themselves the Son of God afresh, and put Him to an open shame." "Cast not away your confidence." "We are made partakers of Christ, if we hold the beginning of our confidence steadfast unto the end."

Observe what the danger was. Christianity had disappointed them — they had not found it in the rest they anticipated. They looked back to the Judaism they had left, and saw a splendid temple service — a line of priests — a visible temple witnessing of God's presence — a religion which was unquestionably fertile in prophets and martyrs. They saw these pretensions and wavered.

But this was all on the eve of dissolution. The Jewish earth and heavens, *i. e.* the Jewish Commonwealth and Church, were doomed and about to pass away. The writer of this epistle felt that their hour was come — see chap. xii. 26, 27; and if their religion rested on nothing better than this, he knew that in the crash religion itself would go. To return to Judaism was to go down to atheism and despair.

Reason alleged — they had contented themselves with a superficial view of Christianity: they had not seen how it was interwoven with all their own history, and how it alone explained that history.

Therefore in this epistle the writer labours to show that Christianity was the fulfilment of the *Idea* latent in Judaism: that from the earliest times, and in every institution, it was implied. In the monarchy — in prophets — in sabbath-days — in psalms — in the priesthood, and in temple-services, Christianity lay concealed: and the dispensation of a Son was the realization of what else was shadows. He therefore alone who adhered to Christ was the true Jew, and to apostatize from Christianity was really to apostatize from true Judaism.

I am to show, then, that the manifestation of God

through a Son was implied, not realized, in the earlier dispensation.

"Sundry portions" of this Truth are instanced in the epistle. The mediatorial dispensation of Moses — the gift of Canaan — the Sabbath, &c. At present I select these:

I. The preparatory Dispensation.
II. The filial and final Dispensation.

1. Implied, not fulfilled in the kingly office. Three Psalms are quoted, all referring to kingship. In Psalm 2nd it was plain that the true idea of a king was only fulfilled in one who was a son of God. The Jewish king was king only so far as he held from God: as His image, the representative of the Fountain of Law and Majesty.

"To Him God hath said, Thou art my Son, this day have I begotten thee."

The 45th Psalm is a bridal hymn, composed on the marriage of a Jewish king. Startling language is addressed to him. He is called God — Lord. "Thy throne, *O God*, is for ever and ever." The bride is invited to worship him as it were a God: "He is thy Lord, and worship thou Him." No one is surprised at this who remembers that Moses was said to be made a God to Aaron. Yet it is startling, almost blasphemous, unless there be a deeper meaning implied: the divine character of the real king.

In the 110th Psalm a new idea is added. The true king must be a priest. "Thou art a priest for ever, after the order of Melchizedek." This was addressed to the Jewish king; but it implied that the ideal king, of which he was for the time the representative, more or less truly, is one who at the same time sustains the highest religious character, and the highest executive authority.

Again, David was emphatically the type of the Jewish regal idea. David is scarcely a personage, so entirely does he pass in Jewish forms of thought into an ideal Sovereign — "the sure mercies of David." David is the name therefore for the David which was to be. Now David was a wanderer, kingly still, ruling men and gaining adherents by force of inward royalty. Thus in the Jewish mind the kingly office disengaged itself from outward pomp and hereditary right as mere accidents, and became a personal reality. The king was an idea.

Further still. The epistle extends this idea to man. The psalm had ascribed (Ps. viii. 6) kingly qualities and rule to manhood — rule over the creation. Thus the idea of a king belonged properly to humanity; to the Jewish king as the representative of humanity.

Yet even in collective humanity the royal character is not realized. "We see not," says the epistle, "all things as yet put under him" — man.

Collect, then, these notions. The true king of men is a Son of God: one who is to his fellow-men, God and Lord, as the Jewish bride was to feel her royal husband to be to her: one who is a priest: one who may be poor and exiled, yet not less royal.

Say, then, whence is this idea fulfilled by Judaism? To which of the Jewish kings can it be applied, except with infinite exaggeration? To David? Why, the Redeemer shows the insuperable difficulty of this. "How then doth David in Spirit call him," *i. e.* the king of whom he was writing, "Lord, saying, the Lord said unto my *Lord*, sit thou on my right hand, until I make thy enemies thy footstool?"

David writing of himself, yet speaks there in the third person, projecting himself outward as an object of contemplation, an idea.

It is fulfilled in the humun race? "We see not yet all things put under him." Then the writer goes on — "But we see Jesus, who was made a little lower than the angels for the suffering of death, crowned with glory and honour; that He by the grace of God should taste death for every man." In Jesus of Nazareth alone all these fragments, these sundry portions of the revealed Idea of Royalty met.

II. Christianity was implied in the race of prophets.

The second class of quotations refer to the prophets' life and history. (Hebr. ii. 11-14.)

Psalm xxii. 22; Psalm xviii. 2; Isaiah xii. 2; Isaiah viii. 18.

Remember what the prophets were. They were not merely predictors of the future. Nothing destroys the true conception of the prophets' office more than those popular books in which their mission is certified by curious coincidences. For example, if it is predicted that Babylon shall be a desolation, the haunt of wild beasts, &c., then some traveller has seen a lion standing on Birs Nimroud: or if the fisherman is to dry his nets on Tyre, simply expressing its destruction thereby, the commentator is not easy till he finds that a net has been actually seen drying on a rock. But this is to degrade the prophetic office to a level with Egyptian palmistry: to make the prophet like an astrologer, or a gipsy fortune-teller — one who can predict destinies and draw horoscopes. But in truth, the first office of the prophet was with the present. He read Eternal principles beneath the present and the transitory, and in doing this of course he prophesied the future; for a principle true to-day is true for ever. But this was, so to speak, an accident of his office: not its essential feature. If, for instance, he read in the voluptuousness of Babylon the secret of Babylon's decay, he also read by anticipation the doom of Corinth, of London, of all cities in Babylon's state; or if Jerusalem's fall was predicted, in it all such judgment comings were foreseen; and the language is true of the fall of the world: as truly, or more so, than that of Jerusalem. A philosopher saying in the present tense the law by which comets move, predicts all possible cometary movements.

Now the prophet's life almost more than his words was predictive. The writer of this epistle lays down a great principle respecting the prophet (ii. 11): "Both he that sanctifieth and they who are sanctified are all of one." It was the very condition of his inspiration that he should be one with the people. So far from making him superhuman, it made him *more* man. He felt with more exquisite sensitiveness all that belongs to man, else he could not have been a prophet. His insight into things was the result of that very weakness, sensitiveness, and susceptibility so tremblingly alive. He burned with their thoughts, and expressed them. He was obliged by the very sensitiveness of his humanity to have a more entire dependence and a more perfect sympathy than other men. The sanctifying prophet was one with those whom he sanctified. Hence he uses those expressions quoted from Isaiah and the Psalms above.

He was more man, just because more divine — more a son of man, because more a son of God. He was peculiarly the suffering Israelite: His countenance marred more than the sons of men. Hence we are told the prophets searched "what, or what manner of time, the Spirit of Christ which was in them did signify, when it testified beforehand the sufferings of Christ, and the glory that should follow." (1 Peter i. 11.)

Observe, it was a spirit *in* them, their own lives witnessing mysteriously of what the Perfect Humanity must be suffering.

Thus especially, Isaiah liii., spoken originally of the Jewish nation: of the prophet as peculiarly the Israelite: no wonder the eunuch asked Philip in perplexity, "Of whom doth the prophet say this? of himself or some other man?" The truth is, he said it of himself, but prophetically of humanity: true of him, most true of the Highest Humanity.

Here then was a new "portion" of the revelation. The prophet rebuked the king: often opposed the priest, but was one with the people. "He that sanctifieth and they who are sanctified are all of one."

If then, One had come claiming to be the Prophet of the Race, and was a Sufferer, claiming to be the Son of God, and yet peculiarly Man; the son of man: the son of man just because the Son of God: more Divine because more human: then this was only what the whole race of Jewish prophets should have prepared them for. God had spoken by the prophets. That God had now spoken by a Son in whom the idea of the True prophet was realized in its entireness.

III. The Priesthood continued this idea latent. The writer of this epistle saw three elements in the priestly idea. 1. That he should be ordained for men in things pertaining to God. 2. That he should offer gifts and sacrifices. 3. That he should be called by God, not be a mere self-assertor.

1. Ordained for men. Remark here the true idea contained in Judaism, and its difference from the Heathen notions. In Heathenism the priest was of a different Race: separate from his fellows. In Judaism he was ordained for men; their representative: constituted in their behalf. The Jewish priest represented the holiness of the nation; he went into the holy of holies, showing it. But this great idea was only implied, not fulfilled in the Jewish priest. He was only by a fiction the representative of holiness. Holy he was not. He only entered into a fictitious Holy of Holies. If the idea were to be ever real, it must be in One who should be actually what the Jewish priest was by a figment, and who should carry our humanity into the real Holy of Holies — the presence of God; thus becoming our invisible and Eternal Priest.

Next it was implied that his call must be Divine. But (in the 110th Psalm) a higher call is intimated than that Divine call which was made to the Aaronic priesthood by a regular succession, or, as it is called in the epistle, "the law of a carnal commandment." Melchizedek's call is spoken of. The king is called a priest after his order. Not a derived or hereditary priesthood: not one transmissible, beginning and ending in himself — Heb. vii. 1 to 3. A priesthood, in other words, of character, of inward right: a call internal, hence more Divine; or, as the writer calls it, a priest "after the power of an endless life." This was the Idea for which the Jewish psalms themselves ought to have prepared the Jew.

Again, the priests offered gifts and sacrifices. Distinguish. Gifts were thank-offerings: first-fruits of harvest, vintage, &c., a man's best: testimonies of infinite gratefulness, and expressions of it. But sacrifices were different: they implied a sense of unworthiness: that sense which conflicts with the idea of any right to offer gifts.

Now the Jewish Scriptures themselves had explained this subject, and this instinctive feeling of unworthiness for which sacrifice found an expression. Prophets and psalmists had felt that no sacrifice was perfect which did not reach the conscience (Ps. li. 16, 17), for instance; also, Heb. X. 8 to 12. No language could more clearly show that the spiritual Jew discerned that entire surrender to the Divine Will is the only perfect Sacrifice, the ground of all sacrifices, and that which alone imparts to it a significance. Not sacrifice.... "Then said I, Lo, I come to do Thy will, O God." *That* is the sacrifice which God wills.

I say it firmly — all other notions of sacrifice are false. Whatsoever introduces the conception of vindictiveness or retaliation; whatever speaks of appeasing fury; whatever estimates the value of the Saviour's sacrifice by the "penalty paid;" whatever differs from these notions of sacrifice contained in psalms and prophets, — is borrowed from the bloody shambles of Heathenism, and not from Jewish altars.

This alone makes the worshipper perfect as pertaining to the conscience. He who can offer it in its entireness, He alone is the world's Atonement; He in whose heart the Law was, and who alone of all mankind was content to do it, His Sacrifice alone can be the Sacrifice all-sufficient in the Father's sight as the proper Sacrifice of humanity: He who through the Eternal Spirit offered Himself without spot to God, He alone can give the Spirit which enables us to present *our* bodies a living sacrifice, holy and acceptable to God.

He is the only High Priest of the Universe.

XIII.

Preached April 25, 1852.

WORLDLINESS.

1 JOHN II. 15-17. — "If any man love the world, the love of the Father is not in him. For all that is in the world, the lust of the flesh, and the lust of the eyes, and the pride of life, is not of the Father, but is of the world. And the world passeth away, and the lust thereof: but he that doeth the will of God abideth for ever."

RELIGION differs from morality in the value which it places on the affections. Morality requires that an act be done on principle. Religion goes deeper, and inquires the state of the heart. The Church of Ephesus was unsuspected in her orthodoxy, and unblemished in her zeal: but to the ear of him who saw the apocalyptic vision, a voice spake, "I have somewhat against thee in that thou hast left thy first love."

In the eye of Christianity he is a Christian who loves the Father. He who loves the world may be in his way a good man, respecting whose eternal destiny we pronounce no opinion: but one of the Children of the Kingdom he is not.

Now, the boundary lines of this love of the world, or worldliness, are exceedingly difficult to define. Bigotry pronounces many things wrong which are harmless: laxity permits many which are by no means innocent: and it is a question perpetually put, a question miserably perplexing to those whose religion consists more in avoiding that which is wrong than in seeking that which is right, — What is Worldliness?

To that question we desire to find to-day an answer in the text; premising this, that our object is to put ourselves in possession of principles. For otherwise we shall only deal with this matter as empirics; condemning this and approving that by opinion, but on no certain and intelligible ground — we shall but float on the unstable sea of opinion.

We confine ourselves to two points.

I. The nature of the forbidden world.

II. The reasons for which it is forbidden.

I. The nature of the forbidden world.

The first idea suggested by "the world" is this green earth, with its days and nights, its seasons, its hills and its valleys, its clouds and brightness. This is not the world the love of which is prohibited; for, to forbid the love of this would be to forbid the love of God.

There are three ways in which we learn to know Him. First, by the working of our minds. Love, Justice, Tenderness: if we would know what they mean in God, we must gain the conception from their existence in ourselves. But inasmuch as humanity is imperfect in us, if we were to learn of God only from His image in ourselves, we should run the risk of calling the evil good, and the imperfect divine. Therefore He has given us, besides this, the representation of Himself in Christ, where is found the meeting-point of the Divine and the human, and in whose Life the character of Deity is reflected, as completely as the sun is seen in the depth of the still, untroubled lake.

But there is a third way still, in which we attain the idea of God. This world is but manifested Deity — God shown to eye, and ear, and sense. This strange phenomenon of a world — what is it? All we know of it — all we know of Matter — is, that it is an assemblage of Powers which produce in us certain sensations: but what those Powers are in themselves we know not. The sensation of colour, form, weight, we have; but what it is which gives those sensations — in the language of the schools, what is the Substratum which supports the accidents or qualities of Being — we cannot tell. Speculative Philosophy replies, It is but our own-selves becoming conscious of themselves. We, in our own being, are the cause of all phenomena. Positive philosophy replies, What the Being of the world is we cannot tell, we only know what it seems to us. Phenomena — appearance — beyond this we cannot reach. Being itself is, and for ever must be, unknowable. Religion replies, That something is God. The world is but manifested Deity. That which lies beneath the surface of all Appearance, the cause of all Manifestation, is God. So that to forbid the love of all this world, is to forbid the love of that by which God is known to us. The sounds and sights of this lovely world are but the drapery of the robe in which the Invisible has clothed Himself. Does a man ask what this world is, and why man is placed in it? It was that the invisible things of Him from the creation of the world might be clearly seen. Have we ever stood beneath the solemn vault of heaven, when the stars were looking down in their silent splendour, and not felt an overpowering sense of His eternity? When the white lightning has quivered in the sky, has that told us nothing of Power, or only something of electricity? Rocks and mountains, are they here to give us the idea of material massiveness, or to reveal the conception of the Strength of Israel? When we take up the page of past history, and read that wrong never prospered long, but that nations have drunk one after another the cup of terrible retribution, can we dismiss all that as the philosophy of history, or shall we say that through blood, and war, and desolation, we trace the footsteps of a presiding God, and find evidence that there sits at the helm of this world's affairs, a strict, and rigorous, and most terrible justice? To the eye that can see — to the heart that is not paralyzed, God is here. The warnings which the Bible utters against the things of this world bring no charge against the glorious world itself. The world is the glass through which we see the Maker. But what men do is this: They put the dull quicksilver of their own selfishness behind the glass, and so it becomes not the transparent medium through which God shines, but the dead opaque which reflects back themselves. Instead of lying with open eye and heart to *receive*, we project ourselves upon the world and *give*. So it gives us back our own false feelings and nature. Therefore it brings forth thorns and thistles. Therefore it grows weeds — weeds to us. Therefore the lightning burns with wrath, and the thunder mutters vengeance. By all which it comes to pass that the very Manifestation of God has transformed itself — the lust of the flesh, and the lust of the eye, and the pride of life: and all that is in the world is no longer of the Father, but is of the world.

By the world, again, is sometimes meant the men that are in the world. And thus the command would run — Love not men, but love God. It has been so read. The Pharisees read it so of old. The property which natural affection demanded for the support of parents — upon that they wrote "Corban," a gift for

God, and robbed men that they might give to God. Yet no less than this is done whenever human affection is called idolatry. As if God were jealous of our love in the human sense of jealousy. As if we could love God the more by loving man the less. As if it were not by loving our brother whom we have seen, that we approximate towards the love of God whom we have not seen. This is but the cloak for narrowness of heart. Men of withered affections excuse their lovelessness by talking largely of the affection due to God. Yet, like the Pharisees, the love on which Corban is written is never given to God, but really retained for self.

No, let a man love his neighbour as himself. Let him love his brother — sister — wife — with all the intensity of his heart's affection. This is not St. John's forbidden world.

Again. By the world is often understood the worldly occupation, trade, or profession, which a man exercises. And, accordingly, it is no uncommon thing to hear this spoken of as something which, if not actually anti-religious, is, so far as it goes, time taken away from the religious life. But when the man from whom the legion had been expelled, asked Jesus for the precepts of a religious existence, the reply sent him back to home. His former worldliness had consisted in doing his worldly duties ill — his future religiousness was to consist in doing those same duties better. A man's profession or trade is not only not incompatible with religion (provided it be a lawful one) — it *is* his religion. And this is true even of those callings which at first sight appear to have in them something hard to reconcile with religiousness. For instance, the profession of a lawyer. He is a worldling in it if he use it for some personal greed, or degrade it by chicanery. But in itself it is an occupation which sifts right from wrong; which in the entangled web of human life, unwinds the meshes of error. He is by profession enlisted on the side of the Right — directly connected with God, the central point of Justice and Truth. A nobler occupation need no man desire than to be a fellow-worker with God. Or take the soldier's trade — in this world generally a trade of blood, and revenge, and idle licentiousness. Rightly understood, what is it? A soldier's whole life, whether he will or not, is an enunciation of the greatest of religious truths, the voluntary sacrifice of one for the sake of many. In the detail of his existence, how abundant are the opportunities for the voluntary recognition of this. Opportunities such as that when the three strong men brake through the lines of the enemy to obtain the water for their sovereign's thirst — opportunities as when that same heroic sovereign poured the untasted water on the ground, and refused to drink because it was his soldiers' lives — he could not drink at such a price. Earnestness in a lawful calling is not worldliness. A profession is the sphere of our activity. There is something sacred in work. To work in the appointed sphere is to be religious — as religious as to pray. This is not the forbidden world.

Now to define what worldliness is. Remark, first, that it is determined by the *spirit* of a life, not the objects with which the life is conversant. It is not the "flesh," nor the "eye," nor "life," which are forbidden, but it is the *lust* of the flesh, and the *lust* of the eye, and the *pride* of life. It is not this earth nor the men who inhabit it — nor the sphere of our legitimate activity, that we may not love; but the way in which the love is given which constitutes worldliness. Look into this a little closer. The lust of the flesh. Here is affection for the outward: Pleasure, that which affects the senses only: the flesh, that enjoyment which comes from the emotions of an hour, be it coarse or be it refined. The pleasure of wine or the pleasure of music, so far as it is only a movement of the flesh. Again, the lust of the eye. Here is affection for the transient, for the eye can only gaze on form and colour — and these are things that do not last.

Once more — the pride of life. Here is affection for the unreal. Men's opinion — the estimate which depends upon wealth, rank, circumstances. Worldliness then consists in these three things: — Attachment to the Outward — attachment to the Transitory — attachment to the Unreal: in opposition to love for the Inward, the Eternal, the True: and the one of these affections is necessarily expelled by the other. If a man love the world, the love of the Father is not in him. But let a man once feel the power of the kingdom that is within, and then the love fades of that emotion whose life consists only in the thrill of a nerve, or the vivid sensation of a feeling: he loses his happiness and wins his blessedness. Let a man get but one glimpse of the King in His beauty, and then the forms and shapes of things here are to him but the types of an invisible loveliness: types which he is content should break and fade. Let but a man feel truth — that goodness is greatness — that there is no other greatness — and then the degrading reverence with which the titled of this world bow before wealth, and the ostentation with which the rich of this world profess their familiarity with title: all the pride of life, what is it to him? The love of the Inward — Everlasting, Real — the love, that is, of the Father, annihilates the love of the world.

II. We pass to the reasons for which the love of the world is forbidden.

The first reason assigned is, that the love of the world is incompatible with the love of God. If any man love the world, the love of the Father is not in him. Now what we observe in this is, that St. John takes it for granted that we must love something. If not the love of the Father, then of necessity the love of the world. Love misplaced, or love rightly placed — you have your choice between these two: you have not your choice between loving God or nothing. No man is sufficient for himself. Every man must go out of himself for enjoyment. Something in this universe besides himself there must be to bind the affections of every man. There is that within us which compels us to attach ourselves to something outward. The choice is not this — Love, or be without love. You cannot give the pent-up steam its choice of moving or not moving. It must move one way or the other: the right way or the wrong way. Direct it rightly, and its energy rolls the engine-wheels smoothly on their track: block up its passage, and it bounds away, a thing of madness and ruin. Stop it you cannot; it will rather burst. So it is with our hearts. There is a pent-up energy of love, gigantic for good or evil. Its right way is in the direction of our Eternal Father; and then let it boil and pant as it will, the course of the man is smooth.

Expel the love of God from the bosom — what then? Will the passion that is within cease to burn? Nay. Tie the man down — let there be no outlet for his affections — let him attach himself to nothing, and become a loveless spirit in this universe, and then there is what we call a broken heart: the steam bursts the machinery that contains it. Or else let him take his course, unfettered and free, and then we have the riot of worldliness — a man with strong affections thrown off the line, tearing himself to pieces, and carrying desolation along with him. Let us comprehend our own nature, ourselves, and our destinies. God is our Rest, the only One that can quench the fever of our desire. God in Christ is what we want. When men quit that, so that "the love of the Father is not in them," then they must perforce turn aside: the nobler heart to break with disappointment — the meaner heart to love the world instead, and sate and satisfy itself, as best it may, on things that perish in the using. Herein lies the secret of our being, in this world of the affections. This explains why our noblest feelings lie so close to our basest — why the noblest so easily metamorphose themselves into the basest. The heart which was made large enough for God, wastes itself upon the world.

The second reason which the apostle gives for not squandering affection on the world is its transitoriness. Now this transitoriness exists in two shapes. It is transitory in itself — the world passeth away. It is transitory in its power of exciting desire — the lust thereof passeth away.

It is a twice-told tale that the world is passing away from us, and there is very little new to be said on the subject. God has written it on every page of His creation that there is nothing here which lasts. Our affections change. The friendships of the man are not the friendships of the boy. Our very selves are altering. The basis of our being may remain, but our views, tastes, feelings, are no more our former self than the oak is the acorn. The very face of the visible world is altering around us: we have the gray mouldering ruins to tell of what was once. Our labourers strike their ploughshares against the foundations of buildings which once echoed to human mirth — skeletons of men, to whom life once was dear — urns and coins that remind the antiquarian of a magnificent empire. To-day the shot of the enemy defaces and blackens monuments and venerable temples, which remind the Christian that into the deep silence of eternity, the Roman world, which was in its vigour in the days of John, has passed away. And so things are going. It is a work of weaving and unweaving. All passes. Names that the world heard once in thunder are scarcely heard at the end of centuries — good or bad, they pass. A few years ago and *we* were not. A few centuries further, and we reach the age of beings of almost another race. Nimrod was the conqueror and scourge of his far-back age. Tubal Cain gave to the world the iron which was the foundation of every triumph of men over nature. We have their names now. But the philologist is uncertain whether the name of the first is real or mythical — and the traveller excavates the sand-mounds of Nineveh to wonder over the records which he cannot decipher. Tyrant and benefactor, both are gone. And so all things are moving on to the last fire which shall wrap the world in conflagration, and make all that has been the recollection of a dream. This is the history of the world, and all that is in it. It passes while we look at it. Like as when you watch the melting tints of the evening sky — purple-crimson, gorgeous gold, a few pulsations of quivering light, and it is all gone: — we are such stuff as dreams are made of.

The other aspect of this transitoriness is, that the lust of the world passeth away. By which the apostle seems to remind us of that solemn truth that, fast as the world is fleeting from us, faster still does the taste for its enjoyments fleet: fast as the brilliancy fades from earthly things, faster still does the eye become wearied of straining itself upon them.

Now there is one way in which this takes place, by a man becoming satiated with the world. There is something in earthly rapture which cloys. And when we drink deep of pleasure, there is left behind something of that loathing which follows a repast on sweets. When a boy sets out in life, it is all fresh — freshness in feeling — zest in his enjoyment — purity in his heart. Cherish that, my young brethren, while you can — lose it, and it never comes again. It is not an easy thing to cherish it, for it demands restraint in pleasure, and no young heart loves that. Religion has only calm, sober, perhaps monotonous pleasures to offer at first. The deep rapture of enjoyment comes in after-life. And that will not satisfy the young heart. Men will know what pleasure is, and they drink deep. Keen delight — feverish enjoyment — that is what you long for: and these emotions lose their delicacy and their relish, and will only come at the bidding of gross excitements. The ecstasy which once rose to the sight of the rainbow in the sky, or the bright brook, or the fresh morning, comes languidly at last only in the crowded midnight room, or the excitement of commercial speculation, or beside the gaming-table, or amidst the fever of politics. It is a spectacle for men and angels, when a man has become old in feeling and worn out before his time — Know we none such among our own acquaintance? Have the young never seen those aged ones who stand amongst them in their pleasures, almost as if to warn them of what they themselves must come to at last? Have they never marked the dull and sated look that they cast upon the whole scene, as upon a thing which they would fain enjoy and cannot? Know you what you have been looking on? A sated worldling — one to whom pleasure was rapture once, as it is to you now. Thirty years more, that look and that place will be yours: and that is the way the world rewards its veterans; it chains them to it after the "lust of the world" has passed away.

Or this may be done by a discovery of the unsatisfactoriness of the world. That is a discovery not made by every man. But there are some at least who have learned it bitterly, and that without the aid of Christ. Some there are who would not live over this past life again even if it were possible. Some there are who would gladly have done with the whole thing at once, and exchange — oh! how joyfully — the garment for the shroud. And some there are who cling to life, not because life is dear, but because the future is dark, and they tremble somewhat at the thought of entering it. Clinging to life is no proof that a man is still longing for the world. We often cling to life the more tenaciously as years go on. The deeper the tree has struck its roots into the ground, the less willing is it to be rooted up. But there is many a one who so hangs on just because he has not the desperate hardihood to quit it, nor faith enough to be "willing to depart." The world and he have understood each other: he has seen through it: he has ceased to hope anything from it. The love of the Father is not in him: but "the lust of the world" has passed away.

Lastly, A reason for unlearning the love of the world is the solitary permanence of Christian action. In contrast with the fleetingness of this world, the apostle tells us of the stability of labour. "He that doeth the will of God abideth for ever." And let us mark this. Christian life is action: not a speculating — not a debating: but a doing. One thing, and only one, in this world has eternity stamped upon it. Feelings pass: resolves and thoughts pass: opinions change. What you have done lasts — lasts in you. Through ages, through eternity, what you have done for Christ, that and only that you are. "They rest from their labours," saith the Spirit, "and their works do follow them." If the love of the Father be in us, where is the thing done which we have to show? You think justly — feel rightly — yes — but your work. Produce it. Men of wealth — men of talent — men of leisure: What are you *doing* in God's world for God?

Observe, however, to distinguish between the act and the actor: — It is not the thing done, but the Doer who lasts. The thing done often is a failure. The cup given in the name of Christ may be given to one unworthy of it: but think ye that the love with which it was given has passed away? Has it not printed itself indelibly in the character by the very act of giving? Bless, and if the Son of peace be there, your act succeeds: but if not, your blessing shall return unto you again. In other words, the act may fail; but the doer of it abideth for ever.

We close this subject with two practical truths.

First of all, let us learn from earthly changefulness a lesson of cheerful activity. The world has its way of looking at all this — but it is not the Christian's way. There has been nothing said to-day that a worldly moralist has not already said a thousand times far better. The fact is a world-fact. The application is a Christian one. Every man can be eloquent about the nothingness of time.

But the application! Let us eat and drink, for to-morrow we die? That is one application. Let us sentimentalize and be sad in this fleeting world, and talk of the instability of human greatness, and the transitoriness of human affection? Those are the only two applications the world knows. They shut out the recollection and are merry: or they dwell on it and are sad. Christian brethren, dwell on it and be happy. This world is not yours: thank God it is not. It is dropping away from you like worn-out autumn leaves; but beneath it, hidden in it, there is another world lying as the flower lies in the bud. That is *your* world, which must burst forth at last into eternal luxuriance. All you stand on, see, and love, is but the husk of something better. Things are passing — our friends are dropping off from us: strength is giving way: our relish for earth is going, and the world no longer wears to our hearts the radiance that once it wore. We have the same sky above us, and the same scenes around us; but the freshness that our hearts extracted from everything in boyhood, and the glory that seemed to rest once on earth and life has faded away for ever. Sad and gloomy truths to the man who is going down to the grave with his work undone. Not sad to the Christian: but rousing, exciting, invigorating. If it be the eleventh hour, we have no time for folding of the hands: we will work the faster. Through the changefulness of life: through the solemn tolling of the bell of Time, which tells us that another, and another, and another, are gone before us: through the noiseless rush of a world which is going down with gigantic footsteps into nothingness. Let not the Christian slack his hand from work: for he that doeth the will of God may defy hell itself to quench his immortality.

Finally, The love of this world is only unlearned by the love of the Father. It were a desolate thing, indeed, to forbid the love of earth, if there were nothing to fill the vacant space in the heart. But it is just for this purpose, that a sublimer affection may find room, that the lower is to be expelled. And there is only one way in which that higher love is learned. The cross of Christ is the measure of the love of God to us, and the measure of the meaning of man's existence. The measure of the love of God. Through the death-knell of a passing universe, God seems at least to speak to us in wrath. There is no doubt of what God means in the Cross. He means love. The measure of the meaning of man's existence. Measure all by the Cross. Do you want success? The Cross is failure. Do you want a name? The Cross is infamy. Is it to be gay and happy that you live? The Cross is pain and sharpness. Do you live that the will of God may be done, in you and by you in life and death? Then and only then the Spirit of the Cross is in you. When once a man has learned that, the power of the world is gone; and no man need bid him, in denunciation or in invitation, not to love the world. He cannot love the world: for he has got an ambition above the world. He has planted his foot upon the Rock, and when all else is gone, he at least abides for ever.

XIV.

Preached November 14, 1852.

THE SYDENHAM PALACE, AND THE RELIGIOUS NON-OBSERVANCE OF THE SABBATH.

ROM. xiv. 5, 6. — "One man esteemeth one day above another; another esteemeth every day alike. Let every man be fully persuaded in his own mind. He that regardeth the day, regardeth it unto the Lord; and he that regardeth not the day, to the Lord he doth not regard it. He that eateth, eateth to the Lord, for he giveth God thanks; and he that eateth not, to the Lord he eateth not, and giveth God thanks."

THE selection of this text is suggested by one of the current topics of the day. Lately, projects have been devised, one of which in importance surpasses all the rest, for providing places of public recreation for the people: and it has been announced, with the sanction of government, that such a place will be held open during a part at least of the day of rest. By a large section of sincerely religious persons this announcement has been received with considerable alarm, and strenuous opposition. It has seemed to them that such a desecration would be a national crime: for, holding the Sabbath to be God's sign between Himself and His people, they cannot but view the desecration of the sign as a forfeiture of His covenant, and an act which will assuredly call down national judgments. By the secular press, on the contrary, this proposal has been defended with considerable power. It has been maintained that the Sabbath is a Jewish institution; in its strictness, at all events, not binding on a Christian community. It has been urged with much force that we cannot consistently refuse to concede to the poor man publicly, that right of recreation which privately the rich man has long taken without rebuke, and with no protest on the part of the ministers of Christ. And it has been said, that such places of recreation will tend to humanize, which if not identical with Christianizing the population, is at least a step towards it.

Upon such a subject, where truth unquestionably does not lie upon the surface, it cannot be out of place if a minister of Christ endeavours to direct the minds of his congregation towards the formation of an opinion; not dogmatically, but humbly remembering always that his own temptation is from his very position, as a clergyman, to view such matters, not so much in the broad light of the possibilities of actual life, as with the eyes of a recluse; from a clerical and ecclesiastical, rather than from a large and human point of view. For no minister of Christ has a right to speak oracularly. All that he can pretend to do is to give his judgment, as one that has obtained mercy of the Lord to be faithful. And on large national subjects there is perhaps no class so ill qualified to form a judgment with breadth as we, the clergy of the Church of England, accustomed as we are to move in the narrow circle of those who listen to us with forbearance and deference, and mixing but little in real life, till in our cloistered and inviolable sanctuaries we are apt to forget that it is one thing to lay down rules for a religious clique, and another to legislate for a great nation.

In the Church of Rome a controversy had arisen in the time of St. Paul, respecting the exact relation in which Christianity stood to Judaism; and consequently, the obligation of various Jewish institutions came to be discussed: among the rest the Sabbath-day. One party maintained its abrogation: another its continued obligation. "One man esteemeth one day above another; another esteemeth every day alike." Now, it is remarkable that in his reply, the Apostle Paul, although his own views upon the question were decided and strong, passes no judgment of censure upon the practice of either of these parties, but only blames the uncharitable spirit in which the one "judged their brethren," as irreligious, and the other "set at nought" their stricter brethren as superstitious. He lays down, however, two principles for the decision of the matter: the first being the rights of Christian conviction, or the sacredness of the individual conscience — "Let every man be fully persuaded in his own mind;" the second, a principle unsatisfactory enough, and surprising, no doubt, to both, that there is such a thing as a religious observance, and also such a thing as a religious non-observance of the day — "He that regardeth the day, regardeth it unto the Lord: and he that regardeth not the day, to the Lord he doth not regard it."

I shall consider,

I. St. Paul's own view upon the question.

II. His modifications of that view, in reference to separate cases.

I. St. Paul's own view.

No one, I believe, who would read St. Paul's own writings with unprejudiced mind could fail to come to the conclusion that he considered the Sabbath abrogated by Christianity. Not merely modified in its stringency, but totally repealed.

For example, see Col. ii. 16, 17: observe, he counts the Sabbath-day among those institutions of Judaism which were shadows, and of which Christ was the realization, the substance or "body;" and he bids the Colossians remain indifferent to the judgment which would be pronounced upon their non-observance of such days. "Let no man judge you with respect to ..... the sabbath-days."

More decisive still in the text. For it has been contended that in the former passage, "Sabbath-days" refers simply to the Jewish Sabbaths, which were superseded by the Lord's day; and that the apostle does not allude at all to the new institution, which it is supposed had superseded it. Here, however, there can be no such ambiguity. "One man esteemeth *every* day alike;" and he only says let him be fully persuaded in his own mind. "Every" day must include first days as well as last days of the week: Sundays as well as Saturdays.

And again, he even speaks of scrupulous adherence to particular days, as if it were giving up the very principle of Christianity: "Ye observe days, and months, and times, and years. I am afraid of you, lest I have bestowed upon you labour in vain." So that his objection was not to Jewish days, but to the very principle of attaching intrinsic sacredness to any days. All forms and modes of particularizing the Christian life he reckoned as bondage under the elements or alphabet of the law. And this is plain from the nature of the case. He struck not at a day, but at a principle. Else, if with all this vehemence and earnestness, he only meant to establish a new set of days in the place of the old, there is no intelligible principle for which he is contending, and that earnest apostle is only a champion for one day instead of another — an assertor of the eternal sanctities of Sunday, instead of the eternal sanctities of Saturday. Incredible indeed.

Let us then understand the principle on which he declared the repeal of the sabbath. He taught that the blood of Christ cleansed *all* things; therefore there was nothing *specially* clean. Christ had vindicated all for God: therefore there was no one thing more God's than another. For to assert one thing as God's more than another, is by implication to admit that other to be less God's.

The blood of Christ had vindicated God's parental right to all humanity; therefore there could be no peculiar people. "There is neither Jew nor Greek, circumcision nor uncircumcision, Barbarian, Scythian, bond, nor free: but Christ is all and in all." It had proclaimed God's property in all places: therefore there could be no one place intrinsically holier than another. No human dedication, no human consecration, could localize God in space. Hence the first martyr quoted from the prophet: "Howbeit the most High dwelleth not in temples made with hands; as saith the prophet, heaven is my throne, and earth is my footstool: what house will ye build for me? saith the Lord."

Lastly, the Gospel of Christ had sanctified all time: hence no time could be specially God's. For to assert that Sunday is more God's day than Monday, is to maintain by implication Monday is His less rightfully.

Here, however, let it be observed, it is perfectly possible, and not at all inconsistent with this, that for human convenience, and even human necessities, just as it became desirable to set apart certain places in which the noise of earthly business should not be heard for spiritual worship, so it should become desirable to set apart certain days for special worship. But then all such were defensible on the ground of wise and Christian expediency alone; they could not be placed on the ground of a Divine statute or command: they rested on the authority of the Church of Christ: and the power which had made could unmake them again.

Accordingly, in early, we cannot say exactly how early times, the Church of Christ felt the necessity of substituting something in place of the ordinances which had been repealed. And the Lord's day arose, not a day of compulsory rest; not such a day at all as modern sabbatarians suppose. Not a Jewish sabbath; rather a day in many respects absolutely contrasted with the Jewish sabbath.

For the Lord's day sprung, not out of a transference of the Jewish sabbath from Saturday to Sunday; but rather out of the idea of making the week an imitation of the life of Christ. With the early Christians, the great conception was that of following their crucified and risen Lord: they set, as it were, the clock of time to the epochs of his history. Friday represented the Death in which all Christians daily die, and Sunday the Resurrection in which all Christians daily rise to higher life. What Friday and Sunday were to the week, that Good Friday and Easter Sunday were to the year. And thus, in larger or smaller cycles, all time represented to the early Christians the mysteries of the Cross and the Risen life hidden in humanity. And as the sunflower turns from morning till evening to the sun, so did the early Church turn for ever to her Lord, transforming week and year into a symbolical representation of His Spiritual Life.

Carefully distinguish this, the true historical view of

the origin of the Lord's day, from a mere transference of a Jewish sabbath from one day to another. For St. Paul's teaching is distinct and clear, that the sabbath is annulled, and to urge the observance of the day as indispensable to salvation, was, according to him, to Judaize: "to turn again to the weak and beggarly elements, whereunto they desired to be in bondage."

II. The modifications of this view.

1. The first modification has reference to those who conscientiously observed the day. He that observeth the day, observeth it to the Lord. Let him act then on that conviction: "Let him be fully persuaded in his own mind."

There is therefore a religious *observance* of the Sabbath-day possible.

We are bound by the spirit of the Fourth commandment, so far as we are in the same spiritual state as they to whom it was given. The spiritual intent of Christianity is to worship God every day in the spirit. But had this law been given in all its purity to the Jews, instead of turning every week-day into a sabbath, they would have transformed every sabbath into a week-day: with no special day fixed for worship, they would have spent every day without worship. Their hearts were too dull for a devotion so spiritual and pure.

Therefore a law was given, specializing a day, in order to lead them to the broader truth that every day is God's.

Now, so far as we are in the Jewish state, the fourth commandment, even in its rigour and strictness, is wisely used by us; nay, we might say, indispensable.

For who is he who needs not the day? He is the man so rich in love, so conformed to the mind of Christ, so elevated into the sublime repose of heaven, that he needs no carnal ordinances at all, nor the assistance of one day in seven to kindle spiritual feelings, seeing he is, as it were, all his life in heaven already.

And doubtless, such the Apostle Paul expected the Church of Christ to be. Anticipating the second Advent at once; not knowing the long centuries of slow progress that were to come, his heart would have sunk within him could he have been told that at the end of eighteen centuries the Christian Church would be still observing days, and months, and times, and years, and still more, needing them.

Needing them, I say. For the sabbath was made for man. God made it for men in a certain spiritual state, because they needed it. The need therefore is deeply hidden in human nature. He who can dispense with it must be holy and spiritual indeed. And he who still unholy and unspiritual, would yet dispense with it, is a man who would fain be wiser than his Maker. We, Christians as we are, still need the law: both in its restraints, and in its aids to our weakness.

No man, therefore, who knows himself, but will gladly and joyfully use the institution. No man who knows the need of his brethren will wantonly desecrate it, or recklessly hurt even their scruples respecting its observance. And no such man can look with aught but grave and serious apprehensions on such an innovation upon English customs of life and thought, as the proposal to give public and official countenance to a scheme which will *invite* millions, I do not say to an irreligious, but certainly an unreligious use of the day of rest.

This then is the first modification of the broad view of a repealed sabbath. Repealed though it be, there is such a thing as a religious observance of it. And provided that those who are stricter than we in their views of its obligation, observe it not from superstition, nor in abridgment of Christian liberty, nor from moroseness, we are bound in Christian charity to yield them all respect and honour. Let them act out their conscientious convictions. Let not him that observeth not, despise him that observeth.

The second modification of the broad view is, that there is such a thing as a *religious non-observance* of the sabbath. I lay a stress on the word religious. For St. Paul does not say that every non-observance of the sabbath is religious, but that he who not observing it, observeth it not to the Lord, is, because acting on conscientious conviction, as acceptable as the others, who, in obedience to what they believe to be His will, observe it.

He pays his non-observance to the Lord, who feeling that Christ has made him free, striving to live all his days in the spirit, and knowing that that which is displeasing to God is not work nor recreation, but selfishness and worldliness, refuses to be bound by a Jewish ordinance which forbade labour and recreation, only with a typical intent.

But he who, not trying to serve God on any day, gives Sunday to toil or pleasure, certainly observes not the day: but his non-observance is not rendered to the Lord. He may be free from superstition: but it is not Christ who has made him free. Nor is he one of whom St. Paul would have said that his liberty on the sabbath is as acceptable as his brother's conscientious scrupulosity.

Here, then, we are at issue with the popular defence of public recreations on the Sabbath-day: not so much with respect to the practice, as with respect to the grounds on which the practice is approved. They claim liberty: but it is not Christian liberty. Like St. Paul, they demand a license for non-observance; only, it is not "non-observance to the Lord." For distinguish well. The abolition of Judaism is not necessarily the establishment of Christianity: to do away with the sabbath-day in order to substitute a nobler, truer, more continuous sabbath, even the sabbath of all time given up to God, is well. But to do away with the special Rights of God to the sabbath, in order merely to substitute the Rights of Pleasure, or the Rights of Mammon, or even the license of profligacy and drunkenness, that, methinks, is not Paul's "Christian liberty!"

The second point on which we join issue is the assumption that public places of recreation, which humanize, will therefore Christianize the people. It is taken for granted that architecture, sculpture, and the wonders of Nature and Art which such buildings will contain, have a direct or indirect tendency to lead to true devotion.

Only in a very limited degree is there truth in this at all. Christianity will humanize: we are not so sure that humanizing will Christianize. Let us be clear upon this matter. Esthetics are not Religion. It is one thing to civilize and polish: it is another thing to Christianize. The Worship of the Beautiful is not the Worship of Holiness; nay, I know not whether the one may not have a tendency to disincline from the other.

At least, such was the history of ancient Greece. Greece was the home of the Arts, the sacred ground on which the worship of the Beautiful was carried to its perfection. Let those who have read the history of her decline and fall, who have perused the debasing works of her later years, tell us how music, painting, poetry, the arts, softened and debilitated and sensualized the nation's heart. Let them tell us how, when Greece's last and greatest man was warning in vain against the foe at her gates, and demanding a manlier and a more heroic disposition to sacrifice, that most polished and humanized people, sunk in trade and sunk in pleasure, were squandering enormous sums upon their buildings and their esthetics, their processions and their people's palaces, till the flood came, and the liberties of Greece were trampled down for ever beneath the feet of the Macedonian Conqueror.

No! the change of a nation's heart is not to be effected by the infusion of a taste for artistic grace. "Other foundation can no man lay than that is laid, which is Christ Jesus." Not Art, but the Cross of Christ. Simpler manners, purer lives: more self-denial; more earnest sympathy with the classes that lie below us; nothing short of that can lay the foundations of the Christianity which is to be hereafter, deep and broad.

On the other hand, we dissent from the views of those who would arrest such a project by petitions to the legislature on these grounds.

1. It is a return backwards to Judaism and Law. It may be quite true that, as we suspect, such non-observance of the day is not to the Lord: but only a

scheme of mere pecuniary speculation. Nevertheless there is such a thing as a religious non-observance of the day: and we dare not "judge another man's servant: to his own master he standeth or falleth." We dare not assert the perpetual obligation of the Sabbath, when an inspired apostle has declared it abrogated. We dare not refuse a public concession of that kind of recreation to the poor man which the rich have long not hesitated to take in their sumptuous mansions and pleasure-grounds, unrebuked by the ministers of Christ, who seem touched to the quick only when the desecration of the Sabbath is loud and vulgar. We cannot substitute a statute law for a repealed law of God. We may think, and we do, that there is much which may lead to dangerous consequences in this innovation: but we dare not treat it as a crime.

The second ground on which we are opposed to the ultra-rigour of Sabbath observance, especially when it becomes coercive, is the danger of injuring the conscience. It is wisely taught by St. Paul that he who does anything with offence, *i. e.*, with a feeling that it is wrong, does wrong. To him it is wrong, even though it be not wrong abstractedly. Therefore it is always dangerous to multiply restrictions and requirements beyond what is essential, because men feeling themselves hemmed in, break the artificial barrier, but breaking it with a sense of guilt, do thereby become hardened in conscience and prepared for transgression against commandments which are divine and of eternal obligation. Hence it is that the criminal has so often in his confessions traced his deterioration in crime to the first step of breaking the Sabbath-day: and no doubt with accurate truth. But what shall we infer from this? Shall we infer, as is so often done upon the platform and in religious books, that it proves the everlasting obligation of the Sabbath? Or shall we, with a far truer philosophy of the human soul, infer, in the language of St. Peter, that we have been laying on him "a yoke which neither we nor our fathers were able to bear?" — in the language of St. Paul, that "the motions of sin were by the law," that the rigorous rule was itself the stimulating, moving cause of the sin: and that when the young man, worn out with his week's toil, first stole out into the fields to taste the fresh breath of a spring-day, he did it with a vague, secret sense of transgression, and that having as it were drawn his sword in defiance against the established code of the religious world, he felt that from thenceforward there was for him no return, and so he became an outcast, his sword against every man, and every man's sword against him? I believe this to be true account of the matter: and believing it, I cannot but believe that the false Jewish notions of the Sabbath-day which are prevalent have been exceedingly pernicious to the morals of the country.

Lastly, I remind you of the danger of mistaking a "positive" law for a moral one. Tho danger is that proportionably to the vehemence with which the law positive is enforced, the sacredness of moral laws is neglected. A positive law, in theological language, is a law laid down for special purposes, and corresponds with statute laws in things civil. Thus laws of quarantine and laws of excise depend for their force upon the will of the legislature, and when repealed are binding no more. But a moral law is one binding for ever, which a statute law may declare, but can neither make nor unmake.

Now when men are rigorous in the enforcement and reverence paid to laws positive, the tendency is to a corresponding indifference to the laws of eternal Right. The written supersedes in their hearts the moral. The mental history of the ancient Pharisees who observed the Sabbath, and tithed mint, anise, and cummin, neglecting justice, mercy, and truth, is the history of a most dangerous but universal tendency of the human heart. And so, many a man whose heart swells with what he thinks pious horror when he sees the letter delivered or the train run upon the Sabbath-day, can pass through the streets at night, undepressed and unshocked by the evidences of the wide-spreading profligacy which has eaten deep into his country's heart. And many a man who would gaze upon the domes of a crystal palace, rising above the trees, with somewhat of the same feeling with which he would look on a temple dedicated to Juggernaut, and who would fancy that something of the spirit of an ancient prophet was burning in his bosom, when his lips pronounced the Woe! Woe! of a coming doom, would sit calmly in a social circle of English life, and scarcely feel uneasy in listening to its uncharitableness and its slanders: would hear without one throb of indignation, the common dastardly condemnation of the weak for sins which are venial in the strong: would survey the relations of the rich and poor in this country, and remain calmly satisfied that there is nothing false in them, unbrotherly and wrong. No, my brethren! let us think clearly and strongly on this matter. It may be that God has a controversy with this people. It may be, as they say, that our Father will chasten us by the sword of the foreigner. But if He does, and if judgments are in store for our country, they will fall, not because the correspondence of the land is carried on upon the Sabbath day: nor because Sunday trains are not arrested by the legislature: nor because a public permission is given to the working-classes for a few hours' recreation on the day of rest: but because we are selfish men: and because we prefer Pleasure to duty, and Traffic to Honour; and because we love our party more than our Church, and our Church more than our Christianity; and our Christianity more than Truth, and ourselves more than all. These are the things that defile a nation: but the labour and the recreation of its Poor, these are not the things that defile a nation.

XV.

Preached January 9, 1853.

THE EARLY DEVELOPMENT OF JESUS.

LUKE ii. 40. — "And the child grew, and waxed strong in spirit, filled with wisdom; and the grace of God was upon him."

THE ecclesiastical year begins with Advent, then comes Christmas-day. The first day of the natural year begins with the infancy of the Son of Man. To-day the gospel proceeds with the brief account of the early years of Jesus.

The infinite significance of the life of Christ is not exhausted by saying that He was a perfect man. The notion of the earlier Socinians that He was a pattern man (ψιλὸς ἄνθρωπος) commissioned from Heaven with a message to teach men how to live, and supernaturally empowered to live in that perfect way Himself, is immeasurably short of truth. For perfection merely human does not attract; rather it repels. It may be copied in form. It cannot be imitated in spirit, — for men only imitate that from which enthusiasm and life are caught, — for it does not inspire nor fire with love.

Faultless men and pattern children — you may admire them, but you admire coldly. Praise them as you will, no one is better for their example. No one blames them, and no one loves them: they kindle no enthusiasm; they create no likeness of themselves: they never reproduce themselves in other lives — the true prerogative of all original life.

If Christ had been only a faultless Being, He would never have set up in the world a new type of character which at the end of two thousand years is fresh and life-giving and inspiring still. He never would have regenerated the world. He never would have "drawn all men unto Him," by being lifted up a self-sacrifice, making self-devotion beautiful. In Christ the Divine and Human blended: Immutability joined itself to Mutability. There was in Him the Divine which remained fixed; the Human which was constantly developing. One uniform idea and Purpose characterized His whole life, with a Divine immutable unity throughout, but it was subject to the laws of human growth. For the soul of Christ was not cast down upon this world a perfect thing at once. Spotless? — yes. Faultless? — yes. Tempted in all points without sin? — yes. But perfection is more than faultlessness. All scripture coincides in telling us that the ripe perfection of His manhood was reached step by step. There was a power and a Life within Him which were to be developed, which could only be developed, like all human strength and goodness, by toil of brain and heart. Life up-hill all the way: and every footprint by which He climbed left behind for us, petrified on the hard rock, and indurated into history for ever, to show us when and where and how He toiled and won.

Take a few passages to prove that His perfection was gained by degrees. "It became Him for whom are all things, and by whom are all things, in bringing many sons to glory, to make the Captain of their salvation *perfect* through suffering."

Again, "Behold, I cast out devils, and do cures to-day and to-morrow, and the third day I shall be *perfected*."

"Though He were a Son, yet *learned* He obedience." And in the context, "Jesus *increased*" . . . .

Now see the result of this aspect of His perfectibility. In that changeless element of His Being which beneath all the varying phases of growth remained Divinely faultless, we see that which we can adore. In the everchanging, ever-growing, subject therefore to feebleness and endearing mutability, we see that which brings Him near to us: makes Him lovable, at the same time that it interprets us to ourselves.

Our subject is the early development of Jesus. In this text we read of a threefold growth.

I. In strength.

II. In wisdom.

III. In grace.

First, it speaks to us simply of his early development, "The child grew."

In the case of all rare excellence that is merely human, it is the first object of the biographer of a marvellous man to seek for surprising stories of his early life. The appetite for the marvellous in this matter is almost instinctive and invariable. All men almost love to discover the early wonders which were prophetic of after-greatness. Apparently, the reason is that we are unwilling to believe that wondrous excellence was attained by slow, patient labour. We get an excuse for our own slowness and stunted growth, by settling it once for all, that the *original* differences between such men and us were immeasurable. Therefore it is, I conceive, that we seek so eagerly for anecdotes of early precocity.

In this spirit the fathers of the primitive church collected legends of the early life of Christ, stories of superhuman infancy: what the infant and the child said and did. Many of these legends are absurd: all, as resting on no authority, are rejected.

Very different from this is the spirit of the Bible narrative. It records no marvellous stories of infantine sagacity or miraculous power, to feed a prurient curiosity. Both in what it tells and in what it does not tell, one thing is plain, that the human life of the Son of God was *natural.* There was first the blade, then the ear, then the full corn. In what it does *not* say: because, had there been anything preternatural to record, no doubt it would have been recorded. In what it *does* say: because that little is all unaffectedly simple. One anecdote, and two verses of general description, that is all which is told us of the Redeemer's childhood.

The child, it is written, grew. Two pregnant facts. He was a child, and a child that grew in heart, in intellect, in size, in grace, in favour with God. Not a man in child's years. No hot-bed precocity marked the holiest of infancies. The Son of Man grew up in the quiet valley of existence — in shadow, not in sunshine, not *forced.* No unnatural, stimulating culture had developed the mind or feelings: no public flattery: no sunning of His infantine perfections in the glare of the world's show, had brought the temptation of the wilderness with which His manhood grappled, too early on His soul. We know that He was childlike, as other children: for in after years His brethren thought His fame strange, and His townsmen rejected him. They could not believe *that one*, who had gone in and out, ate and drank and worked, was He whose Name is Wonderful. The proverb, true of others, was true of Him: "A prophet is not without honour, but in his own country, and among his own kin, and in his own house." You know Him in a *picture* at once, by the halo round His brow. There was no glory in His real life to mark Him. He was in the world, and the world knew Him not. Gradually and gently He woke to consciousness of life and its manifold meaning; found Himself in possession of a self; by degrees opened His eyes upon this outer world, and drank in its beauty. Early He felt the lily of the field discourse to Him of the Invisible Loveliness, and the ravens tell of God His Father. Gradually and not at once, He embraced the sphere of human duties, and woke to His earthly relationships one by one — the Son — the Brother — the Citizen — the Master.

It is a very deep and beautiful and precious truth that the Eternal Son had a human and progressive childhood. Happy the child who is suffered to be and content to be what God meant it to be — a child while childhood lasts. Happy the parent who does not force artificial manners — precocious feeling — premature religion. Our age is one of stimulus and high pressure. We live as it were our lives out fast. Effect is everything. Results produced at once: something to show and something that may *tell*. The folio of patient years is replaced by the pamphlet that stirs men's curiosity to-day, and to-morrow is forgotten. "Plain living and high thinking are no more." The town, with its fever and its excitements, and its collision of mind with mind, has spread over the country: and there is no country, scarcely home. To men who traverse England in a few hours, and spend only a portion of the year in one place, Home is becoming a vocable of past ages.

The result is that heart and brain which were given to last for seventy years, wear out before their time. We have our exhausted men of twenty-five, and our old men of forty. Heart and brain give way: the heart hardens and the brain grows soft.

Brethren! the Son of God lived till thirty in an obscure village of Judea, unknown: then came forth a matured and perfect Man — with mind, and heart, and frame, in perfect balance of humanity. It is a Divine lesson! I would I could say as strongly as I feel deeply. Our stimulating artificial culture destroys depth. Our competition, our nights turned into days by pleasure, leave no time for earnestness. We are superficial men. Character in the world wants *root*. England has gained much: she has lost also much. The world wants what has passed away — and which until we secure, we shall remain the clever shallow men we are: a childhood and a youth spent in shade — a Home.

Now this growth took place in three particulars.

I. In spiritual strength. "The child waxed strong in spirit."

Spiritual strength consists of two things — power of Will, and power of Self-restraint. It requires two things, therefore, for its existence — strong feelings, and strong command over them.

Now it is here we make a great mistake: we mistake strong feelings for strong character. A man who bears all before him — before whose frown domestics tremble, and whose bursts of fury make the children of the house quake: because he has his will obeyed, and his own way in all things, we call him a strong man. The truth is, *that* is the weak man: it is his passions that are strong: he, mastered by them, is weak. You must measure the strength of a man by the power of the feelings which he subdues, not by the power of those which subdue him.

And hence composure is very often the highest result of strength. Did we never see a man receive a flagrant insult, and only grow a little pale, and then reply quietly? That was a man spiritually strong. Or did we never see a man in anguish, stand as if carved out of solid rock, mastering himself? or one bearing a hopeless daily trial, remain silent, and never tell the world what it was that cankered his home-peace? That is strength. He who with strong passions remains chaste: he who keenly sensitive, with manly power of indignation in him, can be provoked, and yet refrain himself, and forgive — these are strong men, spiritual heroes.

The child *waxed* strong — spiritual strength is reached by successive steps. Fresh strength is got by every mastery of self. It is the belief of the savage, that the spirit of every enemy he slays enters into him and becomes added to his own, accumulating a warrior's strength for the day of battle: therefore he slays all he can. It is true in the spiritual warfare. Every sin you slay — the spirit of that sin passes into you transformed into strength: every passion, not merely kept in abeyance by asceticism, but subdued by a higher impulse, is so much character strengthened. The strength of the passion not expended is yours still.

Understand then, you are not a man of spiritual power because your impulses are irresistible. They sweep over your soul like a tornado — lay all flat before them; whereupon you feel a secret pride of strength. Last week men saw a vessel on this coast borne headlong on the breakers, and dashing itself with terrific force against the shore. It embedded itself, a miserable wreck, deep in sand and shingle. Was that brig in her convulsive throes strong? or was it powerless and helpless?

No, my brethren: God's spirit in the soul — an inward power of doing the thing we will and ought — that is strength, nothing else. All other force in us is only our weakness, the violence of driving Passion. "I can do all things through Christ who strengtheneth me:" this is Christian strength. "I cannot do the things I would:" that is the weakness of an unredeemed slave.

I instance one single evidence of strength in the early years of Jesus: I find it in that calm, long waiting of thirty years before He began His Work. And yet all the evils He was to redress were there, provoking indignation, crying for interference — the hollowness of social life — the misinterpretations of Scripture — the forms of worship and phraseology which had hidden moral truth — the injustice — the priestcraft — the cowardice — the hypocrisies: He had long seen them all.

All those years His soul burned within Him with a Divine zeal and heavenly indignation. A mere *man* — a weak, emotional man of spasmodic feeling — a hot enthusiast, would have spoken out at once, and at once been crushed. The Everlasting Word incarnate bided His own time: "Mine hour is not yet come" — matured His energies — condensed them by repression — and then went forth to speak and do and suffer. His hour was come. This is strength: the power of a Divine Silence: the strong will to keep force till it is wanted: the power to wait God's time. "He that believeth," said the wise prophet, "shall not make haste."

II. Growth in wisdom — "filled with wisdom."

Let us distinguish wisdom from two things. From information first. It is one thing to be well-informed, it is another to be wise. Many books read, innumerable facts hived up in a capacious memory, this does not constitute wisdom. Books give it not: sometimes the bitterest experience gives it not. Many a heart-break may have come as the result of life-errors and life-mistakes; and yet men may be no wiser than before. Before the same temptations they fall again in the self-same way they fell before. Where they erred in youth they err still in age. A mournful truth! "Ever learning," said St. Paul, "and never able to come to a knowledge of the truth."

Distinguish wisdom again from talent. Brilliancy of powers is not the wisdom for which Solomon prayed. Wisdom is of the heart rather than the intellect: the harvest of moral thoughtfulness, patiently reaped in through years. Two things are required — Earnestness and Love. First that rare thing Earnestness — the earnestness which looks on life practically. Some of the wisest of the race have been men who have scarcely stirred beyond home, read little, felt and thought much. "Give me," said Solomon, "a wise and understanding heart." A heart which ponders upon life, trying to understand its mystery, not in order to talk about it like an orator, nor in order to theorize about it like a philosopher; but in order to know how to *live* and how to die.

And, besides this, love is required for wisdom — the love which opens the heart and makes it generous, and reveals secrets deeper than prudence or political economy teaches — for example, It is more blessed to give than to receive. Prudence did not calculate *that*, love revealed it. No man can be wise without love. Prudent: cunning: Yes; but not wise. Whoever has closed his heart to love has got wisdom at one entrance quite shut out. A large, genial, loving heart, with that we have known a ploughman wise; without it we know a hundred men of statesman-like sagacity fools, profound, but not wise. There was a man who pulled down his barns and built greater, a most sagacious man, getting on in life, acquiring, amassing, and all for self. The men of that generation called him, no doubt, wise — God said, "Thou fool."

Speaking humanly, the steps by which the wisdom of Jesus was acquired were two.

1. The habit of inquiry. — 2. The collision of mind with other minds. Both these we find in this anecdote: His parents found Him with the doctors in the Temple, both hearing and asking them questions. For the mind of man left to itself is unproductive: alone in the wild woods be becomes a savage. Taken away from school early, and sent to the plough, the country boy loses by degrees that which distinguishes him from the cattle that he drives, and over his very features and looks the low animal expressions creep. Mind is necessary

for mind. The Mediatorial system extends through all God's dealings with us. The higher man is the mediator between God and the lower man: only through man can man receive development.

For these reasons, we call this event at Jerusalem a crisis or turning point in the history of Him who was truly Man.

He had come from Nazareth's quiet valley and green slopes on the hillsides, where hill and valley, and cloud and wind, and day and night, had nourished His child's heart — from communion with minds proverbially low, for the adage was, "Can any good thing come out of Nazareth?" — to the capital of His country, to converse with the highest and most cultivated intellects. He had many a question to ask, and many a difficulty to solve. As for instance, such as this: How could the religion accredited in Jerusalem — a religion of long prayers and church services, and phylacteries, and rigorous sabbaths — be reconciled with the stern, manly righteousness of which He had read in the old prophets: a righteousness not of litany-makers, but of men with swords in their hands and zeal in their hearts, setting up God's kingdom upon earth? a kingdom of Truth, and Justice, and Realities — were *they* bringing in that kingdom? — And if not, who should? Such questions had to be felt, and asked and pondered on. Thenceforth we say therefore, in all reverence, dated the intellectual life of Jesus. From that time "Jesus increased in *wisdom*."

Not that they, the doctors of the Temple, contributed much. Those ecclesiastical pedants had not much to tell Him that was worth the telling. They were thinking about theology, He about Religion.

They about rubrics and church services, He about God His Father, and His Will. And yet He gained more from them than they from Him. Have we never observed that the deepest revelations of ourselves are often made to us by trifling remarks met with here and there in conversation and books, sparks which set a whole train of thoughts on fire? Nay, that a false view given by an inferior mind has led us to a true one, and that conversations from which we had expected much light, turning out unsatisfactorily, have thrown us upon ourselves and God, and so become almost the birth times of the soul? The truth is, it is not the amount which is poured in that gives wisdom: but the amount of creative mind and heart working on and stirred by what is so poured in. That conversation with miserable priests and formalists called into activity the One Creative Mind which was to fertilize the whole spiritual life of man to the end of time; and Jesus grew in wisdom by a conversation with pedants of the law.

What Jerusalem was to Him a town life is to us. Knowledge developes itself in the heated atmosphere of town life. Where men meet, and thought clashes with thought — where workmen sit round a board at work, intellectual irritability must be stirred more than where men live and work alone. The march of mind, as they call it, must go on. Whatever evils there may be in our excited, feverish, modern life, it is quite certain that we know through it more than our forefathers knew. The workman knows more of foreign politics than most statesmen knew two centuries ago. The child is versed in theological questions which only occupied master minds once. But the question is, whether, like the Divine Child in the Temple, we are turning knowledge into wisdom, and whether, understanding more of the mysteries of life, we are feeling more of its sacred law; and whether, having left behind the priests, and the scribes, and the doctors, and the fathers, we are about our Father's business, and becoming wise to God.

III. Growth in grace — "the grace of God was upon Him." And this in three points:

1. The exchange of an earthly for a heavenly home.

2. Of an earthly for a heavenly parent.

3. The reconciliation of domestic duties.

First step: Exchange of an earthly for a heavenly home.

Jesus was in the Temple for the first time. That which was dull routine to others through dead habit, was full of vivid impression, fresh life, and God to Him. "My Father's business"—"My Father's house." How different the meaning of these expressions now from what it had been before! Before all was limited to the cottage of the carpenter: now it extended to the Temple. He had felt the sanctities of a new home. In after-life the phrase which He had learned by earthly experience obtained a Divine significance. "In my Father's house are many mansions."

Our first life is spontaneous and instinctive. Our second life is reflective. There is a moment when the life spontaneous passes into the life reflective. We live at first by instinct; then we look in — feel ourselves — ask what we are and whence we came, and whither we are bound. In an awful new world of mystery, and destinies, and duties — we feel God, and know that our true home is our Father's house which has many mansions.

Those are fearful, solitary moments; in which the heart knoweth its own bitterness, and a stranger intermeddleth not with its joys. Father — Mother — cannot share these; and to share is to intrude. The soul first meets God alone. So with Jacob when he saw the dream-ladder: so with Samuel when the Voice called him: so with Christ. So with every son of man, God visits the soul in secrecy, in silence, and in solitariness. And the danger and duty of a teacher is twofold. 1st, To avoid hastening that feeling, hurrying that crisis-moment which some call conversion. 2nd, To avoid crushing it. I have said that first religion is a kind of instinct; and if a child does not exhibit strong religious sensibilities, if he seem "heedless, untouched by awe or serious thought," still it is wiser not to interfere. He may be still at home with God: he may be worshipping at home; as has been said with not less truth than beauty, he may be

> Lying in Abraham's bosom all the year,
> And worship at the Temple's inner shrine,

God being with him when he knew it not. Very mysterious, and beautiful, and wonderful, is God's communing with the unconscious soul before reflection comes. The second caution is not to quench the feeling. Joseph and the Virgin chid the Child for His absence: "Why hast thou dealt so with us?" They could not understand His altered ways: His neglect of apparent duties: His indifference to usual pursuits. They mourned over the change. And this reminds us of the way in which affection's voice itself ministers to ruin. When God comes to the heart, and His presence is shown by thoughtfulness, and seriousness, and distaste to common business, and loneliness, and solitary musings, and a certain tone of melancholy, straightway we set ourselves to expostulate, to rebuke, to cheer, to prescribe amusement and gaieties, as the cure for seriousness which seems out of place. Some of us have seen that tried; and more fearful still, seen it succeed. And we have seen the spirit of frivolity and thoughtlessness, which had been banished for a time, come back again with seven spirits of evil more mighty than himself, and the last state of that person worse than the first. And we have watched the still small voice of God in the soul silenced. And we have seen the spirit of the world get its victim back again; and incipient Goodness dried up like morning dew upon the heart. And they that loved him did it — his parents — his teachers. They quenched the smoking flax, and turned out the lamp of God lighted in the soul.

The last step was, reconciliation to domestic duties. He went down to Nazareth, and was subject unto them. The first step in spirituality is to get a distaste for common duties. There is a time when creeds, ceremonies, services, are distasteful; when the conventional arrangements of society are intolerable burdens; and when, aspiring with a sense of vague longing after a goodness which shall be immeasurable, a duty which shall transcend mere law, a something which we cannot put in words — all restraints of rule and habit gall the spirit. But the last and highest step in spirituality is made in feeling these common duties again divine and holy. This is the true liberty of Christ, when a free man binds himself in love to duty. Not in shrinking from our distateful occupations, but in fulfilling them, do we realize our high origin. And this is the blessed, second, childhood of Christian life. All the several stages towards it seem to be shadowed forth with accurate truthfulness in the narrative of the Messiah's infancy. First, the quiet, unpretending, unconscious obedience and innocence of home. Then the crisis of inquiry: new strange thoughts, entrance upon a new world, hopeless seeking of truth from those who cannot teach it, hearing many teachers and questioning all: thence bewilderment and bitterness, loss of relish for former duties: and small consolation to a man in knowing that he is farther off from heaven than when he was a boy. And then, lastly, the true reconciliation and atonement of our souls to God — a second springtide of life — a second Faith deeper than that of childhood — not instinctive but conscious trust — childlike love come back again — childlike wonder — childlike implicitness of obedience — only deeper than childhood ever knew. When life has got a new meaning, when "old things are passed away, and all things are become new;" when earth has become irradiate with the feeling of our Father's business and our Father's Home.

XVI.

Preached January 9, 1853.

CHRIST'S ESTIMATE OF SIN.

LUKE xix. 10. — "The Son of Man is come to seek and to save that which was lost."

THESE words occur in the history which tells of the recovery of Zacchéus from a life of wordliness to the life of God. Zaccheus was a publican; and the publicans were outcasts among the Jews, because, having accepted the office under the Roman government of collecting the taxes imposed by Rome upon their brethren, they were regarded as traitors to the cause of Israel. Reckoned a degraded class, they *became* degraded. It is hard for any man to live above the moral standard acknowledged by his own class; and the moral standard of the publican was as low as possible. The first step downwards is to sink in the estimation of others — the next and fatal step is to sink in a man's own estimation. The value of character is that it pledges men to be what they are taken for. It is a fearful thing to have no character to support — nothing to fall back upon — nothing to keep a man up to himself. Now the publicans had no character.

Into the house of one of these outcasts the Son of Man had entered. It was quite certain that such an act would be commented upon severely by people who called themselves religious: it would seem to them scandalous, an outrage upon decency, a defiance to every rule of respectability and decorum. No pious Israelite would be seen holding equal intercourse with a publican. In anticipation of such remarks, before there was time perhaps to make them, Jesus spoke these words: "The Son of Man is come to seek and to save that which was lost."

They exhibit the peculiar aspect in which the Redeemer contemplated sin.

There are two ways of looking at sin: — One is the severe view: it makes no allowance for frailty — it will not hear of temptation, nor distinguish between circumstances. Men who judge in this way shut their eyes to all but two objects — a plain law, and a transgression of that law. There is no more to be said: let the law take its course. Now if this be the right view of sin, there is abundance of room left for admiring what is good, and honourable, and upright: there is positively no room provided for restoration. Happy if you have done well; but if ill, then nothing is before you but judgment and fiery indignation.

The other view is one of laxity and false liberalism. When such men speak, prepare yourself to hear liberal judgments and lenient ones: a great deal about human weakness, error in judgment, mistakes, an unfortunate constitution, on which the chief blame of sin is to rest — a good heart. All well, if we wanted in this mysterious struggle of a life, only consolation. But we want far beyond comfort — Goodness; and to be merely made easy when we have done wrong will not help us to *that!*

Distinct from both of these was Christ's view of guilt. His standard of Right was high — higher than ever man had placed it before. Not moral excellence, but heavenly, He demanded. "Except your righteousness shall exceed the righteousness of the Scribes and

Pharisees, ye shall in no case enter into the kingdom of heaven." Read the Sermon on the Mount. It tells of a purity as of snow resting on an Alpine pinnacle, white in the blue holiness of heaven; and yet, also, He the All-pure had tenderness for what was not pure. He who stood in Divine uprightness that never faltered, felt compassion for the ruined, and infinite gentleness for human fall. Broken, disappointed, doubting hearts, in dismay and bewilderment, never looked in vain to Him. Very strange, if we stop to think of it, instead of repeating it as a matter of course. For generally human goodness repels from it evil men: they shun the society and presence of men reputed good, as owls fly from light. But here was purity *attracting* evil; that was the wonder. Harlots and wretches steeped in infamy gathered round Him. No wonder the purblind Pharisees thought there must be something in Him like such sinners which drew them so. Like draws to like. If He chose their society before that of the Pharisees, was it not because of some congeniality in Evil? But they *did* crowd His steps, and that because they saw a hope opened out in a hopeless world for fallen spirits and broken hearts, ay, and seared hearts. The Son of Man was for ever standing among the lost, and His ever predominant feelings were sadness for the evil in human nature, hope for the Divine good in it, and the Divine image never worn out wholly.

I perceive in this description three peculiarities, distinguishing Christ from ordinary men.

I. A peculiarity in the constitution of the Redeemer's moral nature.

II. A peculiarity in the objects of His solicitude.

III. A peculiarity in His way of treating guilt.

I. In His moral constitution. Manifested in that peculiar title which he assumed — The Son of Man.

Let us see what that implies.

1. It implies fairly His Divine origin: for it is an emphatic expression, and, as we may so say, an unnatural one. Imagine an apostle, St. Paul or St. John, insisting upon it perpetually that he himself was human. It would almost provoke a smile to hear either of them averring and affirming, I am a Son of Man: it would be unnatural, the affectation of condescension would be intolerable. Therefore, when we hear these words from Christ, we are compelled to think of them as contrasted with a higher nature. None could without presumption remind men that He was their Brother and a Son of Man, except One who was also something higher, even the Son of God.

2. It implies the catholicity of His Brotherhood.

Nothing in the judgment of historians stands out so sharply distinct as race — national character: nothing is more ineffaceable. The Hebrew was marked from all mankind. The Roman was perfectly distinct from the Grecian character; as markedly different as the rough English truthfulness is from Celtic brilliancy of talent. Now these peculiar nationalities are seldom combined. You rarely find the stern, old Jewish sense of holiness going together with the Athenian sensitiveness of what is beautiful. Not often do you find together severe truth and refined tenderness. Brilliancy seems opposed to perseverance. Exquisiteness of taste commonly goes along with a certain amount of untruthfulness. By Humanity, as a whole, we mean the aggregate of all these separate excellences. Only in two places are they all found together — in the universal human race; and in Jesus Christ. He having, as it were, a whole humanity in Himself, combines them all.

Now this is the universality of the Nature of Jesus Christ. There was in Him no national peculiarity or individual idiosyncrasy. He was not the Son of the Jew, nor the Son of the carpenter; nor the offspring of the modes of living and thinking of that particular century. He was the Son of Man. Once in the world's history was born a MAN. Once in the roll of ages, out of innumerable failures, from the stock of human nature, one Bud developed itself into a faultless Flower. One perfect specimen of humanity has God exhibited on earth.

The best and most catholic of Englishmen has his prejudices. All the world over our greatest writer would be recognised as having the English cast of thought. The pattern Jew would seem Jewish everywhere but in Judea. Take Abraham, St. John, St. Paul, place them where you will, in China or in Peru, they are Hebrews: they could not command all sympathies: their life could not be imitable except in part. They are foreigners in every land, and out of place in every country but their own. But Christ is the King of men, and "draws all men," because all character is in Him, separate from nationalities and limitations. As if the life-blood of every nation were in his veins, and that which is best and truest in every man, and that which is tenderest, and gentlest, and purest in every woman, were in his character. He is emphatically the Son of *Man*.

Out of this arose two powers of His sacred Humanity — the universality of His sympathies, and their intense particular personality.

The universality of His sympathies: for, compare Him with any one of the sacred characters of Scripture. You know how intensely national they were, priests, prophets, and apostles, in their sympathies: for example the apostles "marvelled that He spake with a woman of Samaria:" — just before His resurrection, their largest charity had not reached beyond this, "Lord, wilt thou at this time restore the kingdom unto *Israel?*" Or, to come down to modern times, when His spirit has been moulding men's ways of thought for many ages: — now, when we talk of our philanthropy and catholic liberality, here in Christian England, we have scarcely any fellow-feeling, true and genuine, with other nations, other churches, other parties, than our own: we care nothing for Italian or Hungarian struggles; we think of Romanists as the Jew thought of gentiles; we speak of German Protestants in the same proud, wicked, self-sufficient way in which the Jew spoke of Samaritans.

Unless we bring such matters home, and away from vague generalities, and consider what we and all men are, or rather are not, we cannot comprehend with due wonder the mighty sympathies of the heart of Christ. None of the miserable antipathies that fence us from all the world, bounded the outgoings of that Love, broad and deep and wide as the heart of God. Wherever the mysterious pulse of human life was beating, wherever aught human was in struggle, there to Him, was a thing not commou or unclean, but cleansed by God and sacred. Compare the daily, almost indispensable language of our life with His spirit. "Common people?"

—Point us out the passage where he called any people that God His Father made, common? "Lower orders?" — Tell us when and where He, whose home was the workshop of the carpenter, authorized you or me to know any man after the flesh as low or high? To Him who called Himself the Son of Man, the link was manhood. And *that* he could discern even when it was marred. Even in outcasts His eye could recognise the sanctities of a nature human still. Even in the harlot "one of Eve's family:" — a "son of Abraham" even in Zaccheus.

Once more, out of that universal, catholic Nature rose another power — the power of intense, particular, personal affections. He was the Brother and Saviour of the human race; but this because He was the Brother and Saviour of every separate man in it.

Now it is very easy to feel great affection for a country as a whole; to have, for instance, great sympathies for Poland, or Ireland, or America, and yet not care a whit for any single man in Poland, and to have strong antipathies to every single individual American. Easy to be a warm lover of England and yet not love one living Englishman. Easy to set a great value on a flock of sheep, and yet have no particular care for any one sheep or lamb. If it were killed, another of the same species might replace it. Easy to have fine, large, liberal views about the working classes, or the emancipation of the negroes, and yet never have done a loving act to one. Easy to be a great philanthropist, and yet have no strong friendships, no deep personal attachments.

For the idea of an universal Manlike sympathy was not new when Christ was born. The reality *was* new.

But before this, in the Roman threatre, deafening applause was called forth by this sentence — "I am a man — nothing that can affect man is indifferent to me." A fine sentiment — that was all. Every pretence of realizing that sentiment, except one, has been a failure. One and but One has succeeded in loving man: and that by loving men. No sublime high-sounding language in His lips about educating the masses, or elevating the people. The charlatanry of our modern sentiment had not appeared then: it is but the parody of His love.

What was His mode of sympathy with men? He did not sit down to philosophize about the progress of the species, or dream about a millennium. He gathered round Him twelve men. He formed one friendship, special, concentrated, deep. He did not give himself out as the Leader of the Publican's cause, or the Champion of the Rights of the dangerous classes; but He associated with Himself Matthew, a publican called from the detested receipt of custom. He went into the house of Zaccheus, and treated him like a fellow-creature — a brother, and a son of Abraham. His catholicity or philantropy was not an abstraction, but an aggregate of personal attachments.

II. Peculiarity in the objects of Christ's solicitude.

He had come to seek and to save *the* "*lost.*" The world is lost, and Christ came to save the world. But by the lost in this place He does not mean the world; He means a special class, lost in a more than common sense, as sheep are lost which have strayed from the flock, and wandered far beyond all their fellows scattered in the wilderness.

Some men are lost by the force of their own passions, as Balaam was by love of gold: as Saul was by self-will, ending in jealousy, and pride darkened into madness: as Haman was by envy indulged and brooded on: as the harlots were, through feelings pure and high at first, inverted and perverted: as Judas was by secret dishonesty, undetected in its first beginnings, the worst misfortune that can befall a tendency to a false life. And others are lost by the entanglement of outward circumstances, which make escape, humanly speaking, impossible. Such were the publicans: men *forced*, like executioners, into degradation. An honest publican, or a holy executioner, would be miracles to marvel at. And some are lost by the laws of society, which while defending society, have no mercy for its outcasts, and forbid their return, fallen once, for ever.

Society has power to bind on earth; and what it binds is bound upon the soul indeed. For a man or woman who has lost self-respect is lost indeed.

And oh! the untold world of agony contained in that expression — "a lost soul!" agony exactly in proportion to the nobleness of original powers. For it is a strange and mournful truth, that the qualities which enable men to shine are exactly those which minister to the worst ruin. God's highest gifts — talent, beauty feeling, imagination, power: they carry with them the possibility of the highest heaven and the lowest hell. Be sure that it is by that which is highest in you that you may be lost. It is the awful warning, and not the excuse of evil, that the light which leads astray is light from heaven. The shallow fishing-boat glides safely over the reefs where the noblo bark strands: it is the very might and majesty of her career that bury the sharp rock deeper in her bosom. There are thousands who are not lost (like the respectable Pharisees), because they had no impetuous impulses — no passion — no strong enthusiasm, by the perversion of which they could be lost.

Now this will explain to us what there was in these lost ones which left a hope for their salvation, and which Jesus saw in them to seek and save. Outwardly men saw a crust of black scowling impenitence. Reprobates they called them. Below that outward crust ran a hot lava-stream of anguish: What was that? The coward fear of hell? Nay, hardened men defy hell. The anguish of the lost ones of this world is not fear of punishment. It was and is, the misery of having quenched a light brighter than the sun: the intolerable sense of being sunk: the remorse of knowing that they were not what they might have been. And He saw that: He knew that it was the germ of life which God's spirit could develope into salvation.

It was His work and His desire to save such, and in this world a new and strange solicitude it was, for the world had seen before nothing like it.

Not half a century ago a great man was seen stooping and working in a charnel-house of bones. Uncouth nameless fragments lay around him, which the workmen had dug up and thrown aside as rubbish. They belonged to some far-back age, and no man knew what they were or whence. Few men cared. The world was merry at the sight of a philosopher groping among mouldy bones. But when that creative mind, reverently discerning the fontal types of living being in diverse shapes, brought together those strange fragments, bone to bone, and rib to claw, and tooth to its own corresponding vertebra, recombining the wondrous forms of past ages, and presenting each to the astonished world as it moved and lived a hundred thousand ages back, then men began to perceive that a new science had begun on earth.

And such was the work of Christ. They saw Him at work among the fragments and mouldering wreck of our humanity, and sneered. But He took the dry bones such as Ezekiel saw in Vision, which no man thought could live, and He breathed into them the breath of life. He took the scattered fragments of our ruined nature, interpreted their meaning, showed the original intent of those powers, which were now destructive only, drew out from publicans and sinners yearnings which were incomprehensible, and feelings which were misunderstood, vindicated the beauty of the original intention, showed the Divine Order below the chaos, exhibited to the world once more a human soul in the form in which God had made it, saying to the dry bones "Live!"

Only what in the great foreigner was a taste, in Christ was love. In the one the gratification of an enlightened curiosity: in the other the gratification of a sublime affection. In the philosopher it was a longing to restore and reproduce the past. In Christ a hope for the future — "to seek and to save that which was lost."

III. A peculiarity in His mode of treatment. How were these lost ones to be restored? The human plans are reducible to three. Governments have tried chatisement for the reclamation of offenders. For ages that was the only expedient known either to church or state.

Time has written upon it Failure. I do not say that penal severity is not needful. Perhaps it is, for protection, and for the salutary expression of indignation against certain forms of evil. But as a system of reclamation it has failed. Did the rack ever reclaim in heart one heretic? Did the scaffold ever soften one felon? One universal fact of history replies: Where the penal code was most sanguinary, and when punishments were must numerous, crime was most abundant.

Again, society has tried exclusion for life. I do not pretend to say that it may not be needful. It *may* be necessary to protect your social purity by banishing offenders of a certain sort for ever. I only say for recovery it is a failure. Who ever knew one case where the ban of exclusion was hopeless, and the shame of that exclusion reformed? Did we ever hear of a fallen creature made moral by despair? Name, if you can, the publican or the harlot in any age brought back to goodness by a Pharisee, or by the system of a Pharisee.

And once more, some governors have tried the system of indiscriminate lenity: they forgave great criminals, trusting all the future to gratitude: they passed over great sins, they sent away the ringleaders of rebellion with honours heaped upon them: they thought this was the gospel: they expected dramatic emotion to work wonders. How far this miserable system has succeeded, let those tell us who have studied the history of our South African colonies for the last twenty years. We were tired of cruelty — we tried sentiment — we trusted to feeling. Feeling failed: we only made hypocrites, and encouraged rebellion by impunity. Inexorable severity — rigorous banishment — indiscriminate and mere forgivingness, — all are failures.

In Christ's treatment of guilt we find three peculiarities: — Sympathy, holiness, firmness.

1. By human sympathy. In the treatment of Zaccheus this was almost all. We read of almost nothing else as the instrument of that wonderful reclamation. One thing only, Christ went to his house self-invited. But that one was everything. Consider it — Zaccheus was, if he were like other publicans, a hard and hardened man. He felt people shrink from him in the streets. He lay under an imputation: and we know how that feeling of being universally suspected and misinterpreted makes a man bitter, sarcastic, and defiant. And so the outcast would go home, look at his gold, rejoice in the revenge he could take by false accusations, felt a pride in knowing that they might hate, but could not help fearing him: scorned the world, and shut up his heart against it.

At last, one whom all men thronged to see, and all men honoured, or seemed to honour, came to him, offered to go home and sup with him. For the first time for many years, Zaccheus felt that he was not despised, and the floodgates of that avaricious, shut heart were opened in a tide of love and generosity. "Behold, Lord, the half of my goods I give to the poor; and if I have taken anything from any man by false accusation, I restore him fourfold."

He was reclaimed to human feeling by being taught that he was a man still; recognised and treated like a man. A Son of Man had come to "seek" him, the lost.

2. By the exhibition of Divine holiness.

The holiness of Christ differed from all earthly, common, vulgar holiness. Wherever it was, it elicited a sense of sinfulness and imperfection. Just as the purest cut crystal of the rock looks dim beside the diamond, so the best men felt a sense of guilt growing distinct upon their souls. When the Anointed of God came near, "Depart from me," said the bravest and truest of them all, "for I am a sinful man, O Lord."

But at the same time the holiness of Christ did not awe men away from Him, nor repel them. It inspired them with hope. It was not that vulgar unapproachable sanctity which makes men awkward in its presence, and stands aloof. Its peculiar characteristic was that it made men enamoured of goodness. It "drew all men unto Him."

This is the difference between greatness that is first-rate and greatness which is second-rate — between heavenly and earthly goodness. The second-rate and the earthly draws admiration on itself. You say, "how great an act — how good a man!" The first-rate and the heavenly imparts itself — inspires a spirit. You feel a kindred something in you that rises up to meet it, and draws you out of yourself, making you better than you were before, and opening out the infinite possibilities of your life and soul.

And such pre-eminently was the holiness of Christ. Had some earthly great or good one come to Zaccheus' house, a prince or a nobleman, his feeling would have been, What condescension is there! But when *He* came whose every word and act had in it Life and Power, no such barren reflection was the result: but instead, the beauty of holiness had become a power within him, and a longing for self-consecration. "Behold, Lord, the half of my goods I give to the poor; and if I have taken anything from any man by false accusation, I restore him fourfold."

By Divine sympathy, and by the Divine Image exhibited in the speaking act of Christ, the lost was sought and saved. He was saved, as alone all fallen men can be saved. "Beholding as in a glass the glory of the Lord, he was changed into the same image." And this is the very essence of the Gospel of Jesus Christ. We are redeemed by the Life of God without us, manifested in the Person of Christ, kindling into flame the Life of God that is within us. Without Him we can do nothing. Without Him the warmth that was in Zaccheus' heart would have smouldered uselessly away. Through Him it became Life and Light, and the lost was saved.

XVII.

Preached January 16, 1853.

THE SANCTIFICATION OF CHRIST.

JOHN xvii. 19. — "And for their sakes I sanctify myself, that they also might be sanctified through the truth."

THE prayer in which these words occur is given to us by the Apostle John alone. Perhaps only St. John *could* give it, for it belongs to the peculiar province of his revelation. He presents us with more of the heart of Christ than the other apostles: with less of the outward manifestations. He gives us more conversations — fewer miracles: more of the inner life — more of what Christ was, less of what Christ did.

St. John's mind was not argumentative, but intuitive. There are two ways of reaching truth: by reasoning it out and by feeling it out. All the profoundest truths are felt out. The deep glances into truth are got by Love. Love a man, that is the best way of understanding him. Feel a truth, that is the only way of comprehending it.

Not that you can put your sense of such truths into words in the shape of accurate maxims or doctrines: but the truth is reached, notwithstanding. Compare 1 Cor. ii. 15, 16.

Now St. John *felt out* truth. He understood his Lord by loving him. You find no long trains of argument in St. John's writings: an atmosphere of contemplation pervades all. Brief, full sentences, glowing with imagery of which the mere prose intellect makes nonsense, and which a warm heart alone interprets, that is the character of his writing: very different from the other apostles. St. Peter's knowledge of Christ was formed by impetuous mistakes, corrected slowly and severely. St. Paul's Christianity was formed by principles wrought out glowing hot, as a smith hammers out ductile iron, in his unresting, earnest fire of thought, where the Spirit dwelt in warmth and light for ever, kindling the Divine fire of inspiration. St. John and St. John's Christianity were formed by personal view of Christ, by intercourse with Him, and by silent contemplation. Slowly, month by month and year by year, he gazed on Christ in silence, and thoughtful adoration: "Reflecting as from a glass the glory of the Lord," he became like Him — caught His tones — His modes of thought — His very expressions, and became partaker of His inward life. A "Christ was formed in him."

Hence it was that this prayer was revealed to St. John alone of the apostles, and by him alone recorded for us. The Saviour's mind touched his: through secret sympathy he was inspired with the mystic consciousness of what had passed and what was passing in the deeps of the soul of Christ. Its secret longings and its deepest struggles were known to John alone.

This particular sentence in the prayer which I have taken for the text was peculiarly after the heart of the Apostle John. For I have said that to him the true life of Christ was rather the inner Life than the outward acts of life. Now this sentence from the lips of Jesus speaks of the Atoning Sacrifice as an inward mental act rather than as an outward deed: a self-consecration wrought out in the Will of Christ. For their sakes I am sanctifying myself. That is a resolve — a secret of the inner Life. No wonder that it was recorded by St. John.

The text has two parts.

I. The sanctification of Jesus Christ.

II. The sanctification of His people.

I. Christ's sanctification of Himself. "For their sakes I sanctify myself, that they also might be sanctified through the truth."

We must explain this word "sanctify;" upon it the whole meaning turns. Clearly, it has not the ordinary popular sense here of making holy. Christ *was* holy. He could not by an inward effort or struggle *make* Himself holy, for He was that already.

Let us trace the history of the word "sanctify" in the early pages of the Jewish history.

When the destroying angel smote the first-born of the Egyptian families, the symbolic blood on the lintel of every Hebrew house protected the eldest born from the plague of death. In consequence, a law of Moses viewed every eldest son in a peculiar light. He was reckoned as a thing devoted to the Lord — redeemed, and therefore set apart. The word used to express this devotion is *sanctify*. "The Lord said unto Moses, *sanctify* unto me all the first-born, whatsoever openeth the womb among the children of Israel, both of man and of beast: it is mine."

By a subsequent arrangement these first-born were exchanged for the Levites. Instead of the eldest son in each family, a whole tribe was taken, and reckoned as set apart and devoted to Jehovah, just as now a substitute is provided to serve in war in another's stead.

Therefore the tribe of Levi were said to be *sanctified* to God.

Ask we what was meant by saying that the Levites were sanctified to God? The ceremony of their sanctification will explain it to us. It was a very significant one. The priest touched with the typical blood of a sacrificed animal the Levite's right hand, right eye, right foot. This was the Levite's sanctification. It devoted every faculty and every power — of seeing, doing, walking, the right hand faculties — the best and choicest — to God's peculiar service. He was a man set apart.

To sanctify, therefore, in the Hebrew phrase, meant to devote or consecrate. Let us pause for a few moments to gather up the import of this ceremony of the Levites.

The first-born are a nation's hope: they may be said to represent a whole nation. The consecration therefore of the first-born was the consecration of the entire nation by their representatives. Now the Levites were substituted for the first-born. The Levites consequently represented all Israel; and by their consecration the life of Israel was declared to be in idea and by right a consecrated life to God. But further still. As the Levites represented Israel, so Israel itself was but a part taken for the whole, and represented the whole human race. If any one thinks this fanciful, let him remember the principle of representation on which the whole Jewish system was built. For example — the first-fruits of the harvest were consecrated to God. Why? — to declare that portion and that only to be God's? No; St. Paul says as a part for the whole, to teach and remind that the whole harvest was his.

"If the first fruits be holy, the lump also is holy." So in the same way, God consecrated a peculiar people to Himself. Why? The Jews say because they alone are His. We say, as a part representative of the whole, to show in one nation what all are meant to be. The holiness of Israel is a representative holiness. Just as the consecrated Levite stood for what Israel was meant to be, so the anointed and separated nation represents for ever what the whole race of man is in the Divine Idea, a thing whose proper life is perpetual consecration.

One step further. This being the true Life of Humanity, name it how you will, sanctification, consecration, devotion, sacrifice, Christ the Representative of the Race, submits Himself in the text to the universal law of this devotion. The true law of every life is consecration to God: therefore Christ says, I consecrate myself: else He had not been a Man in God's idea of manhood — for the idea of Man which God had been for ages labouring to give through a consecrated tribe and a consecrated nation to the world, was the idea of a being whose life-law is Sacrifice, every act and every thought being devoted to God.

Accordingly, this is the view which Christ Himself gave of His own Divine Humanity. He spoke of it as of a thing devoted by a Divine decree. "Say ye of Him, whom the Father hath *sanctified*, and sent into the world, Thou blasphemest; because I said, I am the Son of God?"

We have reached therefore the meaning of this word in the text, "For their sakes I sanctify, *i. e.* consecrate or devote myself." The first meaning of sanctify is to set apart. But to set apart for God is to devote or consecrate; and to consecrate a thing is to make it holy. And thus we have the three meanings of the word, viz., to set apart, to devote, to make holy — rising all out of one simple idea.

To go somewhat into particulars. This sanctification is spoken of here chiefly as threefold: Self-devotion by inward resolve — self-devotion to the Truth — self-devotion for the sake of others.

1. He devoted himself *by inward resolve*. "I sanctify myself." God His Father had devoted him before. He had sanctified and sent Him. It only remained that this devotion should become by His own act — *self*-devotion: completed by His own will. Now in that act of will consisted His sanctification of Himself.

For observe, this was done within: in secret, solitary struggle — in wrestling with all temptations which deterred Him from His work — in resolve to do it unflinchingly: in real human battle and victory.

Therefore this self-sanctification applies to the whole tone and history of His mind. He was for ever devoting Himself to work — for ever bracing His human spirit to sublime resolve. But it applies peculiarly to certain special moments, when some crisis, as on this present occasion, came, which called for an act of will.

The first of these moments which we read of came when He was twelve years of age. We pondered on it a few weeks ago. In the temple, that earnest conversation with the doctors indicates to us that He had begun to revolve His own mission in His mind; for the answer to His mother's expostulations shows us what had been the subject of those questions He had been putting: "Wist ye not that I must be about my

Father's business?" Solemn words, significant of a crisis in His mental history. He had been asking those doctors about His Father's business: what it was, and how it was to be done by Him of whom He had read in the prophets, even Himself. This was the earliest self-devotion of Messias: — the Boy was sanctifying Himself for life and manhood's work.

The next time was in that preparation of the wilderness which we call Christ's Temptation. You cannot look deeply into that strange story without perceiving that the true meaning of it lies in this, that the Saviour in that conflict was steeling His soul against the threefold form in which temptation presented itself to Him in after-life, to mar or neutralize His ministry.

1. To convert the hard, stony life of Duty into the comfort and enjoyment of this life: to barter, like Esau, life for pottage: to use Divine powers in Him only to procure bread of Earth.

2. To distrust God, and try impatiently some wild, sudden plan, instead of His meek and slow-appointed ways — to cast Himself from the temple, as we dash ourselves against our destiny.

3. To do homage to the majesty of wrong: to worship Evil for the sake of success: to make the world His own by force or by crooked policy, instead of by suffering.

These were the temptations of His life as they are of ours. If you search through His history, you find that all trial was reducible to one or other of these three forms. In the wilderness His soul foresaw them all; they were all in spirit met then, fought and conquered before they came in their reality. In the wilderness He had sanctified and consecrated Himself against all possible temptation, and Life thenceforward was only the meeting of that in Fact which had been in Resolve met already — a vanquished foe.

I said He had sanctified Himself against every trial: I should have said, against every one except the last. The temptation had not exhibited the terrors and the form of Death: He had yet to nerve and steel Himself to that. And hence the lofty sadness which characterizes His later ministry, as He went down from the sunny mountain-tops of life into the darkening shades of the valley where lies the grave. There is a perceptible difference between the tone of His earlier and that of His later ministry which by its evidently undesigned truthfulness gives us a strong feeling of the reality of the history.

At first all is bright, full of hope, signalized by success and triumph. You hear from Him joyous words of anticipated victory: "I beheld Satan as lightning fall from heaven." And we recollect how His first sermon in the synagogue of Capernaum was hailed; how all eyes were fixed on Him, and His words seemed full of grace.

Slowly, after this, there comes a change over the spirit of His life. The unremitting toil becomes more superhuman, "I must work the work of Him that sent Me while it is day: the night cometh when no man can work." The cold presentiment of doom hangs more often on Him. He begins to talk to his disciples in mysterious hints of the betrayal and the cross. He is going down into the cloudland, full of shadows where nothing is distinct, and His step becomes more solemn, and His language more deeply sad. Words of awe, the words as of a soul struggling to pierce through thick glooms of Mystery, and Doubt, and Death, come more often from His lips: for instance, "Now is My soul troubled: and what shall I say? Father, save me from this hour: but for this cause came I into the world." "My soul is exceeding sorrowful, even unto death." And here in the text is another of those sentences of mournful grandeur: "For their sakes I sanctify Myself, that they also might be sanctified through the truth."

Observe the present tense. Not I *shall* devote Myself — but I sanctify, *i.e.* I am sanctifying Myself. It was a mental struggle going on then. This prayer was, so to speak, part of His Gethsemane prayer — the first utterances of it, broken by interruption — then finished in the garden. The Consecration and the Agony had begun — the long inward battle — which was not complete till the words came, too solemnly to be called triumphantly, though they were indeed the trumpet-tones of Man's grand victory, "It is finished."

Secondly, the sanctification of Christ was self-devotion to the Truth.

I infer this, because He says, "I sanctify Myself, that they *also* might be sanctified through the truth." "Also" implies that what His consecration was, theirs was. Now theirs is expressly said to be sanctification by the truth. That then was His consecration too. It was the truth which devoted Him and marked Him out for death.

For it was not merely death that made Christ's sacrifice the world's Atonement. There is no special virtue in mere death, even though it be the death of God's own Son. Blood does not please God. "As I live, said the Lord, I have no pleasure in the death of the sinner." Do you think God has pleasure in the blood of the righteous? blood merely as blood? death merely as a debt of nature paid? suffering merely, as if suffering had in it mysterious virtue?

No, my brethren! God can be satisfied with that only which pertains to the conscience and the will; so says the writer of the Epistle to the Hebrews: Sacrifices could never make the comers thereunto perfect. The Blood of Christ was sanctified by the Will with which He shed it: it is that which gives it value. It was a sacrifice offered up to conscience. He suffered as a Martyr to the Truth. He fell in fidelity to a cause. The sacred cause in which He fell was love to the human race: "Greater love hath no man than this, that a man give his life for his friends." Now that Truth was the Cause in which Christ died. We have His own words as proof: "To this end was I born, and for this cause came I into the world, *to bear witness to the Truth*."

Let us see how His death was a martyrdom of witness to Truth.

1. He proclaimed the identity between religion and Goodness. He distinguished religion from correct views, accurate religious observances, and even from devout feelings. He said that to be religious is to be good. "Blessed are the pure in heart . . . Blessed are the merciful . . . Blessed are the meek." Justice, mercy, truth — these He proclaimed as the real righteousness of God.

But because He taught the truth of Godliness, the Pharisees became His enemies: those men of opinions and maxims: those men of ecclesiastical, ritual, and spiritual pretensions.

Again, He taught spiritual Religion. God was not in the temple: the temple was to come down. But Religion would survive the temple. God's temple was man's soul; and because He taught spiritual worship, the priests became His enemies. Hence came those accusations that He blasphemed the temple: that He had said contemptuously, "Destroy this temple, and in three days I will raise it up."

Once more, He struck a deathblow at Jewish exclusiveness: He proclaimed the truth of the character of God. God the Father: the hereditary descent from Abraham was nothing: the inheritance of Abraham's faith was everything. God therefore would admit the Gentiles who inherited that faith. For God loved the world, not a private few: not the Jew only, not the elder brother who had been all his life at home, but the prodigal younger brother too, who had wandered far and had sinned much.

Now because He proclaimed this salvation of the Gentiles, the whole Jewish nation were offended. The first time He ever hinted it at Capernaum, they took Him to the brow of the hill whereon their city was built that they might throw Him thence.

And thus by degrees — Priests, Pharisees, Rulers, rich and poor — He had roused them all against Him: and the Divine Martyr of the Truth stood alone at last beside the cross, when the world's life was to be won, without a friend.

All this we must bear in mind, if we would understand the expression, "I sanctify myself." He was sanctifying and consecrating Himself for this — to be a Witness to the Truth — a devoted one, consecrated in His heart's deeps to die — loyal to truth, even though it should have to give as the reward of allegiance, not honours and kingdoms, but only a crown of thorns.

3. The self-sanctification of Christ was for the sake of others. "For their sakes."

He obeyed the law of self-consecration for Himself, else He had not been man; for that law is the universal law of our human existence. But he obeyed it not for Himself alone, but for others also. It was vicarious self-devotion, *i. e.* instead of others, as the Representative of them. "For their sakes," as an example, "that they also might be sanctified through the truth."

Distinguish between a model and an example. You copy the outline of a model: you imitate the spirit of an example. Christ is our Example: Christ is not our Model. You might copy the life of Christ: make Him a model in every act: and yet you might be not one whit more of a Christian than before. You might wash the feet of poor fishermen as He did, live a wandering life with nowhere to lay your head. You might go about teaching, and never use any words but His words, never express a religious truth except in Bible language: have no home, and mix with publicans and harlots. Then Christ would be your model: you would have copied His life like a picture, line for line, and shadow for shadow; and yet you might not be Christlike.

On the other hand, you might imitate Christ, get His Spirit, breathe the atmosphere of thought which He breathed: do not one single act which He did, but every act in His spirit: you might be rich, whereas He was poor: never teach, whereas He was teaching always; lead a life in all outward particulars the very contrast and opposite of His: and yet the spirit of His self-devotion might have saturated your whole being, and penetrated into the life of every act and the essence of every thought. Then Christ would have become your Example: for we can only imitate that of which we have caught the spirit.

Accordingly, He sanctified Himself that He might become a living, inspiring Example, firing men's hearts by love to imitation — a burning and a shining light shed upon the mystery of Life, to guide by a spirit of warmth lighting from within. In Christ there is not given to us a faultless essay on the loveliness of self-consecration, to convince our reason how beautiful it is: but there is given to us a self-consecrated One: a living Truth, a living Person, a Life that was beautiful, a Death that we feel in our inmost hearts to have been Divine: and all this in order that the Spirit of that consecrated Life and consecrated Death, through love, and wonder, and deep enthusiasm, may pass into us, and sanctify us also to the Truth in life and death. He sacrificed Himself that we might offer *ourselves* a living sacrifice to God.

II. Christ's sanctification of his people: "That they also might be sanctified through the truth."

To sanctify means two things. It means to devote, and it means to set apart. Yet these two meanings are but different sides of the same idea: for to be devoted to God is to be separated from all that is opposed to God.

Those whom Christ sanctifies are separated from two things: from the world's evil, and from the world's spirit.

1. From the world's evil. So in verse 15, "I pray not that thou shouldest take them out of the world, but that thou shouldest keep them from the evil." Not from physical evil, not from pain: Christ does not exempt His own from such kinds of evil. Nay, we hesitate to call pain and sorrow evils, when we remember what bright characters they have made, and when we recollect that almost all who came to Christ came impelled by suffering of some kind or other. For example, the Syrophenician woman had been driven to "fall at His feet and worship Him," by the anguish of the tormented daughter whom she had watched. It was a widow that cast into the treasury all her living, and that widow poor.

Possibly Want and Woe will be seen hereafter, when this world of Appearance shall have passed away, to have been, not evils, but God's blessed angels and ministers of His most parental love.

But the evil from which Christ's sanctification separates the soul is that worst of evils — properly speaking the only evil — sin: revolt from God, disloyalty to conscience, tyranny of the passions, strife of our self-will in conflict with the loving Will of God. This is our foe — our only foe that we have a right to hate with perfect hatred, meet it where we will, and under whatever form, in church or state, in false social maxims, or in our own hearts. And it was to sanctify or separate us from this that Christ sanctified or consecrated Himself. By the blood of His anguish — by the strength of His unconquerable resolve — we are sworn against it — bound to be, in a world of evil, consecrated spirits, or else greatly sinning.

Lastly, the self-devotion of Christ separates us from the world's spirit.

Distinguish between the world's evil and the world's spirit. Many things which cannot be classed amongst things evil are yet dangerous as things worldly.

It is one of the most difficult of all ministerial duties to define what the world-spirit is. It cannot be identified with vice, nor can unworldliness be defined as abstinence from vice. The Old Testament saints were many of them great transgressors. Abraham lied — Jacob deceived — David committed adultery. Crimes dark surely! and black enough! And yet these men were unworldly — the spirit of the world was not in them. They erred and were severely punished; for crime is crime in whomsoever it is found, and most a crime in a saint of God. But they were beyond their age: they were not of the world. They were strangers and pilgrims upon earth. They were, in the midst of innumerable temptations from within and from without, seeking after a better country, *i. e.* an heavenly.

Again, you cannot say that worldliness consists in mixing with many people, and unworldliness with few. Daniel was unworldly in the luxurious, brilliant court of Babylon: Adam, in Paradise, had but one companion; that *one* was the world to him.

Again, the spirit of the world cannot be defined as consisting in any definite plainness of dress or peculiar mode of living. If we would be sanctified from the world when Christ comes, we must be found not stripping off the ornaments from our persons, but the censoriousness from our tongues, and the selfishness from our hearts.

Once more, that which is a sign of unworldliness in

one age is not a certain sign of it in another. In Daniel's age, when dissoluteness marked the world, frugal living was a sufficient evidence that he was not of the world. To say that he restrained his appetites, was nearly the same as saying that he was sanctified. But now when intemperance is not the custom, a life as temperate as Daniel's might coexist with all that is worst of the spirit of the world in the heart; almost no man then was temperate who was not serving God — now hundreds of thousands are self-controlled by prudence, who serve the world and self.

Therefore you cannot define sanctification by any outward marks or rules. But he who will thoughtfully watch will understand what is this peculiar sanctification or separation from the world which Christ desired in His servants.

He is sanctified by the self-devotion of his Master from the world, who has a life in himself independent of the maxims and customs which sweep along with them other men. In his Master's words, "A well of water *in* him, springing up into everlasting life," keeping his life on the whole pure and his heart fresh. His true life is hid with Christ in God. His motives, the aims and objects of his life, however inconsistent they may be with each other, however irregularly or feebly carried out, are yet on the whole above, not here. His citizenship is in heaven. He may be tempted — he may err — he may fall — but still in his darkest aberrations, there will be a something that keeps before him still the dreams and aspirations of his best days — a thought of the Cross of Christ, and the self-consecration that it typifies — a conviction that that is the Highest, and that alone the true Life. And that —

if it were only that — would make him essentially different from other men, even when he mixes with them and seems to catch their tone, among them but not one of them. And that Life within him is Christ's pledge that he shall be yet what he longs to be — a something severing him, separating him, consecrating him. For him and for such as him the consecration prayer of Christ was made. "They are not of the world, even as I am not of the world: Sanctify them through thy Truth: Thy Word is Truth."

XVIII.

Preached January 23, 1853.

THE FIRST MIRACLE.

I. THE GLORY OF THE VIRGIN MOTHER.

John ii. 11. — "This beginning of miracles did Jesus in Cana of Galilee, and manifested forth his glory; and his disciples believed on him."

This was the "beginning of Miracles" which Jesus did, and yet He was now thirty years of age. For thirty years He had done no miracle; and that is in itself almost worthy to be called a miracle. That He abstained for thirty years from the exertion of His wonder-working power is as marvellous as that He possessed for three years the power to exert. He was content to live long in deep obscurity. Nazareth, with its quiet valley, was world enough for Him. There was no disposition to rush into publicity: no haste to be known in the world. The quiet consciousness of power which breathes in that expression, "Mine hour is not yet come," had marked His whole life. He could bide His time. He had the strength to wait.

This was true greatness — the greatness of man, because also the greatness of God: for such is God's way in all He does. In all the works of God there is a conspicuous absence of haste and hurry. All that He does ripens slowly. Six slow days and nights of creative force before man was made: two thousand years to discipline and form a Jewish people: four thousand years of darkness, and ignorance, and crime, before the fulness of the Time had come, when He could send forth His Son: unnumbered ages of war before the thousand years of solid peace can come. Whatever contradicts this Divine plan must pay the price of haste — brief duration. All that is done before the hour is come, decays fast. All precocious things ripened before their time wither before their time: precocious fruit — precocious minds — forced feelings. "He that believeth shall not make haste."

We shall distribute the various thoughts which this event suggests under two heads.

I. The Glory of the Virgin Mother.

II. The Glory of the Divine Son.

I. The Glory of the Virgin Mother.

In the First Epistle to the Corinthians, St. Paul speaks of the glory of the woman as of a thing distinct from the glory of the man. They are the two opposite poles of the sphere of humanity. Their provinces are not the same, but different. The qualities which are beautiful as predominant in one are not beautiful when predominant in the other. That which is the glory of the one is not the glory of the other. The glory of her who was highly favoured among women, and whom all Christendom has agreed in contemplating as the Type and ideal of her sex, was glory in a different order from that in which her Son exhibited the glory of a perfect manhood. A glory different in *degree*, of course: — the one was only human, the other more than human, the Word made flesh; but different in *order* too: the one manifesting forth *her* glory — the grace of womanhood: the other manifesting forth *His* glory — the Wisdom and the Majesty of Manhood, in which God dwelt.

Different orders or kinds of glory. Let us consider the glory of the Virgin, which is, in other words, the glory of what is womanly in character.

Remarkable, first of all, in this respect, is her considerateness. There is gentle, womanly tact in those words, "They have no wine." Unselfish thoughtfulness about others' comforts, not her own: delicate anxiety to save a straitened family from the exposure of their poverty: and moreover, for this is very worthy of observation, carefulness about gross, material things: a sensual thing, we might truly say — wine, the instrument of intoxication: yet see how her feminine tenderness transfigured and sanctified such gross and common things — how that wine which, as used by the revellers of the banquet, might be coarse and sensual, was in her use sanctified, as it was by unselfishness and charity: a thing quite heavenly, glorified by the Ministry of Love.

It was so that in old times, with thoughtful hospitality, Rebekah offered water at the well to Abraham's way-worn servant. It was so that Martha showed her devotion to her Lord even to excess, being cumbered with much serving. It was so that the women ministered to Christ out of their substance — water, food, money. They took these low things of earth, and spiritualized them into means of hospitality and devotion.

And this is the glory of womanhood: surely no common glory: surely one which, if she rightly comprehended her place on earth, might enable her to accept its apparent humiliation unrepiningly; the glory of unsensualizing coarse and common things, sensual things, the objects of mere sense, meat and drink and household cares, elevating them by the spirit in which she ministers them, into something transfigured and sublime.

The humblest mother of a poor family who is cumbered with much serving, or watching over a hospitality which she is too poor to delegate to others, or toiling for love's sake in household work, needs no emancipation in God's sight. It is the prerogative and the glory of her womanhood to consecrate the meanest things by a ministry which is not for self.

2. Submission.

"Whatsoever He saith unto you, do it." Here is the true spirit of Obedience. Not slavishness, but entire loyalty and perfect trust in a Person whom we reverence. She did not comprehend her Son's strange repulse and mysterious words; but she knew that they were not capricious words, for there was no caprice in Him: she knew that the law which ruled His will was Right, and that importunity was useless. So she bade them reverently wait in silence till his time should come.

Here is another distinctive glory of womanhood. In the very outset of the Bible, submission is revealed as her peculiar lot and destiny. If you were merely to look at the words as they stand, declaring the results of the Fall, you would be inclined to call that vocation of obedience a curse; but in the spirit of Christ it is transformed, like Labour, into a blessing. In this passage one peculiar blessing stands connected with it.

Here a twofold blessing is connected with it: Freedom from all doubt; and prevailing power in prayer.

The first is freedom from all doubt. The Virgin seems to have felt no perplexity at that rebuke and seeming refusal; and yet perplexity and misgiving would seem natural. A more masculine and imperious mind would have been startled; made sullen, or begun at once to sound the depths of metaphysics, reasoning upon the hardship of a lot which cannot realise all it wishes: wondering why such simple blessings are refused, pondering deeply on Divine decrees, ending perhaps in scepticism. Mary was saved from this. She could not understand, but she could trust and wait. Not for one moment did a shade of doubt rest upon her heart. At once, and instantly, "Whatsoever He saith unto you, do it." And so, too, the Syrophenician woman was not driven to speculate on the injustice of her destiny by the seeming harshness of Christ's reply. She drew closer to her Lord in prayer. Affection and submissiveness saved them both from doubt. True women both.

Now there are whole classes of our fellow-creatures, to whom, as a class, the anguish of religious doubt never or rarely comes. Mental doubt rarely touches women. Soldiers and sailors do not doubt. Their religion is remarkable for its simplicity and childlike character. Scarcely ever are religious warriors tormented with scepticism or doubts. And in all, I believe, for the same reason, the habits of feeling to which the long life of obedience trains the soul. Prompt, quick, unquestioning obedience: that is the soil for faith.

I call this, therefore, the glory of womanhood. It is the true glory of human beings to obey. It is her special glory, rising out of the very weakness of her nature — God's strength made perfect in weakness. England will not soon forget that lesson left her as the bequest of a great life. Her buried Hero's glory came out of that which was manliest in his character — the Virgin spirit of obedience.

The second glory resulting from it, is prevailing power with God. Her wish was granted. "What have I to do with thee," were words that only asserted His own perfect independence. They were not the language of rebuke. As Messiah, He gently vindicated His acts from interference, showing the filial relation to be in its first strictness dissolved. But as Son He obeyed, or to speak more properly, complied. Nay, probably His look had said that already, promising more than His words, setting her mind at rest, and granting the favour she desired.

Brethren, the subject of prayer is a deep mystery. To the masculine intellect it is a demonstrable absurdity. For, says logic, how can man's will modify the will of God, or alter the fixed decree? And if it cannot, wherein lies the use of prayer? But there is a something mightier than intellect and truér than logic. It is the faith which works by love — the conviction that in this world of mystery, that which cannot be put in words, nor defended by argument, may yet be true. The will of Christ was fixed, what could be the use of intercession? and yet the Virgin feeling was true — she felt her prayer would prevail.

Here is a grand paradox, which is the paradox of all prayer. The heart hopes that which to reasoning seems impossible. And I believe we never pray aright except when we pray in that feminine childlike spirit which no logic can defend, feeling *as if* we modified the will of God, though that will is fixed.

It is the glory of the spirit that is affectionate and submissive that it, ay, and it alone, *can* pray, because it alone can believe that its prayer will be granted; and it is the glory of that spirit too, that its prayer will be granted.

3rdly, In all Christian ages the especial glory ascribed to the Virgin Mother is purity of heart and life. Implied in the term "Virgin." Gradually in the history of the Christian church the recognition of this became idolatry. The works of early Christian art curiously exhibit the progress of this perversion. They show how Mariolatry grew up. The first pictures of the early Christian ages simply represent the woman. By and by, we find outlines of the Mother and the Child. In an after-age, the Son is seen sitting on a throne, with the mother crowned, but sitting as yet below Him. In an age still later, the crowned Mother on a level with the Son. Later still, the Mother on a throne *above* the Son. And, lastly, a Romish picture represents the Eternal Son in wrath, about to destroy the Earth, and the Virgin Intercessor, interposing, pleading by significant attitude her maternal rights, and redeeming the world from his vengeance. Such was, in fact, the progress of Virgin-worship. First the woman reverenced for the Son's sake; then the woman reverenced above the Son and adored.

Now the question is, How came this to be? for we assume it as a principle that no error has ever spread widely, that was not the exaggeration or perversion of a truth. And be assured that the first step towards dislodging error is to understand the truth at which it aims. Never can an error be permanently destroyed by the roots, unless we have planted by its side the truth that is to take its place. Else you will find the falsehood returning for ever, growing up again when you thought it cut up root and branch, appearing in the very places where the crushing of it seemed most complete. Wherever there is a deep truth unrecognised, misunderstood, it will force its way into men's hearts. It will take pernicious forms if it cannot find healthful ones. It will grow as some weeds grow, in noxious forms, ineradicably, because it has a root in human nature.

Else how comes it to pass, after three hundred years of Reformation, we find Virgin-worship restoring itself again in this reformed England, where least of all countries we should expect it, and where the remembrance of Romish persecution might have seemed to make its return impossible? How comes it that some of the deepest thinkers of our day, and men of the saintliest lives, are feeling this Virgin-worship a necessity for their souls; for it is *the* doctrine to which the converts to Romanism cling most tenaciously?

Brethren, I reply, because the doctrine of the worship of the Virgin has a root in truth, and no mere cutting and uprooting can destroy it: no Protestant thunders of oratory: no platform expositions: no Reformation societies. In one word, no mere negations; nothing but the full liberation of the truth which lies at the root of error can eradicate error.

Surely we ought to have learnt that truth by this time. Recollect how, before Christ's time, mere negations failed to uproot paganism. Philosophers had disproved it by argument: satirists had covered it with ridicule. It was slain a thousand times, and yet paganism lived on in the hearts of men: and those who gave it up returned to it again in a dying hour, because the disprovers of it had given nothing for the heart to rest on in its place. But when Paul dared to proclaim of paganism what we are proclaiming of Virgin-worship, that paganism stood upon a truth, and taught that truth, paganism fell for ever. The Apostle Paul found in Athens an altar to the unknown God. He did not announce in Athens lectures against heathen priestcraft; nor did he undertake to prove it, in the Areopagus, all a mystery of iniquity, and a system of damnable idolatries; — that is the mode in which we set about *our* controversies — but he disengaged the truth from the error, proclaimed the truth, and left the errors to themselves. The truth grew up, and the errors silently and slowly withered.

I pray you, Christian brethren, do not join those fierce associations which think only of uprooting error. There is a spirit in them which is more of earth than heaven, short-sighted too and self-destructive. They do not make converts to Christ, but only controversialists, and adherents to a party. They compass sea and land. It matters little whether fierce Romanism or fierce Protestantism wins the day: but it does matter whether or not in the conflict we lose some precious Christian truth, as well as the very spirit of Christianity.

What lies at the root of this ineradicable Virgin-worship? How comes it that out of so few scripture sentences about her, many of them like this rebuke, depreciatory, learned men and pious men could ever have *developed*, as they call it, or as it seems to us, tortured and twisted a doctrine of Divine honours to be paid to Mary? Let us set out with the conviction that there must have been some reason for it, some truth of which it is the perversion.

I believe the truth to be this. Before Christ the qualities honoured as Divine were peculiarly the virtues of the man: Courage — Wisdom — Truth — Strength. But Christ proclaimed the Divine nature of qualities entirely opposite: Meekness — Obedience — Affection — Purity. He said that the pure in heart should see God. He pronounced the beatitudes of meekness, and lowliness, and poverty of spirit. Now observe these were all of the order of graces which are distinctively feminine. And it is the peculiar feature of Christianity that it exalts not strength nor intellect, but gentleness, and lovingness, and Virgin purity.

Here was a new strange thought given to the world. It was for many ages *the* thought: no wonder — it was the one great novelty of the revealed religion. How were men to find expression for that idea which was working in them, vague and beautiful, but wanting substance? the idea of the Divineness of what is pure, above the Divineness of what is strong? Would you have had them say simply, we had forgotten these things; now they are revealed — now we know that Love and Purity are as Divine as Power and Reason? My brethren, it is not so that men *worship* — it is only so that men *think*. They think about qualities — they worship *persons*. Worship must have a form. Adoration finds a Person, and if it cannot find one, it will imagine one. Gentleness and purity are words for a philosopher; but a man whose heart wants something to adore will find for himself a gentle *one* — a pure *one* — Incarnate purity and love — gentleness robed in flesh and blood, before whom his knee may bend, and to whom the homage of his spirit can be given. You cannot adore except a Person.

What marvel if the early Christian found that the Virgin-mother of our Lord embodied this great idea? What marvel if he filled out and expanded with that idea which was in his heart, the brief sketch given of her in the gospels, till his imagination had robed the woman of the Bible with the majesty of the mother of God? Can we not *feel* that it must have been so? Instead of a dry, formal dogma of theology, the Romanist presented an actual woman, endued with every inward grace and beauty, and pierced by sorrows, as a living object of devotion, faith, and hope — a personality instead of an abstraction. Historically speaking, it seems inevitable that the idea could scarcely have been expressed to the world except through an idolatry.

Brethren, it is an idolatry: in modern Romanism a pernicious and most defiling one. The worship of Mary overshadows the worship of the Son. The love given to her is so much taken from Him. Nevertheless let us not hide from ourselves the eternal truth of the idea that lies beneath the temporary falsehood of the dogma. Overthrow the idolatry; but do it by substituting the truth.

Now the truth which alone can supplant the worship of the Virgin is the perfect humanity of Jesus Christ. I say the perfect *humanity:* for perfect manhood is a very ambiguous expression. By man we sometimes mean the human race, made up of man and woman, and sometimes we only mean the masculine sex. We have only one word to express both ideas. The language in which the New Testament was written has two. Hence we may make a great mistake. When the Bible speaks of man the human being, we may think that it means man the male creature. When the

Bible tells us Jesus Christ was the Son of Man, it uses the word which implies human being: it does not use the word which signifies one of the male sex: it does not dwell on the fact that He was *a* man! but it earnestly asserts that He was Man. Son of a man He was not. Son of Man He was: for the blood, as it were, of all the race was in His veins.

Now let us see what is implied in this expression Son of Man. It contains in it the doctrine of the Incarnation: it means the full humanity of Christ. Lately I tried to bring out one portion of its meaning. I said that He belonged to no particular age, but to every age. He had not the qualities of one clime or race, but that which is common to all climes and all races. He was not the Son of the Jew, nor the Son of the Oriental — He was the Son of Man. He was not the villager of Bethlehem: nor one whose character and mind were the result of a certain training, peculiar to Judea, or peculiar to that century — but He was *the Man*. This is what St. Paul insists on, when he says that in Him there is neither Jew nor Gentile, Barbarian, Scythian, bond nor free. A Humanity in which there is nothing distinctive, limited, or peculiar, but universal — your nature and mine, the Humanity in which we all are brothers, bond or free. Now in that same passage St. Paul uses another very remarkable expression: "There is neither Jew nor Greek, there is neither bond nor free, there is neither male nor female." That is the other thing implied in His title to the Son of Man. His nature had in it the nature of all nations: but also His heart had in it the blended qualities of both sexes. Our humanity is a whole made up of two opposite poles of character — the manly and the feminine. In the character of Christ neither was found exclusively, but both in perfect balance. He was the Son of Man — the human being — perfect Man.

There was in Him the woman-heart as well as the manly brain — all that was most manly, and all that was most womanly. Remember what He was in life: recollect His stern iron hardness in the temptation of the desert: recollect the calmness that never quailed in all the uproars of the people, the truth that never faltered, the strict severe integrity which characterized the Witness of the Truth: recollect the justice that never gave way to weak feeling — which let the rich young ruler go his way to perish if he would — which paid the tribute money — which held the balance fair between the persecuted woman and her accuser, but did not suffer itself to be betrayed by sympathy into any feeble tenderness — the justice that rebuked Peter with indignation, and pronounced the doom of Jerusalem unswervingly. Here is one side or pole of human character — surely not the feminine side. Now look at the other. Recollect the twice recorded tears, which a man would have been ashamed to show, and which are never beautiful in man except when joined with strength like His: and recollect the sympathy craved and yearned for as well as given — the shrinking from solitude in prayer — the trembling of a sorrow unto death — the considerate care which provided bread for the multitude, and said to the tired disciples, as with a sister's rather than a brother's thoughtfulness, "Come ye apart into the desert and rest awhile." This is the other side or pole of human character — surely not the masculine.

When we have learnt and felt what is meant by

Divine Humanity in Christ, and when we have believed it, not in a one-sided way, but in all its fulness, then we are safe from Mariolatry; because we do not want it: we have the truth which Mariolatry labours to express, and, labouring ignorantly, falls into idolatry. But so long as the male was looked upon as the only type of God, and the masculine virtues as the only glory of His character, so long the truth was yet unrevealed. This was the state of heathenism. And so long as Christ was only felt as the Divine Man, and not the Divine Humanity, so long the world had only a one-sided truth.

One-half of our nature, the sterner portion of it, only was felt to be of God and in God. The other half, the tenderer and the purer qualities of our souls, were felt as earthly. This was the state of Romanism from which men tried to escape by Mariolatry. And if men had not learned that this side of our nature too, was made Divine in Christ, what possible escape was there for them, but to look to the Virgin Mary as the Incarnation of the purer and lovelier elements of God's character, reserving to her Son the sterner and the more masculine?

Can we not understand too, how it came to pass that the mother was placed above the Son, and adored more? Christianity had proclaimed Meekness, Purity, Obedience, as more Divine than Strength and Wisdom. What wonder if she who was gazed on as the type of Purity should be reckoned more near to God than He who had come through misconception to be looked on chiefly as the type of Strength and Justice?

There is a spirit abroad which is leading men to Rome. Do not call that the spirit of the Devil. It is the desire and hope to find there in its tenderness, and its beauty, and its devotion, a home for those feelings of awe, and contemplation, and love, for which our stern Protestantism finds no shelter. Let us acknowledge that what they worship is indeed deserving of all adoration: only let us say that *what* they worship is, ignorantly, Christ. Whom they ignorantly worship let us declare unto them: Christ their unknown God, worshipped at an idol-altar. Do no let us satisfy ourselves by saying as a watchword, "Christ not Mary:" say rather, "In Christ all that they find in Mary." The Mother in the Son, the womanly in the Soul of Christ. Divine Honour to the Feminine side of His character, jofyul and unvarying acknowledgment that in Christ there is a revelation of the Divineness of submission, and love, and purity, and long-suffering, just as there was before in the name of the Lord of Hosts, a revelation of the Divineness of courage, and strength, and heroism, and manliness.

Therefore it is we do not sympathize with those coarse expositions which aim at doing exclusive honour to the Son of God by degrading the life and character of the Virgin. Just as the Romanist has loved to represent all connection with her as mysterious and immaculate, so has the Protestant been disposed to vulgarize her to the level of the commonest humanity, and exaggerate into rebukes the reverent expressions to her in which Jesus asserted His Divine independence.

Rather reverence, not her, but that Idea and type which Christianity has given in her — the type of Christian womanhood; which was not realized in her, which never was and never will be realized in one single woman — which remains ever a Divine Idea, after which each living woman is to strive.

And when I say reverence that Idea or type, I am but pointing to the relation between the Mother and the Son, and asking men to reverence that which He reverenced. Think we that there is no meaning hidden in the mystery that the Son of God was the Virgin's Son? To Him through life there remained the early recollections of a pure mother. Blessed beyond all common blessedness is the man who can look back to that. God has given to him a talisman which will carry him triumphant through many a temptation. To other men purity may be a name; to him it has been once a reality. "Faith in all things high beats with his blood." He may be tempted: he may err: but there will be a light from home shining for ever on his path inextinguishably. By the grace of God, degraded he cannot be.

XIX.

Preached January 30, 1853.

THE FIRST MIRACLE.

II. THE GLORY OF THE DIVINE SON.

JOHN II. 11. — "This beginning of miracles did Jesus in Cana of Galilee, and manifested forth his glory; and his disciples believed on him."

IN the history of this miracle, two personages are brought prominently before our notice. One is the Virgin Mary; the other is the Son of God. And these two exhibit different orders of glory, as well as different degrees. Different degrees, for the Virgin was only human: her Son was God manifest in the flesh. Different orders of glory, for the one exhibited the distinctive glory of womanhood: the Other manifested forth *His* glory — the glory of perfect manhood.

Taking the Virgin as the type and representative of her sex, we found the glory of womanhood, as exhibited by her conduct in this parable, to consist in unselfish considerateness about others, in delicacy of tact, in the power of ennobling a ministry of coarse and household things, like the wine of the marriage-feast, by the sanctity of affection: in meekness, and lowly obedience, which was in the Fall her curse, in Christ become her glory, transformed into a blessing and a power: and lastly, as the name Virgin implies, the distinctive glory of womanhood we found to consist in purity.

Now the Christian history first revealed these great truths. The gospels which record the life of Christ, first, in the history of the world, brought to light the Divine glory of those qualities which had been despised.

Before Christ came, the heathen had counted for Divine the legislative wisdom of the man, manly strength, manly truth, manly justice, manly courage. The Life and the Cross of Christ shed a splendour from heaven upon a new and till then unheard-of order of heroism — that which may be called the feminine order, meekness, endurance, long-suffering, the passive strength of martyrdom. For Christianity does not say Honour to the Wise, but "Blessed are the Meek." Not Glory to the Strong, but, "Blessed are the pure in heart, for they shall see God." Not The Lord is a man of war, Jehovah is His name, but "God is Love." In Christ not intellect, but love is consecrated. In Christ is magnified, not force of will, but the Glory of a Divine humility. "He was obedient unto death, even the death of the cross: *wherefore* God also hath highly exalted Him."

Therefore it was, that from that time forward womanhood assumed a new place in this world. She in whom these qualities, for the first time declared Divine in Christ, were the distinctive characteristics, steadily and gradually rose to a higher dignity in human life. It is not to mere civilization, but to the spirit of life in Christ, that woman owes all she has, and all she has yet to gain.

Now the outward phases in which this Redemption of the sex appeared to the world have been as yet chiefly three. There have been three ages through which these great truths of the Divineness of purity, and the strength and glory of obedience, the peculiar characteristics of womanhood, have been rising into their right acknowledgment. 1. The ages of Virgin-worship. 2. The ages of Chivalry. 3. The age of the three last centuries. Now during the three Protestant centuries, the place and destinies of womanhood have been every year rising more and more into great questions. Her mission, as it is called in the cant language of the day — what it is — that is one of the subjects of deepest interest in the controversies of the day. And unless we are prepared to say that the truth which has been growing clearer and brighter for eighteen centuries shall stop now exactly where it is, and grow no clearer: unless we are ready to affirm that mankind will never learn to pay less glory to strength and intellect, and more to meekness, and humbleness, and pureness than they do now, it follows that God has yet reserved for womanhood a larger and more glorious field for her peculiar qualities and gifts, and that the truth contained in the Virgin's motherhood is unexhausted still.

For this reason, in reference to that womanhood and its destinies, of which St. Mary is the type, I thought it needful last Sunday to insist on two things as of profound importance.

I. To declare in what her true glory consists. The only glory of the Virgin was the glory of true womanhood. The glory of true womanhood consists in being *herself:* not in striving to be something else. It is the false paradox and heresy of this present age to claim for her as a glory the right to leave her sphere. Her glory lies *in* her sphere, and God has given her a sphere distinct; as in the Epistle to the church of Corinth, when in that wise chapter St. Paul rendered unto womanhood the things which were woman's, and unto manhood the things which were man's.

And the true correction of that monstrous rebellion

against what is natural, lies in vindicating Mary's glory, on the one side, from the Romanist, who gives to her the glory of God; and on the other from those who would confound the distinctive glories of the two sexes, and claim as the glory of woman what is, in the deeps of nature, the glory of the man.

Everything is created in its own order. Every created thing has its own glory. "There is one glory of the sun, another glory of the moon, and another glory of the stars: for one star differeth from another star in glory." There is one glory of Manhood, and another glory of Womanhood. And the glory of each created thing consists in being true to its own nature, and moving in its own sphere.

Mary's glory was not immaculate origin, nor immaculate life, nor exaltation to Divine honours. She had none of these things. Nor on the other hand, was it Force or demanded Rights, social or domestic, that constituted her glory. But it was the glory of simple Womanhood; the glory of being true to the nature assigned her by her Maker; the glory of motherhood; the glory of "a meek and quiet spirit, which in the sight of God is of great price." She was not the Queen of Heaven, but she was something nobler still, a creature content to be what God had made her: in unselfishness, and humbleness, and purity, rejoicing in God her Saviour, content that He had regarded the lowliness of His handmaiden.

The second thing upon which I insisted was, that the only safeguard against the idolatrous error of Virgin-worship, is a full recognition of the perfect Humanity of Christ. *A full* recognition: for it is only a partial acknowledgment of the meaning of the Incarnation when we think of Him as the Divine Man. It was not manhood, but humanity, that was made Divine in Him. Humanity has its two sides: one side in the strength and intellect of manhood; the other in the tenderness, and faith, and submissiveness of womanhood: Man and Woman, not man alone, make up human nature. In Christ not one alone but both were glorified. Strength and Grace — Wisdom and Love — Courage and Purity — Divine Manliness: Divine Womanliness. In all noble characters you find the two blended: in Him — the noblest — blended into one entire and perfect Humanity.

Unless you recognise and fully utter this whole truth, you will find Mariolatry for ever returning, cut it down as you will. It must come back. It will come back. I had well nigh said it *ought* to come back, unless we preach and believe the full truth of God incarnate in Humanity. For while we teach in our classical schools as the only manliness, Pagan heroism of warrior and legislator, can we say that we are teaching both sides of Christ? Our souls were trained in boyhood to honour the heroic and the masculine. Who ever hinted to us that charity is the "more excellent way?" Who suggested that "he which ruleth his spirit is greater than he which taketh a city?"

Again we find our English society divided into two sections: one the men of business and action, exhibiting prominently the masculine virtues of English character, truth and honour, and almost taught to reckon forbearance and feeling as proofs of weakness; taught in the playground to believe that a chaste life is romance; false sentiment and strengthlessness of character taught there: and in after-life, that it is mean to forgive a personal affront.

The other section of our society is made up of men of prayer and religiousness: for some reason or other singularly deficient in masculine breadth and strength, and even truthfulness of character: with no firm footing upon reality, not daring to look the real problems of social and political life in the face, but wasting their strength in disputes of words, or shrinking into a dim atmosphere of ecclesiastical dreaminess, unreal and effeminate. Dare we say that the full Humanity of Christ in its double aspect is practically adored amongst us? Have we not made a fatal separation between the manly and the feminine of character? between the moral and the devout? so that we have men who are masculine and moral, and also men who are effeminate and devout. But where are our Christian men in whom the whole Christ is formed, all that is brave, and true, and wise, and at the same time all that is tender, and devout, and pure? Who ever taught us to adore in Christ all that is most manly, and all that is most womanly, that we might strive to be such in our degree ourselves? And if not, can you wonder that men, feeling their Christianity imperfect, blindly strive to patch it up through Mariolatry?

I gather into a few sentences the substance of what was said last Sunday. I said that Christianity exhibited the Divine glory of the weaker elements of our human nature. Heathenism, nay, even Judaism, had as yet before him only recognised the glory of the stronger and masculine. Now the Romanist personified the masculine side of human nature in Christ. He personified gentleness and purity, the feminine side of human nature in the Virgin Mary. No wonder that with this cardinal error at the outset in his conceptions, he adored; and no wonder since Christianity declared meekness and purity more Divine than strength and intellect, in process of time he came to honour the Virgin more than Christ. That I believe is the true history and account of Virgin-worship.

The Bible personifies both sides of human nature, the masculine and feminine of character in Christ, of whom St. Paul declares in the Epistle to the Galatians, "In him is neither Jew nor Greek, bond nor free, male nor female." Neither *distinctively*, for in Him both the manly and the womanly of character divinely meet. I say therefore, that the Incarnation of God in Christ is the true defence against Virgin-worship.

Think of Christ only as the masculine character, glorified by the union of Godhead with it, and your Christianity has in it an awful gap, a void, a want — the inevitable supply and relief to which will be Mariolatry, however secure you may think yourself; however strong and fierce the language you now use. Men who have used language as strong and fierce have become idolaters of Mary. With a half-thought of Christ, safe you are not. But think of Him as the Divine Human Being, in whom both sides of our double being are divine and glorified, and then you have the truth which Romanism has marred, and perverted into an idolatry pernicious in all; in the less spiritual worshippers sensualizing and debasing.

Now there are two ways of meeting error. The one is that in which, in humble imitation of Christ and His apostles, I have tried to show you the error of the worship of Mary — to discern the truth out of which the error sprung, firmly asserting the truth, forbearing threatening; certain that he in whose mind the truth has lodged, has in that truth the safeguard against error.

The other way of meeting error is to overwhelm it with threats. To some men it seems the only way in which true zeal is shown. Well — it is very easy, requiring no self-control, but only an indulgence of every bad passion. It is very easy to call Rome the mother of harlots and abominations — very easy to use strong language about damnable idolatries — very easy for the apostles to call down fire from heaven upon the Samaritans because they would not receive Christ, and then to flatter themselves that that was Godly zeal. But it might be well for us to remember His somewhat startling comment, "Ye know not what manner of spirit ye are of." There are those who think it a surer and a safer Protestantism to use those popular watchwords. Be it so. But, with God's blessing, *that will not I.* The majesty of truth needs other bulwarks than vulgar and cowardly vituperation. Coarse language and violent, excusable three hundred years ago by the manners of that day, was bold and brave in the lips of the Reformers, with whom the struggle was one of life and death, and who might be called to pay the penalty of their bold defiances with their blood. But the same fierceness of language now, when there is no personal risk in the use of it, in the midst of hundreds of men and women ready to applaud and honour violence as zeal, is simply a dastardliness from which every generous mind shrinks. You do not get the Reformers' spirit by putting on the armour they have done with, but by risking the dangers which those noble warriors risked. It is not their big words, but their large, brave heart, that makes the Protestant. O, be sure that he whose soul has anchored itself to rest on the deep calm sea of Truth, does not spend his strength in raving against those who are still tossed by the winds of error. Spasmodic violence of words is one thing, strength of conviction is another.

When, O when, shall we learn that loyalty to Christ is tested far more by the strength of our Sympathy with Truth than by the intensity of our hatred of Error. I will tell you what to hate. Hate Hypocrisy — hate Cant — hate Intolerance, Oppression, Injustice — hate Pharisaism — hate them as Christ hated them, with a deep, living, God-like hatred. But do not hate *men in intellectual error*. To hate a man for his errors is as unwise as to hate one who in casting up an account has made an error against himself. The Romanist has made an error against himself. He has missed the full glory of his Lord and Master. Well — shall we hate him, and curse, and rant, and thunder at him? Or, shall we sit down beside him, and try to sympathize with him, and see things from his point of view, and strive to understand the truth which his soul is aiming at, and seize the truth for him and for ourselves, "meekly instructing those who oppose themselves?"

Our subject to-day is the glory of the Divine Son.

In that miracle "He manifested forth His glory." Concerning that glory we say: —

1. The glory of Christ did not *begin* with that miracle: the miracle only *manifested* it. For thirty years the wonder-working power had been in him. It was not Diviner power when it broke forth into visible manifestation, than it had been when it was unsuspected

and unseen. It had been exercised up to this time in common acts of youthful life: obedience to His mother, love to His brethren. Well, it was just as divine in those simple, daily acts, as when it showed itself in a way startling and wonderful. It was just as much the life of God on Earth when He did an act of ordinary human love or human duty, as when He did an extraordinary act, such as turning water into wine. God was as much, nay more, in the daily life and love of Christ, than He was in Christ's miracles. The miracle only made the hidden glory visible. The extraordinary only proved that the ordinary was Divine. That was the very object of the miracle. It was done to *manifest forth* His glory. And if, instead of rousing men to see the real glory of Christ in His other life, the miracle merely fastened men's attention on itself, and made them think that the only Glory which is Divine is to be found in what is wonderful and uncommon, then the whole intention of the miracle was lost.

Let us make this more plain by an illustration. To the wise man, the lightning only manifests the electric force which is everywhere, and which for one moment has become visible. As often as he sees it, it reminds him that the lightning slumbers invisibly in the dew-drop, and in the mist, and in the cloud, and binds together every atom of the water that he uses in daily life. But to the vulgar mind the lightning is something unique, a something which has no existence but when it appears. There is a fearful glory in the lightning because he sees it. But there is no startling glory and nothing fearful in the drop of dew, because he does not know, what the Thinker knows, that the flash is there in all its terrors.

So, in the same way, to the half-believer a miracle is the one solitary evidence of God. Without it he could have no certainty of God's existence.

But to the true disciple a miracle only *manifests* the Power and Love which are silently at work everywhere — as truly and as really in the slow work of the cure of the insane, as in the sudden expulsion of the legion from the demoniac — as divinely in the gift of daily bread, as in the miraculous multiplication of the loaves. God's glory is at work in the growth of the vine and the ripening of the grape, and the process by which grape-juice passes into wine. It is not *more* glory, but only glory more *manifested*, when water at His bidding passes at once into wine. And be sure that if you do not feel as David felt, God's presence in the annual miracle, that it is *God*, which in the vintage of every year causeth wine to make glad the heart of man, the sudden miracle at Capernaum would not have given you conviction of His presence, "If you hear not Moses and the prophets, neither will you be persuaded though one rose from the dead." Miracles have only done their work when they teach us the glory and the awfulness that surround our common life. In a miracle, God for one moment shows Himself, that we may remember it is He that is at work when no miracle is seen.

Now this is the deep truth of miracles which most men miss. They believe that the life of Jesus was Divine, because He wrought miracles. But if their faith in miracles were shaken, their faith in Christ would go. If the evidence for the credibility of those miracles were weakened, then to them the mystic glory would have faded off His history. They could not be sure that His Existence was Divine. That love, even unto death, would bear no certain stamp of God upon it. That life of long self-sacrifice would have had in it no certain unquestionable traces of the Son of God. See what that implies. If that be true, and miracles are the best proof of Christ's mission, God can be recognised in what is marvellous: God cannot be recognised in what is good. It is by Divine power that a human Being turns water into wine. It is by power less certainly Divine that the same Being witnesses to truth — forgives His enemies — makes it His meat and drink to do His Father's will, and finishes His work. We are more sure that God was in Christ when He said, "Rise up, and walk," than when He said with absolving love, "Son, thy sins be forgiven thee:" more certain when He furnished wine for wedding guests, than when He said, "Father, forgive them, for they know not what they do." O, a strange, and low, and vulgar appreciation this of the true glory of the Son of God, the same false conception that runs through all our life, appearing in every form — God in the storm, and the earthquake, and the fire — no God in the still small voice. Glory in the lightning-flash — no glory and no God in the lowliness of the dew-drop. Glory to intellect and genius — no glory to gentleness and patience. Glory to every kind of *power* — none to the inward, invisible strength of the life of God in the soul of man.

"An evil and an adulterous generation seeketh after a sign." Look at the feverish eagerness with which men crowd to every exhibition of some newly-discovered Force, real or pretended. What lies at the bottom of this feverishness but an unbelieving craving after signs? some wonder which is to show them the Divine life of which the evidence is yet imperfect? As if the bread they eat and the wine they drink, chosen by God for the emblems of his sacraments because the commonest things of daily life, were not filled with the Presence of his love; as if God were not around their path and beside their bed, and spying out all their daily ways.

It is in this strange way that we have learned Christ. The miracles which were meant to point us to the Divinity of His Goodness, have only dazzled us with the splendour of their Power. We have forgotten what His first wonder-work shows, that a miracle is only *manifested* glory.

2 It was the glory of Christ again to sanctify, *i. e.* declare the sacredness of, all things natural. All natural relationships — all natural enjoyments.

All natural relationship. What He sanctified by His presence was a marriage. Now remember what had gone before this. The life of John the Baptist was the highest form of religious life known in Israel. It was the life ascetic. It was a life of solitariness and penitential austerity. He drank no wine: he ate no pleasant food: he married no wife: he entered into no human relationship. It was the law of that stern and in its way sublime life, to cut out every human feeling as a weakness, and to mortify every natural instinct, in order to cultivate an intenser spirituality. A life in its own order grand, but indisputably unnatural.

Now the first public act of our Redeemer's life is to go with His disciples to a marriage. He consecrates marriage, and the sympathies which lead to marriage. He declares the sacredness of feelings which had been reckoned carnal, and low, and human. He stamps His image on human joys, human connections, human relationships. He pronounces that they are more than human — as it were, sacramental: the means whereby God's presence comes to us; the types and shadows whereby higher and deeper relationships become possible to us. For it is through our human affections that the soul first learns to feel that its destiny is Divine: It is through a mortal yearning, unsatisfied, that the spirit ascends, seeking a higher object: It is through the gush of our human tenderness that the Immortal and the Infinite in us reveals itself. Never does a man know the force that is in him till some mighty affection or grief has humanized the soul. It is by an earthly relationship that God has typified to us and helped us to conceive the only true Espousal — the marriage of the soul to her Eternal Lord.

It was the glory of Christianity to pronounce all these human feelings sacred: therefore it is that the church asserts their sacredness in a religious ceremony; for example, that of marriage. Do not mistake. It is not the ceremony that makes a thing religious: a ceremony can only *declare* a thing religious. The church cannot make sacred that which is not sacred: she is but here on earth as the moon, the witness of the light in heaven; by her ceremonies and by her institutions to bear witness to eternal truths. She cannot by her manipulations manufacture a child of the devil, through baptism, into a child of God: she can only authoritatively declare the sublime truth — he is *not* the devil's child, but God's child by right. She cannot make the bond of marriage sacred and indissoluble: she can only witness to the sacredness of that which the union of two spirits has already made: and such are her own words. Her minister is commanded by her to say — "Forasmuch as these two persons have *consented together*," — there is the sacred Fact of Nature, "I pronounce that they be man and wife" — here is the authoritative witness to the fact.

Again, it was His glory to declare the sacredness of all natural enjoyments.

It was not a marriage only, but a marriage-*feast*, to which Christ conducted His disciples. Now we cannot get over this plain fact by saying that it was a religious ceremony: that would be mere sophistry. It was an indulgence in the festivity of life; as plainly as words can describe here was a banquet of human enjoyment. The very language of the master of the feast about men who had well drunk, tells us that there had been, not excess, of course, but happiness there and merry-making.

Neither can we explain away the lesson by saying that it is no example to us, for Christ was there to do good, and that what was safe for Him might be unsafe for us. For if His life is no pattern for us here in this case of accepting an invitation, in what can we be sure it *is* a pattern? Besides, He took His disciples there, and His mother was there: they were not shielded as he was, by immaculate purity. He was there as a guest at first, as Messiah only afterwards: thereby He declared the sacredness of natural enjoyments.

Here again, then, Christ manifested His peculiar glory. The Temptation of the Wilderness was past: the baptism of John, and the life of abstinence to which it introduced, were over; and now the Bridegroom comes before the world in the true glory of Messiah — not in the life of ascetism, but in the life of Godliness — not separating from life, but consecrating it; carrying a Divine spirit into every simplest act — accepting an invitation to a feast — giving to water the virtue of a nobler beverage. For Christianity does not destroy what is natural, but ennobles it. To turn water into wine, and what is common into what is holy, is indeed the glory of Christianity.

The ascetic life of abstinence, of fasting, austerity, singularity, is the lower and earthlier form of religion. The life of Godliness is the glory of Christ. It is a thing far more striking to the vulgar imagination to be religious after the type and pattern of John the Baptist — to fast — to mortify every inclination — to be found at no feast — to wrap ourselves in solitariness, and abstain from all social joys: yes, and far *easier* so to live, and far easier *so* to win a character for religiousness. A silent man is easily reputed wise. A man who suffers none to see him in the common jostle and undress of life, easily gathers round him a mysterious veil of unknown sanctity, and men honour him for a saint. The unknown is always wonderful. But the life of Him whom men called a gluttonous man and a winebibber, a friend of publicans and sinners, was a far harder and a far heavenlier religion. To shroud ourselves in no false mist of holiness: to dare to show ourselves as we are, making no solemn affectation of reserve or difference from others: to be found at the marriage-feast: to accept the invitation of the rich Pharisee Simon, and the scorned Publican Zaccheus: to mix with the crowd of men, using no affected singularity, content to be "creatures not too bright or good for human nature's daily food:" and yet for a man amidst it all to remain a consecrated spirit, his trials and his solitariness known only to his Father — a being set apart, not *of* this world, alone in the heart's deeps with God: to put the cup of this world's gladness to his lips, and yet be unintoxicated: to gaze steadily on all its grandeur, and yet be undazzled, plain and simple in personal desires: to feel its brightness, and yet defy its thrall: — this is the difficult, and rare, and glorious life of God in the Soul of Man. This, this was the peculiar glory of the life of Christ, which was manifested in that first miracle which Jesus wrought at the marriage-feast in Cana of Galilee.

XX.

Preached March 20, 1853.

THE GOOD SHEPHERD.

JOHN x. 14, 15. — "I am the good shepherd, and know my sheep, and am known of mine. As the Father knoweth me, even so know I the Father: and I lay down my life for the sheep."

As these words stand in the English translation, it is hard to see any connection between the thoughts that are brought together.

It is asserted the Christ is the good Shepherd, and knows His sheep. It is also asserted that He knows the Father; but between these two truths there is no express connection. And again, it is declared that He lays down His life for the sheep. This follows directly after the assertion that He knows the Father. Again, we are at a loss to say what one of these truths has to do with the other.

But the whole difficulty vanishes with the alteration of a single stop and a single word. Let the words "even so" be exchanged for the word "and." Four times in these verses the same word occurs. Three times out of these four it is translated "and," — *and* know my sheep, *and* am known, *and* I lay down my life. All that is required then is, that in consistency it shall be translated by the same word in the fourth case: for "even so" substitute "and:" then strike away the full stop after "mine," and read the whole sentence thus: "I am the good shepherd, and know my sheep, and am known of mine as the Father knoweth me, *and* as I know the Father: and I lay down my life for the sheep."

At once our Redeemer's thought becomes clear. There is a reciprocal affection between the Shepherd and the sheep. There is a reciprocal affection between the Father and the Son; and the one is the parallel of the other. The affection between the Divine Shepherd and His flock can be compared, for the closeness of its intimacy, with nothing but the affection between the Eternal Father and the Son of His Love. As the Father knows the Son, so does the Shepherd know the sheep: as the Son knows the Father, so do the sheep know their heavenly Shepherd.

I. The pastoral character claimed by Christ.

II. The proofs which substantiate the claim.

I. The Son of Man claims to Himself the name of *Shepherd*.

Now we shall not learn anything from that, unless we enter humbly and affectionately into the spirit of Christ's teaching. It is the heart alone which can give us a key to His words. Recollect *how* He taught. By metaphors, by images, by illustrations, boldly figurative, in rich variety — yes, in daring abundance. He calls Himself a gate — a king — a vine — a shepherd — a thief in the night. In every one of these He appeals to certain feelings and associations. What he says can only be interpreted by such associations. They must be understood by a living heart: a cold, clear intellect will make nothing of them. If you take those glorious expressions, pregnant with almost boundless thought, and lay them down as so many articles of rigid, stiff theology, you turn life into death. It is just as if a chemist were to analyze a fruit or a flower, and then imagine that he had told you what a fruit and a flower are. He separates them into their elements, names them, and numbers them: but those elements, weighed, measured, numbered in the exact proportions that made up the beautiful living thing, are not the living thing — no, nor anything like it. Your science is very profound, no doubt; but the fruit is crushed, and the grace of the flower is gone.

It is in this way often that we deal with the words of Christ, when we anatomized them and analyze them. Theology is very necessary, chemistry is very necessary; but chemistry destroys life to analyze, murders to dissect; and theology very often kills religion out of words before it can cut them up into propositions.

Here is a living truth which our cold reasonings have often torn into dead fragments — "I am the good Shepherd." In this northern England, it is hard to get the living associations of the East with which such an expression is full.

The pastoral life and duty in the East is very unlike that of the shepherds on our bleak hill-sides and downs. Here the connection between the shepherd and the sheep is simply one of pecuniary interest. Ask an English shepherd about his flock, he can tell you the numbers and the value; he knows the market in which each was purchased, and the remunerating price at which it can be disposed of. There is before him so much stock convertible into so much money.

Beneath the burning skies and the clear starry nights of Palestine there grows up between the shepherd and his flock an union of attachment and tenderness. It is the country where at any moment sheep are liable to be swept away by some mountain-torrent, or carried off by hill-robbers, or torn by wolves. At any moment their protector may have to save them by personal hazard. The shepherd-king tells us how, in defence of his father's flock, he slew a lion and a bear: and Jacob reminds Laban how, when he watched Laban's sheep in the day, the drought consumed. Every hour of the shepherd's life is risk. Sometimes for the sake of an armful of grass in the parched summer days, he must climb precipices almost perpendicular, and stand on a narrow ledge of rock, where the wild goat will scarcely venture. Pitiless showers, driving snows, long hours of thirst — all this he must endure, if the flock is to be kept at all.

And thus there grows up between the man and the dumb creatures he protects, a kind of friendship. For this is after all the true school in which love is taught, dangers mutually shared, and hardships borne together; these are the things which make generous friendship — risk cheerfully encountered for another's sake. You love those for whom you risk, and they love you; therefore it is that, not as here where the flock is driven, the shepherd goes before and the sheep follow him. They follow in perfect trust, even though he should be leading them away from a green pasture, by a rocky road, to another pasture which they cannot yet see. He knows them all — their separate histories — their ailments — their characters.

Now, let it be observed, how much in all this connection there is of *heart* — of real, personal attachment, almost inconceivable to us. It is strange how deep the sympathy may become between the higher and the lower being: nay, even between the being that has life and what is lifeless. Alone almost in the desert, the Arab and his horse are one family. Alone in those vast solitudes, with no human being near, the shepherd and the sheep feel a life in common. Differences disappear, the vast interval between the man and the brute: the single point of union is felt strongly. One is the love of the protector: the other the love of the grateful life: and so between lives so distant there is woven by night and day, by summer suns and winter frosts, a living network of sympathy. The greater and the less mingle their being together: they feel each other. "The shepherd knows his sheep and is known of them."

The men to whom Christ said these words felt all this and more, the moment He had said them, which it has taken me many minutes to draw out in dull sentences: for He appealed to the familiar associations of their daily life, and calling Himself a Shepherd, touched strings which would vibrate with many a tender and pure recollection of their childhood. And unless we try, by realizing such scenes, to supply what they felt by association, the words of Christ will be only hard, dry, lifeless words to us: for all Christ's teaching is a Divine Poetry, luxuriant in metaphor, overflowing with truth too large for accurate sentences, truth which only a heart alive can appreciate. More than half the heresies into which Christian sects have blundered, have merely come from mistaking for dull prose what prophets and apostles said in those highest moments of the soul, when seraphim kindle the sentences of the pen and lip into poetry. "This is my body." Chill that into prose, and it becomes Transubstantintion. "I am the Good Shepherd." In the dry and merciless logic of a commentary, trying laboriously to find out minute points of ingenious resemblance in which Christ is like a shepherd, the glory and the tenderness of this sentence are dried up.

But try to feel, by imagining what the lonely Syrian shepherd must feel towards the helpless things which are the companions of his daily life, for whose safety he stands in jeopardy every hour, and whose value is measurable to him not by price, but by his own jeopardy, and then we have reached some notion of the love which Jesus meant to represent, that Eternal Tenderness which bends over us — infinitely lower though we be in nature — and knows the name of each and the trials of each, and thinks for each with a separate solicitude, and gave Itself for each with a Sacrifice as special and a Love as personal, as if in the whole world's wilderness there were none other but that one.

To the name Shepherd, Christ adds an emphatic word of much significance: "I am the *Good* Shepherd." Good, not in the sense of benevolent, but in the sense of genuine, true born, of the real kind — just as wine of nobler quality is good compared with the cheaper sort, just as a soldier is good or noble who is a soldier in heart, and not a soldier by mere profession or for pay. It is the same word used by St. Paul when he speaks of a good, *i. e.* a noble soldier of Christ. Certain peculiar qualifications make the genuine soldier — certain peculiar qualifications make the genuine or good shepherd.

Now this expression distinguishes the shepherd from two sorts of men who may also be keepers of the sheep:

shepherds, but not shepherds of the true blood. 1. From robbers. 2. From hirelings.

1. Robbers may turn shepherds: they may keep the sheep, but they guard them only for their own purposes, simply for the flesh and fleece: they have not a true shepherd's heart, any more than a pirate has the true sailor's heart, and the true sailor's loyalty. There were many such marauders on the hills of Galilee and Judea: such, for example, as those from whom David and his band protected Nabal's flocks on Mount Carmel.

And many such nominal shepherds had the people of Israel had in bygone years: rulers in whom the art of ruling had been but kingcraft; teachers whose instruction to the people had been but priestcraft. Government, statesmanship, teachership — these are pastoral callings — sublime, even Godlike. For only consider it: — wise rule, chivalrous protection, loving guidance, — what diviner work than these has the Master given to the shepherds of the people? But when the work is done, even well done, whether it be by statesmen or by pastors, for the sake of party or place, or honour, or personal consistency, or preferment, it is not the spirit of the genuine shepherd, but of the robber. No wonder He said, "All that ever became before Me were thieves and robbers."

Again, hirelings are shepherds, but not good shepherds, of the right pure kind: they are tested by danger. "He that is an hireling, and not the good shepherd, whose own the sheep are not, seeth the wolf coming, and leaveth the sheep, and fleeth; and the wolf catcheth them, and scattereth the sheep."

Now a man is a hireling when he does his duty for

pay. He may do it in his way faithfully. The paid shepherd would not desert the sheep for a shower or a cold night. But the lion and the bear — he is not paid to risk his life against them, and the sheep are not his, so he leaves them to their fate. So, in the same way, a man may be a hired priest, as Demetrius was at Ephesus: "By this craft we get our living." Or a paid demagogue, a great champion of rights, and an investigator of abuses — paid by applause; and while popularity lasts, he will be a reformer — deserting the people when danger comes. There is no vital union between the champion and the defenceless — the teacher and the taught. The cause of the sheep is not *his* cause.

Exactly the reverse of this Christ asserts in calling Himself the *Good* Shepherd. *He* is a good, genuine, or true-born sailor who feels that the ship is as it were his own; whose point of chivalrous honour is to save his ship rather than himself — not to survive her. He is a good, genuine, or true-born shepherd who has the spirit of his calling, is an enthusiast in it, has the true shepherd's heart, and makes the cause of the sheep his cause.

Brethren, the Cause of man was the Cause of Christ. He did no hireling's work. The only pay He got was hatred, a crown of thorns, and the cross. He might have escaped it all. He might have been the Leader of the people and their King. He might have converted the idolatry of an hour into the hosannas of a lifetime: if He would but have conciliated the Pharisees, instead of bidding them defiance and exasperating their bigotry against Him: if He would but have explained, and, like some demagogue called to account, trimmed away His sublime sharp-edged truths about oppression and injustice until they became harmless, because meaningless: if He would but have left unsaid those rough things about the consecrated Temple and the Sabbath-days: if He would but have left undisputed the hereditary title of Israel to God's favour, and not stung the national vanity by telling them that trust in God justifies the Gentile as entirely as the Jew: if He would but have taught less prominently that hateful doctrine of the salvability of the heathen Gentiles and the heretic Samaritans, aud the universal Fatherhood of God: if He would but have stated with less angularity of edge His central truth, that not by mere compliance with law, but by a spirit transcending law, even the spirit of the cross and self-sacrifice, can the soul of man be atoned to God: — that would have saved Him. But that would have been the desertion of the Cause — God's Cause and man's — the Cause of the ignorant defenceless sheep, whose very salvation depended on the keeping of that gospel intact: therefore the Shepherd gave His life a Witness to the truth, and a sacrifice to God. It was a profound truth that the populace gave utterance to when they taunted Him on the cross: "He saved others, Himself He cannot save." No, of course not; He that will save others *cannot* save Himself.

Of that pastoral character He gives here three proofs. I know My sheep — am known of Mine — lay down my life for the sheep.

1. I know my sheep, as the Father knoweth Me. In other words, as unerringly as His Father read His heart, so unerringly did He read the heart of man and recognise His own.

Ask we how? An easy reply, and a common one, would be — He recognised them by the Godhead in Him: His mind was Divine, therefore omniscient: He knew all things, therefore He knew what was in man: and therefore He knew His own.

But we must not slur over His precious words in this way. That Divinity of His is made the pass-key by which we open all mysteries with fatal facility, and save ourselves from thinking of them. We get a dogma and cover truth with it: we satisfy ourselves with saying Christ was God, and lose the precious humanities of His heart and life.

There is here a deep truth of human nature, for He does not limit that recognising power to Himself — He says that the sheep know Him as truly as He the sheep. He knew men on the same principle on which we know men — the same on which we know Him. The only difference is in degree: He knows with infinitely more unerringness than we, but the knowledge is the same in kind.

Let us think of this. There is a certain mysterious tact of sympathy and antipathy by which we discover the like and unlike of ourselves in others' character. You cannot find out a man's opinions unless he chooses to express them; but his feelings and his character you may. He cannot hide them: you feel them in his look and mien, and tones and motion.

There is, for instance, a certain something in sincerity and reality which cannot be mistaken — a certain something in real grief which the most artistic counterfeit cannot imitate. It is distinguished by nature, not education. There is a something in an impure heart which purity detects afar off. Marvellous it is how innocence perceives the approach of evil which it cannot know by experience, just as the dove which has never seen a falcon trembles by instinct at its approach; just as a blind man detects by finer sensitiveness the passing of the cloud which he cannot see overshadowing the sun. It is wondrous how the truer we become, the more unerringly we know the *ring* of truth, discern whether a man be true or not, and can fasten at once upon the rising lie in word and look, and dissembling act. Wondrous how the charity of Christ in the heart finely perceives the slightest aberration from charity in others, in ungentle thought or slanderous tone.

Therefore Christ knew His sheep by that mystic power always finest in the best natures, most developed in the highest, by which Like detects what is like and what unlike itself. He was Perfect Love — Perfect Truth — Perfect Purity: therefore He knew what was in man, and felt, as by another sense, afar off the shadows of unlovingness, and falseness, and impurity.

No one can have read the Gospels without remarking that they ascribe to Him unerring skill in reading man. People, we read, began to show enthusiasm for Him. But Jesus did not trust Himself unto them, "for He knew what was in man." He knew that the flatterers of to-day would be the accusers of to-morrow. Nathaniel stood before Him. He had scarcely spoken a word; but at once unhesitatingly, to Nathaniel's own astonishment, — "Behold an Israelite indeed, in whom there is no guile!" There came to Him a young man with vast possessions: a single sentence, an exaggerated epithet, an excited manner, revealed his character. Enthusiastic and amiable, Jesus loved him:

capable of obedience, in life's sunshine and prosperity, ay, and capable of aspiration after something more than mere obedience, but not of sacrifice. Jesus tested him to the quick, and the young man failed. He did not try to call him back, for He knew what was in him and what was not. He read through Zaccheus when he climbed into the sycamore-tree, despised by the people as a publican, really a son of Abraham: through Judas, with his benevolent saying about the selling of the alabaster-box for the poor, and his false kiss: through the curses of the thief upon the cross, a faith that could be saved: through the zeal of the man who in a fit of enthusiasm offered to go with Him whithersoever He would. He read through the Pharisees, and His whole being shuddered with the recoil of utter and irreconcilable aversion.

It was as if His bosom was some mysterious mirror on which all that came near Him left a sullied or unsullied surface, detecting themselves by every breath.

Now distinguish that Divine power from that cunning sagacity which men call knowingness in the matter of character. The worldly wise have maxims and rules; but the finer shades and delicacies of truth of character escape them. They would prudently avoid Zaccheus — a publican: they —

There is a very solemn aspect in which this power of Jesus to know man presents itself. It is this which qualifies Him for judgment — this perfection of human sympathy. Perfect sympathy with every most delicate line of good implies exquisite antipathy to every shadow of a shade of evil. God hath given Him authority to execute judgment also, because He is the Son of Man. On sympathy the final awards of Heaven and Hell are built: Attraction and Repulsion, the law of the magnet. To each pole all that has affinity with itself: *to* Christ all that is Christlike: *from* Christ all that is not Christlike — for ever and for ever. Eternal judgment is nothing more than the carrying out of these words, "I know my sheep:" — for the obverse of them is, "I never knew *you*, depart from me all ye that work iniquity."

The second proof which Christ alleges of the genuineness of His pastorate is that His sheep know *Him*.

How shall we recognise Truth Divine? What is the test by which we shall know whether it comes from God or not? They tell us we know Christ to be from God because He wrought miracles: we know a doctrine to be from God because we find it written: or because it is sustained by an universal consent of fathers.

That is — for observe what this argument implies — there is something more evident than truth: Truth cannot prove itself: we want something else to prove it. Our souls judge of truth — our senses judge of miracles; and the evidence of our senses — the lowest part of our nature — is more certain than the evidence of our souls, by which we must partake of God.

Now to say so, is to say that you cannot be sure that it is midday or morning sunshine unless you look at the sun-dial: you cannot be sure that the sun is shining in the heavens unless you see his shadow on the dial-plate. The dial is valuable to a man who never reads the heavens — the shadow is good for him who has not watched the sun: but for a man who lives in perpetual contemplation of the sun in heaven, the sunshine needs no evidence, and every hour is known.

Now Christ says, "My sheep know *Me*." Wisdom is justified by her children. Not by some lengthened investigation, whether the shepherd's dress be the identical dress, and the staff and the crozier genuine, do the sheep recognise the shepherd. They know *him*, they hear his voice, they know him as a man knows his friend.

They know him, in short, *instinctively*. Just so does the soul recognise what is of God and true. Truth is like light: visible in itself, not distinguished by the shadows that it casts. There is a something in our souls, of God, which corresponds with what is of God outside us, and recognises it by direct intuition: something in the true soul which corresponds with truth and knows it to be truth. Christ came with truth, and the true recognise it as true: the sheep know the Shepherd, wanting no further evidence. Take a few examples: "God is Love." "What shall a man give in exchange for his soul?" "He that saveth his life shall lose it: and he that loseth his life for my sake shall find it." "All things are possible to him that believeth." "The Sabbath was made for man, not man for the Sabbath." "God is a Spirit."

Now the wise men of intellect and logical acumen wanted proof of these truths. Give us, said they, your credentials. "By what authority doest thou these things?" They wanted a sign from heaven to prove that the truth was true, and the life He led, God-like, and not devil-like. How can we be sure that it is not from Beelzebub, the prince of the devils, that these deeds and sayings come? We must be quite sure that we are not taking a message from hell as one from heaven. Give us demonstration, chains of evidence — chapter and verse — authority.

But simple men had decided the matter already. They knew very little of antiquity, church authority, and shadows of coming events which prophecy casts before: but their eyes saw the light, and their hearts felt the present God. Wise Pharisees and learned doctors said, to account for a wondrous miracle, "Give God the glory."

But the poor unlettered man, whose blinded eye had for the first time looked on a face of love, replied — "Whether this man be a sinner or not, I know not: one thing I know, that whereas I was blind, now I see."

The well-read Jews could not settle the literary question, whether the marks of his appearance coincided with the prophecies. But the Samaritans *felt* the life of God: "Now we believe, not because of thy word, but because we have heard Him ourselves and *know* that this is indeed the Christ."

The Shepherd had come, and the sheep knew His voice. Brethren, in all matters of eternal truth, the soul is before the intellect: the things of God are spiritually discerned. You know truth by being true: you recognise God by being like Him. The scribe comes and says, I will prove to you that this is sound doctrine by chapter and verse, by what the old and best writers say, by evidence such as convinces the intellect of an intelligent lawyer or juryman. Think you the conviction of faith is got in that way?

Christ did not teach like the scribes. He spoke His truth. He said, "If any man believe not, I judge him not; the word which I have spoken, the same shall judge him in the last day." It was true, and the guilt of disbelieving it was not an error of the intellect, but a sin of the heart.

Let us stand upright: let us be sure that the test of truth is the soul within us. Not at second-hand can we have assurance of what is divine and what is not: only at first-hand. The sheep of Christ hear His voice.

The third proof given by Christ was pastoral fidelity: "I lay down my life for the sheep." Now here is the doctrine of vicarious sacrifice: sacrifice of one instead of another: life saved by the sacrifice of life.

Most of us know the meagre explanation of these words which satisfies the Unitarians: they say that Christ merely died as a martyr, in attestation of the truths He taught.

But you will observe the strength of the expression which we cannot explain away, "I lay down my life *for*," *i. e.* instead of "the sheep." If the Shepherd had not sacrificed Himself, the sheep must have been the sacrifice.

Observe, however, the suffering of Christ was not the same suffering as that from which He saved us. The suffering of Christ was death. But the suffering from which He redeemed us by death was more terrible than death. The pit into which He descended was the grave. But the pit in which we should have been lost for ever, was the pit of selfishness and despair.

Therefore St. Paul affirms, "If Christ be not risen, ye are yet in your *sins*." If Christ's resurrection be a dream, and He be not risen from the grave of death, you are yet in the grave of guilt. He bore suffering to free us from what is worse than suffering — sin: temporal death to save us from death everlasting: His life given as an offering for sin to save the soul's eternal life.

Now in the text this sacrificing love of Christ is paralleled by the love of the Father to the Son. As He loved the sheep, so the Father had loved Him. Therefore the sacrifice of Christ is but a mirror of the love of God. The love of the Father to the Son is self-sacrificing Love.

You know that shallow men make themselves merry with this doctrine. The sacrifice of God, they say, is a figment, and an impossibility. Nevertheless this parallel tells us that it is one of the deepest truths of all the universe. It is the profound truth which the ancient fathers endeavoured to express in the doctrine of the Trinity. For what is the love of the Father to the Son — Himself yet not Himself — but the grand truth of Eternal Love losing Itself and finding Itself again in the being of another? What is it but the sublime expression of the unselfishness of God?

It is a profound, glorious truth; I wish I knew how to put it in intelligible words. But if these words of Christ do not make it intelligible to the heart, how can any words of mine? The life of blessedness — the life of love — the life of sacrifice — the life of God, are identical. All love is sacrifice — the giving of life and self for others. God's life is sacrifice — for the Father loves the Son *as* the Son loves the sheep for whom He gave His life.

Whoever will humbly ponder upon this, will, I think, understand the Atonement better than all theology can teach him. O, my brethren, leave men to quarrel as they will about the theology of the Atonement; here in these words is the religion of it — the blessed, all-satisfying religion for our hearts. The self-sacrifice of Christ was the *satisfaction* to the Father.

How could the Father be *satisfied* with the death of Christ, unless He saw in the sacrifice mirrored His own love? — for God can be satisfied only with that which is perfect as Himself. Agony does not satisfy God — agony only satisfied Moloch. Nothing satisfies God but the voluntary sacrifice of Love.

The pain of Christ gave God no pleasure — only the love that was tested by pain — the love of the obedient. He was obedient unto death.

XXI.

Preached Easter Day, March 27, 1853.

THE DOUBT OF THOMAS.

JOHN xx. 29. — "Jesus saith unto him, Thomas, because thou hast seen me, thou hast believed: blessed are they that have not seen, and yet have believed."

THE day on which these words were spoken was the first day of the week. On that day Thomas received demonstration that his Lord was risen from the dead. On that same day, a week before, Thomas had declared that no testimony of others, no eyesight of his own, nothing short of touching with his hands the crucifixion marks in his Master's body, should induce him to believe a fact so unnatural as the resurrection of a human being from the grave. Those seven days between must therefore have been spent in a state of miserable uncertainty. How miserable and how restless none can understand but those who have felt the wretchedness of earnest doubt.

Doubt moreover, observe, respecting all that is dear to a Christian's hopes. For if Christ were not risen, Christianity was false, and every high aspiration which it promised to gratify, was thrown back on the disappointed heart.

Let us try to understand the doubt of Thomas. There are some men whose affections are stronger than their understandings: they feel more than they think. They are simple, trustful, able to repose implicitly on what is told them — liable sometimes to verge upon credulity and superstition, but take them all in all, perhaps the happiest class of minds: for it is happy to be without misgivings about the love of God and our own eternal rest in Him. "Blessed," said Christ to Thomas, "are they that have believed."

There is another class of men whose reflective powers are stronger than their susceptive: they think out truth — they do not feel it out. Often highly gifted and powerful minds, they cannot rest till they have made all their grounds certain: they do not feel safe as long as there is one possibility of delusion left: they prove all things. Such a man was Thomas. He has well been called the rationalist among the apostles. Happy such men cannot be. An anxious and inquiring mind dooms its possessor to unrest. But men of generous spirit, manly and affectionate, they may be: Thomas was. When Christ was bent on going to Jerusalem, to certain death, Thomas said, "Let us go up too, that we may die with Him." And men of mighty faith they may become, if they are true to themselves and their convictions: Thomas did. When such men *do* believe, it is belief with all the heart and soul for life. When a subject has been once thoroughly and suspiciously investigated, and settled once for all, the adherence of the whole reasoning man, if given in at all, is given frankly and heartily as Thomas gave it — "My Lord, and my God."

Now this question of a resurrection which made Thomas restless, is the most anxious that can agitate the mind of man. So awful in its importance, and out of Christ so almost desperately dark in its uncertainty, who shall blame an earnest man severely if he crave the most indisputable proofs?

Very clearly Christ did not. Thomas asked of Christ a sign: he must put his own hands into the prints. His

Master gave him that sign or proof. He said, "Reach hither thy hand." He gave it, it is true, with a gentle and delicate reproof — but He did give it. Now from that condescension, we are reminded of the darkness that hangs round the question of a resurrection, and how excusable it is for a man to question earnestly until he has got proof to stand on. For if it were not excusable to crave a proof, our Master never would have granted one. Resurrection is not one of those questions on which you can afford to wait: it is the question of life and death. There are times when it does not weigh heavily. When we have some keen pursuit before us: when we are young enough to be satisfied to enjoy ourselves — the problem does not press itself. We are too laden with the pressure of the present, to care to ask what is coming. But at last a time comes when we feel it will be all over soon — that much of our time is gone, and the rest swiftly going. And let a man be as frivolous as he will at heart, it is a question too solemn to be put aside — Whether he is going down into extinction and the blank of everlasting silence or not. Whether in those far ages, when the very oak which is to form his coffin shall have become fibres of black mould, and the churchyard in which he is to lie shall have become perhaps unconsecrated ground, and the spades of a generation yet unborn shall have exposed his bones, those bones will be the last relic in the world to bear record that he once trod this green earth, and that life was once dear to him, Thomas, or James, or Paul. Or whether that thrilling, loving, thinking something, that he calls himself, has indeed within it an indestructible existence which shall still be conscious, when everything else shall have rushed into endless wreck. O in the awful earnestness of a question such as that, a speculation and a peradventure will not do: we must have proof. The honest doubt of Thomas craves a sign as much as the cold doubt of the Sadducee. And a sign shall be mercifully given to the doubt of love which is refused to the doubt of indifference.

This passage presents two lines of thought.

I. The naturalness of the doubts of Thomas, which partly excuses them.

II. The evidences of the Christian Resurrection.

The naturalness of the doubts of Thomas.

The first assertion that we make to explain those doubts is, that Nature is silent respecting a future life. All that reason, all that nature, all that religion, apart from Christ, have to show us is something worse than darkness. It is the twilight of excruciating uncertainty. There is enough in the riddle of this world to show us that there *may* be a life to come; there is nothing to make it certain that there *will* be one. We crave as Thomas did, a sign either in the height above or in the depth beneath, and the answer seems to fall back like ice upon our hearts — there shall no sign be given you.

It is the uncertainty of twilight. You strain at something in the twilight, and just when you are beginning to make out its form and colour, the light fails you, and your eyelid sinks down, wet and wearied with the exertion. Just so it is when we strain into Nature's mysteries, to discern the secret of the Great Hereafter. Exactly at the moment when we think we begin to distinguish something, the light goes out, and we are left groping in darkness — the darkness of the grave.

Let us forget for a moment that we ever heard of Christ: what is there in life or nature to strengthen the guess that there is a life to come? There are hints — there are probabilities — there is nothing more. Let us examine some of those probabilities.

First, there is an irrepressible longing in our hearts. We *wish* for immortality. The thought of annihilation is horrible: even to conceive it is almost impossible. The wish is a kind of argument: it is not likely that God would have given all men such a feeling, if He had not meant to gratify it. Every natural longing has its natural satisfaction. If we thirst, God has created liquids to gratify thirst. If we are susceptible of attachment, there are beings to gratify that love. If we thirst for life and love eternal, it is likely that there are an eternal life and an eternal love to satisfy that craving.

Likely, I say: more we cannot say. A likelihood of an immortality of which our passionate yearnings are a presumption, nothing higher than a likelihood. And in weary moments, when the desire of life is not strong, and in unloving moments, there is not even a likelihood.

Secondly, corroborating this feeling we have the traditions of universal belief. There is not a nation perhaps, which does not in some form or other hold that there is a country beyond the grave where the weary are at rest. Now that which all men everywhere and in every age have held, it is impossible to treat contemptuously. How came it to be held by all, if only a delusion? Here is another probability in the universality of belief. And yet when you come to estimate this, it is too slender for a proof: — it is only a presumption. The universal voice of mankind is not infallible. It was the universal belief once on the evidence of the senses that the earth was stationary: — the universal voice was wrong. The universal voice might be wrong in the matter of a resurrection. It might be only a beautiful and fond dream, indulged till hope made itself seem to be a reality. You cannot build upon it.

Once again — In this strange world of perpetual change, we are met by many resemblances to a resurrection. Without much exaggeration we call them resurrections. There is the resurrection of the moth from the grave of the chrysalis. For many ages the sculptured butterfly was the type and emblem of immortality. Because it passes into a state of torpor or deadness, and because from that it emerges by a kind of resurrection — the same, yet not the same — in all the radiance of a fresh and beautiful youth, never again to be supported by the coarse substance of earth, but destined henceforth to nourish its etherealized existence on the nectar of the flowers — the ancients saw in that transformation a something added to their hopes of immortality. It was their beautiful symbol of the soul's indestructibility.

Again, there is a kind of resurrection when the spring brings vigour and motion back to the frozen pulse of the winter world. Let any one go into the fields at this spring season of the year. Let him mark the busy preparations for life which are going on. Life is at work in every emerald bud, in the bursting bark of every polished bough, in the greening tints of every brown hillside. A month ago everything was as still and cold as the dead silence which chills the heart in the highest regions of the glacier solitudes. Life is coming back to a dead world. It is a resurrection surely! The return of freshness to the frozen world is not less marvellous than the return of sensibility to a heart which has ceased to beat. If one has taken place, the other is not impossible.

And yet all this, valuable as it is in the way of suggestiveness, is worth nothing in the way of proof. It is worth everything to the heart, for it strengthens the dim guesses and vague intimations which the heart has formed already. It is worth nothing to the intellect: for the moment we come to argue the matter, we find how little there is to rest upon in these analogies. They are no real resurrections after all: they only look like resurrections. The chrysalis only *seemed* dead: the tree in winter only seemed to have lost its vitality. Show us a butterfly which has been dried and crushed, fluttering its brilliant wings next year again. Show us a tree plucked up by the roots and seasoned by exposure, the vital force really killed out, putting forth its leaves again, then we should have a real parallel to a resurrection. But nature does not show us that. So that all we have got in the butterfly and the spring are illustrations exquisitely in point *after* immortality is proved, but in themselves no proofs at all.

Further still. Look at it in another point of view, and it is a dark prospect. Human history behind and human history before, both give a stern "No," in reply to the question — Shall we rise again?

Six thousand years of human existence have passed away; countless armies of the dead have set sail from the shores of time. No traveller has returned from the still land beyond. More than one hundred and fifty generations have done their work and sunk into the dust again, and still there is not a voice; there is not a whisper from the grave to tell us whether indeed those myriads are in existence still. Besides, why should they be? Talk as you will of the grandeur of man, why should it not be honour enough for him, more than enough to satisfy a thing so mean, to have had his twenty or his seventy years' life-rent of God's universe? Why must such a thing, apart from proof, rise up and claim to himself an exclusive immortality? Man's majesty! man's worth! the difference between him and the elephant or ape is too degradingly small to venture much on. That is not all: instead of looking backwards, now look forwards. The wisest thinkers tell us that there are already on the globe traces of a demonstration that the human race is drawing to its close. Each of the great human families has had its day — its infancy — its manhood — its decline. The two last races that have not been tried are on the stage of earth doing their work now. There is no other to succeed them. Man is but of yesterday, and yet his race is well-nigh done. Man is wearing out as everything before him has been worn out. In a few more centuries the crust of earth will be the sepulchre of the race of man, as it has been the sepulchre of extinct races of palm-trees, and ferns, and gigantic reptiles. The time is near when the bones of the last human being will be given to the dust. It is historically certain that man has quite lately within a few thousand years been called into existence. It is certain that before very long the race must be extinct.

Now look at all this without Christ, and tell us whether it be possible to escape such misgivings, and such reasonings as these which rise out of such an aspect of things. Man, this thing of yesterday, which sprung out of the eternal nothingness, why may he not sink after he has played his appointed part into nothingness again? You see the leaves sinking one by one in autumn, till the heaps below are rich with the spoils of a whole year's vegetation. They were bright and perfect while they lasted: each leaf a miracle of beauty and contrivance. There is no resurrection for the leaves — why must there be one for man? Go and stand some summer evening by the river side: you will see the mayfly sporting out its little hour, in dense masses of insect life, darkening the air, a few feet above the gentle swell of the water. The heat of that very afternoon brought them into existence. Every gauze wing is traversed by ten thousand fibres which defy the microscope to find a flaw in their perfection. The Omniscience and the care bestowed upon that exquisite anatomy, one would think cannot be destined to be wasted in a moment. Yet so it is: when the sun has sunk below the trees, its little life is done. Yesterday it was not: to-morrow it will not be. God has bidden it be happy for one evening. It has no right or claim to a second, and in the universe that marvellous life has appeared once and will appear no more. May not the race of man sink like the generations of the mayfly? Why cannot the Creator, so lavish in his resources, afford to annihilate souls as he annihilates insects?

Would it not almost enhance His glory to believe it?

That, brethren, is the question; and Nature has no reply. The fearful secret of sixty centuries has not yet found a voice. The whole evidence lies before us. We know what the greatest and wisest have had to say in favour of an immortality; and we know how, after eagerly devouring all their arguments, our hearts have sunk back in cold disappointment, and to every proof as we read, our lips have replied mournfully, *that* will not stand. Search through tradition, history, the world within you and the world without, — except in Christ there is not the shadow of a shade of proof that man survives the grave.

I do not wonder that Thomas, with that honest accurate mind of his, wishing that the news were true, yet dreading lest it should be false, and determined to guard against every possible illusion, delusion, and deception, said so strongly, "Except I shall see in his hands the print of the nails, and put my finger into the print of the nails, and thrust my hand into his side, I will not believe."

II. The Christian proofs of a Resurrection.

This text tells us of two kinds of proof: The first is the evidence of the senses — "Thomas, because thou hast seen me, thou hast believed." The other is the Evidence of the Spirit — "Blessed are they that have not seen, and yet have believed."

Let us scrutinize the external evidence of Christ's resurrection which those verses furnish. It is a twofold evidence: The witness of the Apostle Thomas, who was satisfied with the proofs — the witness of St. John, who records the circumstance of his satisfaction. Consider first the witness of St. John: try it by ordinary rules. Hearsay evidence, which comes secondhand, is suspicious, but St. John's is no distant hearsay story. He does not say that he had heard the story from Thomas, and that years afterwards, when the circumstances had lost their exact sharp outline, he had penned it down, when he was growing old and his memory might be failing. St. John was present the whole time. All the apostles were there: they all watched the result with eager interest. The conditions made by Thomas, without which he would not believe, had been made before them all. They all heard him say that the demonstration was complete: they all saw him touch the wounds: and St. John recorded what he saw. Now a scene like that, is one of those solemn ones in a man's life which cannot be forgotten: it graves itself on the memory. A story told us by another may be unintentionally altered or exaggerated in the repetition; but a spectacle like this, so strange and so solemn, could not be forgotten or misinterpreted. St. John could have made no mistake. Estimate next the worth of the witness of Thomas: try it by the ordinary rules of life. Evidence is worth little if it is the evidence of credulity. If you find a man believing every new story, and accepting every fresh discovery so called, without scrutiny, you may give him credit for sincerity; you cannot rest much upon his judgment: his testimony cannot go for much. For example, when St. Peter, after his escape from prison, knocked at Mark's mother's door, there went a maid to open it, who came back scared and startled with the tidings that she had seen his angel or spirit. Had she gone about afterwards among the believers with that tale, that St. Peter was dead and alive again, it would have been worth little. Her fears, her sex, her credulity, all robbed her testimony of its worth.

Now the resurrection of Christ does not stand on such a footing. There was one man who dreaded the possibility of delusion, however credulous the others might be. He resolved beforehand that only one proof should be decisive. He would not be contented with seeing Christ: that might be a dream: it might be the vision of a disordered fancy. He would not be satisfied with the assurance of others. The evidence of testimony which he did reject was very strong. Ten of his most familiar friends, and certain women, gave in their separate and their united testimony; but against all that St. Thomas held out sceptically firm. They might have been deceived themselves: they might have been trifling with him. The possibilities of mistake were innumerable: the delusions of the best men about what they see are incredible. He would trust a thing so infinitely important to nothing but his own scrutinizing hand. It might be some one personating his Master. He would put his hands into real wounds, or else hold it unproved. The allegiance which was given in so enthusiastically, "My Lord, and my God," was given in after, and not before scrutiny. It was the cautious verdict of an enlightened, suspicious, most earnest, and most honest sceptic.

Try the evidence next by character. Blemished character damages evidence. Now the only charge that was ever heard against the Apostle John was that he loved a world which hated him. The character of the Apostle Thomas is that he was a man cautious in receiving evidence, and most rigorous in exacting satisfactory proof, but ready to act upon his convictions when once made, even to the death. Love, elevated above the common love of man, in the one — heroic conscientiousness and a most rare integrity in the other — who impeaches that testimony?

Once more — any possibility of interested motives will discredit evidence. Ask we the motive of John or Thomas for this strange tale? John's reward, — a long and solitary banishment to the mines of Patmos. The gain and the bribe which tempted Thomas, — a lonely pilgrimage to the far East, and death at the last in India. Those were strange motives to account for their persisting and glorying in the story of the resurrection to the last! Starving their gain, and martyrdom their price.

The evidence to which Thomas yielded was the evidence of the senses — touch, and sight, and hearing. Now the feeling which arose from this touching, and feeling, and demonstration, Christ pronounced to be faith: "Thomas, because thou hast seen, thou hast believed." There are some Christian writers who tell us that the conviction produced by the intellect or the senses is not faith: but Christ says it is. Observe then, it matters not *how* faith comes — whether through the intellect, as in the case of St. Thomas — or through the heart, as in the case of St. John — or as the result of long education, as in the case of St. Peter. God has many ways of bringing different characters to faith: but that blessed thing which the Bible calls faith is a *state* of soul in which the things of God become glorious certainties. It was not faith which assured Thomas that what stood before him was the Christ he had known: that was sight. But it was faith, which from the visible enabled him to pierce up to the truth invisible: "My Lord, and My God." And it was faith which enabled him through all life after, to venture everything on that conviction, and live for One who had died for him.

Remark again this: The faith of Thomas was not merely satisfaction about a fact: it was trust in a Person. The admission of a fact, however sublime, is not faith: we may believe that Christ is risen, yet not be nearer heaven. It is a Bible fact that Lazarus rose from the grave, but belief in Lazarus's resurrection does not make the soul better than it was. Thomas passed on from the fact of the resurrection to the Person of the risen: "My Lord, and my God." Trust in the risen Saviour — that was the belief which saved his soul.

And that is our salvation too. You may satisfy yourself about the evidences of the resurrection; you may bring in your verdict well, like a cautious and enlightened judge; you are then in possession of a fact, a most valuable and curious fact: but faith of any saving worth you have not, unless from the fact you pass on like Thomas, to cast the allegiance and the homage of your soul, and the love of all your being, on Him whom Thomas worshipped. It is not belief *about* the Christ, but personal trust *in* the Christ of God, that saves the soul.

There is another kind of evidence by which the Resurrection becomes certain. Not the evidence of the senses, but the evidence of the spirit: "Blessed are they that have not seen, and yet have believed." There are thousands of Christians who have never examined the evidences of the resurrection piece by piece: they are incapable of estimating it if they did examine: they know nothing about the laws of evidence: they have had no experience in balancing the value of testimony: they are neither lawyers nor philosophers: and yet these simple Christians have received into their very souls the Resurrection of their Redeemer, and look forward to their own rising from the grave with a trust as firm, as steady, and as saving, as if they had themselves put their hands into His wounds.

They have never seen — they know nothing of proofs and miracles — yet they believe, and are blessed. How is this?

I reply, there is an inward state of heart which makes truth credible the moment it is stated. It is credible to some men because of what they are. Love is credible to a loving heart: purity is credible to a pure mind: life is credible to a spirit in which, ever, life beats strongly: it is incredible to other men. Because of that such men believe. Of course that inward state could not *reveal* a fact like the resurrection; but it can *receive* the fact the moment it is revealed without requiring evidence. The love of St. John himself never could discover a resurrection; but it made a resurrection easily believed, when the man of intellect, St. Thomas, found difficulties. Therefore with the heart man believeth unto righteousness, and therefore he that believeth on the Son of God hath the witness in himself, and therefore Faith is the substance of things hoped for. Now it is of such a state, a state of love and hope, which makes the Divine truth credible and natural at once, that Jesus speaks: "Blessed are they that have not seen and yet have believed."

There are men in whom the resurrection begun makes the resurrection credible. In them the spirit of the risen Saviour works already; and they have mounted with Him from the grave. They have risen out of the darkness of doubt, and are expatiating in the brightness and the sunshine of a Day in which God is ever Light. Their step is as free as if the clay of the sepulchre had been shaken off: and their hearts are lighter than those of other men; and there is in them an unearthly triumph which they are unable to express. They have risen above the narrowness of life, and all that is petty, and ungenerous, and mean. They have risen above fear — They have risen above self. In the New Testament that is called the spiritual Resurrection, or being risen with Christ: and the man in whom all that is working has got something more blessed than external evidence to rest upon. He has the witness in himself: he has not seen, and yet he has believed: he believed in a resurrection, because he has the resurrection in himself. The resurrection in all its heavenliness and unearthly elevation has begun within his soul, and he knows as clearly as if he had demonstration, that it must be developed in an eternal life.

Now this is the higher and nobler kind of faith — a faith more blessed than that of Thomas. "Because thou hast seen me, *thou* hast believed." There are times when we envy, as possessed of higher privileges, those who saw Christ in the flesh: we think that if we could have heard that calm voice, or seen that blessed presence, or touched those lacerated wounds in His sacred flesh, all doubt would be set at rest for ever. Therefore these words must be our corrective. God has granted us the possibility of believing in a more trustful and more generous way than if we *saw*. To believe, not because we are learned and can prove, but because there is a something in us, even God's own Spirit, which makes us feel light as light, and truth as true — that is the blessed faith.

Blessed, because it carries with it spiritual elevation of character. Narrow the prospects of man to this time-world, and it is impossible to escape the conclusions of the Epicurean sensualist. If to-morrow we die, let us eat and drink to-day. If we die the sinner's death, it becomes a matter of mere taste whether we shall live the sinner's life or not. But if our existence is for ever, then plainly, that which is to be daily subdued and subordinated is the animal within us: that which is to be cherished is that which is likest God within us, — which we have from Him, and which is the sole pledge of eternal being in spirit-life.

XXII.

Preached May 8, 1853.

THE IRREPARABLE PAST.

MARK xiv. 41, 42. — "And he cometh the third time, and saith unto them, Sleep on now, and take your rest: it is enough, the hour is come; behold the Son of man is betrayed into the hands of sinners. Rise up, let us go; lo, he that betrayeth me is at hand."

It is upon two sentences of this passage that our attention is to be fixed to-day — sentences which in themselves are apparently contradictory, but which are pregnant with a lesson of the deepest practical import. Looked at in the mere meaning of the words as they stand, our Lord's first command given to His disciples, "Sleep on now, and take your rest," is inconsistent with the second command which follows almost in the same breath, "Rise, let us be going." A permission to slumber, and a warning to arouse at once, are injunctions which can scarcely stand together in the same sentence consistently.

Our first inquiry therefore is, what did our Redeemer mean? We shall arrive at the true solution of this difficulty if we review the circumstances under which these words were spoken. The account with which these verses stand connected, belongs to one of the last scenes in the drama of our Master's earthly pilgrimage: it is found in the history of the trial-hour which was passed in the garden of Gethsemane. And an hour it was indeed big with the destinies of the world, for the command had gone forth to seize the Saviour's person: but the Saviour was still at large and free. Upon the success or the frustration of that plan the world's fate was trembling. Three men were selected to be witnesses of the sufferings of that hour: three men, the favoured ones on all occasions of the apostolic band, and the single injunction which had been laid upon them was, "Watch with me one hour." That charge to watch or keep awake seems to have been given with two ends in view. He asked them to keep awake, first that they might sympathize with Him. He commanded them to keep awake that they might be on their guard against surprise: that they might afford sympathy, because never in all His career did Christ more stand in need of such soothing as it was in the power of man to give. It is true that was not much: the struggle, and the agony, and the making up of the mind to death had something in them too Divine and too mysterious to be understood by the disciples, and therefore sympathy could but reach a portion of what our Redeemer felt. Yet still it appears to have been an additional pang in Christ's anguish to find that He was left thoroughly alone — to endure, while even His own friends did not compassionate His endurance. We know what a relief it is to see the honest affectionate face of a menial servant, or some poor dependant, regretting that your suffering may be infinitely above his comprehension. It may be a secret which you cannot impart to him: or it may be a mental distress which his mind is too uneducated to appreciate: yet still his sympathy in your dark hour is worth a world. What you suffer he knows not, but he knows you do suffer, and it pains him to think of it: there is balm to you in that. This is the power of sympathy. We can do little for one another in this world. Little, very little, can be done when the worst must come; but yet to know that the pulses of a human heart are vibrating with yours, there is something in that, let the distance between man and man be ever so immeasurable, exquisitely soothing. It was this, and but this, in the way of feeling, that Christ asked of Peter, James, and John: Watch — be awake: let Me not feel that when I agonize, you can be at ease and comfortable. But it would seem there was another thing which He asked in the way of assistance. The plot to capture Him was laid; the chance of that plot's success lay in making the surprise so sudden as to cut off all possibility of escape. The hope of defeating that plot depended upon the fidelity of apostolic vigilance. Humanly speaking, had they been vigilant they might have saved Him. Breathless listening for the sound of footsteps in the distance: eyes anxiously straining through the trees to distinguish the glitter of the lanterns; unremitting apprehension catching from the word of Christ an intimation that He was in danger, and so giving notice on the first approach of anything like intrusion, — that would have been watching.

That command to watch was given twice — first, when Christ first retired aside leaving the disciples by themselves; secondly, in a reproachful way when He returned and found his request disregarded. He waked them up once and said, "What, could ye not watch with me one hour?" He came again, and found their eyes closed once more. On that occasion not a syllable fell from His lips; He did not waken them a second time. He passed away sad and disappointed, and left them to their slumbers. But when He came the third time, it was no longer possible for their sleep to do Him harm, or their watching to do Him good. The precious opportunity was lost for ever. Sympathy — vigilance — the hour for these was past. The priests had succeeded in their surprise, and Judas had well led them through the dark, with unerring accuracy, to the very spot where his Master knelt; and there were seen quite close, the dark figures shown in relief against the glare of the red torchlight, and every now and then the gleam glittering from the bared steel and the Roman armour. It was all over, they might sleep as they liked, their sleeping could do no injury now; their watching could do no good. And therefore, partly in bitterness, partly in reproach, partly in a kind of irony, partly in sad earnest, our Master said to His disciples: Sleep on now: there is no use in watching now: take your rest — for ever if you will. Sleep and rest can do me no more harm now, for all that watching might have done is lost.

But, brethren, we have to observe that in the next sentence our Redeemer addresses Himself to the consideration of what could yet be done; the best thing as circumstances then stood. So far as any good to be got from watching went they might sleep on: there was no reparation for the fault that had been done: but so far as duty went, there was still much of endurance to which they had to rouse themselves. They could not save their Master, but they might loyally and manfully share His disgrace, and if it must be, His death. They could not put off the penalty, but they might steel themselves cheerfully to share it. Safety was out of the question now: but they might meet their fate, instead of being overwhelmed by it: and so, as respected what was gone by, Christ said, "Sleep," what is done cannot be undone: but as respected the duties that were lying before them still, He said, we must make the best of it that can be made: rouse yourselves to dare the worst: on to enact your parts like men. Rise, let us be going — we have something still left to do. Here then we have two subjects of contemplation distinctly marked out for us.

I. The irreparable Past.

II. The available Future.

The words of Christ are not like the words of other men: His sentences do not end with the occasion which called them forth: every sentence of Christ's is a deep principle of human life, and it is so with these sentences: "Sleep on now" — that is a principle. "Rise up, and let us be going" — that is another principle. The principle contained in "Sleep on now" is this, that the past is irreparable, and after a certain moment waking will do no good. You may improve the future, the past is gone beyond recovery. As to all that is gone by, so far as the hope of altering it goes, you may sleep on and take your rest: there is no power in earth or heaven that can undo what has once been done.

Now let us proceed to give illustrations of this principle.

It is true, first of all, with respect to *time* that is gone by. Time is the solemn inheritance to which every man is born heir, who has a life-rent of this world — a little section cut out of eternity and given us to do our work in: an eternity before, an eternity behind; and the small stream between, floating swiftly from the one into the vast bosom of the other. The man who has felt with all his soul the significance ot time will not be long in learning any lesson that this world has to teach him. Have you ever felt it, my Christian brethren? Have you ever realized how your own little streamlet is gliding away, and bearing you along with it towards that awful other world of which all things here are but the thin shadows, down into that eternity towards which the confused wreck of all earthly things are bound? Let us realize that, beloved brethren: until that sensation of time, and the infinite meaning which is wrapped up in it, has taken possession of our souls, there is no chance of our ever feeling strongly that it is worse than madness to sleep that time away. Every day in this world has its work; and every day as it rises out of eternity keeps putting to each of us the question afresh, What will you do before to-day has sunk into eternity and nothingness again? And now what have we to say with respect to this strange solemn thing — Time? That men do with it through life just what the apostles did for one precious and irreparable hour of it in the garden of Gethsemane: they go to sleep. Have you ever seen those marble statues in some public square or garden, which art has so fashioned into a perennial fountain that through the lips or through the hands the clear water flows in a perpetual stream, on and on for ever; and the marble stands there — passive, cold — making no effort to arrest the gliding water?

It is so that time flows through the hands of men — swift, never pausing till it has run itself out; and there is the man petrified into a marble sleep, not feeling what it is which is passing away for ever. It is so, brethren, just so, that the destiny of nine men out of ten accomplishes itself, slipping away from them, aimless, useless, till it is too late. And this passage asks us with all the solemn thoughts which crowd around an approaching eternity, — what has been our life, and what do we intend it shall be? Yesterday, last week, last year — they are gone. Yesterday, for example, was such a day as never was before, and never can be again. Out of darkness and eternity it was born a new fresh day: into darkness and eternity it sank again for ever. It had a voice calling to us, of its own. Its own work — its own duties. What were we doing yesterday? Idling, whiling away the time in light and luxurious literature — not as life's relaxation, but as life's business? thrilling our hearts with the excitements of life — contriving how to spend the day most pleasantly? Was that our day? Sleep, brethren! all that is but the sleep of the three apostles. And now let us remember this: there is a day coming when that sleep will be broken rudely, with a shock: there is a day in our future lives when our time will be counted not by years nor by months, nor yet by hours, but by minutes — the day when unmistakeable symptoms shall announce that the Messengers of Death have come to take us.

That startling moment will come which it is in vain to attempt to realize now, when it will be felt that it is all over at last — that our chance and our trial are past. The moment that we have tried to think of, shrunk from, put away from us, here it is — going too, like all other moments that have gone before it: and then with eyes unsealed at last, you look back on the life which is gone by. There is no mistake about it: there it is, a sleep, a most palpable sleep — self-indulged unconsciousness of high destinies, and God and Christ: a sleep when Christ was calling out to you to watch with Him one hour —, a sleep when there was something to be done — a sleep broken, it may be, once or twice by restless dreams, and by a voice of truth which *would* make itself heard at times, but still a sleep which was only rocked into deeper stillness by interruption. And now from the undone eternity the boom of whose waves is distinctly audible upon your soul, there comes the same voice again — a solemn sad voice — but no longer the same word, "Watch" — other words altogether, "You may go to sleep." It is too late to wake; there is no science in earth or heaven to recall time that once has fled.

Again, this principle of the irreparable past holds good with respect to preparing for temptation. That hour in the garden was a precious opportunity given for laying in spiritual strength. Christ knew it well. He struggled and fought *then:* therefore there was no struggling afterwards — no trembling in the judgment-hall — no shrinking on the cross, but only dignified and calm victory; for he had fought the Temptation on His knees beforehand, and conquered all in the garden. The battle of the Judgment-hall, the battle of the Cross, were already fought and over, in the Watch and in the Agony. The apostles missed the meaning of that hour; and therefore when it came to the question of trial, the loudest boaster of them all shrunk from acknowledging Whose he was, and the rest played the part of the craven and the renegade. And if the reason of this be asked, it is simply this: They went to trial unprepared: they had not prayed: and what is a Christian without prayer but Samson without his talisman of hair?

Brethren, in this world, when there is any foreseen or suspected danger before us, it is our duty to forecast our trial. It is our wisdom to put on our armour — to consider what lies before us — to call up resolution in God's strength to go through what we may have to do. And it is marvellous how difficulties smooth away before a Christian when he does this. Trials that cost him a struggle to meet even in imagination — like the heavy sweat of Gethsemane, when Christ was looking forward and feeling exceeding sorrowful even unto death — come to their crisis; and behold, to his astonishment they are nothing — they have been fought and conquered already. But if you go to meet those temptations, not as Christ did, but as the apostles did prayerless, trusting to the chance impulse of the moment, you may make up your mind to fail. That opportunity lost is irreparable: it is your doom to yield then. Those words are true, you may "sleep on now, and take your rest," for you have betrayed yourselves into the hands of danger.

And now one word about prayer. It is a preparation for danger, it is the armour for battle. Go not, my Christian brother, into the dangerous world without it. You kneel down at night to pray, and drowsiness weighs down your eyelids. A hard day's work is a kind of excuse, and you shorten your prayer and resign yourself softly to repose. The morning breaks, and it may be you rise late, and so your early devotions are not done, or done with irregular haste. No watching unto prayer — wakefulness once more omitted. And now we ask, is that reparable? Brethren, we solemnly believe not. There has been that done which cannot be undone. You have given up your prayer, and you will suffer for it. Temptation is before you, and you are not fit to meet it. There is a guilty feeling on the soul, and you linger at a distance from Christ. It is no marvel if that day in which you suffer drowsiness to interfere with prayer, be a day on which you betray Him by cowardice and soft shrinking from duty. Let it be a principle through life, moments of prayer intruded upon by sloth cannot be made up. We may get experience, but we cannot get back the rich freshness and the strength which were wrapped up in these moments.

Once again this principle is true in another respect. Opportunities of doing good do not come back. We are here, brethren, for a most definite and intelligible purpose — to educate our own hearts by deeds of love, and to be the instrument of blessing to our brother men. There are two ways in which this is to be done — by guarding them from danger, and by soothing them in their rough path by kindly sympathies — the two things which the apostles were asked to do for Christ. And it is an encouraging thought, that he who cannot do the one has at least the other in his power. If he cannot protect he can sympathize. Let the weakest — let the humblest in this congregation remember, that in his daily course he can, if he will, shed around him almost a heaven. Kindly words, sympathizing attentions, watchfulness against wounding men's sensitiveness — these cost very little, but they are priceless in their value. Are they not, brethren, almost the staple of our daily happiness? From hour to hour, from moment to moment, we are supported, blest, by small kindnesses. And then consider: — Here is a section of life one-third, one-half, it may be three-fourths gone by, and the question before us is, how much has been done in that way? Who has charged himself with the guardianship of his brother's safety? Who has laid on himself as a sacred duty to sit beside his brother suffering? Oh! my brethren, it is the omission of these things which is irreparable: irreparable, when you look to the purest enjoyment which might have been your own: irreparable, when you consider the compunction which belongs to deeds of love not done; irreparable, when you look to this groaning world, and feel that its agony of bloody sweat has been distilling all night, and you were dreaming away in luxury! Shame, shame upon our selfishness! There is an infinite voice in the sin and sufferings of earth's millions, which makes every idle moment, every moment that is which is not relaxation, guilt; and seems to cry out, If you will not bestir yourself for love's sake now, it will soon be too late.

Lastly, this principle applies to a misspent youth. There is something very remarkable in the picture which is placed before us. There is a picture of *One* struggling, toiling, standing between others and danger, and those others quietly content to reap the benefit of that struggle without anxiety of their own. And there is something in this singularly like the position in which all young persons are placed. The young are by God's Providence exempted in a great measure from anxiety: they are as the apostles were in relation to their Master: their friends stand between them and the struggles of existence. They are not called upon to think for themselves: the burden is borne by others. They get their bread without knowing or caring how it is paid for: they smile and laugh without a suspicion of the anxious thoughts of day and night which a parent bears to enable them to smile. So to speak they are sleeping — and it is not a guilty sleep — while another watches.

My young brethren — youth is one of the precious opportunities of life — rich in blessing if you choose to make it so, but having in it the materials of undying remorse if you suffer it to pass unimproved. Your quiet Gethsemane is now. Gethsemane's struggles you cannot know yet. Take care that you do not learn too well Gethsemane's sleep. Do you know how you can imitate the apostles in their fatal sleep? You can suffer your young days to pass idly and uselessly away; you can live as if you had nothing to do but to enjoy yourselves: you can let others think for you, and not try to become thoughtful yourselves, till the business and the difficulties of life come upon you unprepared, and you find yourselves like men waking from sleep, hurried, confused, scarcely able to stand, with all the faculties bewildered, not knowing right from wrong, led headlong to evil, just because you have not given yourselves in time to learn what is good. All that is sleep. And now let us mark it. You cannot repair that in after-life. Oh! remember every period of human life has its own lesson, and you cannot learn that lesson in the next period. The boy has one set of lessons to learn, and the young man another, and the grown-up man another. Let us consider one single instance. The boy has to learn docility, gentleness of temper, reverence, submission. All those feelings which are to be transferred afterwards in full cultivation to God, like plants nursed in a hotbed and then planted out, are to be cultivated first in youth. Afterwards, those habits which have been merely habits of obedience to an earthly parent, are to become religious submission to a heavenly parent. Our parents stand to us in the place of God. Veneration for our parents is intended to become afterwards adoration for something higher. Take that single instance; and now suppose that *that* is not learnt in boyhood. Suppose that the boy sleeps to that duty of veneration, and learns only flippancy, insubordination, and the habit of deceiving his father, — can that, my young brethren, be repaired afterwards? Humanly speaking not. Life is like the transition from class to class in a school. The schoolboy who has not learnt arithmetic in the earlier classes cannot secure it when he comes to mechanics in the higher: each section has its own sufficient work. He may be a good philosopher or a good historian, but a bad arithmetician he remains for life; for he cannot lay the foundation at the moment when he must be building the superstructure. The regiment which has not perfected itself in its manœuvres on the parade ground cannot learn them before the guns of the enemy. And just in the same way, the young person who has slept his youth away, and become idle, and selfish, and hard, cannot make up for that afterwards. He may do something, he may be religious — yes; but he cannot be what he might have been. There is a part of his heart which will remain uncultivated to the end. The apostles could share their Master's sufferings — they could not save Him. Youth has its irreparable past.

And therefore, my young brethren, let it be impressed upon you, — NOW is a time, infinite in its value for eternity, which will never return again. Sleep not; learn that there is a very solemn work of heart which must be done while the stillness of the garden of your Gethsemane gives you time. Now — or Never.

The treasures at your command are infinite. Treasures of time — treasures of youth — treasures of opportunity that grown-up men would sacrifice everything they have to possess. Oh for ten years of youth back again with the added experience of age! But it cannot be: they must be content to sleep on now, and take their rest.

We are to pass on next to a few remarks on the other sentence in this passage, which brings before us for consideration the future which is still available: for we are to observe, that our Master did not limit his apostles to a regretful recollection of their failure. Recollection of it He did demand. There were the materials of a most cutting self-reproach in the few words He said: for they contained all the desolation of that sad word *never*. Who knows not what that word wraps up — Never — it *never* can be undone! Sleep on. But yet there was no sickly lingering over the irreparable. Our Master's words are the words of One who had fully recognised the hopelessness of His position, but yet manfully and calmly had numbered His resources and scanned His duties, and then braced up his mind to meet the exigencies of His situation with no passive endurance: the moment was come for action — "Rise, let us be going."

Now the broad general lesson which we gain from this is not hard to read. It is that a Christian is to be for ever rousing himself to recognise the duties which lie before him *now*. In Christ the motto is ever this, "Let us be going." Let me speak to the conscience of some one. Perhaps yours is a very remorseful past — a foolish, frivolous, disgraceful, frittered past. Well, Christ says, — My servant, be sad, but no languor; there is work to be done for me yet — Rise up, be going! Oh, my brethren, Christ takes your wretched remnants of life — the feeble pulses of a heart which has spent its best hours not for Him, but for self and for enjoyment, and in His strange love He condescends to accept them.

Let me speak to another kind of experience. Perhaps we feel that we have faculties which never have and now never will find their right field; perhaps we are ignorant of many things which cannot be learnt now; perhaps the seedtime of life has gone by, and certain powers of heart and mind will not grow now; perhaps you feel that the best days of life are gone, and it is too late to begin things which were in your power once: — still, my repentant brother, there is encouragement from your Master yet. Wake to the opportunities that yet remain. Ten years of life — five years — one year — say you have only that, — Will you sleep *that* away because you have already slept too long? Eternity is crying out to you louder and louder as you near its brink, — Rise, be going: count your resources: learn what you are not fit for, and give up wishing for it: learn what you *can* do, and do it with the energy of a man. That is the great lesson of this passage. But now consider it a little more closely.

Christ impressed two things on His apostles' minds.

1. The duty of Christian earnestness — "Rise."
2. The duty of Christian energy — "Let us be going."

Christ roused them to earnestness when He said, "Rise." A short, sharp, rousing call. They were to start up and wake to the realities of their position. The guards were on them: their Master was about to be led away to doom. That was an awakening which would make men spring to their feet in earnest. Brethren, goodness and earnestness are nearly the same thing. In the language in which this Bible was written there was one word which expressed them both: what we translate a good man, in Greek is literally "earnest." The Greeks felt that to be earnest was nearly identical with being good. But, however, there is a day in life when a man must be earnest, but it does not follow that he will be good. "Behold the bridegroom cometh; go ye out to meet him." That is a sound that will thunder through the most fast-locked slumber, and rouse men whom sermons cannot rouse. But that will not make them holy. Earnestness of *life*, brethren, that is goodness. Wake in death you *must*, for it is an earnest thing to die. Shall it be this, I pray you? — Shall it be the voice of death which first says, "Arise," at the very moment when it says, "Sleep on for ever?" — Shall it be the bridal train sweeping by, and the shutting of the doors, and the discovery that the lamp is gone out? — Shall *that* be the first time you know that it is an earnest thing to live? Let us feel that we have been *doing;* learn what time is — sliding from you, and not stopping when you stop: learn what sin is: learn what "*never*" is: "Awake, thou that sleepest."

Lastly, Christian energy — "Let us be going." There were two ways open to Christ in which to submit to His doom. He might have waited for it: instead of which He went to meet the soldiers. He took up the Cross, the cup of anguish was not forced between His lips, He took it with His own hands, and drained it quickly to the last drop. In after-years the disciples understood the lesson, and acted on it. They did not wait till Persecution overtook them; they braved the Sanhedrim: they fronted the world: they proclaimed aloud the unpopular and unpalatable doctrines of the Resurrection and the Cross. Now in this there lies a principle. Under no conceivable set of circumstances are we justified in sitting

— "By the poison'd springs of life,
Waiting for the morrow which shall free us from the strife."

Under no circumstances, whether of pain, or grief, or disappointment, or irreparable mistake, can it be true that there is not something to be *done*, as well as something to be suffered. And thus it is that the spirit of Christianity draws over our life, not a leaden cloud of Remorse and Despondency, but a sky — not perhaps of radiant, but yet — of most serene and chastened and manly hope. There is a Past which is gone for ever. But there is a Future which is still our own.

END OF VOL. II.

www.ingramcontent.com/pod-product-compliance
Lightning Source LLC
Chambersburg PA
CBHW022122020426
42334CB00015B/723